CONSTRUCTION LAW IN THE 21ST CENTURY

CONSTRUCTION PRACTICE SERIES

Construction Contract Variations
Michael Sergeant and Max Wieliczko
Holman Fenwick Willan LLP

Delay and Disruption in Construction Contracts
Fifth Edition
Andrew Burr

The Law of Construction Disputes
Second Edition
Cyril Chern

Construction Insurance and UK Construction Contracts
Third Edition
Roger ter Haar QC, Marshall Levine and Anna Laney

Construction Law
Second Edition
Julian Bailey

International Contractual and Statutory Adjudication
Andrew Burr

Remedies in Construction Law
Second Edition
Roger ter Haar QC

Professional Negligence in Construction
Second Edition
Ben Patten and Hugh Saunders

Litigation in the Technology and Construction Court
Adam Constable QC, Lucy Garrett QC and Calum Lamont

Chern on Dispute Boards
Practice and Procedure
Fourth Edition
Cyril Chern

The Law of Construction Disputes
Third Edition
Cyril Chern

Construction Arbitration and Alternative Dispute Resolution
Theory and Practice Around the World
Edited by Renato Nazzini

Adjudication in Construction Law
Second Edition
Darryl Royce

International Construction Law
An Overview
Edited by Wolfgang Breyer

Construction Law in the 21st Century
Edited by Renato Nazzini

For more information about this series, please visit:
www.routledge.com/Construction-Practice-Series/book-series/CPS

CONSTRUCTION LAW IN THE 21ST CENTURY

EDITED BY

RENATO NAZZINI

Professor in Law
Director of the Centre of Construction Law & Dispute Resolution at King's College London

informa law
from Routledge

First published 2025
by Informa Law from Routledge
4 Park Square, Milton Park, Abingdon, Oxon OX14 4RN

and by Informa Law from Routledge
605 Third Avenue, New York, NY 10158

Informa Law from Routledge is an imprint of the Taylor & Francis Group, an informa business

© 2025 selection and editorial matter, Renato Nazzini; individual chapters, the contributors

The right of Renato Nazzini to be identified as the author of the editorial material, and of the authors for their individual chapters, has been asserted in accordance with sections 77 and 78 of the Copyright, Designs and Patents Act 1988.

All rights reserved. No part of this book may be reprinted or reproduced or utilised in any form or by any electronic, mechanical, or other means, now known or hereafter invented, including photocopying and recording, or in any information storage or retrieval system, without permission in writing from the publishers.

Trademark notice: Product or corporate names may be trademarks or registered trademarks, and are used only for identification and explanation without intent to infringe.

British Library Cataloguing-in-Publication Data
A catalogue record for this book is available from the British Library

Library of Congress Cataloging-in-Publication Data
Names: Nazzini, Renato, editor.
Title: Construction law in the 21st century/edited by Professor Renato Nazzini.
Other titles: Construction law in the twenty-first century
Description: Abingdon, Oxon [UK]; New York, NY: Routledge, 2024. |
Series: Construction practice series | Includes bibliographical
references and index.
Identifiers: LCCN 2024005544 (print) | LCCN 2024005545 (ebook) |
ISBN 9781032663890 (hardback) | ISBN 9781032663951 (paperback) |
ISBN 9781032663975 (ebook)
Subjects: LCSH: Construction industry–Law and legislation–England. |
Construction industry–Law and legislation–European Union countries. |
Construction contracts–England. | Building laws–England. |
Construction industry–Law and legislation.
Classification: LCC KD2435 .C665 2024 (print) | LCC KD2435 (ebook) |
DDC 343.4207/8624–dc23/eng/20240206
LC record available at https://lccn.loc.gov/2024005544
LC ebook record available at https://lccn.loc.gov/2024005545

ISBN: 978-1-032-66389-0 (hbk)
ISBN: 978-1-032-66395-1 (pbk)
ISBN: 978-1-032-66397-5 (ebk)

DOI: 10.4324/9781032663975

Typeset in Times New Roman
by Deanta Global Publishing Services, Chennai, India

Printed and bound by CPI Group (UK) Ltd, Croydon, CR0 4YY

CONTENTS

Contributors	*vii*
Table of cases	*xi*
Table of legislation	*xxv*
International agreements, conventions and treaties	*xxxi*

INTRODUCTION   1

PART I   THE HISTORICAL AND INTERNATIONAL CONTEXTS

CHAPTER 1   DEVELOPMENTS IN CONSTRUCTION LAW OVER THE LIFE OF THE CENTRE OF CONSTRUCTION LAW & DISPUTE RESOLUTION   7
John Uff

CHAPTER 2   IMPACT OF ENGLISH CONSTRUCTION LAW IN THE INTERNATIONAL MARKET   14
Renato Nazzini

PART II   NEW FRONTIERS IN PROCUREMENT SYSTEMS

CHAPTER 3   'PROCURING TO PREVENT ANOTHER GRENFELL TOWER DISASTER': HOW CAN PROCUREMENT SYSTEMS REDUCE RISKS AND IMPROVE SAFETY?   47
David Mosey

CHAPTER 4   SOLUTIONS FOR PROCURING NET ZERO CARBON CONSTRUCTION   67
David Mosey and Roxana Vornicu

CHAPTER 5   NET ZERO CARBON CHALLENGES IN ITALY   77
Sara Valaguzza

CONTENTS

PART III   KEY CONCEPTS AND DEVELOPMENTS IN COMMON
LAW AND CIVIL LAW

CHAPTER 6   FITNESS FOR PURPOSE OBLIGATIONS: WINDMILLS
OR GIANTS?   91
Julian Bailey

CHAPTER 7   PERFORMANCE BONDS AND BANK GUARANTEES:
35 YEARS OF DEVELOPMENT   101
Richard Wilmot-Smith

CHAPTER 8   ENGLISH RESIDENTIAL BUILDING LAW –
FROM *ANNS* TO GRENFELL AND BEYOND   114
Philip Britton

CHAPTER 9   BUILDING REGULATIONS IN ENGLAND: A HISTORY
OF LURCHING FROM CRISIS TO CRISIS   139
Abdul-Lateef Jinadu and Sam Grimley

CHAPTER 10   QUANTIFYING PROLONGATION COSTS   153
Ronan Champion

CHAPTER 11   LIQUIDATED DAMAGES: A COMMON LAW
PERSPECTIVE   166
Nicholas Gould and Katherine Butler

CHAPTER 12   LIQUIDATED DAMAGES IN THE MIDDLE EAST:
A UAE PERSPECTIVE   181
Gordon Blanke

CHAPTER 13   LIQUIDATED DAMAGES IN CIVIL LAW JURISDICTIONS   198
Cecilia Carrara

PART IV   DISPUTE RESOLUTION

CHAPTER 14   ADJUDICATION SINCE 1998   217
Matt Molloy

CHAPTER 15   ARBITRATION AND INSOLVENCY IN CIVIL LAW
EUROPEAN COUNTRIES   224
Crenguta Leaua and Corina Tanase

CHAPTER 16   CONSTRUCTION PROJECTS IN INVESTOR–STATE
ARBITRATION: INSIGHTS FROM THE LATEST
TRENDS AND STATISTICS   235
Renato Nazzini and Aleksander Godhe

CHAPTER 17   CONSTRUCTION AND THE ENERGY SECTOR:
THE TRANSITION TO A CLEAN ENERGY AND THE
ENERGY CHARTER TREATY   253
Crina Baltag

CHAPTER 18   IS THERE A ROLE FOR AI IN THE DETERMINATION
OF CONSTRUCTION DISPUTES?   261
Paula Gerber

Index   *277*

CONTRIBUTORS

Julian Bailey
Julian Bailey is a Partner at Jones Day specialising in international construction and infrastructure projects. Additionally, he is a Visiting Professor at the Dickson Poon School of Law, King's College London, and an Adjunct Professor of Law at Hamad bin Khalifa University. Julian is also the author of *Construction Law*.

Crina Baltag
Professor Crina Baltag is an Associate Professor in International Arbitration at Stockholm University where she leads the Master of Laws in International Commercial Arbitration. Her academic work focuses on the Energy Charter Treaty. Crina is also a qualified attorney in Romania and an arbitrator acting under various procedural rules.

Gordon Blanke
Dr Gordon Blanke is the Founding Partner of Blanke Arbitration Dubai/London/Paris. He has extensive and wide-ranging experience in all types of international commercial and investment arbitration in both common and civil law jurisdictions, having acted as advising counsel and arbitrator under most leading institutional arbitration rules.

Philip Britton
Professor Philip Britton is a former Visiting Professor of Law at King's College London and a former Director of the Centre of Construction Law & Dispute Resolution. Philip is also the co-author of *Residential Construction Law*, the first book offering a comparative overview of that field.

Katherine Butler
Katherine Butler is a Senior Associate at Fenwick Elliott. She has experience of both domestic and international construction and engineering disputes and advises both contractor and developer clients. Katherine has acted on matters in the Technology and Construction Court, the Court of Appeal, and various international arbitrations.

Cecilia Carrara
Cecilia Carrara is a Partner at Legance. She acts as counsel and arbitrator in international and domestic commercial and investment arbitrations. She is a thought leader in the field of arbitration serving, among others, as a member of the Executive Board of the UN Global Compact Network Italy.

CONTRIBUTORS

Ronan Champion
Dr Ronan Champion is a chartered surveyor with more than 25 years of experience acting as an adjudicator, expert witness, construction cost and delay analyst, and lecturer. He regularly prepares expert reports for courts and tribunals internationally.

Paula Gerber
Professor Paula Gerber is an Australian law academic at Monash University. She is an internationally renowned expert in two distinct areas: construction law (particularly the avoidance, management, and resolution of disputes) and international human rights law. She is the founder of the National Association of Women in Construction in Australia.

Aleksander Godhe
Aleksander Godhe is a Research Associate at the Centre of Construction Law & Dispute Resolution, King's College London and a Visiting Fellow at the Stockholm Centre for Commercial Law, Stockholm University. His speciality is in construction disputes, arbitration, and international economic law.

Nicholas Gould
Nicholas Gould is a Partner at Fenwick Elliott. He is dually qualified as a solicitor advocate and a chartered surveyor. He specialises in international arbitration relating to construction and engineering projects. Nicholas is also a Visiting Professor at King's College London and a Vice President of the International Chamber of Commerce's Arbitration Commission.

Sam Grimley
Sam Grimley is currently training for the Bar after over a decade in the music industry. He is an incoming Pupil Barrister at One Essex Court.

Abdul-Lateef Jinadu
Abdul-Lateef Jinadu is a Barrister and an Arbitrator at Keating Chambers specialising in construction, engineering and energy disputes, and domestic and international arbitration. He is also a Technology & Construction Bar Association adjudicator and a member of the Advisory Board of Africa Construction Law.

Crenguta Leaua
Professor Crenguta Leaua teaches International Arbitration and New Technologies Law at Bucharest University of Economic Studies. In 2005, she founded Leaua Damcali Deaconu Paunescu - LDDP law firm in Romania. An experienced arbitrator and past Vice President of International Chamber of Commerce Paris, she is currently a member of the Board of Silicon Valley Arbitration & Mediation Center and a director of the Swiss Institute for Alternative Thinking.

Matt Molloy
Matt Molloy is a Director at MCMS. He is a chartered quantity surveyor, having been appointed in more than 900 construction and engineering disputes as either adjudicator, arbitrator, mediator, or expert determiner. Matt also chairs the Alternative Dispute Resolution Management Board of the Construction Industry Council.

viii

CONTRIBUTORS

David Mosey
Professor David Mosey CBE is a Professor of Law and a former Director of the Centre of Construction Law & Dispute Resolution at King's College London. David is the author of the *FAC-1 Framework Alliance Contract* and of *Constructing the Gold Standard*, an independent review of construction frameworks commissioned by the United Kingdom government.

Renato Nazzini
Professor Renato Nazzini is the Director of the Centre of Construction Law & Dispute Resolution at King's College London, a Partner at LMS Legal, and an independent arbitrator. He is a qualified English solicitor and Italian advocate. Renato is a member of the International Chamber of Commerce Arbitration and ADR Commission, Italy.

Corina Tanase
Corina Tanase is a Partner at Leaua Damcali Deaconu Paunescu – LDDP and an arbitrator. She has extensive expertise in high-profile disputes settled by international arbitration. Corina also specialises in international transactions, construction law, and aviation law. She holds an Master of Laws in International Arbitration from the Faculty of Law, Bucharest University.

John Uff
Professor John Uff CBE KC is the founding Director of the Centre of Construction Law & Dispute Resolution and an Emeritus Professor of Engineering Law at King's College London. He is dually qualified as a civil engineer and a barrister, having a wide expertise in construction law and public inquiries.

Sara Valaguzza
Professor Sara Valaguzza is the founding Partner of Studio Legale Valaguzza. She is also a Full Professor of Administrative Law at the University of Milan. Sara served as the Scientific Director of the Italian Center of Construction Law & Management. She has wide expertise in procurement, administrative, and environmental law.

Roxana Vornicu
Dr Roxana Vornicu is a Senior Lecturer at the Centre of Construction Law & Dispute Resolution, King's College London and a Partner at Sirbu & Vornicu. She has also held teaching positions at Saïd Business School, Oxford University, and Stuttgart University. Roxana's research focuses on collaborative and net zero procurement.

Richard Wilmot-Smith
Richard Wilmot-Smith KC is a Barrister at 39 Essex Chambers specialising in all aspects of construction and engineering litigation and arbitration. He regularly sits as an arbitrator and adjudicator worldwide in high-value cases. Richard is also an editor of *Wilmot-Smith on Construction Contracts* fourth edition 2021.

TABLE OF CASES

A

A v R [2009] HKCFI 342 209

Abdel-Kader v Royal Borough of Kensington and Chelsea [2022] EWHC 2006 (QB) 124

Actionstrength Ltd v International Glass Engineering SPA [2003] 2 AC 541..............................102

ADF Group Inc v United States of America, ICSID Case No ARB(AF)/00/1
(9 January 2003) 246

AGB Scotland Ltd v McDermott [2023] CSOH 31...136

Alderson v Beetham Organisation Ltd [2003] 1 WLR 1686..92

Alex Genin, Eastern Credit Limited, Inc and AS Baltoil v The Republic of Estonia,
ICSID Case No ARB/99/2, Award (25 June 2001) 246

Alfred McAlpine Capital Projects Ltd v Tilebox Ltd [2005] EWHC 281 (TCC),
(2005) 21 Const LJ 539..166, 169, 170

Alpha Projektholding GmbH v Ukraine, ICSID Case No ARB/07/16,
Award (8 November 2010)..246–247

Alternative Power Solution Ltd v Central Electricity Board [2014] UKPC 31 108

Amalgamated Building Contractors v Waltham Holy Cross Urban District
Council [1952] 2 All ER 452 28

AMEC Civil Engineering Ltd v Secretary of State for Transport [2005] EWCA Civ 291 36

American Cyanamid Co v Ethicom Ltd [1975] AC 396...107, 108

Anns v Merton LBC [1978] AC 728 ....114, 115, 116–118, 119, 120, 123, 125,
126, 127, 128, 129, 137

Apotex Holdings Inc and Apotex Inc v United States of America, ICSID
Case No ARB(AF)/12/1, Award (25 August 2014)...246

Arabtec Construction LLC v Ultra Fuji International LLC [2007] DIFC CFI 0004....................195

Ards Broigh Council v Northern Bank Ltd [1994] NI 121 111

Arnold v Britton [2015] UKSC 36 ....18, 19, 178

ATA Construction, Industrial and Trading Company v The Hashemite Kingdom of
Jordan, ICSID Case No ARB/08/2, Award (18 May 2010)..245, 254

Autoridad del Canal de Panama v Sacyr [2017] EWHC 2228 (Comm)................................16, 17, 18

Aviva Insurance Limited v Hackney Empire Limited [2012] EWCA Civ 1716............................109

B

Barrett v London Borough of Enfield [2001] 2 AC 550...127

Batish v Inspired Sutton Ltd (2023) LON/00BF/HY/2022/002...135

TABLE OF CASES

Bayindir Insaat Turizm Ticaret Ve Sanayi AS v Islamic Republic of Pakistan, ICSID
Case No ARB/03/29, Decision on Jurisdiction (14 November 2005) 244

Beaufort Developments v Gilbert Ash NI [1999] 1 AC 266 12

Beck Interiors Ltd v Russo [2010] BLR 37; [2009] EWHC 3861 (TCC) 110, 111, 112

Bernard Sunley & Co Ltd v Cunard White Star Ltd [1940] 2 All ER 97 163

Bernhard von Pezold and Others v Republic of Zimbabwe, ICSID Case No
ARB/10/15, Award (28 July 2015) 249, 250–251

Biwater Gauff (Tanzania) Ltd v United Republic of Tanzania, ICSID Case No
ARB/05/22, Award (24 July 2008) 248

Bluck v Gompertz [1852] 7 Ex 862 102

Blusun SA, Jean-Pierre Lecorcier and Michael Stein v Italian Republic, ICSID Case No
ARB/14/3, Award (27 December 2016) 242

BMBF (No 12) v Harland & Wolff [2001] EWCA Civ 862 12

Body Corporate 207624 v North Shore City Council (Spencer on Byron) [2012]
NZSC 83, [2013] 2 NZLR 297 129

Bolivinter Oil SA v Chase Manhattan Bank [1984] 1 WLR 392 108

Bowen v Paramount Builders (Hamilton) Ltd [1977] 1 NZLR 394 (NZCA) 128

Bowers v Chapel-en-le-Frith RDC (1910) 9 LGR 339 .... 96, 97, 98

Bramall & Ogden Ltd v Sheffield City Council (1983) 29 BLR 73 .... 173, 174, 175

Bremer Poelstransport GmbH v Drewry [1933] 1 KB 753 111

Bresco Electrical Services Ltd (in liquidation) v Michael J Lonsdale (Electrical)
Ltd [2019] EWCA Civ 27 221

Bridge v Campbell Discount Co Ltd [1962] AC 600 170

British Glanzstoff Manufacturing Co Ltd v General Accident Fire &
Life Assurance Corp Ltd [1913] AC 143 176

Brookfield Multiplex Ltd v Owners Corporation Strata Plan 61288 [2014]
HCA 36 (2014) 254 CLR 185 121

Broster v Galliard Docklands Ltd [2011] EWHC 1722 (TCC), [2011] BLR 569,
137 Con LR 26 118

Brown & Doherty Ltd v Whangarei County Council [1988] 1 NZLR 33 36

Brown-Forman Beverages Europe Ltd v Bacardi UK Ltd [2021]
EWHC (Comm) 1259 .... 102, 108

Bruns v Colocotronis (The Vasso) [1979] 2 Lloyd's Rep 412 .... 110, 111, 112

Buckingham Group Contracting Ltd v Peel L&P Investments and Property Ltd [2022]
EWHC 1842 (TCC) 178, 179

Burlington Resources Inc v Republic of Ecuador, ICSID Case No ARB/08/5:
Decision on Jurisdiction (2 June 2010); Decision on Liability
(14 December 2012) 247, 249

C

Cameron v Mowlem (1990) 52 BLR 24 11

Cannon Corporate Ltd v Primus Build Ltd [2019] EWCA Civ 27 221

Canterbury Pipe Lines Ltd v Christchurch Drainage Board [1979] 2 NZLR 347 .... 28–29, 35–36

Cantillon Limited v Urvasco Limited [2008] EWHC 282 (TCC) 42, 220

Caparo Industries Plc v Dickman [1990] 2 AC 605 127

Carton-Kelly v Darty Holdings SAS [2022] EWHC 3234 (Ch) 117

Caton v Caton [1868] LR 2 HL 127 102

TABLE OF CASES

Cavendish Square Holding BV v Makdessi and ParkingEye Ltd v
   Beavis [2016] AC 1172 ....170, 171, 172, 174, 176, 180
Cavendish Square Holding BV v Talal El Makdessi [2015] UKSC 67 .... 9, 161, 172, 200
Cengiz Ýnþaat Sanayi ve Ticaret AS v Libya, ICC Case No 21537/ZF/AYZ,
   Award (7 November 2018)..250
Cetelem v Roust Holdings [2005] EWCA Civ 618 23
Chambers v Goldthorpe [1901] 1 QB 624...35
Channel Tunnel Group v Balfour Beatty [1993] AC 334..13
Chartbrook Ltd v Persimmon Homes Ltd [2007] EWHC 409 (Ch); [2008]
   EWCA Civ 183; [2009] 1 AC 1101 .... 19, 21
Charter Reinsurance Co Ltd v Fagan [2004] UKHL 54 18
Chelsea Football Club v Mutu 849 FSupp2d 1341.. 209
Chief Constable of Greater Manchester v Carroll [2017] EWCA Civ 1992, [2018]
   4 WLR 32...124
Children's Ark Partnerships Ltd v Kajima Construction Europe (UK) Ltd [2022]
   EWHC 1595 (TCC) 118
Chua Tian Chu v Chin Bay Ching [2011] SGHC 126 28
CIB Properties Limited v Birse Construction [2004] EWHC 2365 (TCC) 220
Civil Liability of Vendors and Lessors for Defective Premises (Law Com No 40, 1970)............. 120
Clarington Developments Ltd v HCC International Insurance [2019] IEHC 630 110
Clydebank Engineering and Shipbuilding Co v Don Jose Ramos Yzquierdo y
   Castaneda [1905] AC 6... 167
Commissioner of Public Works v Hills [1906] AC 368.. 167
Commissioners of the State Savings Bank of Victoria v Costain Australia Ltd (1983)
   2 ACLR 28, 30
Compañiá de Aguas del Aconquija S.A. and Vivendi Universal SA v
   Argentine Republic, ICSID Case No ARB/97/3, Award (20 August 2007) 248
Continental Casualty Company v The Argentine Republic, ICSID Case No ARB/03/9,
   Award (5 September 2008)..249
Corebuild Ltd v Cleaver & Anor [2019] EWHC 2170 (TCC)..222
Costain Ltd v Bechtel Ltd [2005] EWHC 1019 (TCC)...35
Costain Ltd v Charles Haswell & Partners [2009] EWHC B25 (TCC) 155
Council of the Shire of Sutherland v Heyman (1985) 157 CLR 424 129
Cruz City 1 Mauritius Holdings v Unitech Ltd [2013] EWCA Civ 1512 23

D

D&F Estates v Church Commissioners for England [1989] AC 177..8, 115
Dawnays v Minter [1971] 1 WLR 1205 10
Desert Line Projects LLC v The Republic of Yemen, ICSID Case No ARB/05/17,
   Award (6 February 2008) 254
Dodd v Churton [1897] 1 QB 562 ....28, 29
Donoghue v Stevenson [1932] AC 562...119, 125, 130, 268
Doosan Babcock Energy v Comercializaadara de Equipos [2013] EWHC 3201 (TCC).............. 107
Dorchester Hotels Limited v Vivid Interiors [2009] EWHC 70 (TCC).......................................220
Dubai Court of Cassation Petition no. 344/19, the hearing of 23 January 1999 186
Dubai Court of Cassation Petition no. 494/2003, the hearing of 24 April 2004 186

TABLE OF CASES

Dunlop Pneumatic Tyre Co Ltd v New Garage & Motor Co Ltd [1915]
AC 79 HL...166, 167, 168, 169, 170, 171, 173, 179, 200
Dutton v Bognor Regis UDC [1972] 1 QB 373...115, 117, 121, 125, 128

E

Ebury Partners Belgium SA/NV v Technical Touch BV [2022] EWHC 2927 (Comm)......................... 27
Eco World – Ballymore Embassy Gardens Co Ltd v Dobler UK Ltd [2021]
EWHC 2207 (TCC) 174, 175
Edmund Nuttall v RG Carter [2002] EWHC 400 (TCC) 219
Edward Owen Engineering Ltd v Barclays Bank International Ltd [1978] 1 QB 159,
[1983] 1 AC 168 ....104, 105, 107, 108
Electricity Networks Corporation v Herridge Parties [2022] HCA 37 128
Elvia Besil Sampieri and Haffan Properties LLC v Belfiore Developers LLC,
Pierpoint Capital Company LLC, TIC Belfiore LLC, Joseph J Lopez, Giorgio
Borlenghi and Inter-Pier LLC, American Arbitration Association, Case No.
01-16-0001-3080 210
Enterprise Inns Plc v Forest Hill Tavern Public House Ltd [2010] EWHC 2368 (Ch) 106
Etihad Airways PJSC v Flöther [2020] EWCA Civ 1707 25

F

Fiona Trust v Privalov [2007] UKHL 40..22
Fluor Ltd v Shanghai Zhenhua Heavy Industry Co Ltd [2018] EWHC 490 (TCC) 164
Frontier Petroleum Services Ltd v The Czech Republic, UNCITRAL, Final Award
(12 November 2010)...250

G

Garanti Koza LLP v Turkmenistan, ICSID Case No ARB/11/20,
Award (19 December 2016) 241, 242, 243, 244, 245, 246, 248
Gaymark Investments Pty Ltd v Walter Construction Group Ltd (2000) BCL 449............ 28, 31, 32
Geoquip Marine Operations AG v Tower Resources Cameroon SA & Anor [2022]
EWHC 531 (Comm)..109
Gerald Metals SA v Timis & Others [2016] EWHC 2337 (Ch)...23
GHL Pte Ltd v Unitrack Building Construction Pte Ltd [1999] 4 SLR 604...............................108
Gilbert Ash v Modern Engineering [1974] AC 689.. 11
Glencore International AG and CI Prodeco SA v Republic of Colombia,
ICSID Case No ARB/16/6, Award (27 August 2019) 246
Gloucester CC v Richardson [1969] 1 AC 480 10
Golden Ocean Group Ltd v Salgaocar Mining Industries PVT Ltd & Anor [2012]
EWCA Civ 265 .... 102, 103
Goodman-Jones v Hughey [2023] NZHC 180 115
Governors of the Peabody Donation Fund v Sir Lindsey Parkinson & Co Ltd [1985]
AC 210...115
GPP Big Field LLP v Solar EPC Solutions SL (Formerly Prosolua Siglio XXI) [2018]
EWHC 2866 (Comm) 200
Grant v Easton (183) 13 QBD 302.. 110
Greaves & Co (Contractors) Ltd v Baynham Meikle & Partners [1975] 1 WLR 1095 ....94, 95
Gregory v HJ Haynes Ltd [2020] EWHC 911 (Ch)...124

xiv

TABLE OF CASES

H

Hamilton v Moore [1873] OJ No 45, 33 UCR 275 28
Hamlin v Bruce Stirling Ltd [1993] 1 NZLR 374 128
Hancock v B. W. Brazier (Anerley) Ltd [1966] 1 WLR 1317 .... 92, 94
Hedley Byrne v Heller & Partners [1964] AC 465 .... 127, 128
Henry Kendall & Sons v William Lillico & Sons Ltd [1969] 2 AC 31 93
Heyman v Darwin [1942] AC 356 112
Hickman & Co v Roberts [1913] AC 229 35
Holme v Brunskill (1878) LR 3 QBD 495 .... 108, 109, 110
Holme v Guppy (1838) 3 M & W 387 .... 27, 28, 29
Hoshine Silicon Industry Co Ltd v AB Speciality Silicones LLC,
   CIETAC Case No ZJR20190012 211
Hsing Chong Construction (Asia) Ltd v Henble Ltd [2006] HKCFI 965 28
Hussein Nauman Soufraki v United Arab Emirates, ICSID Case No ARB/02/7,
   Award (7 July 2004) 241, 242
HXA v Surrey CC [2022] EWCA Civ 1196 128

I

ICCT Ltd v Pinto [2019] EWHC 2134 (TCC) 136
Imperial Chemical Industries Ltd v Merit Merrell Technology Ltd [2017]
   EWHC 1763 (TCC) 34
Impregilo SpA v Islamic Republic of Pakistan (I), ICSID Case No ARB/02/2;
   Case No ARB/03/3 .... 238, 249, 254
International Ltd v JP SPC 4 [2022] UKPC 18, [2022] 3 WLR 261 128
Invercargill City Council v Hamlin [1994] 3 NZLR 513, 72 BLR 39; [1996]
   AC 624, 78 BLR 78, 50 Con LR 105 (PC) 115, 117, 128, 129, 137
Ioannis Kardassopoulos v the Republic of Georgia, ICSID Case No ARB/05/18,
   Decision on Jurisdiction (6 July 2007) 256
Italian Corte di Cassazione, case 03/8813 201
Italian Corte di Cassazione, case 05/15371 201
Italian Corte di Cassazione, case 15/2491 202
Italian Corte di Cassazione, case 16/12956 201
Italian Corte di Cassazione, case 16/21646 202
Italian Corte di Cassazione, case 18/27994 201
Italian Corte di Cassazione, case 19/22050 201
Italian Corte di Cassazione, case 19/34021 202
Italian Corte di Cassazione, case 21/21398 201
Italian Corte di Cassazione, case 46/910 201
Italian Corte di Cassazione, case 63/1807 201
Italian Corte di Cassazione, case 76/4664 203
Italian Corte di Cassazione, case 91/6561 201
Italian Corte di Cassazione, case 93/96660 201
Italian Corte di Cassazione, case 94/7859 202
Italian Corte di Cassazione, case 95/3549 202
Italian Corte di Cassazione, case 98/10439 202
Italian Corte di Cassazione, case 98/11204 201
Italian Corte di Cassazione, case 99/10511 203
Italian Corte di Cassazione, case 16601/17 208

TABLE OF CASES

J

J J Rhatigan & Co (UK) Ltd v Rosemary Lodge Developments Ltd [2019]
EWHC 1152 (TCC)..222
J&B Hopkins Ltd v A&V Building Solution Ltd [2023] EWHC 1483 (TCC)...............136
Jackson v Barry Railway Co [1893] 1 Ch 238 34
Jan de Nul NV and Dredging International NV v Arab Republic of Egypt, ICSID
Case No ARB/04/13, Decision on Jurisdiction (16 June 2006);
Award (6 November 2008) 242, 254
Jeancharm Ltd (t/a Beaver International) v Barnet Football Club Ltd [2003]
EWCA Civ 58 170
John Doyle Construction Ltd (in Liquidation) v Erith Contractors Ltd [2021]
EWCA Civ 1452...42, 221

K

Karkey Karadeniz Elektrik Uretim AS v Islamic Republic of Pakistan,
ICSID Case No ARB/13/1, Award (22 August 2017) 250
Kitchin, Re [1881] 17 ChD 668 .... 110, 111, 112
Koch Minerals Sàrl and Koch Nitrogen International Sàrl v Bolivarian Republic of
Venezuela, ICSID Case No ARB/11/19, Award (30 October 2017)........................ 251
Krederi Ltd. v Ukraine, ICSID Case No ARB/14/17, Award (2 July 2018) 245

L

LDC (Portfolio One) Ltd v George Downing Construction Ltd [2022]
EWHC 3356 (TCC) 117, 126
Leeman v Stocks [1951] 1 Ch 941 102
Lendlease Construction (Europe) Ltd v AECOM Ltd [2023] EWHC 2620 (TCC)......................100
Lesotho Highlands Development Authority v Impregilo Spa [2006] 1 AC 221 .... 22, 23
The Lessees and Management Company of Herons Court v Heronslea Ltd [2019]
EWCA Civ 1423, [2019] 1 WLR 5849.. 120, 128, 130, 131
Lin Chin San Contractors Pte Ltd v LW Infrastructure Pte Ltd (No.1) [2011] SGHC 162.............28
Lordsvale Finance Plc v Bank of Zambia [1996] QB 752 200

M

MA Mortenson Company Inc v Timberline Software Corporation, et al (1999)
93 Wash App 819 61
Macob Civil Engineering Limited v Morrison Construction [1999] 2 WLUK 258;
All ER (D)..42, 220
Mallonland Pty Ltd v Advanta Seeds Pty Ltd [2023] QCA 24 .... 121, 128
Manchikalapati v Zurich Insurance Plc [2019] EWCA Civ 2163, [2020] BLR 1 118
Manifest Shipping Co Ltd v Uni-Polaris Insurance Co Ltd (The Star Sea) [2003]
1 AC 469 19
Mann v Paterson Constructions Pty Ltd (2019) 267 CLR 560...............................272, 273
Mannai Investment Co v Eagle Star Life Assurance [1997] AC 749 (HL)............................20
Marc Rich & Co AG v Bishop Rock Marine Co Ltd [1996] AC 211 127
Martlet Homes Ltd v Mulalley & Co Ltd [2022]
EWHC 1813 (TCC).. 116, 118, 120, 123, 126, 132

xvi

TABLE OF CASES

Mastrobuono v Shearson Lehman Hutton Inc, 514 US 52 (1995) 209

Mata v. Avianca, Inc., United States District Court, S.D. New York, 22-cv-1461 (PKC),
    22 June, 2023 274

McGlinn v Waltham Contractors Ltd (No 3) [2007] EWHC 149 (TCC), 111 Con LR 1 115

Melville Dundas Ltd v George Wimpey UK Ltd [2007] 1 WLR 1136 39

Melville v Carpenter [1853] OJ No 186, 4 UCCP 159 28

Meritz Fire and Marine Insurance Co Ltd v Jan dee Nul NV [2011] 1 All ER
    (Comm) 1049 106

Mertens v Home Freeholds Co [1921] 2 KB 526 93

Metalclad Corporation v The United Mexican States, ICSID Case No ARB(AF)/97/1,
    Award (30 August 2000) 247, 254

Methanex Corporation v United States of America, UNCITRAL, Final Award
    (3 August 2005) 245, 246

Middle East Cement Shipping and Handling Co SA v Arab Republic of Egypt,
    ICSID Case No ARB/99/6, Award (12 April 2002) 247

Mihaly International Corporation v Democratic Socialist Republic of Sri Lanka,
    ICSID Case No ARB/00/2, Award (15 March 2002) 254

Miller v. Cannon Hill Estates Ltd. [1931] 2 KB 113 94

MT Højgaard A/S v E.On Climate & Renewables UK Robin Rigg East Ltd [2017]
    UKSC 59 ....97, 98, 99

Mul v Hutton Construction Ltd [2014] EWHC 1797 (TCC), [2014] BLR 529 126

Mulalley & Co Ltd v Martlet Homes Ltd [2022] EWCA Civ 32; [2021]
    EWHC 296 (TCC) 117

Multiplex Constructions (UK) Ltd v Honeywell Control Systems Ltd (No. 2) [2007]
    EWHC 447 (TCC) 27, 28, 29, 31, 32

Murdoch v Lockie (1896) 15 NZLR 296 ....28, 34

Murphy v Brentwood (1988) 13 Con LR 96; DC [1990] 2 WLR 944; DC [1991]
    1 AC 398 ....8, 115, 121, 124, 127, 128, 129, 130, 132, 137

MW High Tech Projects UK Ltd v Biffa Waste Services Ltd [2015] EWHC 949 (TCC) 104

N

National Grid plc v The Argentine Republic, UNCITRAL, Decision on Jurisdiction
    (20 June 2006); Award (3 November 2008) 245, 250

National Infrastructure Development Company Ltd v Banco Santander S.A. [2017]
    EWCA Civ 27 108

National Westminster Bank plc v Riley [1986] FLR 213 109

Natura Furniture, UAB v GE Power Sweden AB, ICC Case No 21983/MHM 212

Natural Brands Inc v Beaumont Juice Inc D/B/A Perricone Juicees, American
    Arbitration Association, Case No. 01-20-0000-4293 210

Noble Ventures, Inc v Romania, ICSID Case No ARB/01/11, Award (12 October 2005) 248

Nord Stream 2 AG v European Union, PCA Case No 2020-07, Notice of Arbitration
    (26 September 2019) 256

North Midland Building Ltd v Cyden Homes Ltd [2018] EWCA Civ 1744 ....27, 32

North Shore City Council v Body Corporate 188529 (Sunset Terraces) and Body
    Corporate 189855 (Byron Avenue) [2010] NZSC 158, [2011] 2 NZLR 289 129

Northern RHA v Derek Crouch Construction Co Ltd [1984] QB 644 218

NRHA v Derek Crouch [1984] QB 644 12

TABLE OF CASES

O

Oceanfill Ltd v Nuffield Health Wellbeing Ltd & Anor [2022] EWHC 2178 (Ch) 109
Oceltip Aviation 1 Pty Ltd v Gulfstream Aerospace Corporation, ICDR
    Case No 01-14-0001-3711 210
OGI Group Corporation v Oil Projects Company of the Ministry of Oil, Baghdad,
    Iraq (SCOP), ICC Case No 20994/ZF/AYZ 212
Okaroo Pty Ltd v Vos Construction and Joinery Pty Ltd [2005] NSWSC 45 39
OOO Manolium-Processing v The Republic of Belarus, PCA Case No 2018-06,
    Award (22 June 2021) 247
Ottawa Northern and Western Railway Co v Dominion Bridge Co (1905) 36 SCR 347 28
Owners Corporation No 1 of BS613436T v LU Simon Builders Pty Ltd ('Lacrosse')
    [2019] VCAT 286 ....267, 268
Owners Corporation No 1 of PS613436T v LU Simon Builders Pty Ltd [2019] VCAT 286 130
The Owners – Strata Plan 89041 v Galyan Pty Ltd [2019] NSWSC 619 126

P

Pantechniki SA Contractors & Engineers v the Republic of Albania, ICSID
    Case No ARB/07/21, Award (30 July 2009) 254
Panther Real Estate Development LLC v. Modern Executive Systems Contracting
    LLC [2022] DIFC CA 016 195
Parkingeye Limited v Barry Beavis v The Consumers' Association [2015]
    EWCA Civ 402 ....171, 172, 173
Parkview Constructions Pty Ltd v Futuroscop Enterprises Pty Ltd [2023] NSWSC 178 93
Payne v John Setchell Ltd [2001] EWHC 457 (TCC), [2002] BLR 489, (2001)
    3 TCLR 26 118
Peak Construction (Liverpool) Ltd v McKinney Foundations Ltd [1971]
    1 WLUK 456 ....28, 29, 30, 31
Peninsula Balmain Pty Ltd v Abigroup Contractors Ptd Ltd (2002) 18 BCL 322 36
Perar v General Surety (1994) 66 BLR 72 103
Perini Pacific Ltd v Greater Vancouver Sewerage and Drainage District [1966]
    BCJ No 105, 57 DLR (2d) 307 28
Permasteelisa Japan KK v Bouyguesstroi, Banca Intesa SpA [2007] EWHC 3508 (TCC) 17
Petro-Chem Development Co Inc v Pangang Group International Economic & Trading Co Ltd,
    and Pangang Group Chongqing Titanium Industry Co Ltd, ICC Case No 19574/GFG 211
Petroleum Company of Trinidad and Tobago v Samsung Engineering Trinidad [2017]
    EHWC 3055 (TCC) 16, 17, 18
Philip Morris Brands Sàrl, Abal Hermanos SA v Oriental Republic of Uruguay,
    ICSID Case No ARB/10/7, Decision on Jurisdiction (2 July 2013) 244
Philips Hong Kong v Attorney General of Hong Kong (1993) 9 Const LJ 202 169
Phoenix Action, Ltd. v The Czech Republic, ICSID Case No ARB/06/5, Award (15 April 2009)
   244
Pirelli General Cable Works Ltd v Oscar Faber & Partners [1983] 2 AC 1 (HL) 117
Plama Consortium Ltd v Republic of Bulgaria, ICSID Case No ARB/03/24,
    Award (27 August 2008) 250
Plymouth and South West Co-operative Society Ltd v Architecture Structure and
    Management Ltd [2006] EWHC 5 (TCC) 61
PME Cake Ltd, Re [2022] EWHC 1783 (Ch) 109
Poole BC v GN [2019] UKSC 25, [2020] AC 780 128

TABLE OF CASES

Portsmouth City Council v Ensign Highways [2015] EWHC 1969 (TCC)....................................20
Prenn v Simmonds [1971] 1 WLR 1381 (HL)..20
PSEG Global Inc and Konya Ilgin Elektrik Üretim ve Ticaret Limited Sirketi v
    Republic of Turkey, ICSID Case No ARB/02/5, Award (19 January 2007)..................237–238
PSEG Global Inc, The North American Coal Corporation, and Konya Ingin
    Electrick Üretim ve Ticaret Ltd Sirketi v Republic of Turkey, ICSID Case No
    ARB/02/5, Decision on Jurisdiction (4 June 2004) 254

R

R v Sussex Justices; Ex parte McCarthy [1924] KB 256 269
Raffles Offshore (Singapore) Ltd & Anor v Schahin Holding SA [2013] EWCA Civ 644 109
Rainy Sky SA v Kookmin Bank [2011] UKSC 50 ....18, 20
Rees v Firth [2011] NZCA 668..42
Rendlesham Estates Plc v Barr Ltd [2014] EWHC 3968 (TCC) 131
RGB P&C Ltd v Victory House General Partner Ltd [2019] EWHC 1188 (TCC).......................222
Roberts v Bury Improvement Commissioners (1870) LRCP 310..28
Robinson v Chief Constable of West Yorkshire Police [2018] UKSC 4 128
Robinson v PE Jones (Contractors) Ltd [2011] EWCA Civ 9, [2011] BLR 206,
    134 Con LR 26..117, 124, 126, 127
Rosewood Hotel Abu Dhabi LLC v Skelmore Hospitality Group Ltd, ruling of the
    ADGM Court of Appeal of 16 December 2019 196
Ruling of the Abu Dhabi Court of Cassation Case No. 790/2013 (22 October 2014)............ 189, 190
Ruling of the Abu Dhabi Court of Cassation Case No. 941/2009 (29 September 2009) 189
Ruling of the Abud Dhabi Court of Appeal Case No. 941/2009 (30 May 2006) 189
Ruling of the DIFC Court of First Instance Case No. 008/2007 – Ithmar Capital v.
    8 Investments Inc and 8 Investment Group FZE 195
Ruling of the Dubai Court of Cassation Case No. 48/2005 (29 May 2005)................................192
Ruling of the Dubai Court of Cassation Case No. 138/1994 (13 November 1994) 189, 192
Ruling of the Dubai Court of Cassation Case No. 177/1998 (12 July 1998)...............................192
Ruling of the Dubai Court of Cassation Case No. 205/2002 (23 June 2002)..............................184
Ruling of the Dubai Court of Cassation Case No. 222/2005 (19 June 2006)..............................185
Ruling of the Dubai Court of Cassation Case No. 266/2008 (17 March 2009)...........................192
Ruling of the Dubai Court of Cassation Case No. 402/2004 189
Ruling of the Dubai Court of Cassation Case No. 494/2003 (24 April 2004) 189, 192
Ruling of the UAE Federal Supreme Court Case No. 103/24 (21 March 2004) 186, 187, 188
Ruling of the UAE Federal Supreme Court Case No. 302/21 (17 June 2001).......................189, 190
Ruling of the UAE Federal Supreme Court Case No. 344/19 (23 January 1999) 188
Ruling of the UAE Federal Supreme Court Case No. 414/21 (Civil) (27 March 2001)....................189
Ruling of the UAE Federal Supreme Court Case No. 595/18 (26 April 1998)...........................191
Ruling of the UAE Federal Supreme Court Case No. 742/23 (16 May 2004)..............................188
Ruling of the UAE Federal Supreme Court Case No. 782/22 (7 April 2002).......................186, 188
Ruling of the UAE Federal Supreme Court Case No. 344/19 (23 January 1999) 188
Ruling of the UAE Federal Supreme Court, Petition No. 26 of Judicial Year 24,
    Judgement rendered 1 June 2004 187
Rumeli Telekom AS and Telsim Mobil Telekomunikasyon Hizmetleri AS v
    Republic of Kazakhstan, ICSID Case No ARB/05/16, Award (29 July 2008).......................248
Rusoro Mining Ltd. v Bolivarian Republic of Venezuela, ICSID Case No ARB(AF)/12/5,
    Award (22 August 2016)...249–250
Russell v Russell (1976) 134 CLR 495...271

TABLE OF CASES

S

S&T (UK) Limited v Grove Developments Limited: [2018] EWHC 123 (TCC) 221

Sabah Shipyard v Government of Pakistan [2008] 1 Lloyd's Rep 210...111

Saipem SpA v The People's Republic of Bangladesh, ICSID Case No ARB/05/07,
  Decision on Jurisdiction and Recommendation on Provisional Measures
  (21 March 2007) 243, 254

Salam Air SAOC v Latam Airlines Group SA [2020] EWHC 2414 (Comm)...............................108

Salini Construttori SpA and Italstrade SpA v Hashemite Kingdom of Jordan,
  ICSID Case No ARB/02/13, Award (31 January 2006)...254

Salini Costruttori SpA and Italstrade SpA v Kingdom of Morocco, ICSID Case
  No ARB/00/4, Decision on Jurisdiction (31 July 2001)...243

Saluka Investments BV v The Czech Republic, UNCITRAL, Partial Award
  (17 March 2006)..246, 250

Samsung Engineering Co, Ltd v Sultanate of Oman, ICSID Case No ARB/15/30.....................254

Samuels Finance Group plc v Beechmanor Ltd [1993] 67 P&CR 282..109

Scammell v Dicker [2005] EWCA Civ 405 178

Scheldebouw BV v St James Homes (Gosvenor Dock) Ltd [2006] EWHC 89 (TCC) 34, 36

Scott v Scott [1913] AC 417..271

SD Myers, Inc v Government of Canada, UNCITRAL, Partial Award (13 November 2000)..... 246

Seele Middle East FZE v Drake & Scull International SA Co [2014] EWHC 435 (TCC) 23

Seele Middle East FZE v Raiffeisenlandesbank Oberösterreich
  Aktiengesellschaft Bank [2014] EWHC 343 (TCC)... 17, 18

Sempra Energy International v The Argentine Republic, ICSID Case No ARB/02/16,
  Award (28 September 2007)... 248–249

SGS Société Générale de Surveillance SA v Islamic Republic of Pakistan, ICSID
  Case No. ARB/01/13, Decision of the Tribunal on Objections to Jurisdiction
  (6 August 2003) 248

Shanghai Shipyard Co Ltd v Reignwood International Investment (Group)
  Company Ltd [2021] EWCA Civ 1147 ....105, 107, 110

Shapoorji Pallonji & Company Private Limited v Yumn Ltd v
  Standard Chartered Bank [2021] EWHC 862..23, 108

Sheffield Teaching Hospital Foundation Trust v Hadfield Healthcare
  Partnerships Ltd [2023] EWHC 644 (TCC) 117

Shui on Construction Co Ltd v Shui Kay Co Ltd & Ors [1985] 2 HKC 634 35

Sim Chio Huat v Wong Ted Fui [1983] 1 MLJ 151..28, 29

Simon Carves Ltd v Enus UK Ltd [2011] EWHC 657 (TCC) 107

Sistem Mühendislik Insaat Sanayi ve Ticaret AS v Kyrgyz Republic, ICSID Case No
  ARB(AF)/06/1, Decision on Jurisdiction (13 September 2007)..242

SK Shipping Europe PLC v Capital VLCC Corp and Ano [2020] EWHC 3448 (Comm)........... 111

SKX v Manchester City Council [2021] EWHC 782 (QB)..124

SMK Cabinets v Modern Electrics Pty Ltd [1984] VR 391 ....28, 29

Societe Gaussin et autres v Societe Alstom Power Turbomachines, Cour de
  Cassation (Ch Com), 2 June 2004 228

Société Générale In respect of DR Energy Holdings Limited and Empresa
  Distribuidora de Electricidad del Este, SA v The Dominican Republic,
  UNCITRAL, LCIA Case No UN 7927, Award on Preliminary Objections to
  Jurisdiction (19 September 2008)..245

Solo Industries UK Ltd v Canara Bank [2001] 1 WLR 1800..108

Soulemezis v Dudley (Holdings) Pty Ltd (1987) 10 NSWLR 247 269

TABLE OF CASES

Sparham-Souter v Town & Country Developments (Essex) Ltd [1976] 1 QB 858 (CA)...............117
Sportcity 4 Management Ltd v Countrywide Properties (UK) Ltd [2020]
  EWHC 1591 (TCC), 192 Con LR 131 118
St James's Oncology SPC Ltd v Lendlease Construction (Europe) Ltd [2022]
  EWHC 2504 (TCC)...126
ST-AD GmbH v Republic of Bulgaria, UNCITRAL, PCA Case No 2011-06, Award on
  Jurisdiction (18 July 2013)...245
Standard Chartered Bank v The United Republic of Tanzania, ICSID Case No
  ARB/10/12, Award (2 November 2012) 242
Steel v NRAM Ltd [2018] UKSC 13, [2018] 1 WLR 1190...127
Stevenson v Watson (1879) 4 CPD 148 35
Strabag SE v Libya, ICSID Case No ARB(AF)/15/1, Award
  (29 June 2020)...................................235, 240, 241, 243, 244, 245, 249, 251
Struthers v Davies [2022] EWHC 333 (TCC)...126
Sudbrooke Trading v Eggleton [1983] 1 AC 444...57
Sudlows Ltd v Global Swith Estates 1 Ltd [2022] EWHC 3319 (TCC)...........................42
Suez, Sociedad General de Aguas de Barcelona, SA and Vivendi Universal, SA v
  Argentine Republic, ICSID Case No ARB/03/1, Decision on Liability (30 July 2010).........248
Sutcliffe v Chippendale & Edmondson (a firm) [1982] 18 BLR 149 35
Sutcliffe v Thackrah [1974] AC 727...35
Sztejn v J Henry Schroder Banking Corporation (1941) 31 NYS 2d 631 105

T

Talal El Makdessi v Cavendish Square Holdings BV and another [2013] EWCA Civ 1539.........171
Tanah Merah Vic Pty Ltd v Owners Corporation No 1 of PS613436 (No 1) [2021]
  VSCA 72; (No 2) ('Lacrosse No 2') [2021] VSCA 122.....................................268
Tanah Merah Vic Pty Ltd v Owners Corporation No 1 of PS613436T [2021] VSCA 72 130
Tecnicas Reunidas Saudia for Services and Contracting Co Ltd v Korea Development
  Bank [2020] EWHC 968 (TCC)..17, 18
Tetronics (International) Ltd v HSBC Bank Plc [2018] EWHC 201 (TCC) 104, 108
Thomas-Frederic's (Construction) Ltd v Keith Wilson [2003] WCA Civ 1750 42
Thorn v The Mayor and Commonalty of London (1876) LR 1 HL 120............................92
Trade Indemnity Company Limited v. Workington Harbour and Dock Board [1937] AC 1 104
Trafalgar House Construction (Regions) Limited v General Surety and Guarantee
  Company Limited [1995] AC 199 ....101, 103–104, 105, 108
TransCanada Corporation and TransCanada PipeLines Limited v The United States of
  America, ICSID Case No. ARB/16/21, Request for Arbitration (24 June 2016) 255
Transfield Shipping Inc v Mercator Shipping Inc (The Achilleas) [2008] UKHL 48;
  [2009] 1 AC 61...158
Triple Point Technology Inc v PTT Public Co Ltd [2018] EWHC 45 (TCC), [2019]
  EWCA Civ 230 and [2021] UKSC 29 ....175, 176, 177, 178
Trollope & Colls Ltd v North West Metropolitan Regional Hospital Board [1973]
  1 WLR 601..27, 28, 29
TTI Telecom International v Hutchison 3G UK Ltd [2003] EWHC 762 (TCC)................107
Turner Corporation Ltd (In Provisional Liquidation) v Co-Ordinated
  Industries Pty Ltd & Ors (1995) 11 BCL 202 ....28, 31
Turner Corporation Ltd (Receiver and Manager Appointed) v Austotel Pty Ltd (1997)
  13 BCL 378...28, 31, 32
Tyers v Aegis Defence Services (BVI) Ltd [2023] EWHC 896 (KB)...............................124

xxi

TABLE OF CASES

U

Ulysseas, Inc v The Republic of Ecuador, UNCITRAL, Final Award (12 June 2012) 250
Unaoil v Leighton Offshore Unaoil v Leighton Offshore [2014] EWHC 2965 (Comm)............ 16, 17
United City Merchants (Investments) Limited v Royal Bank of Canada [1983] 1AC 168 104
United States v Spearin, 248 U.S. 132 (1918) 92
University of Warwick v Balfour Beatty [2018] EWHC 3239 (TCC)...20
URS Corporation Ltd v BDW Trading Ltd [2023] EWCA Civ 772, [2021]
    EWHC 2796 (TCC), [2022] EWHC 2966 (TCC), [2023] EWCA
    Civ 189 ....114, 117, 118, 119, 121, 130
Ust-Kamenogorsk Hydropower Plant JSC v AES Ust-Kamenogorsk
    Hydropower Plant LLP [2013] UKSC 35...22

V

Valores Mundiales, SL and Consorcio Andino SL v Bolivarian Republic of
    Venezuela, ICSID Case No ARB/13/11, Award (25 July 2017)...250
Vinci Construction UK Ltd v Eastwood and Partners (Consulting Engineers)
    Ltd [2023] EWHC 1899 (TCC) 118

W

The Wardens and Commonality of the Mystery of Mercers of the City of London v New
    Hampshire Insurance Company Limited [1992] 2 Lloyd's LR 365(1992)
    60 BLR 26.. 101, 109
West Tankers Inc v RAS Riunione Adriatica di Sicurta SpA (The Front Comor) [2007]
    UKHL 4 .... 22, 23
William Ranger v The Great Western Railway Co [1854] 10 ER 824 34
Willow Corp SÀRL v MTD Contractors Ltd [2019] EWHC 1591 (TCC)...................................222
Winterthur Gas & Diesel AG v Nuclebrás Equipamentos Pesados S.A, Ad Hoc
    Arbitration, 2014; ICC Case No 10302 210
Woodlands Oak Ltd v Conwell [2011] EWCA Civ 254, [2011] BLR 365.....................................126
Woolcock Street Investments Pty Ltd v CDG Pty Ltd [2004] HCA 16, 216 CLR 515 121
Workers Trust & Merchant Bank Ltd v Dojap Investments Ltd [1993] AC 573..........................170
Wraight v PHT Holdings 13 BLR 26 157

X

X v Bedfordshire County Council [1995] 2 AC 633...127

Y

Yam Seng Pte Ltd v International Trade Corp Ltd [2013] 1 CLC 662...19
Ying Ho Co Ltd v Secretary for Justice [2004] HKCU 1113 ....28, 29
Young & Marten Ltd v McManus Childs Ltd [1969] 1 AC 454...10, 93
Yuanda (UK) Company Ltd v Multiplex Construction Europe Ltd & Anor [2020]
    EWHC 468 (TCC)... 110
Yves Morael v. France, Communication No. 207/1986 (4 November 1988) 270

xxii

TABLE OF CASES

Z

Zagora Management Ltd v Zurich Insurance Plc [2019] EWHC 140 (TCC),
182 Con LR 180 118
ZCCM Investments Holdings Plc v Konkola Copper Mines Plc [2017]
EWHC 3288 (Comm) 200
Zim Integrated Shipping Services v European Container [2013]
EWHC 3581 (Comm) 23

TABLE OF LEGISLATIONS

United Kingdom

Arbitration Act 1950
  s 7 110
Arbitration Act 1979
  s 68 110
  s 69 110
Arbitration Act 1996 220
  s 1 22
  s 33 22
  s 34 22
  s 34(g) 219
  s 39 .... 11, 12
  s 44 23
  s 44(3) 23
  s 44(5) 23
  s 47 11
  s 67 16
  s 68 22
  s 69 22

Building Act 1984 .... 143, 147
  s 1(2) 132
  s 38 .... 148, 149
  s 38(1)(a) 148
  s 120D 123
  section 38 132
Building Safety Act 2022 .... 3, 10, 48,
        63, 120, 130, 139, 140, 141, 148, 151
  Pt 2 129
  Pt 4 151
  Pt 5 .... 123, 133, 137
  s 2A 130–131
  s 3(1) 149
  s 4 149
  s 31 123
  s 38 132
  ss 91–97 123

s 117 .... 123, 135
s 120 .... 123, 135
ss 121–124 135
s 124 135
s 130 132
s 130(1) 148
s 130(2)(b) 148
s 130(3)(a) 148
s 130(3)(b) 148
s 130(6) 148
s 131 132
s 134 131
s 135 .... 118, 132
s 135(1) 149
ss 136–143 133
s 137 150
s 140(1)(a)-(b) 150
ss 144–145 134
ss 146–150 114
ss 147–150 131
s 148 131
s 148(2) 149
s 148(3) 131
s 148(5) 149
s 148(6) 131
s 148(7) 132
s 149 131
s 149(3) 131
s 150 132
s 151 118
s 156 115
sch 8 135
schs 9–10 133
Building Safety Act (Scotland) 2022
  s 135 118
  s 151 .... 118, 132

TABLE OF LEGISLATIONS

Building Safety Act 2022 (Commencement No 4 and Transitional Provisions) Regulations 2023 (SI 2023/362) 134

Building Safety (Leaseholder Protections) (England) Regulations 2022 (SI 2022/711) 135

Building Safety (Leaseholder Protections) (Information etc) (England) Regulations 2022 (SI 2022/859) 135

Building Safety (Leaseholder Protections) (England) (Amendment) Regulations 2023 (SI 2023/126) 135

Building Safety (Responsible Actors Scheme and Prohibitions) Regulations 2023 (SI 2023/753) 123

Civil Procedure Rules
Pt 6 25
Pt 8 42
s II 25
s IV 25

Companies Act 2006
s 171(1)(d) 68

Constitutional Reform Act 2005 272
s 25 272

Consumer Rights Act 2015
s 2 115
s 10(1) 93
s 10(3) 93
s 49–52 115
ss 54–56 115

Contracts (Rights of Third Parties) Act 1999 58

County Courts Act 1959
s 92 218

Courts Act 1971
Section 25 220

Defective Premises Act 1972 .... 117, 120, 127, 128, 132, 148
s 1 .... 114, 118, 130, 131, 135, 149
s 1(1) 130, 131
s 1(4) 130
s 2A 114, 135, 149
s 2A(7) 131
s 3 120
s 7(2) 120

Environment Act 2021 74

Factories Act 1937 142

Factories Act 1961 142

Fire Precautions Act 1971 142

Fire Safety Act 2021 115

Fire Safety (England) Regulations 2022 (SI 2022/547) 115

Higher-Risk Buildings (Descriptions and Supplementary Provisions) Regulations 2023 (SI 2023/275) 123

Housing Grants, Construction and Regeneration Act 1996 *see also* Construction Act 1996 .... 1, 3, 7–8, 11, 15, 37–42, 103, 137, 217
Pt II 136
ss 104–105 136
s 104(3) 39
s 104(6)(b) 38
s 105 .... 39, 222
s 106 .... 39, 136
s 106(2) 136
s 106(3) 136
s 106A 136
s 107 39
s 108 .... 37, 39, 217
s 108(1) 42, 136
s 109 .... 37, 39
s 109(2) 40
s 110(1) 40
s 110(3) 40
s 112 37

Judicature Act 1873
s 82 220

Latent Damage Act 1986 (England & Wales)
s 3 118

Limitation Act 1980
s 2 117
s 5 117
s 8 .... 117, 118
s 11 124
s 14A 118
s 14A–B 117, 118
s 33 124

Local Democracy, Economic Development and Construction Act 2009
Pt 8 37

London Building Act 1667 .... 140, 141

London Building Act 1772 140

London Building Act 1774 140

Occupiers Liability Act 1957 124

Private International Law (Implementations of Agreements) Act 2020 25

Public Contracts Regulations 2015
reg 67(1) 52
reg 67(2) 52

TABLE OF LEGISLATIONS

reg 67(3) 52
Public Health Act 1936 .... 119, 127, 141
Public Health Act 1961 142
Sale of Goods Act 1979
    s 14(3) 93, 95, 100
Scheme for Construction Contracts (England
    and Wales) Regulations 1998 217
    Art 13 219
Senior Courts Act 1981
    s 37 23
Statute of Frauds 1677
    s 4 102
Unfair Trading Regulations 2008
    (SI 2008/1277) 116

Australia

Building Act 2004 (Australian Capital
    Territory) 129
Building Act 1993 (Northern Territory) 129
Building Amendment Act 2015
    (Victoria) 130
Building and Construction Commission
    Act 1991 (Queensland) 129
Building and Construction Industry
    Security of Payment Act 1999
    (New South Wales) 38, 40
    s 7(1) 39
    s 7(3) 39
    s 7(3)(a) 39
    s 7(4) 38
    s 8 .... 39, 40
    s 12 40
    s 13 40
    s 13(1) 40
    s 13(2) 40
    s 13(7) 40
    s 13(9) 40
    s 14 40
    s 14(3) 40
    s 14(4) 40
    s 17 42
    ss 14(1)–14(2) 40
Building and Construction Industry
    Security of Payment Act 2021
    (Western Australia) 38
    s 17 39
Building (General) Regulation 2008
    (Australian Capital Territory) 129
Building Regulations 1993 (Northern
    Territory) 129

Building Work Contractors Act 1995 (South
    Australia) 129
Domestic Building Contracts
    Act 1995 (Victoria) 130
    s 8 268
Domestic Building Contracts Regulations
    2017 (Victoria) 130
Federal Court of Australia Act 1976
    s 6 (2)(b) 272
Federal Court of Australia Act 1976 (Cth)
    s 6 272
Home Building Act 1989
    (New South Wales) 129
Home Building Contracts Act 1991
    (Western Australia) 130
Home Building Contracts Regulations
    1992 (Western Australia) 130
Residential Building Work Contracts
    and Dispute Resolution Act 2016
    (Tasmania) 129–130

Canada

Builder's Lien (Prompt Payment)
    Amendment Act 2019
    (Saskatchewan) 38
Builders' Lien (Prompt Payment)
    Amendment Act 2020 (Alberta) 38
Construction Act 1990 (Ontario) 41, 42
    s 6.2 39
    s 6.3 39
    s 13.5(1) 42
Federal Prompt Payment for
    Construction Work Act 2019 38

European Union

Commission Delegated Regulation (EU)
    2021/2139 of 4 June 2021
    supplementing Regulation (EU)
    2020/852 of the European
    Parliament and of the Council by
    establishing the technical screening
    criteria for determining the conditions
    under which an economic activity
    qualifies as contributing substantially
    to climate change mitigation or climate
    change adaptation and for determin-
    ing that economic activity causes no
    significant harm to any of the other
    environmental objectives 84

TABLE OF LEGISLATIONS

Council Regulation (EC) No 1346/2000 of
29 May 2000 on insolvency
proceedings
Art 15 226
Directive 2010/31/EU of the European
Parliament and of the Council of 19
May 2010 on the energy performance
of buildings (recast) 79, 81, 82
Directive 2012/27/EU of the European
Parliament and of the Council of 25
October 2012 on energy efficiency,
amending Directives 2009/125/EC and
2010/30/EU and repealing Directives
2004/8/EC and 2006/32/EC 79
Directive 2023/1791 of the European
Parliament and of the Council of 13
September 2023 on energy efficiency
and amending Regulation (EU)
2023/955 (recast) 81
Directive 2014/24/EU of the European
Parliament and of the Council of 26
February 2014 on public
procurement and repealing
Directive 2004/18/EC 52
Regulation (EU) 2015/848 of the
European Parliament and of the
Council of 20 May 2015 on
insolvency proceedings
(recast) 225, 228
Art 3(1) 226
Art 18 .... 226, 227
Art 19(1) 226
Art 32 226
Art 92 226
Regulation (EU) 2020/852 of the European
Parliament and of the Council of 18
June 2020 on the establishment of a
framework to facilitate sustainable
investment, and amending Regulation
(EU) 2019/2088 85
Art 1(2)(f) 85
Art 3 84
Art 17 84
Sch 1 85
Sch 7 85
Regulation (EU) 2021/241 of the
European Parliament and of the
Council of 12 February 2021
establishing the Recovery and
Resilience Facility 84

Regulation (EU) 2021/1119 of the European
Parliament and of the Council of 30
June 2021 establishing the frame-
work for achieving climate neutrality
and amending regulations (EC) No
401/2009 and EU 2018/1999 ('European
Climate Law') 68
Regulation (EC) No 593/2008 of the
European Parliament and of the Council
of 17 June 2008 on the law applicable to
contractual obligations (Rome I)
Art 9 209
Regulation (EU) No 1215/2012 of the
European Parliament and of the Council
of 12 December 2012 on jurisdiction
and the recognition and enforcement of
judgments in civil and commercial mat-
ters (recast) 25
Regulations (EC) No 401/2009 of the
European Parliament and the Council
of 23 April 2009 on the European
Environment Agency and the European
Environment Information and
Observation Network 68
Regulation (EU) 2018/1999 of the European
Parliament and of the Council of 11
December 2018 on the Governance
of the Energy Union and Climate
Action, amending Regulations (EC) No
663/2009 and (EC) No 715/2009 of the
European Parliament and of the Council,
Directives 94/22/EC, 98/70/EC, 2009/31/
EC, 2009/73/EC, 2010/31/EU, 2012/27/
EU and 2013/30/EU of the European
Parliament and of the Council, Council
Directives 2009/119/EC and (EU)
2015/652 and repealing Regulation (EU)
No 525/2013 of the European Parliament
and of the Council 68

France
Civil Code
Art 1231-5 .... 202, 203
Art 2060 230
Commercial Code
Art L 622-17 (I) 228
Art L 622-17 (II) 228
Art L 622-17 (III) 228
Art L 622-21 (I) 228

TABLE OF LEGISLATIONS

Germany
Civil Code
  s 339 .... 203, 204
  s 340 203
  s 340 (2) 203
  s 341 203
  s 342 204
  s 343 203
  s 345 204
Code of Civil Procedure
  s 1030(1) 231
Insolvency Code 229

Ireland
Construction Contracts Act 2013 .... 38, 40
  s 1(1) 39
  s 2(1)(a) 39
  s 2(1)(b) 39
  s 2(2) 39
  s 3 39
  s 3(1) 40
  s 3(2) 40
  s 3(5) 40
  s 4(2) 40
  s 4(3) 40
  s 4(4) 40
  s 6(1) 42

Italy
Civil Code
  Art 1382 201
  Art 1383 201
  Art 1384 201
Insolvency Code
  Art 150 228
  Art 192 230
Insolvency Law 1942
  Art 83-bis 230
Legislative Decree-Law No, 34 of
  19 May 2020
  Art 119 80
  Art 119(1) 80
Legislative Decree No, 28 of 3 March 2011
Annex 3, paragraph 1, letter (c) 79
  Art 2(1) 80
Legislative Decree No, 36 of 31 March 2023
  Art 57 82
Legislative Decree No, 50/2016

Art 211(1-bis) 83
Legislative Decree No, 176 of 18 November
  2022 80
Legislative Decree No, 221 of 28 December
  2015
  Art 18 82

Malaysia
Construction Industry Payment and
  Adjudication Act 2012
  s 2 .... 38, 39
  s 3 39
  s 5 40
  s 6 40
  s 7(1) 42
  s 15 42
  s 30 42
  s 35 40
  s 36 .... 39, 40

New Zealand
Building Act 2004
  Part 4A 130
Construction Contracts Act 2002
  s 6 39
  s9 ... 39
  s 9(a) 38
  s 9(c) 39
  s 11 39
  s 11(a) 39
  s 11(b) 39
  s 13 40
  s 14 40
  s 16 .... 39, 40
  s 17 40
  s 18 40
  s 20 40
  s 21 40
  s 22 40
  s 24 40
  s 24A(1)(a)(iii) 42
  s 25 42
  s 28(3) 137
  s 31A(3) 137
Construction Contracts Amendment
  Act 2015 137
Construction Contracts Regulations 2003
  reg 5 137

xxix

TABLE OF LEGISLATIONS

Poland
Bankruptcy and Reorganization Act
Art 142 232

Portuguese
Insolvency Law
Art 87(1) 232
Art 178(2) 232

Romania
Civil Procedure Code
Art 541–542 224
Art 542(1) 232
Art 1112 224
Art 1115 224
Code of Civil Procedure
Art 542 230
Art 1112 230
Insolvency Law no 85/2014
Art 75(1) 227
Art 178 227

Singapore
Building and Construction Industry
    Security of Payment Act 2004 38
    s 2 39
    s 3 39
    s 4(1) 39
    s 4(2)(a) 39
    s 4(2)(b)(i) 39
    s 4(2)(b)(ii) 38
    s 4(4) 39
    s 5 .... 39, 40
    s 9 40
    s 10 40
    s 11 40
    s 12 42
    s 13 42
    s 18 42
    s 25 42

Spain
Insolvency Law
Art 140 228–229

Switzerland
Code of Obligations
Art 160 204
Art 161 204
Art 163 204
Federal Act on Private International Law 1987
Art 154 233
Art 155(c) 233
Art 177(1) 230

United Arab Emirates
Abu Dhabi Global Market
    Application of English Law
    Regulations 2015 182
Civil Code 182, 183, 197
Art 291 192
Art 389 .... 184, 191
Art 390 .... 183, 184, 185, 186, 187,
                189, 190, 191, 193, 194, 196
Art 390(1) 183, 184, 185, 190, 192
Art 390(2) 183, 184, 185, 186, 189, 190,
                191, 192, 194, 195
Arts 872–896 182
Civil Transactions Law (Federal Law No. 5
    of 1985, Federal Law No. 1 of 1987 and
    Federal Law No. 30/2020) 182
Constitution 1971
    Art 7 182
Dubai International Financial Centre
Implied Terms in Contracts and Unfair
    Terms Law No. 6 of 2005 182
Law of Contract (No. 6 of 2004) 182
    s 122 .... 193, 194, 195, 196
    s 122(1) 193, 194
    s 122(2) 194, 195
Law of Damages and Remedies
    (No. 7 of 2005) 182
    s 21 193
    s 21(1) 193, 194, 195
    s 21(2) 194, 195
Law of Obligations DIFC Law
    (No. 5 of 2005) 182
Law on the Application of Civil and
    Commercial Laws in the DIFC
    (No. 3 of 2004)
    Art 8(1) 182

INTERNATIONAL AGREEMENTS, CONVENTIONS AND TREATIES

Austria–Libya Bilateral Investment
    Treaty 2002 .... 235, 240
    Art 8 249
    Art 15 251
    Art 23(1) 243
Brussels Convention 1968 25
Convention on Choice of Court
    Agreements 2005 (Hague
    Convention) 24–25, 26
    Art 5 25
    Art 8 25
    Art 16 25
    Art 36 25
    Art 39 25
Convention on Contracts for the
    International Sale of Goods
    1976 205
    Art 4 207
    Art 6 211
    Art 7 207
    Art 45(2) 211
    Art 74 211
Convention on the Execution of Foreign
    Arbitral Awards 1927 (Geneva
    Convention) 230
    Art 1 224
Convention on jurisdiction and the recogni-
    tion and enforcement of judgments
    in civil and commercial matters 2007
    (Lugano Convention)
    Art 70 26
    Art 72 26
Convention on the Recognition and
    Enforcement of Foreign Arbitral

Awards 1958 (New York
    Convention) 3, 224, 236
    Art II(1) 230
    Art II(3) 229
    Art V 236
    Art V(2)(b) 209
    Art V(a) 232
Convention on the Settlement of
    Investment Disputes between
    States and Nationals of Other
    States 1965 (ICSID
    Convention) 236, 237, 244
    Art 25 243
    Art 54(1) 236
    Art III-3:712 206–207
Energy Charter Treaty
    1991 .... 254, 258, 259, 260
    Pt III 258
    Annex EM I
    Art 27.11 256
    Art 1(4) 256
    Art 1(5) 257, 258
    Art 1(6) 256, 257, 259
    Art 1(6)(a) 256
    Art 1(6)(c) 256
    Art 1(6)(f) 256
European Convention on
    International Commercial
    Arbitration 1961 230
    Art 1 224
Franco–British Convention on Foreign
    Judgments 1934 25
India–Kuwait BIT 2001
    Art 4.4 251

xxxi

INTERNATIONAL AGREEMENTS, CONVENTIONS AND TREATIES

International Covenant on Civil
  and Political Rights 1966
  Art 14 .... 271, 272
  Art 14(1) 270
UK Model Bilateral Investment Treaty
  Art 2(2) 248

Art 3(3) 245
United Nations Framework Convention on
  Climate Change 1992 259
United Kingdom-Turkmenistan Bilateral
  Investment Treaty 1995
  Art 1 241

INTRODUCTION

Introduction

On 17 and 18 November 2022, the Centre of Construction Law & Dispute Resolution at King's College London held a conference to mark its 35th anniversary. The conference offered an excellent opportunity to reflect on and consider future developments in this unique area of law. This book is a testament to the lively discussions that took place over the course of the conference. However, it is not merely a collection of conference papers. In line with the Centre's research methodology and the approach adopted in previous publications, the contributors have significantly reworked and expanded their contributions. The book also includes chapters by authors who did not participate in the conference in order for the book to be a coherent and standalone publication.

This is the third book published by the Centre that employs the same dynamic and interactive research methodology, drawing insights from academia, legal practice, and industry.[1] The book invites reflection on the historical and international contexts shaping the evolution of construction law, new frontiers in procurement models and outcomes, key concepts and developments in common law and civil law jurisdictions, and, finally, construction dispute resolution.

Chapter 1, written by **Professor John Uff CBE KC** – the founding Director of the Centre – outlines how the Centre, from its very inception in July 1987, spearheaded the academic development of construction law. Its scholarship has notably influenced the key aspects of modern construction law such as risk allocation, quality and time control, prompt payment, and dispute resolution. The chapter also discusses the overarching role of the Centre as an institution of education through its landmark Master of Science in Construction Law and Dispute Resolution – a course that has persistently attracted top calibre students and shaped entire generations of construction professionals.

In Chapter 2, **Professor Renato Nazzini**, the current Director of the Centre, reflects on how English construction law has influenced the international market. In particular, it examines the international appeal of English construction law, the impact of English legal concepts on foreign case law and on standard forms of construction contracts, and the international impact of the payment and adjudication provisions of the UK Housing Grants, Construction and Regeneration Act 1996.

---

1 Renato Nazzini (ed), *Key Themes in International Construction Arbitration* (Routledge 2017) and Renato Nazzini (ed), *Construction Arbitration and Alternative Dispute Resolution: Theory and Practice around the World* (Routledge 2021).

DOI: 10.4324/9781032663975-1

The Centre has a rich history of driving policy change. The second part of this book explores how the Centre's research influenced procurement policy in the UK and beyond.

In Chapter 3, **Professor David Mosey CBE**, a former Director of the Centre, explains how collaborative procurement can support building safety so as to prevent another Grenfell disaster, which claimed 71 lives and shook British society, prompting an urgent reconsideration of building safety standards.

In Chapter 4, Professor Mosey and **Dr Roxana Vornicu**, a Research Associate at the Centre, advocate for harnessing the potential of collaborative procurement not only to improve safety but also to achieve the net zero target by 2050.

Both contributions advocate for early supply chain involvement, supply chain collaboration, use of long-term alliance contracts, joint contract governance and risk management, and use of digital tools such as building information modelling.

In Chapter 5, **Professor Sara Valaguzza**, Scientific Director of the Centre of Construction Law & Management at the University of Milan, observes that such collaborative and sustainable procurement methods are already employed by the Milan contracting authorities to foster net zero construction. The solutions framed by Professor Mosey and the Centre team, therefore, can have international application.

Surrounded by the Royal Courts of Justice, the Technology and Construction Court, and the historic Inns of Court, the Centre is located right in the heart of legal London. Thus, English law often constitutes the starting point of its research. Nevertheless, the Centre does not shy away from engaging with matters of international and transnational law to produce cutting-edge research of global relevance. In line with this research paradigm, the third part of the present book traces the development of key concepts in common and civil law.

Fitness for purpose obligations constitute an integral part of English commercial law and reflect the business reality in the construction sector. In Chapter 6, **Julian Bailey**, Partner at Jones Day and a Visiting Professor at the Centre, examines how they arise and influence risk allocation between the parties. It discusses the key ingredient of implied fitness for purpose obligations: the employer's reliance on the contractor's judgement or skill in design or selecting goods or materials.

Continuing the debate on English commercial law, Chapter 7, authored by **Richard Wilmot-Smith KC**, a Barrister at 39 Essex Chambers, surveys the jurisprudence concerning the law of guarantee and indemnity. It concludes that while the law has not changed considerably over the past 35 years, reforms of other areas of law and the development of industry practices have resulted in new financial instruments arriving on the market, such as adjudication bonds stemming from the interim binding nature of decisions.

Retention and maintenance bonds allow commercial parties to mitigate the risk of latent defects. However, as **Professor Philip Britton**, a former Director of the Centre, observes in Chapter 8, English law does not afford a judicial remedy to homeowners for latent construction defects in the absence of a contractual link between the claimant and the defendant. Professor Britton draws on comparative insights from other jurisdictions, including New Zealand and various Australian states and territories to critique this position.

Reflecting on how to prevent construction defects and ensure building safety, Chapter 9, by **Abdul-Lateef Jinadu**, a Barrister at Keating Chambers, and **Sam Grimley**, an incoming Pupil Barrister at One Essex Court, offers a historical account of building regulation in England. It observes that, from the outset, the impetus for change has been a disaster, followed by piecemeal legislation. The chapter also enquires whether reforms introduced by the Building Safety Act 2022 can properly address the shortcomings of the preceding regime highlighted by the Grenfell Tower tragedy.

Under most standard forms, the employer must reimburse the contractor only the additional costs or losses when the delays were caused by certain prescribed causes or matters for which the employer has taken the delay risk and when the contractor has fulfilled the relevant claims notification requirements. Usually, the contracts do not specify how much is due or how that amount is to be calculated. Chapter 10, authored by **Dr Ronan Champion**, a Lecturer in construction law at the University of Reading, addresses these questions by comparing different approaches to quantifying prolongation costs arising under the JCT, NEC and FIDIC forms, such as valuation based on costs, valuation based on contract rates and prices, valuation by agreement, or valuation by formula.

The next three chapters contrast the common law and civil law approaches to liquidated damages.

In Chapter 11, **Nicholas Gould**, a Partner at Fenwick Elliott and a Visiting Professor at the Centre, and **Katherine Butler**, a Senior Associate at Fenwick Elliott, show how the courts developed the law on liquidated damages to better reflect commercial reality and respect the autonomy of the parties.

In Chapter 12, **Dr Gordon Blanke**, the founding Partner at Blanke Arbitration, observes how the civil law and common law positions on liquidated damages converge in the United Arab Emirates. UAE law grants a significant margin of discretion to the judge or arbitral tribunal to adjust the pre-agreed amount of liquidated damages, as required by the UAE's public policy in respecting the Islamic Shari'ah. This public policy requirement is also imported into the law of the Dubai International Financial Centre (DIFC). Although English law has strongly influenced the DIFC law, Dr Blanke shows that the DIFC courts' jurisprudence has evolved to accommodate public policy considerations.

Chapter 13 contributes to this discussion as **Cecilia Carrara**, Partner at Legance, compares the approach to liquidated damages, or contractual penalties as they are known in civil law jurisdictions, under English, French, and Swiss law as well as under the UNIDROIT Principles of International Commercial Contracts.

The final part of the book reflects the Centre's wide expertise in the field of dispute resolution.

Since May 1998, when the Housing Grants, Construction and Regeneration Act 1996 entered into force, statutory adjudication has become a deeply embedded and successful part of the dispute resolution landscape. In Chapter 14, **Matt Molloy**, a leading adjudicator and Director at MCMS, reflects on the causes of its success. In particular, he examines the role of the Technology and Construction Court in strengthening the role of the adjudicator. Since the passing of the Construction Act, adjudication has been introduced in common law jurisdictions around the globe, and various interim dispute resolution methods have been picked up by standard forms of construction contracts. However, international construction disputes are still primarily resolved through arbitration, benefiting from relatively easy enforcement under the New York Convention.

Chapter 15, written by **Professor Crenguta Leaua**, Professor of Law at the Bucharest University of Economic Studies and the founding Partner of LDDP, and **Corina Tanase**, Partner at LDDP, compares how the clash between insolvency and arbitration is resolved in several civil law jurisdictions such as Romania, France, Italy, Spain, Germany, and

INTRODUCTION

Switzerland. It investigates whether insolvency can affect the jurisdiction of the arbitral tribunal, the subject-matter arbitrability, or the legal standing of the insolvent party.

In Chapter 16, Professor Nazzini and **Aleksander Godhe**, a Research Associate at the Centre, discuss investor–State dispute settlement as a unique avenue for redress for contractors involved in foreign construction projects. It notices that the number of construction sector-related cases is increasing, justifying a deeper appreciation of this subject among professionals. It demonstrates that multiple standards of investment protection can be successfully invoked, provided that the various jurisdictional requirements are met and quantum aspects are meticulously assessed, correctly presented, and substantiated to the satisfaction of the tribunal.

This is important as the energy transition drives foreign investments in sustainable energy infrastructure. In Chapter 17, **Professor Crina Baltag**, an Associate Professor in international arbitration at Stockholm University, contributes to the debate by discussing the recent controversies surrounding the reform of the Energy Charter Treaty. The Treaty provided a basis for numerous investment claims but is now facing heavy criticism from the states.

Finally, in Chapter 18, **Professor Paula Gerber**, a Professor at Monash University, contemplates whether there is scope for deploying artificial intelligence to resolve construction disputes. Noting current technological deficiencies and various moral considerations, she concludes, to the relief of all those who practice in the field, that it is highly unlikely that robot judges will be deciding construction disputes anytime soon.

The above survey of the themes touched upon in the chapters forming the present work shows that it cuts across all key areas of construction law, both substantive and procedural, ranging from contract law through procurement to construction arbitration. It also takes an international approach to construction law, drawing insights from international and transnational law as well as the practice of several common and civil law jurisdictions. Therefore, it will be of interest to a truly international audience composed of academics, students, and practitioners around the world. The contributors must be congratulated on achieving, in their individual chapters and collectively, a result that is impressive in depth and scope.

This publication not only marks the 35th anniversary of the Centre, but also, more importantly, it celebrates the hard work of the Centre staff, its visiting professors and fellows, all the other authors of this book who have shaped construction law as we know it, and our alumni and students, many of whom are now leading practitioners, who never fail to push us to think about the law differently and imaginatively. To all, I express my unreserved gratitude.

Professor Renato Nazzini
Old Watch House, London
30 November 2023

PART I

THE HISTORICAL AND INTERNATIONAL CONTEXTS

CHAPTER 1

Developments in construction law over the life of the Centre of Construction Law & Dispute Resolution

John Uff [1]

A brief history of the Centre

The Centre of Construction Law & Dispute Resolution was launched in July 1987 to run a two-year, part-time course in construction law and took in its first cohorts of students in September of the same year. Since that time, the course has continued to operate, with just a few tweaks, on the same basis as in the first year: lectures and tutorials up to April, exams in May, and thereafter preparation for the dissertation to be presented in September, the second anniversary of the start of the course. The student composition has remained the same, being of mixed professions extending from lawyers, barristers and solicitors, architects, and surveyors and to every sort of engineering discipline. This mixture was inherited from the Society for Construction Law, founded five years earlier, which had established, beyond question, that interest in the subject was spread evenly across all the professions involved in the construction process. It was the Centre which was the first to put this interest onto the firm academic footing from which it has now expanded to cover the whole construction world.

Among the tweaks which have been introduced was the switch, with the approval of the University of London, in 1988 from the award of a college diploma to a full master's degree, a benefit which, fortunately we were able to make available to the first intake as well as all the subsequent intakes of students. Another significant tweak was the change from evening lectures to the 'thick' weekend, a change which had been pioneered in Australia where the construction law master's degree was run between the universities of Sydney and Melbourne, with lectures held on alternative weekends in each venue. Weekend lectures also made it possible for the course to be undertaken by students residing outside of London, some remaining resident abroad. And this also facilitated some students undertaking the part-time course as full-time students over one year.

From the first year, the Centre has also participated in and often led other academic activities, from professional and government committees and bodies to the development of new forms of procurement, in most cases being marked by significant publications which have continued to document the development of construction law. But despite these developments and changes, the subject itself has retained the same body of principles, which have evolved slowly through case law and new forms of contract, with the Construction

---

1 Founding director of the King's Centre, 1987–2000, Nash Professor of Engineering Law 1988–2000, and Emeritus Professor since 2000.

DOI: 10.4324/9781032663975-3

7

Act of 1996 introducing new statutory rights and obligations. This chapter will consider the changes that have occurred over the lifetime of the Centre and examine to what extent the subject of construction law can be said to have changed.

The establishment of construction law

In September 1988, when the Centre was gearing up for its second year of teaching, it was decided to run a conference at the college on construction law themes. This was almost certainly the first academic-based construction law conference held in London,[2] and the interest of those who agreed to participate was such that the event was programmed to run for a full three days, including papers and working parties. The topic chosen for the conference was 'Construction Contract Policy', reflecting the then current view that the form of the contract would be an influential element in the success of a project. The conference sections included risk assessment, project management and quality control, and control of programme and payment. Participants included judges of the High Court and of the (then) Official Referee's court, representatives of the major law firms and chambers, and academic writers and authorities. Individuals contributing to the proceedings included Martin Barnes (subsequently the author of the NEC form) and Professor Ian Duncan Wallace QC. The conference was opened by the Solicitor General, Sir Nicholas Lyell, who reminded us, in the words of Sir Francis Drake, that it was 'not the beginning of any great venture but the continuing of the same until it be thoroughly finished which yieldeth the true glory'.

The first conference was followed by a succession of annual conferences covering all aspects of construction law and the construction process including, particularly, dispute resolution. For the third annual conference, Donald Keating QC gave a keynote address in which he noted that '[c]onstruction law either has already, or will in the future, become the most important stimulus to the development of business law in its widest sense. It may replace shipping law as a prime generator of English law'. That prediction was already in process of fulfilment by 1991 with the House of Lords' judgement in *Murphy v Brentwood*[3] following *D&F Estates v Church Commissioners*.[4] The proceedings of the first and subsequent annual conferences were edited and published in a series of publications from the Centre, which, while originally intended to benefit subsequent students at the Centre, achieved a wider circulation and provide a convenient record of the state of construction law of some three decades ago and from which emerges various answers to the question 'what has changed'.

Changes to valuation

The answer revealed by these publications, as regards valuation or quantum issues including disputes, in particular, is that there has been a progression but little change in substance. The problems of valuation and payment for construction operations remain subject to the same issues of measurement expressed through the art of the quantity surveyor.

---

2 An earlier one-day conference had been organised by the law school at the University of Bristol.
3 [1991] 1 AC 398.
4 [1989] AC 177.

This is, however, subject to some undoubted changes, particularly in the introduction and development of target price contracts in which the sums payable in respect of the cost of the work are subject to addition or deduction reflecting the contractor's performance against the target price. The calculation of the sum due is intended to be entirely formulaic but, in practice, the disputes which can arise are the same as those which have traditionally arisen under more direct methods of payment, namely measurement disputes, disputes over allocation of operations, and delay-related payment issues. It is also the case that some target cost contracts have been designed to reflect complex measurement and payment arrangements which have given rise to correspondingly complex contractual issues in which events have led to different interpretations of the contractual outcome, often representing major financial differences.

The time dimension

Time has always been one of the three essential elements of construction (along with cost and quality). Time is important to both parties in the case of employer or promoter delays representing lost opportunity to put the works to use and in the case of the contractor representing additional cost without additional income. From the employer's position, liquidated damages have remained the overwhelmingly popular or at least usual choice, reflecting the uncertainties that would surround an attempt to prove actual loss as well as the likely objection of contractors to face unspecified and unlimited damages in the event of culpable delay. Frequently, liquidated damages are subject to a cap and to other provisions such as an escalating scale. But it remains the case that the consequences of contractor delay are still, in the great majority of cases, specified in sums not requiring proof. English law on the topic has remained substantially as it has been for well over a century, with no suggestion of joining the more liberal approach of most other commercial jurisdictions in which tribunals are empowered to reduce specified damages. English law has maintained its view of the recovery of liquidated damages as all or nothing, perhaps reflecting its underlying respect for competitive sport. The Supreme Court has recently rationalised its view of liquidated damages[5] and penalties, but the basic approach remains.

In the case of contractor delay damages, the position also remains substantially as it was in the 1980s, despite suggestions for a more rational and certain approach, perhaps, using liquidated damages as a model. What has developed, rather than changed, is the degree of sophistication now possible with the use of greatly increased computing power to assist the quantum experts. This has been accompanied by the development of delay analysis into a technical discipline with its own sophisticated rules which has generated its own literature. Among the important topics which have engaged both technical expertise and legal authorities is the identification of concurrent delay and its consequences in translating the facts, once disentangled, into an award of time and money.

Quality and fitness

The United Kingdom (UK) construction industry has been beset from time to time by apparent crises of quality standards. 'Apparent' here means the occurrence of a

---

5 *Cavendish Square Holdings v Makdessi* [2015] UKSC 67.

well-publicised failure, often involving loss of life and which has led to the setting up of inquiries, the publishing of reports, and, sometimes, action including legislation. From the years immediately preceding the setting up of the Centre, the structural collapse at Rhonan Point might be mentioned, which led to changes in the practice of 'system' or industrialised building. In the late 1980s, there was general concern about latent defects regarding the corporate structure of the industry, which often resulted in the culprit – whether designer, supplier, or builder – no longer being in business to be held to account. This led to the setting up of a Department of Trade and Industry committee chaired by Professor Donald Bishop,[6] which produced, in 1988,[7] a recommendation for the adoption of insurance based on the French Decennial cover, which adopted the acronym BUILD (Building Users Insurance against Latent Defects). The report was generally accepted by the construction industry, and BUILD Insurance became available but, obviously, at additional cost and, therefore, not universally put in place. It is of no consolation that BUILD insurance, had it become a general requirement in respect of cladding on high-rise residential blocks, would have provided some measure of protection for apartment owners whose properties have become unsaleable as a result of the Grenfell disaster. That tragedy, which followed other serious fires, has finally given rise to government action in the form of a number of inquiries and the recently enacted Building Safety Act 2022.

The law regarding quality and fitness for purpose in the context of construction was largely settled by two decisions of the House of Lords some 18 years before the launch of the Centre[8] and has not changed in substance since then. Under English law, parties generally remain free to agree whatever obligations they wish. But the practice of avoiding an obligation of fitness for purpose is well ingrained, largely as a result of insurers refusing to cover such risk. Thus, claims against professionals have continued to be based on allegations of negligence, and contractors undertaking design obligations have continued to shelter behind the same barrier. This is in marked contrast to obligations imposed under foreign legal codes. French contractors and professionals have not been seen to change their practices despite being under a legal obligation to deliver products and works which are fit for purpose.

The holy grail of cash flow

The UK construction industry had, by 1986, already gone through more than one cycle of attempts to secure prompt payment to contractors and subcontractors who might otherwise face insolvency through non-payment for work done. Many cases had addressed the special nature of certificates of the architect or engineer. In 1971 the Court of Appeal led by Lord Denning decided that certificates were of such a special nature that they could not be subject to a set-off to reduce or avoid payment.[9] A total of nine appeal cases reached the same conclusion until the House of Lords was persuaded to examine the issue and concluded that the ordinary right of equitable set off was not removed by the wording of the

---

6 A firm supporter and frequent lecturer at the Centre

7 'Building Users' Insurance Against Latent Defects' (*Designing Buildings The Construction Wiki*, 18 November 2020) <https://www.designingbuildings.co.uk/wiki/Building_Users%27_Insurance_Against_Latent_Defects> accessed 27 September 2023.

8 *Young & Martin v McManus* [1969] 1 AC 454; *Gloucester CC v Richardson* [1969] 1 AC 480.

9 *Dawnays v Minter* [1971] 1 WLR 1205.

standard forms of contract.[10] There the matter rested until the professional bodies issuing the standard forms began to address the issue. This led in the 1980s to the ICE introducing mediation and, in the case of the JCT, a form of contractual adjudication,[11] in both cases motivated by the apparent inability of arbitration to offer any timely relief.

By the 1990s, the problem of bankruptcies in the construction industry was becoming acute and led to the government setting up what became the Latham inquiry, which in turn led to the Construction Act of 1996 and, incidentally in the same year, the Arbitration Act 1996. Both pieces of legislation, promoted by two different government departments,[12] would have been unlikely to reach the statute book but for the fact that the Tory Government under John Major had lost its majority and was prepared to offer parliamentary time to Bills which were regarded as uncontroversial and commanded general support.

So it was that the two Bills were passed in the same year, each offering its own remedy to the problems of unpaid contractors and subcontractors. The solution offered by the Construction Act is well known but it is worth pausing to consider the alternative contained in the Arbitration Act. It is also noteworthy that, while the Arbitration Bill was preceded by at least a decade of well-informed debate, the Construction Bill was the product of a hybrid procedure involving an appointed chairman[13] undertaking consultations organised and directed by a small group of advisors. In the result, many informed observers regarded the consultation process preceding the Construction Act as far from thorough and prone to adopt ready-made solutions.[14]

By contrast, the Arbitration Bill was produced by the DTI Departmental Advisory Committee, composed of arbitration specialists, and including a number of construction practitioners. As a result, the committee adopted for the Bill specific measures addressing both cash-flow and the problem of potentially lengthy technical disputes. The solution contained in the subsequent Act was to empower an arbitrator to give a 'provisional' decision, equivalent to an interim order available in the High Court, in a case where liability could be substantially established but where quantum remained in issue. The new provision as finally enacted was section 39 of the Act, as follows:

Power to make provisional awards
(1)   The parties are free to agree that the tribunal shall have power to order on a provisional basis any relief which it would have power to grant in a final award.
(2)   This includes, for instance, making –
    (a)   a provisional order for the payment of money or the disposition of property as between the parties, or
    (b)   an order to make an interim payment on account of the costs of the arbitration.
(3)   Any such order shall be subject to the tribunal's final adjudication; and the tribunal's final award, on the merits or as to costs, shall take account of any such order.
(4)   Unless the parties agree to confer such power on the tribunal, the tribunal has no such power. This does not affect its powers under section 47 (awards on different issues, &c.).

This provision, whilst requiring the parties' consent, is included in the Construction Industry Model Arbitration Rules (CIMAR), widely adopted throughout the industry

---

10 *Gilbert Ash v Modern Engineering* [1974] AC 689.
11 See *Cameron v Mowlem* (1990) 52 BLR 24.
12 Respectively the Department of Education (DOE) and the DTI.
13 Sir Michael Latham.
14 Such as the New Engineering Contract.

including by the JCT (which issues the most widely used domestic standard form contract). The provision has the potential to allow arbitrators to cut through complex disputes by giving a decision which would reduce the extent and amount of the dispute, allowing the parties to attempt to resolve or further reduce the matters in issue. It has been adopted in one reported shipbuilding case[15] where the arbitrators made a provisional award on the quantum of sums payable where liability had been established.

Unfortunately, the potential of section 39 has not been further developed by the UK construction industry which has, as is well known, adopted and embraced Adjudication as the preferred method of seeking a quick resolution of construction disputes. This has without doubt achieved an impressive success rate of well over 90% in terms of decisions of adjudicators leading to final resolution of the original dispute. This is not the occasion to question the merits of adjudication; but it should be said that the debate on the relative merits of Adjudication against section 39 of the Arbitration Act is still to take place. Among the merits of the latter is that the arbitrator does not become functus after giving the Decision and can if required continue the case with other section 39 decisions up to a final award. It is also regrettable that the huge volume of case law now available in regard to Adjudication is specific to England and (although operating under its own legislation) Scotland and possibly Ireland too. By contrast Arbitration generates an international jurisprudence which contributes materially to the international success and arguably the dominance of English law and English lawyers in international arbitration.

Dispute Resolution

Whilst in domestic terms this subject could be seen as synonymous with adjudication, the fact that the Centre has now added 'Dispute Resolution' to its formal title[16] recognises that much more is encompassed within the topic. In historical terms the first meeting of interested parties from which grew the Centre for Effective Dispute Resolution (CEDR) took place within the King's Centre and was followed by mediation and conciliation being added to the syllabus. It is also apposite to remember that at the Centre's inception in 1987 construction disputes taken to court were subject to the 'Crouch' doctrine, by which the court's jurisdiction was limited by a decision of the Court of Appeal,[17] which was only reversed through a Northern Irish case that surmounted the hurdles necessary to reach the House of Lords.[18] It is thus clear that dispute resolution in the context of construction covers a very wide and developing range of topics from mediation through all the domestic formal processes and then on to international dispute resolution, particularly in arbitration, both commercial and, now, investment.

The King's Centre has devoted a substantial portion of its annual conferences and publications to dispute resolution in its many forms. Thus, the second annual conference in 1988 took as its subject ICC and International Arbitration; and the eighth annual conference in 1995 was on the resolution of construction disputes with the Channel Tunnel litigation having recently reached the House of Lords. It was particularly apposite to have

---

15 *BMBF (No 12) v Harland & Wolff* [2001] EWCA Civ 862.

16 The original formal title of the Centre also referred to 'Management', a subject which earlier was formally taught as part of the curriculum.

17 *NRHA v Derek Crouch* [1984] QB 644.

18 *Beaufort Developments v Gilbert Ash* NI [1999] 1 AC 266.

on the platform Sir Alastair Morton, Co-Chairman of Eurotunnel, who delivered a paper on the Channel Tunnel contract; and as Keynote speaker, Lord Mustill, who had recently delivered the lead judgement in the House of Lords, which decided that the Court did have jurisdiction to issue the injunction sought by the Eurotunnel against its contractors, but decided in its discretion that no injunction should be given.[19] The Centre's publications also included a volume of edited student dissertations on dispute resolution themes.

Apart from domestic construction disputes, the Centre has taken particular account of developments in international practice and procedure. Members of the Centre's staff have been involved, through their professional practices, in international arbitrations conducted in many different jurisdictions and, with the passage of time, graduates of the centre have developed practices in international arbitration as lawyers, advocates, experts, or as arbitrators. The Centre has also maintained links with the major international bodies, including the ICC and LCIA as arbitration institutions, and with FIDIC as a promotor of the most widely used international construction contract forms. International arbitration forms a significant element in the Centre's core studies and remains one of the developing areas in construction law.

KCCLA and the King's Centre

King's College Construction Law Association is the alumnus body which from the 1990s has organised regular meetings of former students with, in addition to social events, regular talks and lectures. In addition, KCCLA organises events for current students at the centre to give guidance on topics such as dissertation writing. The obvious success of the Association is due, not only to the wish to repay some of what students have gained during their period of study, but to an appreciation of the benefits of maintaining contacts with members of the other professions that make up the construction law community, both in the case of lawyers and of construction professionals.

The enthusiastic support for KCCLA mirrors the growth of support for and the activities of the Society of Construction Law, which continues in its multi-disciplinary format to organise lectures and events throughout the UK and now in other jurisdictions including Scotland and the Republic of Ireland. Both SCL and KCCLA are dedicated not only to keeping abreast of developments in the subject but also in seeking new solutions to the intractable problems of construction law. Both organisations along with the Centre itself offer platforms for new ideas and proposals aimed at addressing the inherent problems that the past decades of studies in construction law have exposed.

It is also of considerable note that construction law is now recognised as an inter-disciplinary subject in many jurisdictions outside the UK including many civil law jurisdictions. One of the remarkable developments is that construction law courses in foreign institutions are reportedly conducted in the English language and make use of English sources. There is an unfortunate overuse of the term 'world-class', especially in institutions that have little claim to its use. However, in the case of construction law there can be no doubt that construction law at the King's Centre is genuinely world class and that the King's Centre remains the world leader in the field.

---

19 *Channel Tunnel Group v Balfour Beatty* [1993] AC 334

CHAPTER 2

Impact of English construction law in the international market

Renato Nazzini

Introduction

This chapter discusses the role and contribution of English construction law in the international construction market. English law is widely recognised for its attractiveness as one of the preferred governing laws in international commercial transactions.[1] Construction law is no different. However, the impact of English construction law on the international market extends far beyond its adoption as the governing law of construction contracts. Within common law jurisdictions, legal concepts endemic to English construction law have spread internationally.[2] This impact is attributable to the decisions of the English courts, particularly the Official Referees, established in 1873 and perhaps the first specialist construction court in the world, and its successor, the Technology and Construction Court (TCC).[3] Alongside the development of this distinct body of case law and legal doctrine, English legal practitioners and English universities, with their international outlook and vocation, have played a key role in exporting English law solutions to construction law, also beyond common law jurisdictions.

This chapter is divided into three parts. The first part discusses the use of English law in international construction contracts. It surveys the extent to which English law is the law of choice in international construction contracts, as evidenced by decisions of the English courts, the TCC in particular. Next it analyses distinct substantive and procedural advantages offered by English law specifically in the construction context, asking whether these advantages will erode following Brexit.

The second part of the chapter explores the international influence of some quintessentially English construction law concepts and features such as the prevention principle or the role of the contract administrator. It traces their impact on the law of other common law jurisdictions and international construction contracting, in particular through the FIDIC forms.

---

1 The Law Society, 'International Data Insights Report 2023 Global Position of English Law' (*The Law Society*, 30 October 2023) <https://www.lawsociety.org.uk/topics/research/international-data-insights-report> accessed 10 December 2023; Louise Merrett and Antonia Sommerfeld, 'Incentives for Choice of Law and Forum in Commercial Contracts: Predicting the Impact of Brexit' (2020) 3 *European Review of Private Law* 627.

2 Vivian Ramsey, 'Construction Law: The English Route to Modern Construction Law' (2022) 75 Ark L Rev 251, 252.

3 ibid.

DOI: 10.4324/9781032663975-4

Finally, the third part investigates the international impact of the payment and adjudication provisions of the UK Housing Grants, Construction and Regeneration Act 1996 as an inspiration for legislation or procedures in other common law jurisdictions.

The use of English contract law internationally

Parties to international business transactions tend to select the law to govern their contracts that is most commercially attractive, even if different to the law of their home jurisdiction.[4] For this reason, the extent to which English law is applied to international construction contracts can serve as an indicator of its impact in the international market.

Although no comprehensive empirical analysis exists in relation to construction contracts, studies surveying all international commercial agreements are indicative. These consistently conclude that English law is the preferred law selected by international parties to govern their contracts.[5] Some suggest that English law may govern as much as half of all international contracts.[6] This is also true for parties and transactions with little to no connection to the UK, for instance, in fast growing Asian markets.[7] In a recent report, The Law Society of England & Wales found that English Law governs international trade, deals and contracts worth trillions of pounds, including £10 trillion in metals trading and £250 billion in M&A transactions.[8]

Turning to construction contracts, perhaps the best evidence of the application of English law to international construction contracts is that the English courts frequently

---

4 Parties participating in international commercial transactions are willing to choose the law of a third state as the law applicable to the contract for at least 40% of agreements they enter into. See Giles Cuniberti, 'The International Market for Contracts: The Most Attractive Contract Laws' (2014) 34 NW J Int'l L & Bus 455, 474.

5 English law is 'the preferred choice of governing contract law'. See 'Civil Justice Systems in Europe: Implications for Choice of Forum and Choice of Contract Law. A Business Survey. Final Results' (*Foundation Pour La Droit Continental*, 1 October 2008) <https://www.fondation-droitcontinental.org/fr/wp-content/uploads/2013/12/oxford_civil_justice_survey_-_summary_of_results_final.pdf> accessed 30 November 2021 (Oxford Civil Justice Survey); In international commercial arbitration, English law is the most chosen governing law other than the 'law of home jurisdiction' being on average three time more attractive than US State laws and French law, and almost five times more attractive than German law. See Queen Mary University of London and White & Case, '2010 International Arbitration Survey: Choices in International Arbitration (*Queen Mary University of London*) <https://arbitration.qmul.ac.uk/media/arbitration/docs/2010_Internation alArbitrationSurveyReport.pdf> accessed 30 November 2022; Cuniberti, (n 4); Similarly, in 2021, parties to arbitrations before the London Court of International Arbitration chose English law to govern their agreements in 76% of cases. See LCIA, '2021 Annual Casework Report' (*LCIA*) <https://www.lcia.org/lcia/reports.aspx> accessed 30 November 2022.

6 More than half of respondents has agreed upon or recommended a choice of law clause in favour of English law between 2010 and 2015 as well as uses choice of English law clause in 60-100% of their work. See Eva Lein and others, 'Factors Influencing International Litigants' Decisions to Bring Commercial Claims to the London Based Courts' (*British Institute of International and Comparative Law*, 1 January 2015) <https://www.biicl.org/publications/factors-influencing-international-litigants-decisions-to-bring-commercial-disputes-to-the-london-based-courts> accessed 30 November 2022.

7 43% of respondents who were legal practitioners and in-house counsel dealing with cross-border transactions in Singapore and the region selected English law as the most frequently used governing law. See Singapore Academy of Law and Ipsos, '2019 Study on Governing Law & Jurisdictional Choices in Cross-Border Transactions' (*SAL.org*) <https://www.sal.org.sg/sites/default/files/PDF%20Files/Newsroom/News _Release_PSL%20Survey_2019_Appendix_A.pdf> accessed 30 November 2021; TheCityUK, 'Legal Excellence Internationally Renowned: UK Legal Services 2020' (*TheCityUK*, 26 November 2020) <https://www.thecityuk.com/media/hllopd1i/legal-excellence-internationally-renowned-uk-legal-services-2020.pdf> accessed 27 October 2022.

8 The Law Society (n 1).

resolve disputes under these contracts. For instance, the case of *Autoridad del Canal de Panama v Sacyr*[9] concerned a construction contract for the widening of the Panama Canal. The claimant, Autoridad del Canal de Panama, a Panamanian public corporation, employed a consortium consisting of Spanish, Italian, Belgian, and Panamanian companies, to design and construct a third set of locks on the canal.[10]

The main construction contract was governed by Panamanian law. However, the claimant made several advanced payments to the consortium secured by Advance Payment Guarantees. English law applied to some of these Guarantees. The claimant applied to the English High Court for a 'summary judgment under the [Advance Payment Guarantees] on the basis that [they were] first demand instruments'.[11]

English law played an even more central role in *Petroleum Company of Trinidad and Tobago v Samsung Engineering Trinidad*[12] – a dispute arising out of the construction of new refinery facilities in Trinidad and Tobago. Petrotrin, a state-owned company, entered into three contracts – the Onshore Agreement with Samsung Engineering Trinidad, the Offshore Agreement with SECL, another Samsung's local affiliate, and a tripartite Linkage Agreement. The purpose of the Linkage Agreement was to ensure that Petrotrin was not disadvantaged by the contract splitting.[13] Accordingly, it provided, among others, for the close integration of the onshore and the offshore operations, construction of both agreements as if they were one, the mutual attribution of responsibility by both the onshore and the offshore contractors, and a liquidated damages cap amounting to the 10% of the aggregate price of both contracts.[14] It also contained a choice of law clause in favour of English law.

The arbitration concerned the question of whether the Petrotrin's counterclaim was subject to a 10% cap based on the value of the Onshore Agreement or the total value of both agreements (onshore and offshore) as stipulated by the Linkage Agreement.[15] The issue was significant because applying a lower cap, as the arbitral tribunal did, meant that Samsung was the overall winner and should be paid US$9.3 million; had the higher cap been used instead, it would have been Petrotrin that should be paid US$11.6 million.[16]

Petrotrin argued that the tribunal lacked jurisdiction to make a determination of the liability cap, and brought an application under section 67 of the Arbitration Act 1996.[17] Coulson J (as he then was) dismissed the application because 'Petrortin's essential complaint is about the result, and it has been uncomfortably shoehorned into a jurisdictional challenge when, on proper analysis, it is no such thing'.[18]

Finally, in *Unaoil v Leighton Offshore*,[19] a dispute arose out of a Memorandum of Understanding entered into by Unaoil, a company incorporated in the British Virgin Islands, and Leighton Offshore, a company incorporated in Singapore, in relation to the

---

9 [2017] EWHC 2228 (Comm) [2].
10 ibid [2] and [10].
11 ibid [3].
12 [2017] EHWC 3055 (TCC).
13 ibid [2].
14 ibid [11].
15 ibid [3].
16 ibid [4].
17 ibid [1].
18 ibid [27].
19 [2014] EWHC 2965 (Comm).

Table 2.1 Examples of TCC cases where English law governed international contracts related to construction

Case	Nationality of the claimant(s)	Nationality of the defendant(s)	Location of the project	Nature of the contract
Permasteelisa Japan v Bouyguesstroi, Banca Intesa	Japan	Russia	Russia	Performance Bond
Seele Middle East v Raiffeisenlandesbank Oberösterreich Aktiengesellschaft Bank	United Arab Emirates, Dubai	Austria	Saudi Arabia	Performance Guarantee
Unaoil v Leighton Offshore	British Virgin Islands	Singapore	Iraq	Memorandum of Understanding
Autoridad del Canal de Panama v Sacyr	Panama	Spain, Italy, Belgium, Panama	Panama	Advance Payment Guarantee
Petroleum Company of Trinidad and Tobago v Samsung Engineering Trinidad	Trinidad and Tobago	Trinidad and Tobago	Trinidad and Tobago	Linkage (Umbrella) Agreement connecting the Onshore and Offshore Agreements
Tecnicas Reunidas Saudia for Services and Contracting Co Ltd v Korea Development Bank	Spain	South Korea	Saudi Arabia	On-Demand Guarantee

construction of oil infrastructure in Iraq. In the Memorandum, Leighton Offshore agreed to appoint Unaoil as its contractor for the project, although this was later halted by the project employer. In its claim, Unaoil alleged repudiatory breach of contract claiming liquidated and unliquidated damages as well as debt arising due to non-payment of the advance payments. The Memorandum contained a choice of law clause in favour of English law and the claimant decided to litigate the dispute in the English High Court.[20]

There are many more construction-related cases like the ones above.[21] They show that international parties apply English law to govern their construction contracts even where (i) the project is located outside of the UK and/or (ii) the parties to the contract have little or no connection to the UK.

The cases in Table 2.1 demonstrate a further point illustrated well by *Autoridad del Canal de Panama v Sacyr* – in international construction projects, the construction contract itself will often be governed by the law of the host state. However, ancillary contracts

---

20 ibid [14].

21 *Permasteelisa Japan KK v Bouyguesstroi, Banca Intesa SpA* [2007] EWHC 3508 (TCC); *Seele Middle East FZE v Raiffeisenlandesbank Oberösterreich Aktiengesellschaft Bank* [2014] EWHC 343 (TCC); *Tecnicas Reunidas Saudia for Services and Contracting Co Ltd v Korea Development Bank* [2020] EWHC 968 (TCC).

such subcontracts, split contracts, and especially bonds and guarantees will often apply English law.[22] The next section will explore some of the advantages of selecting English law in the international market.

Prevalence of English law explained

There are many reasons why international parties apply English law to their construction contracts. Softer reasons include the authoritative role of English law in other common law jurisdictions,[23] the relative stability of the English legal system,[24] the availability of commercial law expertise to assist the parties,[25] and the spread of the English language.[26] This section, however, focuses on the substantive and procedural reasons for selecting English law.

Substantive advantages of English law

Several studies conclude that the substance of contract law influences the choice of law.[27] Arguably, sophisticated commercial parties prefer a textualist or formalistic approach to contract interpretation.[28] English courts have recognised that it is essential for commercial parties 'to be confident that they can rely on the court to enforce their contract according to its terms'.[29] As, traditionally, English law has adopted a textualist approach to contract construction that could explain the high international demand for English law.

Following *Arnold v Britton*,[30] the aim of contractual interpretation, especially in the commercial context,[31] is to ascertain the parties' intention by reference to what a reasonable person with all the background knowledge which would have been available to the parties would have understood the parties to mean. This exercise is informed by the 'natural and ordinary meaning' of a given clause, any other relevant clauses, the overall

---

22 For memoranda of understanding see *Unaoil* (n 21). For split contracts see *Petroleum Company of Trinidad and Tobago* (n 13). For bonds and guarantees see *Permasteelisa Japan KK* (n 24); *Seele Middle East* (n 24); *Autoridad del Canal de Panama* (n 9); *Tecnicas Reunidas Saudia for Services and Contracting* (n 24).

23 Common law is considered authoritative in 27% of the world's jurisdictions. See TheCityUK, (n 7) 40.

24 The UK has consistently been ranked among the top 16 jurisdictions by the World Justice Project Rule of Law Index. See World Justice Project, 'WJP Rule of Law Index (Historical)' (*World Justice Project*, 2022) <https://worldjusticeproject.org/rule-of-law-index/global/2022/historical> accessed 7 December 2022.

25 John McGrath, 'Global Law and the English Lawyer Country Survey' (1994) 13(2) *International Financial Law Review* 23, 24.

26 Martina Künnecke, 'English as Common Legal Language: Its Expansion and the Effects on Civil Law and Common Law Lawyers' (2016) 24(5) *European Review of Private Law* 733.

27 Oxford Civil Justice Survey (n 5); Lein and others (n 6); Merrett and Sommerfeld (n 1).

28 There is some evidence, particularly in the US context, that sophisticated parties prefer textualist or formalist approach to contract interpretation. See, e.g., Alan Schwartz and Robert E Scott, 'Contract Interpretation Redux' (2010) 119 Yale LJ 926; Geoffrey P Miller, 'Bargains Bicoastal: New Light on Contract Theory' (2010) 31 Cardozo L Rev 1475. This is reflected by the prevalence of the New York Law in the US. See, e.g., Theodore Eisenberg and Geoffrey P Miller, 'The Flight to New York: An Empirical Study of Choice of Law and Choice of Forum Clauses in Publicly-Held Companies' Contracts' (2009) 30 Cardozo L Rev 1475. However, this contention is not made out in the context of disputes relating to international commercial contracts arbitrated under the auspices of the ICC. In the ICC context the market for international contracts is dominated by formalist English contract law and more contextual Swiss contract law. See, e.g., Giles Cuniberti, 'The International Market for Contracts: The Most Attractive Contract Laws' (2014) 34 Nw J Int'l L & Bus 455.

29 *Charter Reinsurance Co Ltd v Fagan* [2004] UKHL 54 [19].

30 [2015] UKSC 36.

31 *Rainy Sky SA v Kookmin Bank* [2011] UKSC 50 [14].

purpose of the clause and the agreement, 'the facts and circumstances known or assumed by the parties at the time that the document was executed', and commercial common sense.[32] Importantly, however, commercial common sense and other contextual considerations can neither 'undervalue the importance of the language of the provision' nor be applied retrospectively.[33] The inquiry is, therefore, objective. Moreover, unlike some civil law jurisdictions, English law does not permit pre-contractual negotiations to determine the meaning of a given clause.[34]

Similarly, commitment to freedom and sanctity of contract means that in contrast to many civil law jurisdictions, English law has no general duty of good faith.[35] While parties are free to provide for an obligation of good faith in their contract, and this is becoming increasingly common in the construction sector,[36] 'it is difficult to see what these aspirational provisions add to the black letter terms of the contract'.[37] Moreover, there are wider policy considerations militating against generalised reliance on good faith obligations. Construction projects involve complex relationships and numerous stakeholders. All those involved, such as employer's or contractor's employees, certifiers or subcontracts must comply with the contract. It is essential that they can understand the contract requirements by simply reading the black letter provisions without recourse to legal advice.[38] Therefore, English law's emphasis on textual interpretation and scepticism towards good faith may be considered an advantage by the construction sector.

Moreover, English common law has a more practical approach to construction contracts than contract laws rooted in a civilian tradition.[39] In many civil contract laws, the legal analysis begins with a 'qualification' i.e., 'the determination of legal category (e.g., sale of goods or a novation of contract) to which a given situation belongs, from which flow all the relevant legal consequences'.[40] In contrast, categorisation of construction contracts in English law is, by and large, a non-issue. A contract will be enforced according to its terms. Turnkey contracts are particularly difficult to categorise. Under French law, for example, they include elements associated with both contracts concerning the sale of goods (*contrat de vente*) and provision of services (*contrat d'enterprise*).[41] This poses practical difficulties because treatment of warranties under the former contract differs significantly from the latter.[42] Consequently, English law may be more appropriate to such contracts.[43] By choosing English law, legal metaphysics is avoided, pragmatism prevails.

---

32 *Arnold* (n 33) [15].

33 ibid [17] and [19].

34 *Chartbrook Ltd v Persimmon Homes Ltd* [2009] 1 AC 1101 [39].

35 *Manifest Shipping Co Ltd v Uni-Polaris Insurance Co Ltd (The Star Sea)* [2003] 1 AC 469. A duty of good faith has also been recognised in the context of relational contracts. See, e.g., *Yam Seng Pte Ltd v International Trade Corp Ltd* [2013] 1 CLC 662.

36 See, e.g., Engineering and Construction Contract, NEC3, Cl 10.1; Engineering and Construction Contract, NEC4, Cl 10; Rupert Jackson, 'Does good faith have any role in construction contracts?' (2018) 34(5) Const LJ 313, 324.

37 Jackson (n 39) 324.

38 ibid.

39 P Durand-Barthez, 'The Governing Law Clause: Legal and Economic Consequences of the Choice of Law in International Contracts' (2012) 2012 Int;l Bus LJ 505, 509.

40 ibid 507.

41 ibid.

42 ibid.

43 The 'appropriateness for type of contract' was ranked as the second most important factor when choosing the governing law of the contract. See Queen Mary University of London, School of International Arbitration

On the other hand, what we have described as the 'textualist' approach of English law to contractual interpretation does not mean that English courts do not construe contracts reasonably and flexibly, and according to their commercial purpose. A long line of authorities supports the proposition that commercial considerations constitute an important factor in contractual construction.[44] A survey of case law reveals that commercial common sense involves the following guidelines:

> (1) commercial documents are to be read from the perspective of commercial users; in particular, the commercial reader abhors pedantry, including excessive technicality or semantic logic; (2) the court should avoid frustrating the parties' commercial object or purpose revealed by the contractual text and its factual matrix; (3) the adjudicator must understand the trade practices and market assumptions within the relevant contractual pigeonhole; (4) inapt words can be overridden when manifestly inconsistent with business common sense (this overlaps with both 'corrective construction' (...), and Rectification (...); (5) absurd constructions are to be avoided; (6) [construction common sense] can be used as a compass to point the way when the court is confronted by rival meanings.[45]

Construction contracts concern bespoke projects, bring together many parties, and have a long duration.[46] Their complexity therefore warrants contractual interpretation that takes account of the factual background and the commercial purpose of the agreement. *Portsmouth City Council v Ensign Highways*,[47] for example, concerned a dispute arising out of a 25-year long PFI contract whereby the Council employed Ensign Highways primarily to bring the Council's highway network to a defined standard and, second, to maintain it over the contract's life cycle.[48] The agreement incorporated a regime for awarding service points for breaches by the contractor.[49] The dispute concerned the manner of awarding service points.[50] While the contractor alleged that service points were to be awarded on a sliding scale depending on the gravity of the breach, the employer argued that that they were supposed to be awarded by reference to the figure set out in the contract as a fixed tariff.[51] The TCC preferred the former construction because it better aligned with commercial common sense. As explained by Edwards-Stuart J 'it does not (...) make sense to have a system which requires the authority to impose the same number of points irrespective of the gravity or duration of the breach'.[52]

Similarly, in *University of Warwick v Balfour Beatty*,[53] the TCC considered the factual background and commercial common sense to clarify the meaning of an amended JCT 2011 Design and Build Contract. The contract provided for the works to be divided in

---

and White & Case, '2010 International Arbitration Survey: Choices in International Arbitration' (*Queen Mary University of London*, 2010) <https://arbitration.qmul.ac.uk/media/arbitration/docs/2010_InternationalArbitrationSurveyReport.pdf> accessed 27 October 2022, 11.

44 See, e.g., *Prenn v Simmonds* [1971] 1 WLR 1381 (HL), 1389; *Mannai Investment Co v Eagle Star Life Assurance* [1997] AC 749 (HL), 771; *Rainy Sky* (n 34); *Arnold* (n 33) [15].

45 Neil Andrews, 'Interpretation of Contracts and "Commercial Common Sense": Do Not Overplay This Useful Criterion' (2017) 76(1) *Cambridge Law Journal* 36, 37.

46 Michael Curtis, 'Differences between construction contracts and other contracts' in Humphrey Lloyd and Andrew Bartlett (eds), *Emden's Construction Law* (LexisNexis 2023).

47 [2015] EWHC 1969 (TCC).

48 ibid [1]–[2].

49 ibid [4].

50 ibid [24].

51 ibid.

52 ibid [70].

53 [2018] EWHC 3239 (TCC).

sections with different applicable completion dates and liquidated damages rates.[54] The contract also set out the requirements for practical completion, one of them being that the level of completeness achieved must 'allow the Property to be occupied or used'[55] where 'the property comprised of the completed Works'.[56] The dispute arose out of the question of whether 'on the proper construction of the definition of Practical Completion within the Contract, the entire Works were to be complete before a single Section could be certified as complete'.[57] The TCC ruled that for sectional completion it was sufficient that the requirements for the practical completion were satisfied in relation to a given section; there was no need 'for the Works as a whole to be complete or the Property as a whole to be ready for occupation'.[58] A different construction would have defeated the sectional completion provisions and would have been contrary to business common sense.[59]

In *Chartbrook v Persimmon Homes*,[60] the Court had to decide on the proper construction of the payment provisions in a contract for the development of residential and commercial premises. Both the High Court and the Court of Appeal adopted a purely textualist approach to contractual interpretation.[61] The House of Lords, however, overturned the Court of Appeal's ruling because, as explained by Lord Hoffman, interpretation 'in accordance with the ordinary rules of syntax [made] no commercial sense'.[62] *Chartbrook* constituted one of the rare cases where it was clear that something had gone wrong with the language of the contract.[63] Consequently, the Court was entitled to correct the parties' mistake by construing the contract in light of the commercial context, as long as the meaning of the contract was clear to a reasonable person.[64]

Importantly, *Chartbrook v Persimmon* also confirmed the English law rule that what was said or done during the course of the negotiations is inadmissible in evidence for the purposes of drawing inferences of what a contract means.[65] However, as Lord Hoffmann explained, the rule that does not prevent such evidence from being admitted for other purposes, for example, 'to establish that a fact which may be relevant as background was known to the parties, or to support a claim for rectification or estoppel', although these were held to be separate principles rather than exceptions.[66] Again, this would appear to be a sensible solution as to admit evidence of contractual negotiations would open the floodgates to endless arguments about the meaning of disputed contractual clauses and be inconsistent with the objective approach to contractual interpretation under English law.

---

54 ibid [4]–[6].
55 ibid [7]–[10].
56 ibid [7]–[10].
57 ibid [2].
58 ibid [20].
59 ibid [21].
60 *Chartbrook* (n 37) [5]–[13].
61 *Chartbrook Ltd v Persimmon Homes Ltd* [2007] EWHC 409 (Ch) [52]–[62]; *Chartbrook v Persimmon Homes Ltd* [2008] EWCA Civ 183.
62 *Chartbrook* (n 37) [16].
63 ibid [21]–[25].
64 ibid [21]–[25].
65 ibid.
66 ibid [42].

Procedural advantages of English law

Choice of substantive law and dispute resolution forum are interlinked.[67] It often makes sense to have a dispute governed by English law resolved by arbitration in London or by the English courts. Therefore, procedural advantages offered by English law such as institutional support for arbitration[68] as well as litigation in the TCC[69] further incentivise parties to select it.

As regards arbitration, English courts have recognised that excessive judicial interference in arbitral proceedings can deter commercial parties from selecting a jurisdiction as a dispute resolution forum.[70] One of the objectives of the Arbitration Act 1996 is 'to reduce drastically the extent of intervention of courts in the arbitral process'.[71] Accordingly, section 1 provides that the courts should refrain from intervention, except as provided in the Act itself.[72] Moreover, the Act offers only limited avenues to challenge an arbitral award. Section 67 allows a challenge on the ground that the tribunal lacked substantive jurisdiction. Procedural challenges under section 68 require the application of the strict test of 'serious irregularity' that has led or will lead to 'substantial injustice'.[73] Appeals on points of law are possible, under section 69, only with the leave of the court.[74] Importantly, however, the operation of section 69 can be excluded and, if that is the case, the courts will not allow a review of errors of law through the back door under section 68.[75] In addition, sections 33 and 34 of the Arbitration Act give parties significant freedom to agree on procedural and evidentiary rules in their arbitrations. The English courts have been fully supportive of the principle of limited court intervention in arbitration. In *Fiona Trust v Privalov*,[76] for instance, the House of Lords construed the arbitration clause applying a presumption that the parties intended all their disputes to be resolved by arbitration, as a result of which allegations of bribery to enter into the contract were held to fall within the scope of the arbitration clause. In addition, the House of Lords ruled that due to the principle of separability the invalidity of the contract does not necessarily entail the invalidity of the arbitration agreement.[77]

However, arbitration cannot be self-sustaining – it needs the support of the courts.[78] Judicial practice shows that, while usually English courts show deference to arbitration, they do not hesitate to intervene where necessary. For example, in *Ust-Kamenogorsk Hydropower Plant JSC v AES Ust-Kamenogorsk Hydropower Plant LLP*,[79] the Supreme Court widened the discretion of English courts to issue anti-suit injunctions. The judgment

---

67 Oxford Civil Justice Survey (n 5); Lein and others (n 6).

68 'Arbitration Friendliness' has been described as a pull-factor in the choice of law. See Merrett and Sommerfeld, (n 1) 639.

69 Ramsey (n 2) 257.

70 *Lesotho Highlands Development Authority v Impregilo Spa* [2006] 1 AC 221 [18].

71 ibid [25].

72 Arbitration Act 1996, s 1.

73 Arbitration Act 1996, s 68.

74 Arbitration Act 1996, s 69.

75 *Lesotho Highlands Development Authority* (n 74).

76 [2007] UKHL 40.

77 ibid [17].

78 *West Tankers Inc v RAS Riunione Adriatica di Sicurta SpA (The Front Comor)* [2007] UKHL 4 [20].

79 [2013] UKSC 35 [48].

clarified that the proper legal basis for the grant of an anti-suit injunction is section 37 of the Senior Courts Act 1981, and not section 44 of the Arbitration Act 1996.[80]

Similarly, in *Cetelem v Roust Holdings*,[81] the Court of Appeal construed 'assets' in section 44(3) of the Arbitration Act to include contractual rights. By adopting a wide definition, it widened the scope for judicial intervention in support of the arbitral proceedings. At the same time, English courts have been careful not to extend the definition too far. For example, in *Zim Integrated Shipping Services v European Container*,[82] the Commercial Court ruled that contractual rights being the subject-matter of the arbitration did not fall within the meaning of 'assets' under section 44(3). Males J in the Commercial Court went on to say that even if he was wrong and such rights were indeed assets, and consequently the court did have a jurisdiction to grant an injunction such an exercise of discretion was not appropriate[83] – '[t]he closer any injunction comes to determining a matter which it is for the arbitrators to decide, the more wary the court should be as a matter of discretion'[84].

Importantly, the court shall only exercise its powers under section 44 of the Arbitration Act 'if or to the extent that the arbitral tribunal (...) has no power or is unable for the time being to act effectively'.[85] Therefore, the availability of an emergency arbitrator may lead the court not to exercise its jurisdiction to grant interim relief.[86] This depends on whether an emergency arbitrator can 'act effectively'. After all, there may be cases where an emergency arbitrator will not be able to do so, an application without notice for a freezing injunction[87] or an application without notice for an anti-suit injunction being relevant examples. A refusal by the relevant arbitral institution to appoint an emergency arbitrator does not automatically mean that the condition set forth in section 44(5) is satisfied.[88]

Therefore, what becomes evident is that English law struck a good balance between judicial non-interference and judicial support. This reflects the fact that English law supports arbitration as a matter of policy.[89] Commercial considerations are at the forefront of this policy. As observed by the House of Lords in *Lesotho Highlands Development Authority v Impregilo*, the purpose of the Arbitration Act 1996 was to set out logically and in clear language the most important principles of English arbitration law so that it can be easily accessible by commercial parties.[90] Likewise, English courts have recognised that in their auxiliary role their aim 'is to serve the business community'[91] and the support they can offer, for instance, in the form of granting anti-suit injunctions can be regarded by commercial actors as a distinct advantage of the English forum.[92] This

---

80 ibid.

81 [2005] EWCA Civ 618 [70].

82 [2013] EWHC 3581 (Comm) [24].

83 ibid [24]–[26].

84 ibid.

85 Arbitration Act 1996, s 44(5).

86 *Gerald Metals SA v Timis & Others* [2016] EWHC 2337 (Ch) [58]; *Shapoorji Pallonji & Company Private Limited (a company incorporated under the laws of India) v Yumn Ltd (a company incorporated under the laws of Rwanda) v Standard Chartered Bank* [2021] EWHC 862 (Comm); cf *Seele Middle East FZE v Drake & Scull International SA Co* [2014] EWHC 435 (TCC).

87 *Gerald Metals* (n 91) [53].

88 ibid [56].

89 *Cruz City 1 Mauritius Holdings v Unitech Ltd* [2013] EWCA Civ 1512 [36].

90 *Lesotho Highlands Development Authority* (n 74) [19].

91 *The Front Comor* (n 82) [22].

92 ibid.

is significant because construction disputes are often resolved through arbitration[93] and London becomes a forum of choice for such arbitrations.

As regards courts procedures, these are relevant in two ways. First, when there are court applications relating to arbitration and, second, when the parties litigate before the English courts. In both cases, disputes relating to construction contracts are likely to be listed in the TCC. The TCC, established in 2004 as a division of the High Court, has since been at the forefront of procedural innovation. It replaced evidence-in-chief with witness statements[94] and allowed expert witnesses to meet 'without prejudice' with an aim to reach agreement with their conclusions being summarised in a joint statement.[95] Additionally, it introduced the use of lists of issues in complex cases[96] and the 'Scott Schedules' allowing parties to outline their arguments on multiple claims in a single document[97]. The TCC also widely recognises the need for active case management by the judge trying the case.[98]

Procedural advantages offered by English law and English dispute resolution fora are considerable pull-factors influencing the choice of law. The TCC has been part of this success story. With its unparalleled international reputation, it comes as no surprise that 'parties to construction and engineering contracts from all over the world specify the TCC as the court to resolve their disputes'[99] and that its procedures are emulated in the emerging specialist construction dispute resolution fora.[100]

Prevalence of English law in the future

Despite the above advantages of English law, its leading position on the international market is not guaranteed as English law and its dispute resolution fora face the aftermath of Brexit and increasing competition from emerging specialist commercial courts in Europe and elsewhere.[101] This being said, the attractiveness of English law for parties to international commercial contracts is independent of the UK's membership in the EU. As harmonisation of contract law in the EU has been limited, substantive and procedural advantages of English law have endured Brexit and will continue to do so in the future.[102]

Furthermore, the status of exclusive jurisdiction clauses has been preserved. The UK has, in its own right, ratified the 2005 Hague Convention on the Choice of Court

---

93 Ramsey (n 2) 268.

94 HM Courts & Tribunals Service, *The Technology and Construction Court Guide* (2nd edn, 2015), paras 12.1, 12.1.3 and 12.2.5.

95 ibid paras 7.6, 13.6, 13.8.2.

96 ibid para 13.8.1.

97 ibid para 5.6.

98 ibid para 5.1.

99 Ramsey (n 2) 257.

100 Procedural rules of the Technology and Construction Division of the Dubai International Financial Centre Courts, the Technology, Infrastructure and Construction List of the Singapore International Commercial Court, the Hong Kong Construction and Arbitration List have been influenced by the procedure in the TCC. See Pinsent Masons, 'Specialist construction courts around the world' (*Pinsent Masons*, 18 January 2022) <https://www.pinsentmasons.com/out-law/guides/specialist-construction-courts> accessed 8 March 2023.

101 See, e.g., Olga Sendetska and Marti Bär, 'Checking In With Competition in Europe: Where Do International Commercial Courts Stand?' (*Kluwer Arbitration Blog*, 26 April 20211) <https://arbitrationblog.kluwerarbitration.com/2021/04/26/checking-in-with-competition-in-europe-where-do-international-commercial-courts-stand-2/> accessed 8 March 2023.

102 Merrett and Sommerfeld (n 1) 657.

Agreements[103] to which the EU is a party.[104] The Convention ensures the enforcement of exclusive jurisdiction clauses in favour of the courts of contracting parties and the resulting judgments of the relevant national courts.[105] Therefore, courts of the EU Member States have to respect exclusive jurisdiction clauses in favour of English law and resulting English judgments.

There remain doubts as to the recognition and enforceability of English judgments in the EU and vice versa beyond the scope of The Hague Convention. This is because the Brussels I Regulation (Recast),[106] which provides for mutual recognition and enforceability of judgments as between EU Member States, ceased to apply to the UK. Previously, English judgments could be recognised and enforced by courts of other EU Member States without the need for any special procedure.[107] While this route is no longer available, there exist three alternative avenues for the enforcement of English judgements in the EU. First, the 2005 Hague Convention, to which both the UK and EU are parties, provides for the recognition and enforcement of judgements resulting from exclusive jurisdiction clauses. However, this does not include other jurisdiction clauses, for example, non-exclusive or asymmetric clauses[108] as well as jurisdiction based on other factors, such as service within the jurisdiction or permission to serve the claim outside the jurisdiction respectively under sections II and IV of Part 6 of the Civil Procedure Rules. Thus, its scope is much narrower than that of the Brussels regime. Moreover, it appears that the 2005 Hague Convention only applies to contracts concluded, and to legal proceedings instituted, after its entry into force on 1 January 2021.[109]

Parties may be able to enforce an English judgment in an EU Member State under a bilateral treaty applicable before the entry into force of the 1968 Brussels Convention and the later Brussels Regulations, e.g., the 1934 Franco–British Convention on Foreign Judgments.[110]

However, if neither the 2005 Hague Convention nor a pre-Brussels treaty applies a party wishing to enforce a foreign judgment will have to rely on the national regime of the State where recognition or enforcement is being sought.

Recognition and enforceability of judgements is particularly important for construction companies operating both in the UK and EU. If they wish to resolve their disputes in the

---

103 Private International Law (Implementations of Agreements) Act 2020.

104 Council Decision of 26 February 2009 on the signing on behalf of the European Community of the Convention on Choice of Court Agreements (2009/397/EC) [2009] OJ L 133/1; Council Decision of 4 December 2014 on the approval, on behalf of the European Union, of the Hague Convention of 30 June 2005 on Choice of Court Agreements (2014/887/EU) [2014] OJ L 353/5.

105 Convention on Choice of Court Agreements (The 2005 Hague Convention) arts 5 and 8.

106 Regulation (EU) No 1215/2012 of the European Parliament and of the Council of 12 December 2012 on jurisdiction and the recognition and enforcement of judgments in civil and commercial matters (recast) [2012] OJ L 351/1.

107 ibid arts 36 and 39.

108 *Etihad Airways PJSC v Flöther* [2020] EWCA Civ 1707 [92]–[94]; Brooke Marshall, 'Asymmetric Jurisdiction Clauses and the Anomaly Created by Article 31(2) of the Brussels I Recast Regulation' (2022) 71 ICLQ 297.

109 The 2005 Hague Convention art 16; Andrew Dickinson, 'Close the Door on Your Way Out – Free Movement of Judgments in Civil Matters – A 'Brexit' Case Study (2017) 3 *Zeitschrift für Europäisches Privatrecht* 539.

110 The Law Society, 'Enforcement of foreign judgements after Brexit' (*The Law Society*, 13 January 2021) <https://www.lawsociety.org.uk/topics/brexit/enforcement-of-foreign-judgments-after-brexit> accessed 13 December 2022.

UK and enforce English judgments in the EU, they should opt for exclusive jurisdiction clauses as covered by the 2005 Hague Conventions. Otherwise, they will be faced either with outdated bilateral agreements or a national regime of the state of enforcement.[111] The British government has recently announced that the UK will accede to the 2019 Hague Convention on the Recognition and Enforcement of Foreign Judgements in Civil or Commercial Matters 'as soon as practicable'.[112] That move should further strengthen the enforcement of judgments between a considerable number of jurisdictions, including the majority of EU Member States.

Despite uncertainty surrounding the recognition of English judgments in the EU and vice versa, there appears to be consensus in the literature that Brexit may increase the competitiveness of English law on the market for international contracts. Arguably it could enhance the perceived neutrality of English law.[113] Since English law has become independent of EU law it can be perceived as neutral ground for agreements between EU and non-EU businesses.[114] Furthermore, the proceedings in the UK may be cheaper and faster as the option to refer a case to the Court of Justice of the European Union has been removed.[115] These aspects should give English law and English courts a competitive edge against their European competitors.[116]

As regards arbitration, as explained in detail elsewhere,[117] the impact of Brexit should be minimal and even positive as English law is now free of the constraints of EU law, such as the concept of 'EU public policy', largely out of the control of English courts, and English courts can once again issue anti-suit inunctions in relation to court proceedings in EU Member States. The EU Brussels I Regulation, and, therefore, also the EU Brussels I Regulation Recast, prevented English courts from issuing anti-suit injunctions against parties litigating the dispute, in breach of the arbitration agreement, in EU Member

---

111 To preserve the enforceability of English judgments in the EU, the UK has applied to accede to the 2007 Lugano Convention. See Federal Department of Foreign Affairs FDFA (Switzerland), Notification to the Parties of the Convention on Jurisdiction and the Recognition and Enforcement of Judgments in Civil and Commercial Matters, concluded at Lugano on 30 October 2007 (14 April 2020). The Lugano Convention is open for accession by any State but requires unanimous consent of the Contracting Parties. See Convention on jurisdiction and the recognition and enforcement of judgments in civil and commercial matters [2007] OJ L339/3 (Lugano Convention) arts 70 and 72. In the case of the UK's accession, unanimous consent has not yet been forthcoming. See European Commission, 'Communication from the Commission to the European Parliament and the Council. Assessment on the application of the United Kingdom of Great Britain and Northern Ireland to accede to the 2007 Lugano Convention' (*European Commission*, 4 May 2021) <https://commission.europa.eu/system/files/2021-05/1_en_act_en.pdf> accessed 3 January 2023. To address the problem of recognition and enforcement of foreign judgments, the British government plans to join the 2019 Hague Convention. See Ministry of Justice, 'Consultation on the Hague Convention of 2 July 2019 on the Recognition and Enforcement of Foreign Judgments in Civil or Commercial Matters (Hague 2019)'. It is, however, difficult to predict how much time it will take. The 2005 Hague Convention, for instance took ten years to come into force. Thus, it is unlikely that the 2019 Hague Convention will assist parties in the short-term.

112 Ministry of Justice, 'Government response to the Hague Convention of July 2019 on the Recognition and Enforcement of Foreign Judgements in Civil or Commercial Matters (Hague 2019)' (*gov.uk*, 23 November 2023)   <https://www.gov.uk/government/consultations/hague-convention-of-2-july-2019-on-the-recognition-and-enforcement-of-foreign-judgments-in-civil-or-commercial-matters-hague-2019/outcome/government-response-to-the-hague-convention-of-july-2019-on-the-recognition-and-enforcement-of-foreign-judgements-in-civil-or-commercial-matters-hagu> accessed 10 December 2023.

113 Merrett and Sommerfeld (n 1) 658.

114 ibid 658.

115 ibid 662.

116 Renato Nazzini, 'Brexit and Arbitration' in Andrea Biondi and others (eds), *Brexit: The Legal Implications* (Kluwer Law International 2018).

117 Nazzini (n 123).

States.[118] This is no longer the case. For instance, in *Ebury Partners Belgium SA/NV v Technical Touch BV*,[119] the Commercial Court granted an anti-suit injunction to restrain proceedings in Belgium.

Impact of English contract law

English legal concepts and principles have influenced the development of construction law in other common law jurisdictions and international construction contracting.

The following section highlights these influences by reference to the prevention principle and the role of the contract administrator.

Prevention principle

The English case of *Holme v Guppy* explains that 'the essence of the prevention principle is that the promisee cannot insist upon the performance of an obligation which he has prevented the promisor from performing'.[120] Its international application provides one of the best examples of the impact of English construction law on other common law jurisdictions and on standard forms of construction contracts.

The prevention principle can be traced back to *Holme v Guppy*,[121] which concerned a delay in completing carpentry and joinery works at a brewery. The parties agreed on a time for completion of four and a half months with a liquidated damages of £40 per week.[122] The works began four weeks later because of the employer's failure to give possession. They were subsequently delayed by one week due to contractor's own default and by four further weeks because of another contractor's default. Ultimately, the completion was delayed by the total of five weeks.[123] The employer sought to deduct liquidated damages. However, the Court found 'clear authorities, that if the party be prevented, by the refusal of the other contracting party, from completing the contract within the time limited, he is not liable in law for the default'.[124] Consequently, the contractors were excused from performing the original agreement and 'left at large'.[125] This general rule may be conceptualised as an implied term of contract rather than a free-standing common law rule.[126] While it can be applied to contracts generally,[127] it is not widely recognised in contexts other than construction.[128] It is, thus, one of 'the particular construction law concepts which have derived from the English common law'.[129]

---

118 TheCityUK (n 7) 9.

119 *Ebury Partners Belgium SA/NV v Technical Touch BV* [2022] EWHC 2927 (Comm).

120 *Multiplex Constructions (UK) v Honeywell Control Systems Ltd* [2007] EWHC 447 (TCC) [47] (Jackson J).

121 (1838) 3 M & W 387, 389 (Parke B).

122 Ramsey (n 2) 268.

123 *Holme* (n 130).

124 ibid.

125 ibid.

126 *North Midland Building Ltd v Cyden Homes Ltd* [2018] EWCA Civ 1744 [28]–[38] (Coulson LJ).

127 *Trollope & Colsl Ltd v North West Metropolitan Hospital Board* [1973] 1 WLR 601.

128 Matthew Bell, 'Scaling the Peak: The Prevention Principle in Australian Construction Contracting [2006] ICLR 318, 319.

129 Ramsey (n 2) 252.

The prevention principle has been 'exported' from England to other common law juris-dictions like Australia, Singapore, and Canada where it has generated a wealth of judicial decisions and legal scholarship.[130]

What constitutes an act of prevention?
Courts have extensively discussed the prevention principle and particularly what consti-tutes as an act of prevention. Preventing conduct may range from a breach of contract, to conduct that is morally blameworthy or simply innocent (e.g., ordering variations in accordance with the contract).[131]

The employer's conduct in *Holme v Guppy* was neither in breach of contract nor culpa-ble in the moral sense and the contractor themselves contributed to the delay. Nevertheless, the employer was unable to recover liquidated damages. Later cases, however, showed little to no consistency. Some confined the operation of prevention principle to delays caused by a breach of contract.[132] Others support the proposition that there is need for neither blame nor breach of contract on the part of the employer to trigger the prevention principle.[133]

Courts in different Canadian jurisdictions has considered and applied the ratio in *Holme v Guppy* since the 1850s.[134] For example, in *Hamilton v Moore*,[135] the Ontario Court of Queen's Bench held that the employer could not recover liquidated damages where the contractor was prevented from performing their obligations under the contract by a delay caused by another contractor.

Similarly, courts of New Zealand have been applying *Holme v Guppy* since the late 19th century; in *Murdoch v Lockie*,[136] the Supreme Court confirmed that the prevention prin-ciple operated under the law of New Zealand. In *Canterbury Pipe Lines v Christchurch*

---

130 For judicial decisions in England see, e.g., *Holme* (n 130); *Dodd v Churton* [1897] 1 QB 562; *Peak Construction (Liverpool) Ltd v McKinney Foundations Ltd* [1971] 1 WLUK 456; *Trollope* (n 137); *Honeywell* (n 129); in Singapore see, e.g., *Lin Chin San Contractors Pte Ltd v LW Infrastructure Pte Ltd (No.1)* [2011] SGHC 162; *Chua Tian Chu v Chin Bay Ching* [2011] SGHC 126; in Canada see, e.g., *Melville v Carpenter* [1853] OJ No 186, 4 UCCP 159; *Hamilton v Moore* [1873[OJ No 45, 33 UCR 275; *Ottawa Northern and Western Railway Co v Dominion Bridge Co* (1905) 36 SCR 347; *Perini Pacific Ltd v Greater Vancouver Sewerage and Drainage District* [1966] BCJ No 105, 57 DLR (2d) 307; in New Zealand see, e.g., *Murdoch v Lockie* (1896) 15 NZLR 296; *Canterbury Pipe Lines Ltd v Christchurch Drainage Board* [1979] 2 NZLR 347; in Malaysia see, e.g., *Sim Chio Huat v Wong Ted Fui* [1983] 1 MLJ 151, 154-155; in Australia see, e.g., *Commissioners of the State Savings Bank of Victoria v Costain Australia Ltd* (1983) 2 ACLR; *SMK Cabinets v Modern Electrics Pty Ltd* [1984] VR 391; *Turner Corporation Ltd (Receiver and Manager Appointed) v Austotel Pty Ltd* (1997) 13 BCL 378; *Turner Corporation Ltd (In Provisional Liquidation) v Co-Ordinated Industries Pty Ltd & Ors* (1995) 11 BCL 202; *Gaymark Investments Pty Ltd v Walter Construction Group Ltd* (2000) BCL 449; in Hong Kong see, e.g., *Ying Ho Co Ltd v Secretary for Justice* [2004] HKCU 1113; *Hsing Chong Construction (Asia) Ltd v Henble Ltd* [2006] HKCFI 965. For academic commentary see, e.g., Ellis Baker, James Bremen and Anthony Lavers, 'The Development of the Prevention Principle in English and Australian Jurisdictions' [2005] ICLR; Matthew Bell, 'Scaling the Peak: The Prevention Principle in Australian Construction Contracting [2006] ICLR 318; Katrina Mae, 'Preventing Improper Liability for Delay But Not Preventing Disputes: Re-Thinking the Implications of the Prevention Principle in Australia and Abroad' (2019) 36(1) ICLR 24; Crispin Winser, 'Shutting Pandora's box: the prevention principle after Multiplex v Honeywell' (2007) 23(7) Const LJ 511.

131 Baker, Bremen and Lavers, (n 140) 198.

132 *Roberts v Bury Improvement Commissioners* (1870) LRCP 310, 324 (Kelly CB).

133 *Dodd* (n 140); *Amalgamated Building Contractors v Waltham Holy Cross Urban District Council* [1952] 2 All ER 452.

134 See, e.g. *Melville* (n 140); *Hamilton* (n 140); *Ottawa Northern and Western Railway Co* (n 140); *Perini Pacific* (n 140).

135 *Hamilton* (n 140) [8].

136 *Murdoch* (n 140).

Drainage Board,[137] the Court of Appeal ruled that 'wrongful withholding of a progress payment' can constitute the act of prevention – '[although] (...) there is no precedent for applying the principle to a case involving a failure to pay money under contract, its application (...) would appear to be no more than a legitimate extension of a rule of justice which the Courts have applied to a variety of circumstances' such as failure to give possession or to supply the necessary documentation.[138]

In Malaysia, the prevention principle has been recognised on the basis on *Holme v Guppy*[139] and *Dodd v Churton*[140]. As a result, the courts in that jurisdiction have adopted a morally neutral definition of the acts of prevention.[141]

The watershed case, however, came in the form of the Court of Appeal decision in *Peak Construction (Liverpool) Ltd v McKinney*.[142] All three members of the Court of Appeal stressed the importance of culpability. Salmon LJ could not see how 'the employer can insist on compliance with a condition if it [was] partly his own fault that it [could] not be fulfilled'.[143] Edmund Davis LJ also emphasised the importance of 'the employer's own default'.[144] Likewise, Phillimore LJ highlighted 'the fault of the employer'.[145] *Peak* found some support in Hong Kong. In *Ying Ho Co Ltd v Secretary for Justice*, the court preferred a morally loaded definition under *Peak* to a morally neutral under *Holme*.[146]

Nevertheless, there has been some pushback both in England and Wales and in Victoria against the proposition that an act of prevention must be culpable. In *Trollope & Colls Ltd v North West Metropolitan Regional Hospital Board*, the House of Lords, without any reference to *Peak*, approved the proposition that 'when there is a stipulation for work to be done in a limited time, if one party by his conduct – it may be quite legitimate conduct, such as ordering extra work – renders it impossible or impracticable for the other party to do his work within the stipulated time, then the one whose conduct caused the trouble can no longer insist upon strict adherence to the time stated'.[147] As evidenced by *SMK Cabinets v Hili Modern Electrics Pty Ltd*,[148] in Victoria, the morally neutral definition in *Trollope* has prevailed over the morally loaded characterisation in *Peak*.[149]

Therefore, it appears that the issue of the nature of the preventive conduct has now been settled. Culpable conduct on the part of the employer will trigger the operation of the prevention principle. But so will perfectly legitimate conduct, provided that it contributes to the delay,[150] provided, however, that the act of prevention bears on the contractor's ability to complete the works by the prescribed time.[151]

---

137 *Canterbury Pipe Lines* (n 140) 369–371.
138 ibid.
139 *Holme* (n 130).
140 *Dodd* (n 140).
141 See, e.g., *Sim Chio Huat* (n 140) 154–155.
142 *Peak* (n 140).
143 ibid (Salmon LJ).
144 ibid (Edmund Davis LJ).
145 ibid (Phillimore LJ).
146 *Ying Ho* (n 140) [142]–[144].
147 *Trollope* (n 137).
148 *SMK Cabinets* (n 140).
149 Bell (n 140) 328–329.
150 *Multiplex* (n 129)
151 *Lim Chin San Contractors* (n 140).

Can extension of time clauses oust the operation of the prevention principle?
The operation of the prevention principle can have severe consequences for the employer. Although there is no culpability or breach of contract on the part of the employer and the contractor contributes to the delay, the employer may lose the right to apply liquidated damages. The prevention principle operates on an all or nothing basis where the employer is entitled either to the full amount of liquidated damages or nothing at all.[152] If apportionment of liquidated damages is not possible, the only option the employer is often left with is an action for unliquidated damages.[153] The employer is thus put in a considerably worse position because it cannot automatically apply liquidated damages; it must instead prove loss and may be restricted by any limitations in unliquidated damages clauses.[154] This usually has detrimental effects on the employer's cashflow.[155] Therefore, it is paramount for the employers to protect their right to recover liquidated damages.

In *Peak v McKinney*, Salmon LJ, while excluding the possibility of apportionment, hinted at an alternative avenue for the preservation of the employer's right to liquidated damages – a contractual clause expressing the parties' intention to the effect that liquidated damages are to be recoverable despite the employer's responsibility in part or in full for the delay.[156] Consequently, it is possible to oust the operation of the prevention principle altogether.[157] However, a more common way to preserve the right to liquidated damages is the inclusion of extension of time clauses. Salmon LJ said in *Peak* that 'if the employer wishes to recover liquidated damages for failure by the contractors to complete on time in spite of the fact that some of the delay is due to the employers' own fault or breach of contract, then the extension of time clause should provide, expressly or by necessary inference, for an extension on account of such a fault or breach on the part of the employer'.[158] Importantly, however, following Salmon LJ, the extension of time must actually be granted to protect the right to liquidated damages.[159]

Australian courts, in particular in Victoria and New South Wales, on the other hand, have pushed back against *Peak*'s second limb towards more relaxed approach. In *Commissioners of the State Savings Bank of Victoria v Costain Australia Ltd*, the contractor relied on *Peak* to argue that mere availability of an extension of time clause is insufficient because the extension of time must in fact be granted to preserve the right to liquidated damages.[160] The court in *Costain* reviewed decisions from England, New Zealand, and the USA to form an Australian position. The existence of the prevention principle in Victorian law can, of course, be traced back to the early English cases that the court in *Costain* analysed.[161] However, as to the effect of an extension of time clause, *Costain* constitutes a significant departure from the two requirements in *Peak*. Without engaging directly with *Peak*, the Court shifted the focus from the actual approval of an extension of time to its mere availability: 'Neither on principles nor on the authorities is

---

152 *Peak* (n 140) (Edmund Davis LJ).
153 Baker, Bremen and Lavers (n 140) 202.
154 ibid.
155 ibid.
156 *Peak* (n 140) 121 (Salmon LJ).
157 *Hsing Chong Construction* (n 140) [17].
158 *Peak* (n 140) 121 (Salmon LJ).
159 ibid 122 (Salmon LJ).
160 *Costain* (n 140), 8.
161 ibid.

it in my opinion necessary to have a clause that is both capable of providing an extension and in fact brings about an extension in every case'.[162]

Following the decision of the Supreme Court of New South Wales in *Turner Corporation Ltd (Receiver and Manager Appointed) v Austotel Pty Ltd*, the availability of an extension of time clause modifies the effect of the prevention principle:

> If the builder, having a right to claim an extension of time fails to do so, it cannot claim that the act of prevention which would have entitled it to an extension of time for Practical Completion resulted in its inability to complete by that time (...) The act of the Proprietor does not prevent performance of the contractual obligations within time: it entitles the Builder to apply for a contractual variation extending time for performance.[163]

The meaning of this paragraph is twofold. First, it seems that the availability of an extension of time clause is sufficient to disapply the prevention principle. Second, it appears that the key question is that of causation.[164] Soon after it was handed down, *Austotel* was applied in *Turner Corporation Ltd (In Provisional Liquidation) v Co-Ordinated Industries Pty Ltd & Ors*.[165] The analysis again focused on the first limb in the *Peak* test and the relevant contractual clauses.[166] Mere availability of an extension of time displaced the operation of the prevention principle.[167]

The decision of the Supreme Court of the Northern Territory in *Gaymark Investments Pty Ltd v Walter Construction Group Ltd*,[168] involved a contractor who failed validly to apply for an extension of time. The employer relied on *Austotel* to argue that when the contractor fails to apply for an extension of time their inability to comply with the stipulated time for completion no longer results from the employer's preventive conduct.[169] However, while contracts in *Austotel* and *Co-Ordinated Industries* empowered the superintendent to extend the time unilaterally, in *Gaymark* that power was removed. Instead, an extension of time was dependent on strict compliance with the condition precedent in the amended clause.[170] The court, thus, upheld the arbitrator's finding that the employer elected to bear the risk of losing the right to liquidated damages where the employer causes delay and the contractor fails to comply with the condition precedent.[171]

Gaymark, therefore, creates a paradoxical situation – a contractor is essentially better off by not complying with the contractual condition precedent for an extension of time then it would have been if it had.[172] The decision also fails to appreciate the purpose of notice provisions – efficient contract management.[173] These issues were addressed in an English case of *Multiplex Constructions (UK) Ltd v Honeywell Control Systems Ltd (No.2)*, where Jackson J, said:

---

162 ibid.
163 *Austotel* (n 140) 384–385.
164 Bell (n 140) 331.
165 *Co-Ordinated Industries* (n 140).
166 Bell (n 140) 332.
167 ibid 332.
168 *Gaymark* (n 140).
169 ibid [63].
170 ibid [69].
171 ibid.
172 Keith Pikavance, 'Calculation of a Reasonable Time to Complete When Time is At Large' ICLR, 173-174; Bell (n 140); Winser (n 140) 513.
173 Winser (n 140) 516.

Whatever may be the law of the Northern Territory of Australia, I have considerable doubt that *Gaymark* represents the law of England. Contractual terms requiring a contractor to give prompt notice of delay serve a valuable purpose; such notice enables matters to be investigated while they are still current. Furthermore, such notice sometimes gives the employer the opportunity to withdraw instructions when the financial consequences become apparent. If *Gaymark* is good law, then a contractor could disregard with impunity any provision making proper notice a condition precedent. At his option the contractor could set time at large.[174]

Furthermore, *Gaymark* is problematic because, as it will be demonstrated later in this chapter, most of the standard construction contracts both aimed for domestic and international use resemble the contract in *Gaymark*. They provide for specific delay events and set conditions precedent to the application for an extension of time. They do not empower the contract administrator to extend the date for completion unilaterally. Australian construction contracts are outliers in that regard.[175] The TCC, having regard to English, Scottish, and Australian jurisprudence, including *Austotel*, as well as academic literature, ruled that *Gaymark* is neither good law nor does it constitute the law of England.[176]

However, it seems that, in *Multiplex*, Jackson J did not address the second limb in the *Peak* test that the extension of time must actually be granted to oust the operation of the prevention principle.[177] Nevertheless, *Multiplex* appears to represent the current or at least the preferable position in English law as it was applied by the Court of Appeal in *North Midland Building Ltd v Cyden Homes Ltd*.[178]

It is evident that the availability and wording of an extension of time clause are key to preserving the employer's right to liquidated damages and preventing time from being set at large. The following paragraphs look at the wording of extension of time clauses in some of the most common construction contracts.

Extension of time clause in standard form contracts internationally
The Joint Contracts Tribunal (JCT) forms of contract are standard construction contracts developed in England for domestic use. Accordingly, they are most commonly used for major construction projects in England and Wales.[179] However, they have been exported abroad, for example, to Nigeria.[180] Each of the JCT forms of contract includes an extension of time clause.[181] In addition to listing specific events warranting an extension of time (e.g., variations, delay in giving possession of the site, exceptionally adverse weather conditions or civil commotion or the use or threat of terrorism and/or the activities of the relevant authorities in dealing with such event or threat),[182] they provide for a sweeping provision entitling the contractor to extension of time as a result of 'any impediment , prevention or default, whether by act or omission by the Employer, the Architect/Contract Administrator, the Quantity Surveyor or any Employer's Person, except to the extent

---

174 *Multiplex* (n 129) [103].
175 Mae (n 140) 35.
176 *Multiplex* (n 129) [95]–[103].
177 ibid [53].
178 [2018] EWCA Civ 1744.
179 PLC Cross-border, *International standard forms of contract* (Thomson Reuters 2010).
180 Muhammad Muktar and others, 'Contractual Shift towards Collaborative Forms of Contract in the Nigerian Construction Industry' (2017) *3rd Annual Research Conference of the Nigerian Institute of Quantity Surveyors (NIQS)* 3.
181 Mae (n 140) 32.
182 JCT Standard Building Contract, cl 29.

caused or contributed to by any default, whether by act or omission, of the Contractor or any Contractor's person'.[183]

New Zealand Standards' contracts such as NZS 3916 use a similar mechanism. They include specific delay events ranging from variations though inclement weather to natural disasters.[184] They also provide for extensions of time for 'any circumstances not reasonably foreseeable by an experienced contractor at the time of tendering and not due to the fault of the contractor; and default by the principal or any other person for whose acts or omission the principal is responsible'.[185]

Australian Standard contracts such as AS4300-1995 are unique. Just like their English and New Zealander counterparts they list specific delay events entitling a contractor to an extension of time.[186] However, they do not rely on sweeping 'catch-all' clauses to oust the operation of the prevention principle. Instead, they empower the superintendent to extend the date for practical completion unilaterally.[187] For instance, Clause 35.5 of AS4300-1995 provides:

> Notwithstanding that the contractor is not entitled to or has not claimed an extension of time, the Superintendent may at any time and from time to time before the issue of the Final Certificate by notice in writing to the contractor extend the time for Practical Completion for any reason.[188]

However, what shows the truly global reach of the prevention principle is the inclusion of extension of time clauses in the FIDIC suite of contracts. In contrast to the above contracts, the FIDIC suite of contracts is intended to be used internationally.[189] As such they are widely used around the world, even in civil law jurisdictions.[190] The extension of time clause in the 1999 FIDIC Red and Yellow, and Silver Book contracts resembles that in the JCT and the New Zealand Standard because it entitles contractors to claim for an extension of time not only as a result of specific delay events but also based on a 'catch all' provision. Sub-Clause 8.4 of the 1999 Red and Yellow, and Silver Books entitles the contractor to an extension of where the delay is caused, for example, by variations, substantial change in quantity of an item of work, adverse climatic conditions, and shortages of personnel or goods due to epidemic or governmental actions.[191] It also entitles the contractor to an extension of time when the completion is delayed by 'any delay, impediment or prevention caused by or attributable to Employer, the Employer's Personnel, or the Employer's other contractors'.[192] This approach is generally followed in the 2017 editions of the Red and Yellow, and Silver Books.[193]

---

183 JCT Standard Building Contract, cl 29(7).

184 Mae (n 140) 33.

185 See, e.g., Standards New Zealand, NZS 3916:2013 Conditions of contract for building and civil engineering – Design and construct, Cl 10.3.1.

186 See, e.g., AS4300-1995, Cl 35.5; AS4000-1997, Cl 34.3; AS2124-1992, Cl 35.5; AS4902-2000, CL 34.3.

187 See, e.g., AS4300-1995, Cl 35.5; AS4000-1997, Cl 34.5; AS2124-1992, Cl 35.5; AS4902-2000, CL 34.5.

188 AS4300-1995, Cl 35.5.

189 Ellis Baker and others, *FIDC Contracts Law and Practice* (1st edn, Routledge 2009), 279 [1.60].

190 Mae, (n 140) 33.

191 FIDIC Conditions of Contract for Construction (1st edn, 1999) (FIDIC Red Book 1999), Sub-Cl 8.4; Baker and others (n 202) [8.242].

192 FIDIC Red Book 1999; FIDIC Conditions of Contract for Plant and Design-Build (1st edn, 1999) (FIDIC Yellow Book 1999), Sub-Cl 8.4(e).

193 FIDIC Conditions of Contract for Construction (2nd edn, 2017) (FIDIC Red Book 2017); FIDIC Conditions of Contract for Plant and Design-Build (2nd edn, 2017) (FIDIC Yellow Book 2017), Sub-Cl 8.5.

The role of the contract administrator

Appointment of a third party by the employer to administer the contract is a long-established practice in construction contracts with English heritage.[194] Historically, contract administration was merged with the design of the project.[195] Thus, the role has often been undertaken by specialists like engineers or architects.[196] Although it is now recognised that the functions of a contract administrator and that of a designer are completely separate, many of the standard form construction contracts still use the traditional terminology.[197]

Generally, when carrying out his or her duties, the contract administrator acts as an agent of the employer.[198] However, the role of contract administrator also entails some decision-making functions which require independent judgment and fairness as between the parties.[199] This duality of the contract administrator's role has a long history under English law and remains one of the most controversial aspects of construction contracts with an English pedigree.[200] This is because, as some commentators argue, 'the dual roles create unavoidable conflicts of interest for the Engineer'.[201]

Initially the role of the contract administrator was purely to protect the interests of the employer.[202] Thus, in early cases the engineer was treated as 'the impersonation' of the employer.[203] Accordingly, contractual clauses stipulating that certain questions shall be decided by a contract administrator appointed by the employer were construed as meaning that these questions shall be decided by the employer albeit acting through an agent.[204] Thus, even when performing decision-making functions, the contract administrator was deemed to act as the employer's agent. This has also meant that, when performing their decision-making functions, the contract administrator was not deemed to act judicially.[205] Consequently, they were not bound by any rules of evidence.[206] The standards of impartiality were also relaxed as it was not intended 'that [the contract administrator] should come with a mind free from human weakness of preconceived opinion'.[207] The contractor's only right in the decision-making process was to insist that the contract administrator hear the contractor's arguments and decide the issue 'as fairly as he could' as guided by their professional honour, position, and intelligence.[208]

However, in the late 19th century, English courts began differentiating between engineers' administrative and certification duties thereby developing the duality of the

---

194 Baker and others (n 202) [6.53].

195 John Murdoch and Will Hughes, *Construction Contracts: Law and Management* (3rd edn, Taylor & Francis 2000), 237.

196 ibid.

197 *Scheldebouw BV v St James Homes (Gosvenor Dock) Ltd* [2006] EWHC 89 (TCC) [33]–[34]; *Imperial Chemical Industries Ltd v Merit Merrell Technology Ltd* [2017] EWHC 1763 (TCC) [128-130].

198 *Scheldebouw* (n 210) [33]–[34]; *Imperial Chemical Industries* (n 210) [128-130].

199 Murdoch and Hughes (n 208).

200 Baker and others (n 202) [6.1].

201 Nick Gillies, 'We Need to Talk about the Engineer: A New Zealand Perspective' (2018) 34 BCL 179, 180.

202 ibid 190.

203 *William Ranger v The Great Western Railway Co* [1854] 10 ER 824, 831.

204 ibid.

205 Edward J Rimmer, 'The Conditions of Engineering Contracts' (1939) 11(4) *Journal of Institution of Civil Engineers* 3, 23–24.

206 ibid.

207 *Jackson v Barry Railway Co* [1893] 1 Ch 238, 246–247.

208 ibid.

Engineers' role.[209] At first the distinction was drawn between 'ministerial duties' and those that required 'professional judgment and skill'.[210]

By the early 20th century this had evolved in a distinction between those duties that a contract administrator carries out as an agent of the employer and those that require them to remain impartial.[211] The former include for instance the supervision of building works or quality assurance.[212] Accordingly, the contract administrator must 'follow the progress of the work and to take steps to see that those works comply with the general requirements of the contract in specification and quality (...) If he should fail to exercise his professional care and skill in this respect, he would be liable to his employer for any damage attributable to that failure'.[213]

The latter include, for example, the determination of an amount due under the contract, whether the contractor is entitled to an extension of time, or whether the work is defective.[214] When carrying out these duties, the contract administrator has been held to have a 'high duty (...) to maintain his judicial position' and express 'fair and judicial view with regard to the rights of the parties'.[215] Accordingly, this standard was not met when an architect deferred to the employer's instructions instead of reaching their own judgment.[216]

In *Sutcliffe v Thackrah*,[217] Lord Reid explained that in relation to the determination of the aforementioned issues the contract administrator is required to 'form and act on his own opinion'.[218] In doing so, they must act 'in a fair and unbiased manner'.[219] They must also 'reach such decisions fairly, holding the balance between his client and the contractor'.[220] This duty has also been described as an obligation to act 'impartially and fairly.[221] In *Costain v Bechtel*, Jackson J, when interpreting the agreement, held that he was 'unable to find anything which militates against the existence of a duty to act impartially in matters of assessment and certification'.[222] Thus, in England the duty appears to act as a kind of presumption which comes into life unless negated by express contractual clauses.[223]

The English jurisprudence has also influenced the position in other common law jurisdictions. For instance, in the Hong Kong case of *Shui on Construction v Shui Kay Co*, Hunter J held, relying on the cases mentioned above, and especially on the dicta in *Sutcliffe*, that the contract administrator has a duty to the employer and the contractor alike to act fairly using professional care.[224] Similarly, in the New Zealand case of *Canterbury Pipe Lines Ltd v Christchurch Draining Board*, the Court of Appeal held

---

209 *Stevenson v Watson* (1879) 4 CPD 148.
210 ibid 157–158.
211 *Chambers v Goldthorpe* [1901] 1 QB 624, 634.
212 ibid.
213 *Sutcliffe v Chippendale & Edmondson (a firm)* [1982] 18 BLR 149, 162.
214 *Sutcliffe v Thackrah* [1974] AC 727.
215 *Hickman & Co v Roberts* [1913] AC 229, 234
216 ibid 229.
217 *Sutcliffe* (n 227).
218 ibid 737A.
219 ibid
220 ibid 737D.
221 ibid 751C.
222 *Costain Ltd v Bechtel Ltd* [2005] EWHC 1019 (TCC) [46].
223 Baker and others (n 202) [1.1].
224 *Shui on Construction Co Ltd v Shui Kay Co Ltd & Ors* [1985] 2 HKC 634.

that the contract administrator must act fairly and impartially.[225] The standard was not met when the contract administrator unjustifiably failed to certify progress payments and requested the contractor to rectify the works within the time specified where the contract had been allowed to continue with no new completion date.[226]

In another case from New Zealand a contract administrator failed to satisfy the standard of fairness where they did not give the contractor a clear warning before recommending termination to the employer.[227]

A similar position has been reached in New South Wales where the Court of Appeal held that:

> the superintendent is the owner's agent in all matters only in a very loose sense, and ... when exercising certifying functions in respect of which the superintendent must act honestly and impartially, the superintendent is not acting as the owner's agent, in the strict legal sense. In my opinion, this is confirmed by the consideration that the issue of a certificate by the superintendent does not bind the owner to any extent beyond what is prescribed by the building contract itself, so that the owner can challenge such certificates. If the superintendent was acting as the owner's agent in the strict sense, the issue of the certificate would be an act done by the owner through its agent, which the owner could not then challenge.[228]

The dual role of the contract administrator has had a significant impact on the FIDIC forms of contract since 1987 when the fourth edition of the Red Book imposed an express duty of impartiality on the engineer when exercising their discretion in relation to, for instance, expressing approval and determining value.[229] In the FIDIC 2017 Rainbow Suite, the 2017 Red and Yellow Books use the term 'Engineer' instead of contract administrator. The 2017 Silver Book uses the language of 'Employer's Representative'. However, the duty to act impartially applies equally under all three forms of contract.[230]

Under sub-clause 3.1 of the 2017 Red and Yellow Books the employer shall appoint an engineer[231] who, pursuant to sub-clause 3.2, 'shall be deemed to act for Employer' when carrying out their duties or exercising their authority under the contract.[232] The strong connection between the engineer and the employer is further emphasised by the fact that the engineer is defined as part of the 'Employer's Personnel'.[233] However, under sub-clause 3.7, in some instances, particularly when making determinations as to the parties' entitlements, the engineer 'shall not be deemed to act for the Employer' and must act 'neutrally between the Parties' as well as 'make fair determinations'.[234] Sub-clause 3.2 provides that the employer shall not impose further constraints to the engineer's authority.[235] Thereby,

---

225 *Canterbury Pipe Lines* (n 140) 98.

226 ibid 99.

227 *Brown & Doherty Ltd v Whangarei County Council* [1988] 1 NZLR 33.

228 *Peninsula Balmain Pty Ltd v Abigroup Contractors Ptd Ltd* (2002) 18 BCL 322 [50].

229 FIDIC Conditions of Contract for Works of Civil Engineering Construction (4th edn, 1987) (FIDIC Red Book1987)), Sub-cl 2.6; Baker and others, (n 202) [6.73].

230 FIDIC Red Book 2017, Sub-cl 3.7; FIDIC Yellow Book 2017, Sub-cl 3.7; FIDIC Conditions of Contract for EPC/Turnkey Projects (2nd edn, 2017) (FIDIC Silver Book 2017), Sub-cl 3.5. As to the general duty of a certified to act impartially see *Sutcliffe* (n 227); *AMEC Civil Engineering Ltd v Secretary of State for Transport* [2005] EWCA Civ 291; *Scheldebouw BV v St James Homes (Gosvenor Dock) Ltd* [2006] EWHC 89 (TCC).

231 FIDIC Red Book 2017, Sub-cl 3.1; FIDIC Yellow Book, Sub-cl 3.1.

232 FIDIC Red Book 2017, Sub-cl 3.2; FIDIC Yellow Book, Sub-cl 3.2.

233 FIDIC Red Book 2017, Sub-cl 1.1.33; FIDIC Yellow Book, Sub-cl 1.1.32.

234 FIDIC Red Book 2017, Sub-cl 3.7; FIDIC Yellow Book, Sub-cl 3.7.

235 FIDIC Red Book 2017, Sub-cl 3.2; FIDIC Yellow Book, Sub-cl 3.2.

it additionally strengthens the neutrality of the engineer.[236] Under the 2017 Red Book, the engineer has also some independent powers in evaluating the work.[237] The engineer has a duty to issue Interim Payment Certificates 'stating the amount that the Engineer fairly considers to be due' under sub-clause 14.6;[238] conversely the engineer has also the authority to withhold payments that they consider not to be due. The duty of fairness extends to that evaluation.

Although the 2017 Silver Book uses the language of 'Employer's Representative', its role resembles that of the engineer under the Red and Yellow Books. Sub-clause 3.1 of the Silver Book stipulates that the employer shall appoint an employer's representative who is vested with 'the full authority of the Employer' when carrying out its functions.[239] However, when carrying out its decision-making functions, the employer's representative 'shall not be deemed to act for the Employer' and must make a 'fair determination' in accordance with the contract within 42 days, as set forth in sub-clause 3.5.[240]

As explained above, two key elements of constructions contracts worldwide, that is, extension of time clauses and the role of the engineer or employer's representative are directly derived from English law. While the construction and application of such clauses is also influenced by the governing law of the contract, which may be that of any common law or civil law jurisdiction, their language and operation are, quintessentially, the product of English law and a lasting legacy of the deep influence that English law has had on construction law internationally.

International impact of the Housing Grants, Construction and Regeneration Act 1996

The UK was the first jurisdiction to enact security of payment legislation in the form of the Housing Grants, Construction and Regeneration Act 1996 (UK Act).[241] To facilitate cash flow, the UK Act conferred on the parties to construction contracts a new statutory right to receive stage payments.[242] This new entitlement was bolstered by the right to refer disputes to adjudication and the right to suspend performance for non-payment.[243] The UK Act has since been amended by the Local Democracy, Economic Development and Construction Act 2009 (LDEDCA 2009), among others, to extend its application to oral contracts, improve the payment mechanisms by providing for the giving of notices by the payer and the payee, strengthened the right to suspend performance, introduced the slip rule, and restrict the use of *Tolent* clauses.[244]

---

236 Eugenio Zoppis, 'The Role of the Engineer: A Contractor's Viewpoint' (2018) *FIDIC Conference* 1, 6.

237 ibid 7.

238 FIDIC Red Book 2017, Sub-cl 14.6; FIDIC Yellow Book, Sub-cl 14.6.

239 FIDIC Silver Book 2017, Sub-cl 3.1.

240 FIDIC Silver Book 2017, Sub-cl 3.5.

241 MEC Munaaim, 'Security of Payment Regimes in the United Kingdom, New South Wales (Ausralia), New Zealand and Singapore: A Comparative Analysis' <https://www.irbnet.de/daten/iconda/CIB19017.pdf> accessed 11 December 2023.

242 Housing Grants, Construction and Regeneration Act 1996 (HGCRA 1996), s 109.

243 HGCRA 1996, ss108 and 112.

244 For a summary of these amendments, see Muhammad Ehsan Che Munaaim, 'Part 8 of the Local Democracy, Economic Development and Construction Act 2009: amendments and missed opportunities' (2017) 33(1) Const LJ 19, 25–34.

These novel solutions revolutionised the construction industry and developed the very concept of the security of payment.[245] They have since been adopted in all Australian and some Canadian jurisdictions as well as in Ireland, New Zealand, Singapore, and Malaysia. The following section draws comparisons between the UK Act and its foreign counterparts. Particularly, it compares and contrasts their scopes of application as well as the operation of payment and adjudication mechanisms, the two hallmarks of security of payment legislation. The aim of this exercise is to demonstrate how foreign security of payment legislation borrows from and builds on top of the UK Act.[246]

The focus is on the statutes from the UK, Ireland, New Zealand, Malaysia, New South Wales, Singapore, and Ontario. New South Wales was selected among the Australian jurisdictions because its Building and Construction Industry Security of Payment Act 1999 (NSW Act), despite serving similar policy goals to, and being loosely based on, the UK Act,[247] is sufficiently different from the UK Act to serve as an alternative model of security of payment legislation.[248] It is also a prime example of the east coast model that is leading in Australia.[249] The Singaporean Building and Construction Industry Security Payment Act 2004 (SG Act) also follows the NSW model, but has been amended to include some unique features.[250] Ontario was chosen among Canadian jurisdictions because it was the first Canadian jurisdiction to introduce security of payment legislation.[251]

Scope of application

The scope of application of security of payment and adjudication provisions is delimitated territorially as well as by reference to types of arrangements and contracts. These aspects differ among jurisdictions. All statutes discussed, apart from the Construction Contracts Act 2013 (Irish Act), expressly limit the scope of their application to construction carried out in their respective jurisdictions.[252] A typical arrangement covered by the Acts is a

---

245 Munaaim, (n 254).

246 Roy Goode, 'Insularity or Leadership? The Role of the United Kingdom in the Harmonisation of Commercial Law' (2001) 50(4) ICLQ 751, 751.

247 Julian Bailey, *Construction Law* (3rd edn, London Publishing Partnership 2020), 484.

248 Munaaim (n 254).

249 The Australian West Coast model is more similar to the UK Act. Only Western and Northern Territories has followed the West Coast model. See Department of Jobs and Small Business, 'Review of Security of Payment Laws: Building Trust and Harmony' (2017). However, Western Australia has introduced the Building and Construction Industry (Security of Payment) Act 2021 bringing it closer to the East Coast model. See Stuart Downes, 'Show Me The Money: Western Australia's Security of Payment Act 2021' (*FTI Consulting*, 28 July 2022)' <https://www.fticonsulting.com/insights/articles/show-money-western-australias-security-payment-act-2021> accessed 2 March 2023.

250 Munaaim, (n 254) 431.

251 Attempts to introduce security of payment legislation are still largely in infancy. Federal Prompt Payment for Construction Work Act 2019, Nova Scotia's the Builder's Lien Bill (amended), Saskatchewan's the Builder's Lien (Prompt Payment) Amendment Act 2019, and Alberta's Builders' Lien (Prompt Payment) Amendment Act 2020 have already received royal assent but are still yet to come into force. Similarly, the Manitoba Law Commission and the Legislative Services Branch of the Office of the Attorney General recommended adoption of the security of payment legislation. For an overview see Darryl Royce, *Adjudication in Construction Law* (2nd edn, Routledge 2022) section 7.6.

252 HGCRA 1996, s 104(6)(b); Construction Contracts Act 2002 (NZ) (CCA 2002 (NZ)), s 9(a); Construction Industry Payment and Adjudication Act 2012 (Malaysia) (CIPAA 2012 (Malaysia)), s 2; Building and Construction Industry Security of Payment Act 1999 (NSW) (BCISOPA 1999 (NSW), 7(4); Building and Construction Industry Security of Payment Act 2004 (Singapore) (BCISOPA 2004 (Singapore), s 4(2)(b)(ii).

contract.[253] However, the SG Act is an outlier because it applies also to non-contractual arrangements.[254] The types of contracts covered by the security of payment legislation is also jurisdiction dependent. Some contracts are excluded from the outset, employment contracts[255] and contracts with residential occupiers[256] being the usual examples.[257] Generally, security of payment legislation applies to construction contracts.[258] Depending on the jurisdiction a construction contract may mean a contract for the carrying out of construction operations or construction work, supply of services, and supply of goods.[259] Whereas the UK and the Irish Act use the language of 'construction operations' the NZ, NWS as well as Malaysian and Singaporean Acts all use the term 'construction works'. Their meaning, however, is very similar.[260] There is, in this respect, strong international convergence.[261] Under the UK Act some activities are excluded from the meaning of construction operations. Some of these exclusions, for example concerning extractive activities, are followed in the NZ and NSW Act. On the other hand, the NSW and SG Acts include, for example contracts for the supply of goods, which are not covered by the UK Act.

Payment mechanisms

Progress payments play an important role in preserving the contractors' cash flow and allowing them to perform their duties under the contract.[262] The right to progress payments is now protected by statutes in the UK, Ireland, New Zealand, Singapore, Malaysia, as well as all Australian and some Canadian jurisdictions.[263] Generally, the payment process involves three steps: the making the progress claims by contractor, its assessment by

---

253 HGCRA 1996, s 107; Construction Contracts Act 2013 (Ireland) (CCA 2013 (Ireland), s 1(1); CCA 2002 (NZ), s 9(c); Only the Malaysian and the Singaporean Acts limit their application to contracts concluded in writing. See CIPAA 2012 (Malaysia), s 2; BCISOPA 2004 (Singapore), s 4(1); Interestingly, under the latter Act an oral contract can, in some circumstances, be treated as a written one. See BCISOPA 2004 (Singapore), s 4(4).

254 BCISOPA 1999 (NSW), 7(1); *Okaroo Pty Ltd v Vos Construction and Joinery Pty Ltd* [2005] NSWSC 45 [41].

255 HGCRA 1996, s 104(3); CCA 2013 (Ireland), s 2(2); CCA 2002 (NZ), s 11(a); BCISOPA 1999 (NSW), 7(3)(a); BCISOPA 2004 (Singapore), s 4(2)(b)(i); Employment contracts are not expressly excluded in Malaysia.

256 HGCRA 1996, s 106; CCA 2013 (Ireland), s 2(1)(b); CIPAA 2012 (Malaysia), s 3; BCISOPA 1999 (NSW), 7(3)(a); BCISOPA 2004 (Singapore), s 4(2)(a); The NZ Act applies to residential contracts. See CCA 2002 (NZ), s 11(a).

257 Some jurisdictions impose further exclusions. The NZ and SG Acts exclude contracts forming part of a loan agreement. See CCA 2002 (NZ), s 11; BCISOPA 1999 (NSW), s 7(3); The NZ Act does not apply to contracts for professional services. See CCA 2002 (NZ), s 11(b); The Irish Act applies only t contracts exceeding the value of €10,000. See CCA 2013 (Ireland), s 2(1)(a).

258 HGCRA 1996, s108 and s109; BCISPA 1999 NSW, s 7(1); BCISPA 2004 SG, s 4(1) and s 2; CCA 2002 NZ, s9.

259 MEC Munaaim, (n 254) 434.

260 HGCRA 1996, s105, CCA 2002 NZ, s6; BCISPA 1999 NWS, s5; BCISPA 2004 SG, s3.

261 CCA 2013 (Ireland), s 1(1); CCA 2002 (NZ), s 6; BCISPA 1999 NWS, s5; BCISPA 2004 SG, s3.

262 *Melville Dundas Ltd v George Wimpey UK Ltd* [2007] 1 WLR 1136 (Lord Hoffmann).

263 HGCRA 1996, s 109; BCISOPA1999 (New South Wales), s 8; Building and Construction Industry Security of Payment Act 2021 (Western Australia), s 17; BCISOPA 2004 (Singapore), s 5; CCA 2002 (New Zealand), s 16; CCA 2013 (Ireland), s 3; CIPAA 2012 (Malaysia), s 36; Construction Act 1990 (Ontario), ss 6.2 and 6.3.

the contract administrator, and the payment itself.[264] The nature of the payment mechanism, however, depends on the specific jurisdiction.

The legislation in all discussed jurisdictions provides for a mechanism for prompt payment. A distinction can be drawn between legislation that imposes minimum requirements on construction contracts[265] and statues that fully outline the payment procedure.[266]

The UK Act belongs to the former group. '[P]arties are free to agree the amounts of the payments, and the intervals at which, or circumstances in which, they become due'.[267] Thus, parties are afforded flexibility to agree the payments timeframe; monthly payments are as acceptable as biannual or milestone payments.[268] However, their agreed payment scheme must comply with the minimal requirements of the UK Act. The bare minimum imposed by the Act is that a construction contract must include an 'adequate payment mechanism for determining what payments become due under the contract, and when, and (…) a final date for payment in relation to any sum which becomes due'.[269] If or to the extent that these conditions are not satisfied default provisions contained in the Scheme for Construction Contracts applies.[270]

In contrast, the Building and Construction industry Security of Payment Act 1999 (the NSW Act) 'sets out a detailed and prescriptive code as to how a progress payment may be obtained pursuant to the Act'.[271] The mechanism for obtaining payment is based on payment claims and schedules. Under the NSW Act, 'a person who is or who claims to be entitled to a progress payment may serve a payment claim on the person who, under the construction contract concerned, is or may be liable to make the payment'.[272] In doing so, the party issuing a payment claim must identify the relevant construction work, the amount claimed, and indicate that the claim is made under the Act.[273] If the claim is made by the head contractor on the owner it must also include a 'supporting statement' in the form required declaring that the subcontractors have been paid in relation to the work subject to the claim.[274] A party on whom the payment claim is served may respond with a payment schedule identifying the relevant payment claim and the amount that the payer intends to pay.[275] If the scheduled amount is less than the claimed amount the schedule must also include reasons for the difference including any reasons for withholding payment if that is the case.[276] A failure to issue a payment schedule results in the liability to pay the claimed amount.[277]

---

264 Bailey (n 260) 467.

265 Apart from the UK Act the Irish Act, the NZ Act, and the Malaysian Act belong to this group. See respectively: CCA 2013 Ireland, ss 3(1), (2), (5), 4(2), (3), and (4); CCA 2002 NZ, ss 13, 14, 16, 17, 18, 20, 21, 22, 24; Construction Industry Payment and Adjudication Act 2012 (CIPAA 2012 Malaysia), ss 5, 6, 35, and 36.

266 The NSW and the SG Acts belong to this group. See respectively: Building and Construction Industry Security of Payment Act 1999 (BCISPA 1999 NSW), ss 8, 12, 13, and 14; Building and Construction Industry Security of Payment Act 2004 (BCISPA 2004 Singapore), ss 5, 9, 10, and 11.

267 HGCRA 1996, s 109(2).

268 Bailey (n 260) 482.

269 HGCRA 1996, s 110(1).

270 HGCRA 1996, s 110(3).

271 Bailey, (n 260) 484.

272 BCISPA 1999 NSW, s 13(1).

273 BCISPA 1999 NSW, s 13(2).

274 BCISPA 1999 NSW, ss 13(7) and 13(9).

275 BCISPA 1999 NSW, ss 14(1)–14(2).

276 BCISPA 1999 NSW, s 14(3).

277 BCISPA 1999 NSW, s 14(4).

Another difference relates to the level of detail of the payment mechanism provisions. The NSW, NZ, and SG Acts, for example, impose a prescriptive mechanism centred around payment claims and schedules.[278] The UK and Irish Act, on the other hand, opt for a less prescriptive mechanism payment mechanism based on the requirement of 'adequate payment mechanism' and payment notices.[279] The Ontario Act is an outlier because its payment provisions are not based on the UK Act but on the US federal legislation.[280]

The scope of the prohibition of conditional payment provisions is a further differentiating factor. All jurisdictions discussed above apart from Ontario prohibit 'pay-when-paid' clauses. The scope of prohibition in the UK is a bit wider as a 'pay-when-certified' clause will not constitute an adequate payment mechanism under the UK Act.

Despite these differences, all of the above statutes preserve the main characteristic introduced by the UK Act – a right to progress payments and a payment mechanism enabling to obtain payments quickly.

The scope, application, and enforcement of adjudication

The success of construction adjudication is reflected by the fact that it has spread across common law jurisdictions. It has already been implemented in all Australian and some Canadian jurisdictions, New Zealand, Singapore, Malaysia, and Ireland. The introduction of statutory adjudication has also been contemplated in South Africa and Hong Kong. Additionally, at the transnational level, UNCITRAL Working Group II is developing a model clause on interim binding adjudication[281] and a Model Law is currently being drafted by the International Statutory Adjudication Forum.[282] UK Statutory adjudication has also influenced dispute resolution clauses in the 1999 and 2017 FIDIC Suite of contracts.[283]

As regards construction adjudication, the differences between the jurisdictions relate, inter alia, to types of disputes that can be referred to adjudication, the enforcement mechanism, and the availability of review. Under the UK Act, a party to construction contract has a right to refer any dispute arising under the contract to

---

278 Muhammad EC Munaaim, 'Developing a Framework for the Effective Operation of a Security of Payment Regime in Common Law Jurisdictions' (PhD thesis, King's College London 2012)

279 ibid.

280 Bruce Reynolds and others, 'A Report on the Introduction of Prompt Payment and Adjudication Legislation in the Province of Ontario' [2019] ICLR 73, 73–74.

281 UNCITRAL Working Group II (Dispute Settlement), 'Technology-related dispute resolution and adjudication: Model clauses and guidance text' A/CN.9/WG.II/WP.234.

282 Justice Philip Jeyaretnam, 'Speech delivered at the International Statutory Adjudication Forum Joint Conference' (SG Courts, 21 September 2023) <https://www.judiciary.gov.sg/news-and-resources/news/news-details/justice-philip-jeyaretnam-speech-delivered-at-the-international-statutory-adjudication-forum-joint-conference> accessed 10 December 2023.

283 Dispute Adjudication Boards introduced by the 1999 FIDIC Red Book contract were partly inspired by the introduction of construction adjudication in the UK. See Volker Mahnken, 'On Construction Adjudication, the ICC Dispute Board Rule, and the Dispute Board Provisions of the 2017 FIDIC Conditions of Contracts' (2018–2019) 5 McGill J Disp Resol 60, 68–70. While the 2017 Red Book introduced major changes to the dispute resolution clauses, the new Dispute Avoidance and Adjudication Boards still have some of the feature typical to adjudication: prescribed time for reaching the decision and the ability to enforce the decision in an expedited procedure. See Frederic Gullion and others, 'The New FIDIC Suite 2017: Significant Developments and Key Changes' [2018] ICLR 384; Red Book 2017, Sub-cl 21.1, 21.4.3, and 21.7.

adjudication.[284] In other jurisdictions such as New South Wales only payment disputes can be referred to adjudication.[285] Ontario, constitutes an interesting middle ground because the Ontario Act sets out a list of matters that are capable of being adjudicated: 'the valuation of services or materials provided under the contract', payment, 'disputes that are subject to the notice of non-payment', amounts retained as set-offs, and 'payment of holdback'.[286]

Another difference concerns the enforcement of the adjudicator's decisions. Under the UK Act the adjudicator's decision is binding until finally determined by litigation, arbitration or agreement and is enforced by an expedited summary judgment procedure.[287] Other jurisdictions, however, equip parties with further remedies such as the right to suspend works,[288] direct payment from the employer,[289] or exercising lien over goods supplied under the contract.[290]

In line with the 'pay now, argue later' policy of the UK Act, it is not possible to appeal the adjudicator's decision. However, there are three ways of effectively challenging the decision. First, the losing party can refuse to comply with the decision and attempt to resist the enforcement proceedings[291] by raising defences of lack of jurisdiction or breach of natural justice by the adjudicator[292] or certain other limited grounds, for example in relation to the ability of the payee to repay the adjudicated sum.[293] Second, it can initiate proceedings under Part 8 of the Civil Procedure Rules seeking a declaration that the adjudicator's decision was invalid.[294] Thirdly, it can start court proceedings or arbitration seeking the final determination of the dispute.[295] Other jurisdictions, however, provide for various review mechanisms such as judicial review,[296] statutory procedure to set an adjudication decision aside,[297] or merits review by a review adjudicator.[298]

There is a considerable divergence in the adjudication provisions discussed above. The main differentiating factors relate to the scope of adjudication, the remedies

---

284 HGCRA 1996, s 108(1); Other jurisdictions in this group include New Zealand. See CCA 2002 NZ, s 25.

285 BCISPA 1999 NSW, s 17; Other jurisdictions in this group include Ireland, Malaysia, and Singapore. See CCA 2013 Ireland, s 6(1); CIPAA 2012 Malaysia, s 7(1); BCISPA 2004 Singapore, ss 12 and 13.

286 CA 1990 Ontario, s 13.5(1).

287 Renato Nazzini and Aleksander Kalisz, '2022 Construction Adjudication in the United Kingdom: Tracing trends and guiding reform' (*King's College London*, 3 November 2022) <https://doi.org/10.18742/pub01 -160> accessed 10 December 2023; Renato Nazzini and Aleksander Kalisz, '2023 Construction Adjudication in the United Kingdom' (*King's College London*, 30 November 2023) <https://kclpure.kcl.ac.uk/portal/files /239951018/2023_KCL_Adjudication_Report.pdf> accessed 10 December 2023.

288 See, e.g., CCA 2002 NZ, s 24A(1)(a)(iii).

289 See, e.g., BCISPA 2004 Singapore, s 25.

290 See, e.g., CIPAA 2012 Malaysia, s 30.

291 *Macob Civil Engineering Ltd v Morrison Construction Ltd* [1999] All ER (D) [28]; Bailey (n 260) 534.

292 For a jurisdictional objection see, e.g., *Thomas-Frederic's (Construction) Ltd v Keith Wilson* [2003] EWCA Civ 1750. For a natural justice objection see, e.g., *Cantillon v Uvasco Ltd* [2008] EWHC 282 (TCC). See also Nazzini and Kalisz, 2022 Construction Adjudication in the United Kingdom: Tracing trends and guiding reform (n 304).

293 See, e.g., *John Doyle Construction Ltd (in liquidation) v Erith Contractors* [2021] EWCA Civ 1452.

294 See e.g., *Sudlows Ltd v Global Swith Estates 1 Ltd* [2022] EWHC 3319 (TCC); Bailey (n 260) 534.

295 *Macob* (n 308); Bailey (n 260) 534.

296 *Rees v Firth* [2011] NZCA 668. On judicial review in Ireland see Samer Skaik, 'Taking Statutory Adjudication to the Next Level: A Proposal for Review Mechanism of Erroneous Determinations' [2016] ICLR 287, 292-293.

297 CIPAA 2012 Malaysia, s 15.

298 BCISPA 2004 Singapore, s 18.

available, and the availability of review. Despite these differences, however, they all provide for a speedy dispute resolution mechanism leading to a provisionally binding decision that can be enforced. English case law is often cited in these foreign jurisdictions.

Conclusion

This chapter discussed the impact and role of English construction law in the international market. English construction law has distinct advantages that make it competitive as the governing law in international construction contracts. The factors contributing to the competitiveness of English law in the market for international contracts were not dependent on the UK's membership in the EU. Thus, Brexit has would not have a material impact on the prevalence of English law internationally. On the contrary, particularly when it comes to English contract law and arbitration, the fact that the UK is no longer a member of the EU may well have advantages in terms of the neutrality and purity of English contract law and the strong pro-arbitration approach of the English courts, previously constrained by EU law.

However, the influence of English law in the global construction market goes beyond the choice of English law as governing law of international construction contracts. First, English law doctrines specific to construction law such as the prevention principle and the dual role of the engineer as employer's agent and impartial decision-maker have been adopted in other jurisdictions but, perhaps more importantly, have had a profound influence on construction contracting. Standard extension of time clauses and clauses on the dual role of the engineer or employer's representative are ubiquitous not only in UK JCT and NEC contracts, but also abroad, for example through FIDIC forms of contract that have gained wide international acceptance.

Finally, the Housing Grants, Construction and Regeneration Act 1996, as amended, has revolutionised the construction sector by giving rise to the very concept of security of payment and a statutory right to adjudication. This mode has been adopted in many jurisdictions like Australian states and territories, New Zealand, and Singapore. The comparative analysis of these statutes demonstrated how they follow and expand on the UK's regime, so much so that English case law is often cited in the foreign courts in cases involving their domestic statutes.

There are many reasons behind this phenomenon but perhaps three should be highlighted in closing. The first is the sophisticated and yet commercial and pragmatic nature of English contract law that commands the confidence of businesspeople throughout the world. While, when a dispute arises, one of the parties often looks for solutions that would allow the court or the arbitral tribunal to construe the contract flexibly or 'in good faith', going beyond a literal interpretation, there is no doubt that, *ex ante*, the vast majority of people in commerce place a premium on certainty and would not sign up to legal systems where their carefully drafted contract will be imaginatively and unpredictably interpreted based on legal metaphysics or overridden by unexpected mandatory rules dictated by all sorts of parochial policy considerations.

The second is the dispute resolution fora that the English jurisdiction offer. Whether in the Technology and Construction Court or in an arbitral tribunal seated in London (with arbitrators wisely chosen by the parties themselves or by the relevant institution), parties to international construction contract can rely on a truly first-class legal system with procedures and remedies well suited to the cost-effective resolution of complex construction disputes.

Third, England has been one of the very first jurisdictions, if not the first and still one of the few, to develop construction law as a field of study, scholarship and practice in its own right, with specialist courts going back 150 years, a specialist bar and legal profession, and university courses at postgraduate level focusing exclusively on the teaching of construction law to experience professionals from all over the world. These advantages, whilst never to be taken for granted, are not easily replicated.

PART II

NEW FRONTIERS IN PROCUREMENT SYSTEMS

CHAPTER 3

'Procuring to prevent another Grenfell Tower disaster'

How can procurement systems reduce risks and improve safety?

David Mosey

This paper examines recommendations in the 'Guidance on Collaborative Procurement for Design and Construction to Support Building Safety' ('the Guidance'),[1] which was commissioned from the King's College London Centre of Construction Law & Dispute Resolution ('CCL') by the Department for Levelling Up, Housing and Communities ('DLUHC'), and the publication of which was announced by Secretary of State Michael Gove MP in the House of Commons in January 2022. The Guidance was developed to support clients and industry in adopting and implementing procurement practices that will deliver safer buildings. The Centre led the development of the Guidance, working with co-author Russell Poynter-Brown and in cooperation with DLUHC, the Health and Safety Executive ('HSE') and a Procurement Advisory Group that included representatives from Constructing Excellence, CIoB, CIPS, Crown Commercial Service, RIBA and RICS.

The Guidance has since been embodied in UK Government construction procurement polices set out in the September 2022 'Construction Playbook', which is endorsed by 49 construction industry professional organisations, consultants, and contractors.[2]

The Grenfell Tower fire in 2017 represented the greatest loss of life in a residential fire since the Second World War. When Dame Judith Hackitt assessed the Grenfell fire tragedy in an 'Independent Review of Building Regulations and Fire Safety', she said:

- A key issue underpinning system failure is 'indifference' where 'the primary motivation is to do things as quickly and cheaply as possible rather than to deliver quality homes which are safe for people to live in'.
- 'Improving the procurement process will play a large part in setting the tone for any construction project. This is where the drive for quality and good outcomes, rather than lowest costs must start'.

---

1 Department for Levelling Up, Housing & Communities, 'Guidance on Collaborative Procurement for Design and Construction to Support Building Safety' (*Gov.uk*, 10 January 2022) <https://assets.publishing .service.gov.uk/government/uploads/system/uploads/attachment_data/file/1046501/Guidance_on_collaborative_procurement_for_design_and_construction_to_support_building_safety.pdf> accessed 29 September 2023 (DLUHC Guidance).
2 Cabinet Office, 'Construction Playbook: Government Guidance on sourcing and contracting public works projects and programmes' (*Gov.uk*, September 2022) <https://assets.publishing.service.gov.uk/government/uploads/system/uploads/attachment_data/file/1102386/14.116_CO_Construction_Playbook_Web.pdf> accessed 29 September 2023 (Construction Playbook).

DOI: 10.4324/9781032663975-6

- 'The procurement process kick-starts the behaviours that we then see throughout design, construction, occupation and maintenance'.[3]

The Guidance shows why, in line with Dame Judith's findings, it is essential to adopt collaborative practices on projects that are 'in-scope' of the regulatory regime introduced through the new Building Safety Act (the 'Act').[4] The Act is intended to introduce a new era of accountability, making it clear where the responsibility for managing safety risks lies throughout the design, construction, and occupation of buildings that are in-scope, with more onerous sanctions for those that fail to meet their obligations.

Dame Judith identified the procurement processes used across the construction industry as one of the many areas that urgently need to be improved. At the time of the publication of the Guidance, the Grenfell Tower public inquiry was still underway but there had been significant criticism of the procurement process that governed the Grenfell Tower refurbishment project. The Guidance examines evidence of the ways in which collaborative procurement can lead to safer, better-quality outcomes, and it explains how clients and their project teams can use collaborative procurement in practice.

Collaborative practices have been proven to reduce risks and improve value on construction projects in the public sector and the private sector. Numerous case studies are cited in the Guidance, and these include audited Government 'Trial Projects' which show how collaborative procurement can improve project outcomes.[5] Yet the construction industry and its clients remain cautious and collaborative practices have not become the norm. Instead, many clients, consultants, and contractors continue to use procurement models and contracts that endanger building safety by:

- Gambling on lowest price bids without joint review of detailed costs.
- Focusing primarily on transferring risk down the supply chain and preparing the ground for potential claims and disputes.

Effective collaborative practices need to be clearly connected to the underlying commercial needs and issues that arise on any project, and they will not succeed if they depend on vague or idealistic concepts. The Guidance explains a range of specific issues that should be considered when implementing the procurement of in-scope projects in the public sector or the private sector. These include:

- How can a procurement process avoid a 'race to the bottom'?[6]
- How can 'early supply chain involvement' improve safety and reduce risks?[7]
- How can collaboration improve commitments and involve residents?[8]

---

3 Judith Hackitt, *Building a Safer Future Independent Review of Building Regulations and Fire Safety: Final Report* (Command Paper, Cm 9607, 2018) Foreword pages 5 and 8 and Section 9.1 page 108.

4 Building Safety Act 2022

5 Cabinet Office, 'Government Construction: Construction Trial Projects' (*Gov.uk*, 15 May 2012) <https://assets.publishing.service.gov.uk/government/uploads/system/uploads/attachment_data/file/62628/Trial-Projects-July-2012.pdf> accessed 29 September 2023.

6 DLUHC Guidance (n 1) Section 5.

7 ibid Section 6.

8 ibid Section 7.

- How can a digital 'golden thread' integrate design, construction, and operation?[9]
- What systems sustain and enhance a collaborative culture?[10]
- How can strategic collaboration embed improved safety?[11]
- What improved economic, social, and environmental value can collaborative procurement achieve?[12]
- What are the benefits of collaborative techniques and lessons from other industries?[13]

The Construction Playbook supports adoption of the Guidance and states that:

- '[P]rojects need to be procured and contracts managed to make sure the right behaviours are embedded from the outset and that safety and quality is valued throughout'.
- '[M]eaningful and lasting change requires visible and collaborative leadership at each stage of the project'.
- '[I]f you are working on a project or a higher-risk building that is in scope for the building safety regulatory regime, alongside the Playbook please read DLUHC's guidance on 'Collaborative Procurement for Design and Construction to Support Building Safety' to ensure compliance and commitment to higher safety and quality standards'.[14]

The Guidance is intended to provide support for:

- Public and private sector clients and their advisers when implementing collaborative processes, relationships and systems as features of their procurement strategies, procedures and contracts for projects in-scope and when addressing questions that are relevant to each 'Gateway' point as described below.
- The parties identified in the Act comprising 'duty-holders' during design and construction (namely the 'Client', 'Principal Designer', 'Principal Contractor', 'Designers', and 'Contractors'), 'Accountable Persons', 'Building Safety Managers' and all other consultants, subcontractors, and suppliers when using collaborative processes, relationships, and systems to inform, support, and integrate the design, construction, supply, and operation of an in-scope project and when implementing risk management so as to prioritise safety and quality issues, and the needs of residents.
- The Building Safety Regulator when establishing how the industry moves to safer practices across the lifecycle of buildings in-scope of the new regulatory regime.

Rather than prescribing particular procurement models or contract forms, the Guidance recognises that clients in the public and private sectors adopt varying approaches; it

---

9 ibid Section 8.
10 ibid Section 9.
11 ibid Section 10.
12 ibid, Section 11.
13 ibid Section 12.
14 Construction Playbook (n 2) 5–6.

summarises ways in which all public and private sector duty-holders can demonstrate to the Building Safety Regulator how they have created and used collaborative processes, relationships and activities in order to improve safety and quality outcomes.

Dame Judith Hackitt's Independent Review concluded that:

- '[T]he way in which procurement is often managed can reduce the likelihood that a building will be safe'.
- '[T]he contracting process determines the relationships, competencies and processes that exist between all the parties in the build and management processes'.
- '[P]rocurement sets the tone and direction of the relationships between the client, designer, contractor, and their subcontractors, as well as determining the formal specification of the building'.
- '[I]ssues at this stage, for example inadequate specification, focus on low cost, or adversarial contracting, can make it difficult (and most likely, more expensive) to produce a safe building'.[15]

The Guidance shows how collaborative procurement preserves reasonable legal and commercial protections while using early planning, clear roles, full consultation, and accurate information to reduce the potential for failures, errors, misunderstandings, and disputes. The Government's response to the 'Building a Safer Future' consultation stated that:

'Fire and structural safety issues can be exacerbated by poor procurement, including:
- poorly designed tender specifications and processes
- eleventh hour contractor appointments
- lack of appropriate engagement with the supply chain and
- contract forms which prioritise low-cost solutions at the expense of building safety.

These practices can result in poor value for money and poor building safety outcomes. The Government believes that collaborative procurement approaches can help to mitigate some of the poor behaviours identified above.'[16]

Balanced qualitative selection criteria

The Guidance highlights the dangers of a 'race to the bottom', where the lowest price wins a contract but at the expense of safety and quality.[17] Farmer reports that 'clients tend to fixate on lowest initial tendered price and this is often perpetuated by their advisors, who, in a traditional procurement model, are implicitly employed (at least partly) to manage a fixed and adversarial transactional interface between clients and industry. The cost-based procurement model often hinders the ability to focus on value, outcomes or performance if appropriate weightings are not made'.[18]

---

15 Hackitt (n 4) Section 9.7, page 109.

16 Ministry of Housing, Communities & Local Government, 'A reformed building safety regulatory system: Government response to the "Building a Safer Future" consultation' (*Gov.uk*, April 2020) <https://assets.publishing.service.gov.uk/media/5e85ca81d3bf7f134714636a/A_reformed_building_safety_regulatory_system_-_gvt_response_to_the_Building_a_Safer_Future_consultation.pdf> accessed 29 September 2023 (MHCL Response).

17 DLUHC Guidance (n 1) Section 5.1.

18 Mark Farmer, 'The Farmer Review of the UK Construction Labour Model: Modernise or Die, Time to decide the industry's future' (*Construction Leadership Council*, October 2016) <https://www.cast-consultancy.com/wp-content/uploads/2021/03/Farmer-Review-1-1.pdf> accessed 29 September 2023, page 24.

A balanced evaluation process can assess not only price but also a wide range of capabilities and proposals, for example:

- '[T]echnical knowledge and skills – experience in engineering specialist elements; appropriate design capacity'.
- '[A] number of management skills: (...) managing time (...) managing cost (...) managing value (...) managing quality (...) managing risk (...) managing health and safety'.
- '[E]ffective internal organisation – clear communications; sound administration; empowered staff'.
- '[C]ollaborative culture – record of "partnering"; positive lead from the top; client focus'.
- '[A]ppropriate human resources – qualified and enthusiastic personnel available to do the job'.
- '[S]upply chain management – sound dealing with subcontractors/suppliers; established relationships'.
- '[F]inancial resources – sound balances and cash flow; reliable references'.
- '[G]enerally – a sound, relevant and demonstrable track record'.[19]

Evaluation by reference to these criteria is more demanding for the client and its consultants than a straightforward comparison of prices. However, the bidders' qualitative submissions provide valuable information that should assist the client in making the right choice in terms of safety and quality, and that should also provide stronger foundations for commercial relationships.

A successful balanced evaluation process depends on the quality of the client's brief, which should set out the maximum information as to the client's business needs and all relevant external factors, including:

- '[T]he initial goals and objectives of the project, signed off by the client as the definition of the business need to be met'.
- '[A]ll project specific requirements and constraints that may be pertinent'.
- '[A]ny time and budgetary constraints'.[20]

The UK Office of Government Commerce included among its critical factors for success:

- '[A]ward of contract on the basis of best value for money over the whole life of the facility, not just lowest tender price'.
- '[A]n integrated process in which design, construction, operation and maintenance are considered as a whole'.
- '[P]rocurement and contract strategies that ensure the provision of an integrated project team'.[21]

---

19 Construction Industry Research and Information Association, *Selecting Contractors by Value* (1998) 15.
20 Construction Industry Council, *Selecting the Team* (2005) 4-5 (Selecting the Team).
21 Office of the Government Commerce, *Achieving Excellence in Construction Procurement Guide* (Nos 1-11, 2007).

Balanced evaluation criteria can also include assessment of each organisation's commitment to collaborative working, including for example:

- '[C]ollaborative profile and experience'.
- '[C]ultural compatibility'.
- '[C]ustomer relationship management'.
- '[S]upplier relationship management'.
- '[S]takeholder implications'.[22]

UK Cabinet Office research found that 'the best projects [we saw] and the best private sector clients put time into getting the right team. They assessed the quality of the individuals, their ability to work together and their experience'.[23] The Cabinet Office recommended, for example, that interviewing the individuals who will actually work on the project should be normal practice.[24] Interviews are an important feature of collaborative procurement, providing 'the opportunity to compare the applicant's creative approaches to the design process, as well as their interpretation and understanding of the project implementation' plus 'an important insight into each applicant's management style and communications abilities'.[25]

Selection by a public sector client pursuant to the Public Contracts Regulations[26] is not restricted to price comparisons, but it is required to be on the basis of the 'most economically advantageous tender'.[27] The most economically advantageous tender should 'be identified on the basis of the price or cost, using a cost-effectiveness approach, such as life-cycle costing', and 'may include the best price-quality ratio, which shall be assessed on the basis of criteria, such as qualitative, environmental and/or social aspects, linked to the subject-matter of the public contract in question'.[28]

Such criteria may comprise, for example, of:

- '[Q]uality, including technical merit, aesthetic and functional characteristics, accessibility, design for all users, social, environmental and innovative characteristics and trading and its conditions'.
- '[O]rganisation, qualification and experience of staff assigned to performing the contract, where the quality of the staff assigned can have a significant impact on the level of performance of the contract'.[29]

---

22 The British Standards Institution, *ISO 44001:2017 Collaborative business relationship management systems- Requirements and framework* (2017), Section 8.4.6 (ISO 44001:2017).

23 Cabinet Office Efficiency Unit (1995), *Construction Procurement by Government – an Efficiency Unit Scrutiny.* Efficiency Unit (1995) Section 253, 76.

24 ibid.

25 Selecting the Team (n 22) 13.

26 The Public Contracts Regulations 2015 require and regulate specific competitive procedures in respect of the award by public sector clients (known as contracting authorities), of contracts for works, services and supplies of a value over stated thresholds. These regulations implement the European Public Contracts Directive 2014/24/EU and, at the time of writing, there is no indication as to how these regulations may change following Brexit.

27 Public Contracts Regulations 2015, Reg. 67(1).

28 ibid Reg 67(2).

29 ibid Reg 67(3).

A persistent concern is that any financial evaluation will inevitably dominate a selection procedure and will tempt bidders to undercut each other regardless of other criteria.[30] Overcoming this problem requires the client and its advisers to make clear their priorities in a way that bidders respond to, for example by evaluating quality first and then evaluating cost, taking the benchmark price from the highest quality bid. Specialist commentators have suggested other evaluation models 'that seek to protect the contracting authority and the bidders from an unrealistic pricing risk':

- 'The optimum pricing model in which the contracting authority sets out the optimum price which it considers appropriate for the contract, based on market research. The tenderer is then incentivised to make the effort to reach the optimum price without undercutting it. The tenderer closest to the optimum price receives the highest mark. This should protect against abnormally low bids but arguably curbs the potential for truly innovative approaches'.[31]
- '[T]he fixed price model where the contracting authority fixes the price for the contract and then undertakes a value for money evaluation on the non-price element of the contract's delivery, such as the quality and experience of the team, choice of materials, health and safety standards, liaison with residents, or environmental and social aspects of the project. By fixing the price and considering alternative value for money proposals, the contracting authority will again be neutralising the effect of any abnormally low bids on the overall evaluation'.[32]

Early supply chain involvement

The Guidance recommends early supply chain involvement ('ESI') because problems in the construction industry by way of unpredictable outturn costs, delays, and defects can often be traced to a single-stage procurement and contracting process by which the contractor is expected to assess a correct market price for a project that it has not previously built on a site in respect of which there is little information, adopting a design which may still be incomplete or subject to revision and using a labour force and supply chain not yet recruited.[33]

Critics of a single-stage approach note that it:

- Can provide an incomplete assessment of the costs and capabilities of prospective team members because it depends on a process of 'adverse selection' where the principal is not informed of certain important characteristics of bids at the time when the contract is awarded, for example the bidders' actual underlying costs.[34]
- Can increase the risk of later claims and disputes because selection 'on a take-it-or-leave-it basis' by 'short and sharp consent' and, without joint examination

---

30 'Used in the wrong way (with the wrong price/quality split or the wrong sub-criteria), price can still become and overriding factor in selecting the preferred bidder and, consequently, quality is compromised', The Housing Forum, 'Stopping building failures: How a collaborative approach can improve quality and workmanship' (*The Housing Forum*, June 2018) <https://housingforum.org.uk/reports/building-safety-existing-stock/stopping-building-failures/> accessed 29 September 2023.

31 ibid Case Study 4 18.

32 ibid Case Study 4 18.

33 Rory Burke, *Project Management Planning and Control Techniques* (3rd edn, Wiley 2002) 237.

34 Paul Milgrom and John Roberts, *Economics Organisation and Management* (Prentice-Hall Inc 1992) 129.

of all relevant issues, denies the opportunity for mutual planning and creates 'a process heavily laden with conflict'.[35]

- Does not achieve the price certainty it claims and, in terms of predictability between contract prices and final prices, has proven the least likely to provide predictable cost results, with only 56% of projects completed within plus or minus 5% of the contract price.[36]

Single-stage procurement and contracting by reference to incomplete information can lead bidders to include arbitrary contingencies or premiums to their quoted prices, with the following possible consequences:

- Inflation of the prices quoted to cover perceived risks, with difficulty for the client in then challenging the pricing of a bidder's risk assessments after selection if the client wishes to negotiate reduced risk contingencies.
- A windfall by way of additional profit for the successful bidder, and therefore wasted money for the client, if the contingency is higher than necessary to cover the bidder's actual costs.
- A loss for the successful bidder, resulting in pressure to make additional claims on the client, if the contingency is insufficient to cover the bidder's actual costs.

These failings are not necessarily the result of deliberate tactics and instead may be attributable to the lack of time and available information, because:

- '[U]nder traditional single stage tendering arrangements the opportunity to plan for the construction stage is restricted'.
- [Bidders] will do enough preparatory work to be successful at tender but are unlikely to be able to understand fully all aspects of the project or have sufficient time to identify and consider how to manage the potential risks to the project'.[37]

ESI can be combined with robust competitive processes, commencing with selection of the main contractor through 'a preliminary competition based on an outline, in which the offers of selected firms are considered in the light of such factors as management and plant capacity, and the basis of their labour rates, prices and overheads'.[38] Under a second-stage procedure 'the chosen contractor works as a member of the team, while details are developed and bills of quantities drawn up, and at the end of this time submits a more detailed

---

35 Ian R Macneil, 'The Many Futures of Contracts' (1974) 47 *Southern California Law Review* 691, 770, 771, 777.

36 National Economic Development Office, *The Public Client and the Construction Industry*, (1975) Section 5.5 43 (NEDO).

37 Martin Howe and Giles Dixon, *JCT – Constructing Excellence Contract Guide 2016* (Sweet & Maxwell 2017) Section 35.6; This is known as 'information impactedness which refers to the limited knowledge of the parties to a transaction which denies them the ability to make correct purchasing or selling decisions. (...) Opportunism (...) occurs whenever firms take advantage of the information impactedness of the co-transactor', Stephen Gruneberg and Will Hughes, 'Understanding construction consortia: theory, practice and opinions' (2006) 6(1) *RICS research paper series*, 18.

38 Banwell Report, *The Placing and Management of Contracts for Building and Civil Engineering Work* (1964) Section 3.14, 10.

price which if satisfactory becomes the formal contract sum'.[39] This two-stage system can provide 'competition in a new sense' while at the same time enabling 'the contractor to join the team at a time which is precluded by existing procedures'.[40]

ESI also reduces the overall number of tendering exercises conducted in the marketplace and the costs and time that these incur. Instead of prospective subcontractors, manufacturers, suppliers, and operators each wasting time and money bidding to one or more of a number of main contractors who are themselves bidders, and somehow having to recover that wasted cost from the clients on whose projects their bids are successful, they will be in the position of bidding to a pre-selected main contractor. This significantly increases their chances of success and their likely commitment to the tender process.

Contractors have their own preferred supply chains which they use regularly and which they appoint on competitive terms under their own systems. These subcontractors and suppliers know the main contractor procurement teams and are familiar with their ways of working. Trial Project[41] case studies have shown that ESI does not undermine the potential efficiency of contractors using their established relationships. Instead, it tests the value of these relationships and at the same time exposes prospective supply chain members to direct contact with the client and consultants, in ways that have been demonstrated to:

- Provide additional time for joint reviews of designs, programmes, and risk assessments.
- Enable team members to agree improvements on the brief and proposals that formed the basis of the main contractor's selection.
- Enable more accurate costing of service, supply, and work packages, and the build-up of cost data that is available to the client and consultants as well as the main contractor.
- Reinforce integration among team members through their joint activities and shared knowledge.[42]

The UK Government noted that 'the Two Stage Open Book model reduces industry bidding costs, enables faster mobilisation and provides the opportunity for clients to work earlier with a single integrated team testing design, cost and risk issues ahead of start on site following full project award at the end of the second stage'.[43]

PPC2000[44] and NEC4 Option X 22[45] create two-stage conditional contracts, and for early contractor selection to comply with the Public Contracts Regulations depends on

---

39 ibid Section 3.13, 10.

40 ibid Section 3.15, 10.

41 Such as the SCMG and Project Horizon Trial Project case studies summarised in David Mosey, 'Constructing the Gold Standard: An Independent Review of Public Sector Construction Frameworks' (*Gov .uk*, 2021) <https://assets.publishing.service.gov.uk/government/uploads/system/uploads/attachment_data/file /1041002/Constructing_The_Gold_Standard_Final.pdf> accessed 29 September 2023.

42 ibid.

43 Cabinet Office and King's College London, 'Project Procurement and Delivery Guidance Using Two Stage Open Book and Supply Chain Collaboration', (*Gov*.uk, 2014) <https://www.gov.uk/government/uploads/ system/uploads/attachment_data/file/325014/Two_Stage_Open_Book_Guidance.pdf> accessed 29 September 2023.

44 Association of Consultant Architects, *PPC2000: ACA Standard Form of Contract for Project Partnering 2000. Amended 2013* (2013) (PPC2000 2013).

45 Thomas Telford, *NEC4 Engineering and Construction Contract* (4th edn, 2017) (NEC4).

this contract structure. By comparison, the JCT Pre-Construction Services Agreement (PCSA)[46] does not set out second stage pricing processes and is also vulnerable to breach of public procurement rules because it treats the PCSA as a separate contract distinct from the JCT2016 construction phase contract: this may cause a problem unless both contracts are awarded to the same contractor simultaneously following a single competitive process.[47] If the JCT preconstruction phase appointment is awarded later than the construction phase contract, it is arguable that two separate selection exercises should be undertaken, one for preconstruction phase services and another for the construction phase works.[48]

The Construction Playbook mandates procurement using ESI which 'extends the principle of early contractor involvement by formally engaging the tier 1 contractor alongside tier 2 and 3 subcontractors and suppliers in the pre-construction phase to input into the design (including the use of standards for products and interfaces), costing, risk management and structuring of a project or programme'. The Construction Playbook states that ESI is 'key to reducing end-to-end programme timescales, identifying opportunity and mitigating risk early and accessing the industry experts' knowledge and experience in all tiers of the supply chain early in the project or programme lifecycle', and that 'investing time in ESI can lead to more effective designs, reducing changes and potential cost increases downstream. This results in faster delivery when construction starts'.[49]

In practice ESI can produce the most predictable results in terms of contract prices corresponding to final prices:

- '[I]f the selection process has been properly managed and documented (for example, by an elemental cost plan)'.
- '[I]f a reliable basis of pricing has been established by the client's cost advisers'.
- '[I]f there are no significant changes in the client's brief or design concept'.[50]

In addition, an ESI model by which the parties can build up additional shared information as to underlying costs can contribute substantially to efficient working[51] and will help them focus on accuracy through 'incentive-efficient mechanisms'.[52] A survey of predictability between contract prices and final prices, analysed according to the method of main contractor selection, concluded that two-stage selection was the most likely to produce predictable results, namely 82% of projects successful within plus or minus 5% of the contract price.[53]

The means by which ESI can achieve improved cost certainty and agreed cost savings include:

---

46 JCT PCSA 2016: Pre-Construction Services Agreement (General Contractor) 2016 (Sweet & Maxwell 2017).

47 Shy Jackson and John Barber, 'Pre-Construction Services Agreements – Early Lessons from Experience' (2010) 26(3) Const LJ 168, 181.

48 The vulnerability of separating the contracts governing each phase is considered in the Construction Playbook. See Construction Playbook (n 2) 28.

49 ibid 26-28.

50 NEDO (n 38) Section 5.42 50.

51 As to 'informational asymmetrics' see Milgrom (n 36) 140.

52 ibid 143.

53 NEDO (n 38) Section 5.5 43.

- The separate agreement of profit and overheads.
- The use of a budget as a cost ceiling.
- The use of fixed prices or target costs according to the features of the project.
- The use of appropriate incentives to manage costs.

ESI enables the client and cost consultant to work with the design consultants, the main contractor, and its prospective supply chain members to establish detailed costs more accurately and to identify opportunities for agreement of cost savings in conjunction with other improved value. It is important to set out in a two stage contract the detailed machinery for agreeing costs and prices that is governed by the early provisional appointment of alliance members. However, if this pricing machinery breaks down, the court may substitute its own machinery to determine a fair and reasonable price if, on a true construction, the machinery is a subsidiary and non-essential part of the contract.[54]

Collaborative relationships

There is no universal business morality that creates collaborative norms of behaviour or that builds an underlying basis for trust or good faith. To demonstrate competence and translate goodwill into actions, team members need a clear and balanced understanding of what a collaborative culture means in practical terms and how they are expected to create and sustain it. To anticipate and avoid misunderstandings or breakdowns in good working relationships, team members need to establish procurement processes and contracts that reflect and support their collaborative practices.

The Guidance recognises that collaborative procurement cannot thrive in a parallel universe separate from team members' commercial expectations and commitments. In the absence of a binding contract, collaborative arrangements are likely to be seen as an option overlaying other, less-collaborative arrangements for the members to fall back on at any time.

The Construction Playbook 'Compact with Industry' emphasises the need to 'work more collaboratively at all levels of the supply chain' and 'to place more focus on social value, sustainability and asset performance'.[55] As regards the use of collaborative contracts, the Playbook states that:

- '[O]ne of the most effective ways to deliver outcomes is to create contracting environments that promote collaboration and reduce waste'.
- '[C]ontracts should create positive relationships and processes designed to integrate and align multiple parties' commercial objectives and incentives'.[56]

Collaborative activities require coordination and agreed timelines in order to create mutual confidence among team members that each will create and share the data that they all need to deliver the project. Collaborative contracts provide the machinery for coordination and

---

54 *Sudbrooke Trading v Eggleton* [1983] 1 AC 444.
55 Construction Playbook (n 2) 8.
56 ibid 46.

the mutual commitments to agreed activities and timelines.[57] The value of coordination provisions in contracts has been recognised where 'common knowledge structures such as shared language and routinized interactions emerge that make it easier for the parties to communicate their ability to meet each other's needs'.[58] Coordination provisions have been distinguished from control provisions in collaborative contracts and, unlike control provisions, can 'increase the likelihood of continued collaboration after a dispute and that perceptions of competence mitigate this effect'.[59]

ISO44001 recognises that collaborative contracts can:

- '[E]nsure a defined process and clear guidelines (...) to capture and manage knowledge creation and sharing between organisations (...) [which] shall include, where appropriate designated areas which are to be protected from unintended knowledge transfer to collaborative partners'.[60]
- '[E]stablish and agree a formal foundation for joint working, including contractual frameworks or agreements, roles, responsibilities and ethical principles'.[61]
- '[D]etermine clarity of purpose, encourage appropriate behaviour and identify the potential impacts on or conflict with the aims of collaborative working'.[62]

The strengths of collaborative contracts have been demonstrated in case studies such as the AmicusHorizon and Morrison Facilities Services who used a TPC2005 term partnering contract to establish:

- '[A]greement of prices initially on the basis of a schedule of rates with agreed TPC timetable to move to establishment of an 'Open-book' approach'.
- '[D]evelopment and use of a Risk Register'.
- '[D]evelopment of incentivisation through pain and gain'.
- '[U]se of alternative dispute resolution procedures'.
- '[D]escription of all key activities in the Partnering Timetable'.[63]

Most construction contracts create only two-party relationships, even in respect of their collaborative provisions.[64] Collateral warranties or third-party rights provisions establish additional direct contractual links between team members,[65] but they are designed only

---

57 These roles are explored in David Mosey, 'Contract or Co-operation? Trends and changes within the UK construction industry – an overview' (2003) *Society of Construction Law Paper D039*.

58 Deepak Malhotra and Fabrice Lumineau, 'Trust and Collaboration in the Aftermath of Conflict: The Effects of contract Structure' (2011) 54(5) *Academy of Management Journal* 983.

59 Malhotra and Lumineau whose research found 'that contract design affects the degree of trust that exists after a conflict has arisen, and, through this effect, the likelihood of relationship continuance'. They concluded that 'control provisions have a negative effect on the willingness to continue a damaged relationship, and goodwill trust mediates this effect', whereas 'coordination provisions increase the likelihood of continued collaboration after a dispute and that perceptions of competence mitigate this effect' See ibid 993.

60 ISO 44001:2017 (n 24) Section 8.3.4.

61 ibid Section 8.6.2.1.

62 ibid Section 8.6.10.

63 David Mosey (ed), *10 Years of ACA Project Partnering Agreements* (2010) 9.

64 For example, all JCT 2016 contracts except the JCT CE Project Team Agreement (2016) and all the NEC4 contracts except the NEC4 Alliance Contract (2018).

65 For example, through collateral warranties or pursuant to the UK Contracts (Rights of Third Parties) Act 1999.

to extend a duty of care rather than to integrate the team members' working relationships. However, if team members' interests under contracts are not properly aligned, this 'leaves room for self-interested behaviour to thwart the realisation of efficient plans'.[66]

There is an argument that collaborative procurement creates clearer relationships and more integrated processes if relationships and commitments are expressed in a multi-party contract which establishes:

- The ability of each team member to see the role and responsibilities of the other alliance members so as to check that these correspond to their expectations and so as to ensure that there are no gaps or duplications.
- Transparency that can help to create a level playing field that builds trust and confidence because each team member can see that it is engaged on the same terms as all other team members.
- The ability of team members to establish and build a system of direct peer group rights and mutual reliance, without routing all contractual concerns via the client as an intermediary.
- Simpler contract structures such as direct mutual intellectual property licences, a single integrated set of timeframes and deadlines, and a single governance structure agreed among team member representatives.[67]

Concerns may be expressed that multi-party contracts confuse the roles and responsibilities of different team members, create additional liability of alliance members for other members' acts and omissions and may be harder to insure as a consequence. Whether any of this is true depends on the drafting of the multi-party contract itself but in practice:

- A multi-party contract can restrict the agreed liability of the team members to their respective roles, expertise, and responsibilities, and can exclude each party's responsibility for any error or omission in or discrepancy between any documents, for example to the extent that it is agreed that a party will rely on contributions and information provided by other signatories to the contract.[68]
- A multi-party contract can help team members to distinguish their roles and responsibilities, because each team member can see, for example, the contractor's project brief and the various consultant services schedules, and can see where its own role and responsibilities fit in.[69]

The Guidance emphasizes that a collaborative culture should extend to all members of the team, and where applicable to residents as the stakeholders most directly affected by an in-scope project or programme of work.[70] Collaborative procurement can ensure that residents' voices are heard if a clear communication system ensures that their views are

---

66 Milgrom (n 36) 129.

67 'The success of PPC2000, and TPC2005, rest on their clear commitment to integration of the partnering team around a single contractual hub' See Michael Latham, 'Introduction' in David Mosey (ed), *10 Years of ACA Project Partnering Agreements* (2010) 1.

68 See, for example PPC2000 2013 Cl 2.4.

69 See, for example, PPC2000 2013 Cl 2.4 as to responsibility for 'Partnering Documents'.

70 DLUHC Guidance (n 1) Section 7.5.

notified, considered, discussed, and taken into account. This system needs to be reliable and fully understood. It needs to go beyond informal lines of contact, standard complaints procedures and the points raised at meetings convened for other purposes. ISO 44001 notes that a collaborative team should 'establish, maintain and actively manage an effective communication process, including the messages for key stakeholders (including all collaborative parties), the vision, the objectives behind the collaboration and how concerns will be managed'.[71]

The Guidance explains how, in communications with residents, a system of feedback is imperative to ensure that the meaning and intent of issues raised are clear and unambiguous. For example, communication should be assisted by structured meetings between the representatives of team members and those resident representatives who are authorised to address issues when they arise. Clear procedures and terms of reference for these meetings, linked to mechanisms for the incremental agreement of new information, will increase the chances of preserving the relationships between team members and residents while also respecting their different interests.[72]

A golden thread of information

The Guidance recognises that digital information management can increase the scope and speed of data exchanges, but that digital technology is not a substitute for collaborative construction procurement. To implement one without the other is a serious missed opportunity, and commentators have suggested that:

- 'What partnering needed to succeed was BIM and this risk-managing collaboration concept will probably return to favour in supply chain relationships'.[73]
- 'The industry's route map to collaboration and high efficiency new delivery models can only be underpinned by BIM and the importance of its adoption cannot be overestimated'.[74]
- 'Establishing a 'single source of truth' on projects for monitoring projects early, potentially supported by collaborative technology, helps to minimize misalignments and enable corrective action'.[75]

If BIM is intended to support an integrated and transparent approach to building safety, it should be used with procurement and delivery models that obtain early BIM model contributions from the main contractor and from subcontractors, suppliers, manufacturers, and operators without causing delay or fragmenting the warranties relied on by the client. This is no longer an optional extra in a world where:

---

71 ISO 44001:2017 (n 24) Section 8.6.2.6.

72 Ibid Section 7.5

73 Richard G Saxon, *Growth through BIM* (CIC 2013) 5.27.

74 Farmer (n 20) 36.

75 McKinsey Global Institute, 'Reinventing Construction Through a Productivity Revolution' (*McKinsey*, 2017) <https://www.mckinsey.com/industries/capital-projects-and-infrastructure/our-insights/reinventing -construction-through-a-productivity-revolution>, 8.

- Incorrect advice on procurement models can create liability for advisers.[76]
- Miscalculations by bidders resulting from software errors in procurement can give rise to significant disputes.[77]

Effective collaborative procurement through BIM can be developed by adopting a procurement model:

- That brings all BIM contributors onto the team at the optimum time.
- That uses BIM to build reliable shared data and mutual confidence.
- That considers the operational impact of BIM on those who will operate, repair, and maintain the completed capital project.
- That creates a set of contracts which integrate all the team members' roles.

The 2011 UK Government Construction Strategy recommended BIM in conjunction with ESI and collaborative working.[78] The 2016 UK Government Construction Strategy confirmed that 'BIM is a way of working that facilitates early contractor involvement, underpinned by the digital technologies which unlock more efficient methods of designing, creating and maintaining our assets'.[79] The majority of projects reviewed in the King's CCL BIM research adopted a procurement model that involved ESI.[80] Interviewee comments linked successful BIM to a procurement model under which 'early contractor involvement and bringing tier 2 & tier 3 in early to advise on design has brought in efficiencies'.[81] This evidence and the Trial Project case studies suggest that BIM needs planned and integrated contributions from the main contractor and specialist trades working alongside consultants, and that will be difficult to deliver through a traditional single stage procurement system.

Digital Built Britain described incremental progression in the development of BIM were, at Level 3A.[82] The future of BIM outlined in BIM 2050 includes the prediction that 'design consultants and principal contractors will be appointed simultaneously, early in the lifecycle, to enable concurrent working at outline business case stage'.[83]

---

76 For example, consultant liability for lack of fully informed procurement recommendations in *Plymouth and South West Co-operative Society Ltd v Architecture Structure and Management Ltd* [2006] EWHC 5 (TCC).

77 For example, the US case of *MA Mortenson Company Inc v Timberline Software Corporation, et al* (1999) 93 Wash App 819 where a software error resulted in a bid being too low.

78 Cabinet Office, Government Construction Strategy (*Gov.uk*, 2011) <https://assets.publishing.service .gov.uk/government/uploads/system/uploads/attachment_data/file/61152/Government-Construction-Strategy _0.pdf> accessed 29 September 2023.

79 Infrastructure and Projects Authority, 'Government Construction Strategy 2016–20' (*Gov.uk*, March 2016) <https://assets.publishing.service.gov.uk/government/uploads/system/uploads/attachment_data/file /510354/Government_Construction_Strategy_2016-20.pdf> accessed 29 September 2023, Section 22.

80 King's College Centre of Construction Law and Dispute Resolution, 'Enabling BIM Through Procurement and Contracts' (*Kcl.ac.uk*, 2016) <https://www.kcl.ac.uk/construction-law/assets/bim-research -report-1-jul-2016.pdf> accessed 29 September 2023, Appendix A Part 3 Question 2.2 (KCL CCLDR 2016).

KCL Centre of Construction Law (2016), Appendix A Part 3 Question 2.2.

81 Paul Davis, Information Modelling & Management Capacity Programme (IMMCP) Delivery Team, Transport for London quoted in KCL CCLDR 2016 (n 82).

82 'Digital Built Britain: Level 3 Building Information Modelling – Strategic Plan' (*Gov.uk*, February 2015) <https://assets.publishing.service.gov.uk/government/uploads/system/uploads/attachment_data/file /410096/bis-15-155-digital-built-britain-level-3-strategy.pdf> accessed 29 September 2023, 23.

83 *Built Environment 2050: A Report on Our Digital Future* (2014), 23.

In order to achieve these objectives, BIM can be more closely connected to integrated procurement models such as project alliances, framework alliances, and term alliances. The Cookham Wood Trial Project adopted a collaborative approach to ESI procurement, for example by providing for agreed individuals comprising the 'Core Group' to meet and review design development proposals and to resolve questions and problems arising from BIM clash detection.[84] The Cookham Wood team reported that:

- '[T]he implementation of BIM has created improved value in the pre-commencement and construction phases of the project'.
- '[V]irtual and actual prototypes have been produced to engineer out potential defects and clashes'.
- '[T]he data that BIM will capture will positively inform the future facilities management of the project'.[85]

ISO 19650 provides a new international standard for digital information management, and it states that 'collaboration between the participants involved in construction projects and in asset management is pivotal to the efficient delivery and operation of assets'.[86] King's CCL research led to the recommendation of the FAC-1 Framework Alliance Contract as an 'integrated information management contract' ('IIMC')[87] because:

- [U]nlike two party BIM protocols/contracts, an IIMC creates a bridge and integrator between multiple two-party consultant appointments, main contracts, and subcontracts for all project phases or one or more projects.
- [U]nlike traditional BIM protocols, an IIMC can combine BIM with ESI , collaborative working, strategic thinking, and whole life asset management.
- [A]n alliance contract such as FAC-1 supports its use as an IIMC through recognition of BIM.[88]

Gateways

As part of its regulatory reforms, the Government established three 'Gateways' at key stages in design and construction that will apply to higher-risk buildings:

---

84 PPC2000 2013, Cl 3.3 (Core Group and members), Cl 3.4 (Responsibility for Core Group members) and Cl 3.5 (Core Group meetings).

85 Cabinet Office, 'Procurement trial projects case study report – Ministry of Justice: Cookham Wood Prison' (*Gov.uk*, 19 July 2013) <https://www.gov.uk/government/publications/procurement-trial-case-study-cookham-wood-prison> accessed 29 September 2023.

86 The British Standards Institution, *ISO19650-1:2018 Organization and digitization of information about buildings and civil engineering works, including building information modelling (BIM) – Information management using building information modelling* (2018).

87 David Mosey, 'White Paper on Procurement Strategies for Incentivizing Collaborative Delivery to Optimize Whole-Life Outcomes' (*Centre for Digital Built Britain*, 2022) <https://www.cdbb.cam.ac.uk/files/white_paper_on_procurement_strategies.pdf> accessed 29 September 2023.

88 Association of Consultant Architects and Association for Consultancy and Engineering, *FAC-1 Framework Alliance Contract* (FAC-1).

For example, the FAC-1 (n 90) definitions of 'Framework Brief' and 'Project Brief' and the notes in FAC-1 Schedules 4 and 5.

- 'Planning gateway one' – at the planning application stage.
- 'Gateway two' – before building work starts.
- 'Gateway three' – when building work is completed.[89]

The Guidance sets out a checklist of questions for teams to use in preparing for each Gateway and the new 'Building Safety Regulator' has confirmed that responses to these questions will be used as a measure of compliance in respect of each Gateway.

Planning gateway one

In relation to Planning gateway one (planning application stage), the Government response to the 'Building a Safer Future' consultation stated that 'to aid the local planning authority in their decision as to whether to grant planning permission, the developer will be required to submit a Fire Statement setting out fire safety considerations specific to the development with their planning application'.[90] The Guidance recommends that Planning gateway one compliance is assessed by reference to the following questions:

Question A: Have the Client's processes for identifying the person drafting the 'Fire Statement', and for other professionals who are involved in preparing the planning application, demonstrated a balanced approach to value and evidence of suitable competencies? [Guidance Section 5]

Question B: Have the Client's contract terms for professionals who are involved in preparing the planning application stated their integrated commitments (within the scope of their agreed roles and contributions) to the safety and quality compliance of their proposals? [Guidance Section 7]

Question C: Have the Client's selection process and contract terms for the professionals involved in preparing the planning application made clear their capabilities and commitments to use suitable digital information management tools for the creation, sharing, storage and use of information? [Guidance Section 8]

Gateway two

In relation to Gateway two (building control stage, before construction can begin), the government's response to the 'Building a Safer Future' consultation stated that:

- '[A]t Gateway two, the Client will also be required to ensure they are satisfied that the Principal Designer and Principal Contractor can demonstrate the necessary competence to discharge their responsibilities effectively'.
- '[T]he Client will be required to submit key information to the Building Safety Regulator demonstrating how they are complying with building regulations through the submission of full plans, the construction control plan, fire and emergency file, and other supporting documentation that will help the assessment team determine whether the application meets the building regulations

---

89 MHCL Response (n 18).
90 ibid.

requirements and that the dutyholder has sufficiently demonstrated that they are managing building safety risks'.

- '[K]ey information related to fire and structural safety submitted during the three Gateways will form part of the golden thread of data, which will be kept up to date and made accessible to relevant people throughout the lifecycle of the building'.[91]

The Guidance recommends that Gateway two compliance is assessed by reference to the following questions:

Question D: Have the Client's procurement processes for identifying and appointing the Principal Designer, the Principal Contractor and the other professionals involved in preparing the building control application submitted at Gateway two (including plans, construction control plan, fire and emergency file and other supporting documentation), and for identifying and appointing all other parties who will be working on the project during design and construction, demonstrated a balanced approach to value and evidence of suitable skills, knowledge, experience and behaviours? (also shown in the Client's signed declaration of competence at Gateway two) [Guidance Section 5]

Question E: Have the Client's procurement processes for identifying and appointing the Principal Designer, the Principal Contractor and the other professionals involved in preparing the building control application submitted at Gateway two (including plans, construction control plan, fire and emergency file and other supporting documentation), and for identifying and appointing all other parties that will be working on the project during design and construction, used early supply chain involvement ('ESI') so as to optimise their contributions to improved safety and quality within agreed periods of time after their appointment and in advance of Gateway two? [Guidance Sections 6 and 10]

Question F: Have the Client's contract terms for the Principal Designer, the Principal Contractor and the other professionals involved in preparing the building control application submitted at Gateway two (including plans, construction control plan, fire and emergency file and other supporting documentation), and the contract terms for all other parties that will be working on the project during construction, stated their legal obligations as dutyholders (within the scope of their agreed roles and contributions) to safety and quality compliance? [Guidance Sections 7, 9 and 10]

Question G: Have the Client's procurement processes for the Principal Designer, the Principal Contractor and the other professionals involved in preparing the building control application submitted at Gateway two (including plans, construction control plan, fire and emergency file and other supporting documentation), and the procurement processes for all other parties that will be working on the project during design and construction, made clear their capabilities and commitments to use suitable digital information management tools for the creation, sharing, storage and use of information comprising a golden thread of information? [Guidance Section 8]

---

91 ibid.

Question H: Is there a collaborative system by which the Client, the Principal Designer, the Principal Contractor, and the other professionals involved in preparing the building control application submitted at Gateway two (including plans, construction control plan, fire and emergency file and other supporting documentation), and all other parties that will be working on the project during design and construction, have regularly consulted with each other and with residents (where applicable) in advance of Gateway two in relation to the safety and quality compliance of all designs and specifications and all related cost, time, supply, construction, maintenance and risk management information? [Guidance Sections 7 and 9]

Question I: Is there a transparent decision-making process by which the Client, the Principal Designer, the Principal Contractor and other professionals involved in preparing the building control application submitted at Gateway two (including plans, construction control plan, fire and emergency file and other supporting documentation), and those that will be working on the project during design and construction, have agreed the Gateway two application, based on and to the extent of their agreed roles and their contributions as dutyholders to safety and quality compliance? [Guidance Sections 7 and 9]

Between Gateways two and three

During construction (between Gateways two and three), the government's response to the 'Building a Safer Future' consultation stated that 'the change control strategy submitted as part of the construction control plan at Gateway two will need to be updated and maintained throughout the construction phase, to record all changes from the original plans as submitted, together with:

- A complete construction control plan.
- An updated fire and emergency file.
- A complete key dataset'.[92]

At this stage the Guidance recommends that compliance is assessed by reference to the following questions:

Question J: Is there a collaborative system by which the Client, the Principal Designer and the Principal Contractor, and the others working on the project during design and construction, regularly consult with each other in accordance with their agreed roles and contributions as dutyholders:
- To implement the construction control plan?
- To update, maintain and implement the change management strategy approved at Gateway two and to record all changes from the application approved at Gateway two?
- To monitor and update the golden thread of information, ensuring that it is accurate and up to date?

---

92 ibid.

- To ensure the safety, quality and regulatory compliance of all designs, specifications and related supply, construction, maintenance and risk management activities including the implementation of appropriate site controls and change control procedures? [Guidance Sections 7 and 9]

Gateway three

In relation to Gateway three (completion and handover, before occupation), the Guidance recommends that compliance is assessed by reference to the following questions:

Question K: Is there a collaborative system by which the Client, the Principal Designer and the Principal Contractor, and the other professionals involved in preparing the Gateway three application (including as-built plans and other prescribed documents), have regularly engaged with residents (where applicable) in advance of Gateway three, based on and to the extent of their agreed contributions as dutyholders, in relation to safety, quality and regulatory compliance? [Guidance Sections 7 and 9]

Question L: Is there an integrated system by which the Client, the Principal Designer and the Principal Contractor, and the other professionals involved in preparing the Gateway three application (including as-built plans and other prescribed documents), have confirmed, based on and to the extent of their agreed roles and contributions as duty holders, the safety, quality and regulatory compliance of all designs and specifications and all related supply, construction, maintenance and risk management information and activities at regular stages before work is covered up during construction, and before work is handed over on completion at Gateway three? [Guidance Sections 7 and 9]

Question M: Have the Client's procurement processes made clear its capability and commitment to hand over the golden thread of information and other prescribed?

In conclusion, the Guidance provides a direct response to serious concerns in relation to construction procurement that were raised by Dame Judith Hackitt, and her Foreword to the Guidance makes clear her support for its recommendations.[93] The inclusion of the Guidance in the Construction Playbook is also a good sign.

This high-level support for the Guidance now needs to be converted into obligations that will ensure adoption of its proven safety and quality benefits.

---

93 DLUHC Guidance (n 1), 3.

CHAPTER 4

Solutions for procuring net zero carbon construction

David Mosey and Roxana Vornicu

A panel at the *Centre of Construction Law and Dispute Resolution*'s 35th Anniversary Conference dealt with the net zero carbon challenges faced by the construction industry. Speakers from industry, private practice, and the public sector, as well as various jurisdictions, reflected on topics spanning legislative measures to good procurement practices. Our paper looks at solutions that can and should be immediately applied in adopting a holistic approach – from the procurement strategy to the procurement process, through to the contractual model and the management of the contract. These recommended solutions were developed identified in a King's College research paper, 'Procuring Net Zero Construction', that was published in March 2022 by the Society of Construction Law.[1] That KCL paper on Net Zero Construction has been picked up by the UK Government and mentioned in its updated Construction Playbook,[2] and in its Guidance on 'Promoting Net Zero Carbon and Sustainability in Construction'.[3]

The first section of this chapter will include some introductory remarks, with brief reflections on the construction industry's carbon emissions and the international and national agenda in this regard; we will then present the main concepts of the KCL paper on Net Zero Construction and show how it was picked up in the Playbook and Net Zero Construction Guidance; the fourth section will present case studies and reflect briefly on action plans in the UK, whilst the last section will include conclusions.

Introduction

Construction operations and real estate are responsible for 39% of all carbon emissions in the world, and in 2016, the Paris Agreement required that global emissions must be net zero by 2050. A global rethink and reform in our commercial and industrial practices is necessary in order to tackle climate change. The UK has set an innovative path ahead of

---

1 David Mosey and others, 'Procuring Net Zero Construction' (*Society of Construction Law*, 30 March 2022) <https://www.scl.org.uk/resources/news/scl-and-procuring-net-zero-carbon-construction> accessed 9 November 2023.

2 Cabinet Office, 'The Construction Playbook: Government Guidance on sourcing and contracting public works projects and programmes' (*GOV.UK*, September 2022) <https://www.gov.uk/government/publications/the-construction-playbook> accessed 9 November 2023 (The Construction Playbook).

3 Government Commercial Function, 'Promoting Net Zero Carbon and Sustainability in Construction Guidance Note' (*GOV.UK*, September 2022) <https://assets.publishing.service.gov.uk/government/uploads/system/uploads/attachment_data/file/1102389/20220901-Carbon-Net-Zero-Guidance-Note.pdf> accessed 9 November 2023 (The Net Zero Guidance).

DOI: 10.4324/9781032663975-7

67

other countries, being the first developed economy to commit to reach net zero greenhouse gas emissions by 2050. The European Union is also determined to reach the net zero target by 2050 and the European Climate Law turned this political commitment into a legal obligation.[4]

The 2022 United Nations Conference of the Parties, more commonly referred to as COP27, was held between 6 November and 18 November 2022, in Egypt, and recognised again the built environment's major role in ensuring that sustainability targets are achieved.[5] One of the COP27 initiatives is the creation of the 'Clean Construction Accelerator', to support the built environment sector in halving emissions by 2030 for all new buildings and infrastructure projects.[6] This is an initiative led by the C40 NGO, an association of 40 municipalities committed to using an inclusive, science-based and collaborative approach to halve their share of emissions by 2030.[7] Their strategy includes actions for municipal procurement which: (i) requires life cycle assessments, demand zero emission construction machinery, and reward resource efficient circular design and zero waste construction sites as well as (ii) demanding transparency and accountability in requiring life cycle assessments in planning permissions and embedding them in planning policies.[8]

This is in line with the UK strategic actions under the September 2022 Construction Playbook,[9] which establishes that:

> All contracting authorities should set out strategies and plans for achieving net zero GHG emissions by or ahead of 2050 for their entire estate/infrastructure portfolio. These should be aligned under an overarching sustainability framework, and systems and processes should be in place to ensure their projects and programmes deliver on the targets set. Furthermore, the statutory duties of all UK company directors include a duty to have regard to 'the impact of the company's operations on the community and the environment'.[10]

However, these duties cannot be fulfilled by any construction organisation acting alone, and the net zero strategies and systems that each company adopts need to be integrated with those of multiple other parties across the successive stages of planning, design, construction, operation, and demolition that comprise the lifecycle of each asset. In fact, the first net zero carbon challenge for procurement and legal advisers is to overcome the prevailing inefficient adherence of the construction sector to the single stage, lowest price

---

4 The European Climate Law writes into law the goal set out in the European Green Deal for Europe's economy and society to become climate-neutral by 2050. The law also sets the intermediate target of reducing net greenhouse gas emissions by at least 55% by 2030, compared to 1990 levels. Climate neutrality by 2050 means achieving net zero greenhouse gas emissions for EU countries as a whole, mainly by cutting emissions, investing in green technologies and protecting the natural environment. See Regulation (EU) 2021/1119 of the European Parliament and of the Council of 30 June 2021 establishing the framework for achieving climate neutrality and amending Regulations (EC) No 401/2009 and (EU) 2018/1999 ('European Climate Law') [2021] OJ L243/1, pp 1–17.

5 On the outcomes of the Summit for the construction industry see, e.g., Maria-Cristina Florian, 'What COP27 Meant for Architecture and the Construction Industry' (*ArchDaily*, 24 January 2023) <https://www.archdaily.com/992583/what-cop27-means-for-architecture-and-the-construction-industry> accessed 9 November 2023.

6 'Clean Construction Accelerator' (*C40 Cities*) <https://www.c40.org/accelerators/clean-construction/?utm_medium=website&utm_source=archdaily.com> accessed 9 November 2023.

7 'About C40' (*C40 Cities*) <https://www.c40.org/about-c40/> accessed 9 November 2023.

8 See more on such actions here Clean Construction Accelerator (n 6).

9 The Construction Playbook (n 2) p 6.

10 Companies Act 2006, s 171(1)(d).

tendering of one project at a time and to the use of contracts primarily as a tool for risk transfer and administration.[11]

The King's College London report 'Procuring Net Zero Construction'

Prior to the publication of the 2022 updated Construction Playbook and the Net Zero Construction Guidance, a King's College team of researchers from the Centre for Construction Law and Dispute Resolution published a paper examining how clients, advisers, and all construction sector organisations can use procurement and contracting systems to meet net zero carbon targets.[12] The recommendations under this paper drew on evidence that included the following previous work undertaken by the King's College London Centre of Construction Law from 2013 to 2022, testing and developing the ways that procurement systems and construction contracts can improve economic, social, and environmental value:

- 'Trial Projects' led by Cabinet Office and Constructing Excellence from 2013 to 2017.[13]
- 'Enabling BIM Through Procurement and Contracts', a 2016 report part-funded by the Society of Construction Law.[14]
- The 2016 'FAC-1 Framework Alliance Contract', a standard form contractual integrator that defines 'Sustainability' as a feature of 'Improved Value' and has been used in multiple common law and civil law jurisdictions.[15]
- A 2018 'Research Report and Draft Model Forms for Long-Term Strategic Relationships for the CLC Innovation in Buildings Workstream'.[16]
- 'Constructing the Gold Standard', a 2021 independent review of public sector construction frameworks13 which was a policy commitment in the Construction Playbook.[17]

---

11 Mosey (n 1) p 7.

12 ibid.

13 'Implementing New Models of Construction Procurement: The annual report of the Trial Projects Working Group to the Infrastructure and Projects Authority' (*Constructing Excellence*, March 2017) <https:// constructingexcellence.org.uk/wp-content/uploads/2018/12/Trial-Projects-Working-Group-final-report-2017 .pdf> accessed 9 November 2023.

14 David Mosey and others, 'Enabling BIM Through Procurement and Contracts' (*King's College London Centre of Construction Law and Dispute Resolution*, 2016) <https://www.kcl.ac.uk/construction-law/assets/ bim-research-report-1-jul-2016.pdf> accessed 9 November 2023.

15 'Activity' (*King's College London Centre of Construction Law and Dispute Resolution*) <https://www .kcl.ac.uk/construction-law/activity> accessed 9 November 2023; 'FAC-1' (*Alliance Contracts*) <https://alli-anceforms.co.uk/about-fac-1/> accessed 9 November 2023.

16 David Mosey, 'Research Report and Draft Model Forms for Long-Term Strategic Relationships for CLC Innovation in Building Workstream' (*King's College London Centre of Construction Law and Dispute Resolution*, 2018) <https://www.kcl.ac.uk/construction-law/assets/report-long-term-strategic-relationships-for -clc-innovation-in-buildings-workstream.pdf> accessed 9 November 2023.

17 David Mosey, 'Constructing the Gold Standard: An Independent Review of Public Sector Construction Frameworks' (*GOV.UK*, 16 December 2021) <https://www.gov.uk/government/publications/an-independent -review-of-public-sector-construction-frameworks> accessed 9 November 2023.

- 'Guidance on Collaborative Procurement for Design and Construction to Support Building Safety', a 2022 guide prepared for the Department of Levelling Up Housing and Communities.[18]
- A 2022 'White Paper on Procurement Strategies for Incentivizing Collaborative Delivery to Optimize Whole-life Outcomes', comprising the outcomes from two years of research for the Centre for Digital Built Britain.[19]

The KCL Paper on Net Zero Construction sets out recommendations and case studies designed to help deliver sustainable construction by identifying elements of a procurement strategy and exercise that are designed to deliver sustainable results. They include:

- Client strategy and expectations: The construction procurement strategy should clearly state the client's commitments to tackling climate change and the ways in which the client expects these to be matched by commitments from the construction industry.
- Team evaluation and bidder proposals: The system for selection of construction team members should use balanced evaluation criteria that take into account net zero carbon proposals submitted by prospective consultants, contractors, and supply chain members, and should make clear the procedures by which the approved net zero carbon proposals from successful bidders will be developed, agreed, and implemented.
- Early supply chain involvement and preconstruction activities: Contractors and supply chain members should be appointed early during the pre-construction phase of a project on the basis of clear contractual systems through which they work with the client and consultants in developing and agreeing viable and affordable net zero carbon proposals in line with the client's stated brief and budget, as preconditions to commencement of the construction phase of the project.
- Long-term contracts and industry investment: The procurement strategy, team selection processes and construction contracts should make clear how the award of long-term contracts for pipelines of work will attract industry investments in net zero carbon innovations such as offsite manufacture.
- Specialists and supply chain collaboration: Clients, consultants, and contractors should commit to contractual systems by which they explore systematically the best ways for specialist supply chain members to contribute their net zero carbon expertise and the best ways for local and regional supply chain members to offer a lower carbon footprint.
- Contract governance and joint risk management: Clients should ensure that their construction contracts include a definition of sustainability that includes net zero carbon and should describe systems of collaborative governance and joint

---

18 David Mosey and Russell Poynter-Brown, 'Guidance on Collaborative Procurement for Design and Construction to Support Building Safety' (*GOV.UK*, 10 January 2022) <https://www.gov.uk/government/publications/collaborative-procurement-guidance-for-design-and-construction-to-support-building-safety> accessed 9 November 2023.

19 David Mosey and others, 'White Paper on Procurement Strategies for Incentivizing Collaborative Delivery to Optimize Whole-Life Outcomes' (*Centre for Digital Build Environment*, 2022) <https://www.cdbb.cam.ac.uk/files/white_paper_on_procurement_strategies.pdf> accessed 9 November 2023.

risk management by which the client, consultants, contractors, and supply chain members will achieve net zero carbon and other sustainable outcomes.

- Framework alliances and shared learning: Clients, consultants, contractors, and supply chain members should create multi-party 'Gold Standard' framework alliances through which to integrate the net zero carbon commitments of multiple parties on multiple projects and through which to share learning while protecting intellectual property rights and other confidential information.
- Whole life procurement and digital information: Clients, consultants, contractors, and supply chain members should agree and implement net zero carbon commitments to whole life procurement through digital information management supported by a multi-party 'Integrated Information Management Contract' that governs accurate exchanges of data in relation to design, cost, time, risk, and operation.
- Action plans and leadership: Clients and consultants should lead and manage the urgent implementation of net zero carbon objectives under new and existing construction contracts, including through the agreement of net zero carbon action plans with binding timetables.[20]

All these measures can be integrated in a strategic approach to procurement looking at the '4 I's' of Mosey, namely, Intention, Information, Integration, and Incentivization. Each relates to a particular phase of the procurement process and pushes clients and team members to answer specific questions, such as:

- Intention – Strategy: How do clients and advisers establish an appropriate strategy for obtaining improved environmental value throughout the lifecycle of a construction project or programme of work?
- Information – Procurement process: What information needs to be exchanged during the procurement process in order to help clients, advisers, consultants, contractors, and supply chain members (including subcontractors, manufacturers, suppliers, and operators) to understand each other's positions and to reconcile their differing interests in ways that will achieve net zero outcomes?
- Integration – Contract: How are relationships between clients, consultants, contractors, and supply chain members integrated through contracts so as to ensure that exchanges of ideas, information, and learning take place at the times when they will be of most value in achieving net zero outcomes?
- Incentivisation – Contract management: How will management motivate clients, consultants, contractors, and supply chain members to honour their mutual commitments to achieve net zero outcomes?

The KCL Paper showed how the Net Zero Challenge entails government leadership, industry leadership, and a new approach to procurement and contracts. Finally, the paper showed how new relationships, processes, and tools will enable clients, advisers, and the construction industry to achieve net zero carbon targets and address key questions of effective procurement. In answer to these questions, the report argued that a coherent

---

20 Mosey (n 1) p 3.

approach to achieving net zero targets on any construction project or programme of works requires:

- Strategies that establish the intention of clients in terms of credible plans, commitments, and timescales for meeting net zero carbon targets, with clear requirements for project outcomes and clear expectations for improved value and reduced risks.
- Procurement processes that exchange relevant information between clients and prospective consultants, contractors, and supply chain members in advance of making appointments, demonstrating, and evaluating how plans, commitments, and timescales to meet net zero carbon targets will be implemented.
- Contracts that create and sustain the integration of the plans, commitments, and timescales agreed by clients, consultants, contractors, and supply chain members to implement the agreed steps to achieve net zero carbon targets.
- Management that achieves incentivisation through instructions, support, guidance, and motivation for clients, consultants, contractors, and supply chain members to deliver their integrated net zero carbon targets.[21]

Framework alliances are also presented as an essential tool in facing the net zero carbon challenge. Through strategic collaboration among framework providers, clients, managers, consultants, contractors, and supply chain members, the proposals designed to achieve net zero carbon targets and other sustainability initiatives can be assessed and costed objectively for adoption on multiple framework projects. Framework alliances also support joint net zero carbon initiatives by enabling a joint approach to early supply chain involvement ('ESI') and tier 1/2/3 'Supply Chain Collaboration' so that these collaborative systems facilitate the sharing of net zero innovations obtained, for example, through building information modelling ('BIM'), modern methods of construction ('MMC'), and the expertise offered by SMEs.

For a framework to deliver net zero targets that are reconciled with other measures of value and industry profitability, the framework contract should include 'alliance' features that provide expressly for:

- Shared net zero objectives, success measures, targets, and incentives.
- Analysis, agreement, and adoption of industry net zero carbon proposals.
- Integrated activities and systems governing ESI and Supply Chain Collaboration.
- Whole life procurement and digital information.
- Action plans and leadership for net zero improvements over the life of the framework.
- Collaborative contract governance and joint risk management.

Alliance features appear in a range of bespoke framework contracts, but the use of bespoke forms causes its own inefficiencies because they lack consistency and give rise to additional procurement costs and potential confusion for clients and industry. The only current standard framework alliance contract is the 'FAC-1' form published by the Association of

---

21 ibid p 54.

Consultant Architects in 2016 and, so far, adopted on over £100 billion of procurements. It is important to stress that FAC-1 defines 'Sustainability' as:

> measures intended to reduce carbon emissions, to reduce use of energy and or natural and manmade resources, to improve waste management, to improve employment and training opportunities and otherwise to protect or improve the condition of the Environment or the well-being of people.[22]

The FAC-1 contractual machinery governs joint actions to develop and implement net zero objectives and includes Supply Chain Collaboration among tier 1, 2, and 3 supply chain members linked to incentives such as additional or longer-term subcontracts.

Well-structured frameworks – can draw together all the other King's recommendations for net zero procurement, while also adopting related findings and recommendations from 'Constructing the Gold Standard', the 2021 review of public sector construction frameworks.[23]

The Construction Playbook and the Guidance on Net Zero and Sustainable Construction

Many of the tools and strategies listed as solutions in the KCL paper Procuring Net Zero Construction were picked up by the UK Government. For instance, when requiring that 'projects and programmes should adopt an outcome-based approach focused on whole life value, performance, sustainability and cost', the September 2022 version of the Construction Playbook lists the KCL paper as further reading on the topic.[24] It also states that 'The FAC-1 framework is a good example of a standard form framework contract that can achieve this and many of the ambitions set out in this Playbook',[25] and recommends the use of FAC-1 as an effective contract for creating sustainable environments that promote collaboration and reduce waste.[26]

The UK Government Guidance on Promoting Net Zero Carbon and Sustainability in Construction, published in September 2022, stresses the need for forward thinking and innovation, especially on high-value construction projects, and is structured around the themes of (i) long-term contracting, pipelines, and portfolios, (ii) early market engagement and clear specification, (iii) delivery model assessments and effective contracting, and (iv) successful delivery and transition to operation.

Under its section on integration of contracts with strategy procurement and management, the Guidance states that '[c]ontractual clauses alone will not deliver improved sustainability, carbon or environmental performance outcomes, and an effective strategic approach depends on new contractual relationships and processes being aligned with the client's strategy', and it refers to the KCL paper on Procuring Net Zero Construction by quoting the following elements that are required for a strategic approach to delivering net zero carbon through construction procurement:

---

22 FAC-1, Appendix 1.
23 Mosey (n 19).
24 The Construction Playbook (n 2) p 32.
25 ibid p 48.
26 ibid p 49.

- Team evaluation and bidder proposals.
- Early supply chain involvement and preconstruction activities.
- Long-term contracts and industry investment.
- Specialists and supply chain collaboration.
- Contract governance and joint risk management.
- Framework alliances and shared learning.
- Whole life procurement and digital information.
- Action plans and leadership.[27]

The Guidance proposes solutions that mirror tools and solutions recommended in the KCL paper. For example in 'Pipelines, Portfolios and Long-term contracting', the Guidance suggests the need for '(i) Supply chain decarbonisation '[where] Contracting authorities should work with their supply chains to increase awareness of shared decarbonisation and how this can be achieved';[28] '(ii) Digital and MMC '[where] Adopting digital and offsite manufacturing technologies in the delivery is essential to improving carbon and sustainability outcomes';[29] and (iii) waste and resource efficiency, which highlights relevant principles under the Environmental Act,[30] namely:

- The integration principle.
- The prevention principle.
- The rectification at source principle.
- The polluter pays principle.
- The precautionary principle.[31]

For the second theme, of 'Early Market Engagement', the Guidance states the need for (i) '[e]mbedding a whole life approach at an early stage [that] will enable greater consistency in delivering higher quality and sustainable outcomes across the life of projects and built assets'; for (ii) '[i]ncluding sustainability in outcome based specifications and that 'Clear and measurable outcomes should be set at the outset of a project or programme'.

As regards **'Effective Contracting'**, the Guidance suggests the use of various tools such as Climate and Sustainability contract clauses, Framework Contracts, and related Performance Incentives. It mentions the 'Chancery Lane' project on climate change contractual clauses[32] but highlights the more complex matter of integrating contracts with strategy procurement as made clear in the KCL paper

Finally, in 'Successful Delivery and the Transition to Operation', similarly to the KCL paper, the Guidance suggests the need for adequate evaluation and contract award, for capturing lessons learned and disseminating good practice, and the fact that the Government Major Projects Portfolio is required to publish close out reports that include carbon reduction lessons.

---

27 The Net Zero Guidance (n 3) p 34.
28 ibid p 8.
29 ibid p 10.
30 Environment Act 2021.
31 The Net Zero Guidance (n 3) p 11.
32 ibid p 32.

Action plans

The KCL paper or Net Zero Construction states that clients and consultants should lead and manage the implementation of net zero carbon objectives under new and existing construction contracts, including through the agreement of net zero carbon 'action plans' with binding timetables. This recommendation was picked up by the Government Guidance and is also an important recommendation of 'Constructing the Gold Standard', the independent review of public sector construction frameworks approved and adopted by the UK Government.[33]

Recommendation 5 under the Gold Standard Review sets the need to create an action plan that will show:

- How improvements consistent with Playbook policies will be agreed between the framework provider, clients, manager, and suppliers, both preceding and in parallel with the award and delivery of individual framework projects, and how and when these innovations and other improvements will be adopted for use by framework clients and suppliers on framework projects.
- How and when innovations and other improvements consistent with Playbook policies will be captured from framework projects, how and when they will be shared and agreed between the framework provider, clients, manager, and suppliers, and how and when these innovations and other improvements will be adopted for use by framework clients and suppliers on other framework projects.

Similarly, the KCL paper on Procuring Net Zero Construction shows that a net zero carbon action plan can capture the agreement of clients, consultants, contractors, and supply chain members to implement a shared timetable of specific activities that reflect the net zero strategy for each new procurement and each existing contract:

- How and when innovations and other improvements consistent with net zero carbon targets will be developed and agreed between clients, consultants, contractors, and supply chain members, and how and when these innovations and other improvements will be adopted on specific projects.
- How and when innovations and other improvements consistent with net zero targets will be captured from completed projects, and how and when these innovations and other improvements will be shared and agreed between clients, consultants, contractors, and supply chain members for adoption on other projects.

A good case study on effective action plans and strategic procurement of net zero carbon construction is the Oxfordshire County Council (OCC) and Skanska net zero transitional framework alliance contract. In this case, OCC and Skanska supplemented their £40 million per annum term contract for maintenance, capital renewals and new infrastructure to identify new opportunities for net zero improvements. The parties created an FAC-1 transitional framework alliance contract to describe new binding procedures through which opportunities to capture improved environmental value were formalised and linked to extension of an underlying NEC term call-off contract.

---

33 Mosey (n 17) p 30.

The project teams identified significant opportunities, including carbon consumption reductions and financial savings. Strategic net zero carbon outputs, using FAC-1 and supporting Oxfordshire County Council's and Skanska's carbon neutral targets, included:

- A suite of low carbon design solutions and associated action plans.
- Development of a 'Partnership Carbon Reduction Strategy' and associated action plan.
- Creation of a 'Whole Life Cost & Carbon' tool.
- Focused training on lower carbon alternative materials.
- Trials of new lower carbon materials.
- Calculating carbon baselines for schemes to identify 'Hotspots'.[34]

Another case study showing leadership and strategic contracting techniques that can achieve net zero carbon targets is the multi-party transitional framework alliance led by Crown Commercial Services, integrating the work of 16 consultants appointed under separate pre-existing framework contracts; the integration allowed for establishment and governance of joint initiatives exploring the potential of ESI, digital technologies, and MMC to deliver improved value for clients. Through this framework, CCS appointed suppliers Aecom, AHR Architects, AMEC Foster Wheeler Environmental and Infrastructure, Arcadis, Capita, Faithful & Gould, Gleeds, Kier Business Services, Mace, McBains, Mott McDonald, Ridge, Turner & Townsend, and WYG; they all worked together 'to deliver improved value for framework clients' by:

- Sharing and monitoring best practice intelligence.
- Sharing and monitoring learning between projects and programmes of work.
- Establishing, agreeing, and monitoring consistent and more efficient working practices.
- Agreeing and monitoring techniques for better team integration.
- Agreeing and monitoring improved procurement and delivery systems on projects and programmes of work.[35]

Conclusions

The tools and techniques explored in the KCL paper 'Procuring Net Zero Carbon Construction' and in the UK Government's Guidance are complementary and suggest the need for innovative and strategic thinking. More importantly, as the KCL paper showed, solutions exist but they will not deliver change unless applied holistically, following the strategy of the 4I's of Intention, Information, Integration and Incentivisation. Only by implementing this coherent approach will new relationships, processes, and tools, enable clients, advisers, and the construction industry to play their part in ensuring that the procurement of projects and programmes of work achieve essential net zero carbon targets.

---

34 'News and Users' (*Alliance Contracts*, November 2022) <http://allianceforms.co.uk/news-and-users/> accessed 9 November 2023.

35 Mosey (n 17) p 32.

CHAPTER 5

Net zero carbon challenges in Italy

Sara Valaguzza

Net zero carbon: the courage of innovation and the fear of bureaucracy

Currently, the construction sector in Italy plays a fundamental and leading role in the economy. After ten years of crisis, thanks to the exceptional season of incentives and the impetus of post-Covid recovery funds, the construction market has experienced exponential growth: over 232 billion investments in construction were recorded in the 2020–2023 triennium, 91 billion more than in 2019 – the year before the Covid-19 – marking a development of 20.4% in 2021 and 14.9% in 2022.[1] This led to an increase in the employment rate, with 460,000 more jobs in 2022 compared to 2019, and a significant contribution to the gross domestic product, amounting to 13.9%: the highest in Europe and the second among Western countries.

According to an ISTAT (National Institute of Statistics) study, in 2022, the driving force behind construction as a prime mover for industrial and business economies is the supply chain's extension: the construction industry activates a supply chain interconnected with almost 90% of other economic activities.[2] This phenomenon can be defined as a 'diffuse field transmission', i.e., a sector that is able to transmit impacts across a wide array of economic areas in an extensive and fast manner.

Beside the increasing demand and recent robust investment performance in construction related to European funds, the construction sector is expected to be increasingly important for environmental and social issues, especially environmental pollution and carbon dioxide emissions.[3] For example, demolition and construction waste are crucial for policies and environmental strategies.[4]

---

1 It is interesting to notice that the production is growing especially in the area of residential building renovations. This is due to the fact that, as we will see in the following paragraphs, the incentives assigned for energy efficiency and refurbishment of buildings are the relevant factors of this growth. See 'Mercato delle costruzioni: le previsioni per il 2023' (*lavoripubblici.it*, 12 December 2022) <https://www.lavoripubblici.it/news/mercato-costruzioni-previsioni-per-il-2023-29918> accessed 4 October 2023.

2 Nadia Mignoli and others (eds), 'Rapporto sulla competitività dei settori produttivi. Edizione 2022' (*Istat*, 2022) <https://www.istat.it/storage/settori-produttivi/2022/Rapporto-competitività.pdf> accessed 4 October 2023.

3 In fact, in Italy, despite the most significant CO2 emissions derive from the energy industries (26.9%) and transport (30.7%), the manufacturing and construction industry accounts for 14.4%.

4 These are the emissions associated with so-called embedded carbon, i.e., those resulting from the production, transport, and disposal of building materials and the construction process itself. In this regard, it is worth mentioning that the construction supply chain is one of the main responsible parties for pollutant behaviours: for one-third of drinking water consumption and for one third of global electricity consumption, with the extraction and processing of raw materials. For example, the production of cement, the main material

---

DOI: 10.4324/9781032663975-8

The data suggests considering the following complementary aspects: on the one hand, construction is one of the most harmful sectors to the health of the environment; on the other hand, it offers the opportunity to invest in innovation and research, facilitating the development of sustainable solutions to reduce the negative impact on the environment. Furthermore, its cross-cutting scope should be considered across several fronts:

- Strategically, for example, by employing intelligent contract management, especially using collaborative construction procurement.[5]
- Industrially, in relation to the supply chain.
- Politically, considering the expectation of the community pushing for new services, products, buildings, and infrastructures capable of responding to the climate crisis.

Therefore, the debate on Net Zero Carbon will become fundamental in the Italian legal framework in the near future.

Although Net Zero Carbon represents an ambitious goal, Italian legislation has yet to fully embrace it by introducing obligations able to drive transformation in the construction process.

Public clients' attitudes, the lack of competencies, and very rigid procurement procedures that prioritize competitiveness over qualitative elements hinder rapid progress towards achieving Net Zero Carbon. Moreover, the need to protect SMEs, unprepared to respect Net Zero Carbon targets, is creating a barrier to the implementation policies. Nevertheless, the carbon-neutral approach[6] is being promoted by both legislators and public authorities through requirements like Nearly Zero Energy Buildings (NZEB), CAM, and DNSH.

In greening up the construction processes, we should consider that the Italian construction context is characterized by a strong fragmentation and polarization in which few big operators are opposed by a myriad of small and medium-sized enterprises[7] reluctant to embrace the challenges of Net Zero Carbon, at least for the following reasons:

---

in construction, is almost stable and is estimated at 4,256 billion tonnes per year globally. See Federbeton Confindustra, *Rapporto di Filiera* (2021). For an interesting study on the impact of building materials and about future strategies, see Città Metropolitana di Milano, University of Milan and Centre of Construction Law & Management 'L'economia circolare nel settore delle costruzioni – analisi e prospettiv e partire dal contesto milanese' (2022) <http://www.assimpredilance.it/doc_portale/cont/20221011_UNIMI_CMETRO.pdf> accessed 4 October 2023.

5 See Sara Valaguzza, *Governing by contract procuring for value* (Editoriale Scientifica 2021); David Mosey, *Collaborative Construction Procurement and Improved Value* (Wiley 2019); David Mosey, *Dialogo sugli appalti collaborativi* (Eduardo Parisi and Nicola Posteraro eds, Editoriale Scientifica 2019); Sara Valaguzza, 'Gli accordi collaborativi nell'interesse pubblico: dagli schemi antagonistici ai modelli dialogici' (2019) 65(99) *Il diritto dell'economia* 255; Sara Valaguzza, *Governare per contratto* (Editorial Scientfica 2018).

6 Carbon neutral means that all carbon dioxide (CO_2) released in the atmosphere by a company's activities is offset by an equivalent amount removed (for example by purchasing carbon credits, financing sustainable activities, and so on). Net Zero Carbon is similar in principle to carbon neutrality but is expanded in scale because indicates that the company's activities don't release carbon dioxide and any other greenhouse gases in the atmosphere.

7 The fragmentation is also evident when limiting the analysis to the 200 largest companies in the sector: only the first two companies in the sector – Webuild and Itinera – had a turnover in 2021 above 1 billion euros. Then, the market is followed by much smaller companies. According to the 2021 Report on the Italian Architecture, Engineering, and Construction Industry edited by A Norsa, the reason why the Italian construction market is more fragmented than other European countries is cultural. Both in the private and public market, works are widespread throughout the territory, owners are numerous, many companies are still family-run and rarely pursue growth and value the role of managers. See Aldo Norsa (ed), 'Report 2021 on the Italian

- High costs: transitioning to a Net Zero Carbon model may involve significant investments in green and energy-efficient technologies, which may be difficult to sustain for SMEs with limited budgets.
- Lack of access to financing: SMEs may have difficulty accessing the funding needed to implement the changes required for achieving Net Zero Carbon.
- Limited knowledge: some SMEs may lack the expertise needed to comprehend and implement the most effective practices for reducing carbon emissions.
- Regulatory challenges: SMEs may struggle to adapt to the regulatory changes necessary for achieving Net Zero Carbon.
- Competitiveness concerns: SMEs' biggest fear is that transitioning to Net Zero Carbon may negatively impact their competitiveness compared to competitors who have not adopted sustainable practices.
- Lack of collaboration among market players: insufficient performance is generated compared to that of European competitors, thus preventing the desired results from being achieved at the European and international levels.

Legal framework: challenges and opportunities

Consequences of the EPBD directive: NZEB requirements

Italy has consistently shown commitment to enhancing the energy efficiency of buildings.

This is probably the consequence of the energy performance of buildings Directive 2010/31/EU and the energy efficiency Directive 2012/27/EU.

Directive 2010/31/EU introduced the concept of 'nearly zero energy buildings' (NZEB), referring to buildings with very high energy performance due to very low or almost zero emissions, achieved through the adoption of renewable technologies, materials, and sources.[8]

This Directive was transposed in Italy by Decree-Law No. 63 of 4 June 2013, converted into Law No, 90 of 3 August 2013, and further implemented by the Interministerial Decree of 26 June 2015 (the so-called 'Minimum Requirements Decree'), which defines the methods for calculating energy performance and the use of renewable sources, thus laying down the requirements for NZE buildings. Regarding compliance with the European requirements, the norms provided outlined specific deadlines: starting from 1 January 2018, newly constructed buildings owned by public administrations had to be nearly zero energy buildings, while from 1 January 2021, the abovementioned provision was extended to private buildings.[9]

Architecture, Engineering and Construction Industry' (*www.guamari.it*, November 2021) <https://www.inar-check.it/wp-content/uploads/2021/12/report2021_web4.pdf> accessed 4 October 2023.

8 It should be noted that during the implementation of the Directive in Italy, the Interministerial Decree of 26 June 2015 (the so-called 'Minimum Requirements Decree') specified that from a technical point of view, any building, whether new or existing, that meets the technical requirements is considered a nearly zero energy building when:

- The energy parameters and thermal characteristics are lower than the minimum requirements in force.

- The requirements for integrating renewable sources are met in compliance with the minimum principles set out in Annex 3, paragraph 1, letter c) of Legislative Decree No, 28 of 3 March 2011.

9 It is worth noting that some particularly virtuous Regions have anticipated the legislator's timetable: Lombardy has made NZEB compulsory from 1 January 2016 and Emilia-Romagna from 1 January 2019.

In other words, from the beginning of 2021, NZE buildings have become mandatory for both the private and public sectors for all new constructions or significant renovation projects.[10]

A series of economic incentives were introduced to nudge the private sector toward the green transition, among which 'Superbonus' 110% has proved to be the most effective.

The 'Superbonus' 110%, governed by articles 119 et seq. of Decree-Law No, 34 of 19 May 2020, (the so-called 'Relaunch Decree') converted into Law No. 34 of 19 May 2020, is a tax incentive aimed at encouraging energy requalification and seismic safety works on buildings. This incentive offered the owner of the building a tax deduction of 110% on the expenses incurred for specific interventions. Alternatively, it was possible to opt for a discount on the invoice granted directly from the company that carried out the intervention. The peculiarity was that the credit accrued by the company after the discount could be assigned to banks, in an almost cost-free transaction for both clients and companies, in order to obtain a loan. Interventions included, in particular:

- Thermal insulation work on enclosures.
- Replacement of winter air-conditioning systems in the building's common areas (roof, facades, and staircases).
- Replacement of winter air-conditioning systems in single-family buildings or functionally independent units in multi-family buildings.
- Earthquake-proof interventions.[11]

This incentive has been widely used over the past three years and has generated a strong flow of investments.[12] However, although enterprises and clients have widely exploited it, it has developed quite a few problems. Issues arose due to material shortages, depletion of financial resources, and difficulties in dealing with banks. This caused a boomerang effect for companies that could no longer apply the invoice discount and were forced to increase the prices. Moreover, there was institutional distrust due to instances of tax fraud (in other words, many companies billed works not actually carried out).

As a result, and also in order to contain public spending, with the Legislative Decree No. 176 of 18 November 2022 (the so-called 'Aid Decree Quarter'), converted into Law No. 6 of 13 January 2023, the legislator reduced the 'Superbonus' 110% from 110% to 90% for the entirety of 2023 and plans are in place to reduce it further (70% in 2024 and 65% in 2025) or eliminate it altogether.

---

10 Significant renovation building interventions concern 'a building that falls into one of the following categories: i) existing building having a usable floor area of more than 1,000 square meters, subject to complete renovation of the building elements constituting the envelope; ii) existing building subject to demolition and reconstruction, including extraordinary maintenance'. See Legislative Decree No, 28 of 3 March 2011, art 2(1) (m).

11 In addition to the leading interventions listed above, expenses for interventions carried out together with at least one of the aforementioned main interventions are also covered by the Superbonus 110%. These are: i) energy efficiency interventions; ii) installation of photovoltaic solar systems and storage systems; iii) infrastructure for recharging electric vehicles; and iv) interventions to eliminate architectural barriers. See Decree-Law No, 34 of 19 May 2020, art 119(1).

12 According to ENEA (Italian National Agency for New Technologies, Energy and Sustainable Economic Development) data published on 31st January 2023, investments at the national level amounted to about 65.2 billion euros and the assets linked to the Superbonus 110% were more than 372,000.

This is why, to date, the 'Superbonus' 110% is defined as a 'false benefit' and is at the centre of numerous controversies: many companies (around 50,000) are experiencing difficulties due to credit assignment and the new rules. These companies have carried out renovation works, accepting tax credits as payment instead of money, thus applying the discount on the invoice, but, when they tried to monetize them, they found the system blocked. Hence, companies have carried out works by anticipating money for the State, finding themselves in a situation of great uncertainty and economic loss for the entire construction chain.[13]

The prospects for reforms

The topic of energy efficiency is primarily used to promote carbon neutrality. However, there are several challenges now on the table of European institutions discussing the new Directive proposal on the subject.[14]

Precisely, the European Union, in implementing the 'Fit for 55' package – which aims to reduce CO2 emissions by 55% no later than 2030 compared to 1990 levels – is drafting a new directive to enhance the energy performance of buildings beyond the NZEB requirements. This European strategy represents a robust commitment to Net Zero Carbon policies both at supranational and national levels, aligning with the 'energy efficiency first' principle.[15]

The current version of the proposal, recently amended by the European Parliament, drawing up an energy consumption rating from A (the most efficient) to G (the most polluting), provides that from 2028 all new buildings should be zero-emissions, but new buildings occupied, operated, or owned by public authorities, should be zero-emissions as early as 2026.[16]

Despite the prescriptions above, since the text of the Directive will have to be transposed into each Member State's legal framework, each of them will be responsible for developing its own national plan for buildings renovation.

The entire process will be driven by national evaluations with significant challenges for all Member States.

By the way, also considering the extensive discretionary powers of Member States weakening the Directive impulse, the proposal was widely criticised by the Italian

---

13 More than 40% of companies are struggling to pay taxes and fees, while 60% are considering suspending the current construction sites and 86% say they will not open new ones.

14 See European Commission, 'Proposal for a Directive of the European Parliament and of the Council on energy performance of buildings (recast)' COM (2021) 802 final, as amended by the European Parliament with the 'Amendments adopted by the European Parliament on 14 March 2023 on the proposal for a directive of the European Parliament and of the Council on the energy performance of buildings (recast)' (COM(2021)0802 – C9-0469/2021 – 2021/0426(COD).

15 The recent 'EU Directive 2023/1791 of the European Parliament and of the Council of 13 September 2023 on energy efficiency and amending Regulation (EU) 2023/955 (recast) (Text with EEA relevance)' defines the 'energy efficiency first' principle as an 'overarching principle that should be taken into account across all sectors, going beyond the energy system, at all levels, including in the financial sector'. See Directive 2023/1791, Whereas n. 15.

16 The Directive proposal, as amended by the European Parliament, introduces new minimum performance standards, under which all buildings will have to be upgraded to at least class E, in several stages and depending on the type of building: *i)* public and non-residential buildings will have to achieve at least class E by 2027, and class D by 2030; *ii)* residential buildings, on the other hand, will have until 2030 to bring their certificate up to class E, and until 2033 to bring it up to class D.

government because 74.1% of Italy's building stock was built before the 2010/31/EU directive on the energy performance of buildings. Thus, meeting the proposed scenario set by the European Commission imposes a heavy burden on public funds and private capacities, making compliance daunting.

Therefore, according to data processed from ANCE (National Association of Building Constructors), the implementation of the scenario above should involve, until 2033, about 2 million buildings, requiring an investment of nearly 40/60 billion euros each year.[17] In a nutshell, this goal is highly challenging for companies and, at the same time, difficult to implement if we consider, for example, that with the 110% 'Superbonus' incentives, just under 100,000 interventions were completed in 2021 and 260,000 in 2022.[18]

In addition, the Real Estate Owners' Confederation (CONFEDILIZIA) expressed scepticism about the proposed timing. The Confederation's claim is that millions of residential buildings are supposed to be renovated in just a few years but, in many cases, the required interventions will not even be materially feasible due to the particular characteristics of the buildings concerned.[19]

More generally, to make the EU goals possible, it will be required to structure a new award system based on incentives and adequate financial tools as critical elements.

Other tools: Minimum Environmental Criteria and Do No Significant Harm principle

Other tools for greening constructions can be found in the public sector.

Within the Italian legislative framework, the introduction of CAM ('Minimum Environmental Criteria') has been used to promote the effective integration of environmental policies into the activities of contracting authorities, especially in construction procurement.

CAM can be defined as environmental standards fixed by law to be met by the contractor for the supply of goods and services and the execution of works. Their effectiveness was ensured through art. 18 of Law No, 221 of 28 December 2015. Lastly, art. 57 of the Italian code of public contracts (Legislative Decree No, 36 of 31 March 2023) made their application mandatory for all contracting authorities.

These criteria were officially adopted with the Decree of the Ministry of the Environment on 11 October 2017, substituted by the Decree of the Ministry of the Ecological Transition on 23 June 2022, containing useful provisions to optimise environmental sustainability in construction. It provided for:

1. Selection criteria

    The contracting authority may require economic operators to possess technical and professional capacities in addition to those typically demanded, like having realised projects that achieve high-performance levels. Moreover, the

---

17 See European Commission, 'Communication from the Commission to the European Parliament, the Council, the European Economic and Social Committee and the Committee of the Regions: Enforcing EU law for a Europe that delivers' COM (2022) 518 final.

18 This means that at these rates, the decarbonisation of the building stock, set for 2050, would be completed in a horizon of 3,800 years. In light of the draft directive, the first step, set at 15% of buildings, would not be reached for 630 years.

19 See Confedilizia press release, 13 January 2023.

economic operator can be asked to have executed a project using construction materials and technologies with a low environmental impact alongside their life cycle, verified through the application of life cycle assessment (LCA) methodologies in accordance with UNI EN ISO 15804 and UNI EN ISO 15978.

2. Award criteria

The contractor obtains a reward during the evaluation process by demonstrating EMAS registration or an environmental certification following the standard UNI ISO14001 to meet environmental criteria in the execution of the contract.

3. Contractual performance clauses

The contractor may be required to draft a 'CAM report' including, for each CAM criterion: i) a description of the project choices ensuring compliance with the criteria; ii) the indication of the project documents that prove compliance with the criterion; iii) details on the requirements for sustainable construction materials and products; iv) identification of the documents to be submitted to the director of works.

The CAM tools have proved to be less effective than expected.

Although they should be inserted in tender documents, frequently they are not. This happens because the regulatory framework on CAM is quite complicated: the annex to Ministry Decree No. 256 of 2022 counts more than 60 pages full of requirements and prescriptions to be fulfilled.

The rigidity of the requirements is perceived to be a significant disadvantage for the contractors: especially small and medium-sized enterprises, which may not be in a position to make a serious offer, either due to a lack of expertise or adequate economic resources for innovation. To solve this problem, the National Anti-Corruption Authority (ANAC) started to draw up an outline of guidelines to reconcile the principle of equal treatment with the focus on environmental protection. Unfortunately, following the Ministry for the Environment and Protection of Land and Sea's start with the activities for revising the Ministerial Decree of 11 October 2017, the Authority temporarily suspended the activities to adopt the guidelines. To date, ANAC seems not to have resumed activity on the guidelines, and the new Ministerial Decree on CAM (No, 256/2022) seems to ignore the problem as there is no mention of SMEs in the document.

Moreover, another problem is that compliance with the Minimum Environmental Criteria entails a cost for economic operators that must be adequately remunerated. The contracting authorities seem to be not so aware of the cost increase due to CAM. Economic operators have made several claims against inadequate work remuneration, including CAM requirements. It is worth mentioning Judgment No. 8088 of 27 November 2019, in which the Council of State held it was illegitimate to set a base auction price, asking for the adoption of CAM equal to that of an identical tender launched a few years earlier without CAM.

Lastly, it is surprising that no public authority can spread the proper use of CAM.[20]

---

20 See Fabrizio Fracchia and Pasquale Pantalone, 'Verso una contrattazione pubblica sostenibile e circolare secondo l'agenda ONU 2030' [2022] Riv It Dir Pubb Com 243. The authors believe that legitimacy solely in the hands of the excluded contractor does not seem sufficient to ensure compliance with the rules and principles that preside over the sustainability of contracts. Interesting is the reasoning carried out around art 211(1-bis) of Legislative Decree no 50/2016, which allows ANAC direct access to the administrative court to

Certainly, CAM is a clear example of the strategic use of procurement. Indeed, regardless of the purpose of the individual contract, they introduce an overall regulation of the sector-oriented toward achieving environmental objectives.[21]

However, their application appears to be very complex and requires a complete revision of the normative framework. More precise rules are necessary to favour companies and contracting authorities in their application, especially if one intends CAM as mandatory and considers the possibility of declaring illegitimate the tender documents drawn up without taking into account the technical specifications and contractual clauses contained in the minimum environmental criteria.

The second interesting tool used in the public sector is the 'Do Not Significant Harm' principle (also known as 'DNSH').

It was introduced as part of the EU Regulation No. 852 of 18 June 2020 – a source that produces binding legal effects in EU countries – which in art. 3 provides that economic activity is considered eco-sustainable if: i) it makes a substantial contribution to at least one of six environmental objectives, namely climate change mitigation; climate change adaptation; sustainable use and protection of water and marine resources; transition to a circular economy; pollution prevention and control; protection and restoration of biodiversity and ecosystem; ii) it does not significantly harm any of the environmental objectives;[22] iii) it is carried out in compliance with the minimum safeguards; iv) it complies with technical screening criteria established by the European Commission.

These eco-sustainability criteria were subsequently specified by the Delegated Regulation 2021/2139/EU of the European Commission, detailing for each area the minimum requirements to avoid significant environmental harm. Finally, Regulation 2021/241/EU provided that all the recovery and resilience plans adopted by the Member States to benefit from EU funds must fulfil the DNSH constraint and prove their compliance. Consequently, the DNSH principle became one of the fundamental pillars of the National

---

challenge notices, other general acts and measures relating to contracts of significant impact if it considers that they violate the rules on public contracts for works, services and supplies. Following this interpretation, 'the violation of CAM could be asserted in court directly by the Regulatory Authority, even if-and this constitutes a not insignificant limitation-the subject matter of the jurisdictional action is limited only to contracts of significant impact'.

21 ibid.

22 Under art. 17, an 'economic activity shall be considered to significantly harm:
   (a) climate change mitigation, where that activity leads to significant greenhouse gas emissions;
   (b) climate change adaptation, where that activity leads to an increased adverse impact of the current climate and the expected future climate, on the activity itself or on people, nature, or assets;
   (c) the sustainable use and protection of water and marine resources, where that activity is detrimental: (i) to the good status or the good ecological potential of bodies of water, including surface water and groundwater; or (ii) to the good environmental status of marine waters;
   (d) the circular economy, including waste prevention and recycling, where: (i) that activity leads to significant inefficiencies in the use of materials or in the direct or indirect use of natural resources such as non-renewable energy sources, raw materials, water, and land at one or more stages of the life cycle of products, including in terms of durability, reparability, upgradability, reusability or recyclability of products; (ii) that activity leads to a significant increase in the generation, incineration or disposal of waste, with the exception of the incineration of non-recyclable hazardous waste; or (iii) the long-term disposal of waste may cause significant and long-term harm to the environment;
   (e) pollution prevention and control, where that activity leads to a significant increase in the emissions of pollutants into air, water, or land, as compared with the situation before the activity started;
   (f) the protection and restoration of biodiversity and ecosystems, where that activity is: (i) significantly detrimental to the good condition and resilience of ecosystems; or (ii) detrimental to the conservation status of habitats and species, including those of Union interest'.

Recovery and Resilience Plan (also known as 'PNRR'). This means that within the field of the techniques necessary to select PNRR works, it is essential to structure key acts and documents in a way capable of 'driving' investments and reforms by tying them to the principle of Do No Significant Harm to the environment.

Further confirmation of the importance of the analysed criteria and principles can be found in the delegated law of the forthcoming reform of public contracts (Law No. 78 of 21 June 2022), which establishes the adoption of measures to ensure compliance with energy and environmental responsibility criteria in the awarding of public contracts and concession contracts (in particular through the definition of Minimum Environmental Criteria). It also calls for the simplification of procedures aimed at implementing investments in green and digital technologies in innovation and research, as well as social innovation, also in order to achieve the 2030 Sustainable Development goals, adopted by the United Nations General Assembly on 25 September 2015. Moreover, it aims to increase the degree of eco-sustainability of public investments and economic activities in accordance with the criteria set out in Regulation (EU) 2020/852 of the European Parliament and of the Council of 18 June 2020.[23]

The key role of local authorities: the importance of the urban planning regulations

Local authorities are among the political players most committed to introducing green policies.

It is not by coincidence that a fascinating example is given by the policies adopted in Milan's urban planning regulations: the city has exploited the building and urban planning rules, directing them toward sustainability standards.

The 'Building Regulations of the Municipality of Milan', through offset and incentive systems, promote the improvement of indoor comfort conditions, the reduction of polluting emissions, rational energy use, and the development of renewable energy sources. In particular, the Schedules attached to the document devote significant attention to the theme of energy efficiency in buildings to reduce consumption and pollution: i) Schedule 1 introduces a global energy performance index and eco-sustainability levels for each type of intervention, linked to incentives in the form of increased building gross surface area (ranging from 3% to 15%); ii) Schedule 7, in response to the need to reduce the consumption of non-renewable materials and resources and the production of waste, promotes the use of materials with a recycled content (defined by the international standard UNI EN ISO 14021) of at least 10% of the total value of the materials used in the project.

Lastly, it is also interesting to mention the 'Piano Aria e Clima' (the Air-quality and Climate Plan) approved by the Municipality of Milan on 21 February 2022, which is a strategic tool that aims to enable the city to achieve the goals set by the European Union, i.e., the transition towards a CO2 – free city in the medium-long term. It is evident that this plan introduces a new holistic approach to adaptation policies for decarbonisation, merging building and urban design with city planning. For example, under intervention No. 3 ('Milan with positive energy: a city that consumes less and better'), the local authority proposes: i) creating one or more carbon-neutral pilot areas; ii) implementing an energy efficiency plan covering both public residential and non-residential buildings;

---

23 See Law No. 78 of 21 June 2022, art 1(2)(f).

iii) initiating a pilot project for the installation of photovoltaic panels on municipal buildings; iv) defining a strategy for the energy efficiency of private buildings; v) developing a financial system for decarbonisation actions.[24]

Best practices to enhance net zero carbon

Looking at the tender procedure level, the implementation of the NZEB requirements, and in general the application of sustainable criteria, has been integrated into the design contest 'Futura, la scuola per l'Italia di domani' issued by the Italian Ministry of Education. This contest aims to acquire 212 projects to execute investment 1.1 Construction of new schools through the replacement of buildings' of the Mission 2 – Component 3 – of the National Recovery and Resilience Plan, concerning the construction of innovative highly sustainable, energy-efficient, inclusive, accessible schools under the architectural, structural and plant engineering points of view.[25]

The tender documentation outlined specific requirements. Firstly, proposals needed to be designed with a low environmental impact, aligned with the guidelines approved by Decree of the Minister of Education No. 106 of 26 April 2022, and with the following criteria:

- Ensuring that at least 70% of the non-hazardous waste generated during the demolition is directed towards re-use, recovery, or recycling.
- Avoiding an increase in land consumption, except up to a maximum of 5% of the covered *ante operam* area.
- Designing new school buildings to achieve primary energy consumption at least 20% lower than the NZEB requirement under Italian law.
- Developing electrical and thermos-fluidic systems that advanced management and automatic control of the systems themselves, as well as high environmental comfort conditions, possibly also in terms of adequately controlled mechanical ventilation of the rooms, always in compliance with the achievement of primary energy consumption limits.

Another example of best practices is Gruppo CAP, a publicly-owned contracting authority operating the integrated water service in the Metropolitan City of Milan.

Gruppo CAP is particularly active in adopting a sustainable and responsible business model, adopting collaborative agreements. This example represents a new approach, different from the one adopted in the previously described case.

Gruppo CAP published a tender stipulating that the contractor would receive specific rewards upon achieving objectives of broad public interest (so called 'collateral objectives') listed by the public client at the end of the execution of the contract.

Specifically, the collateral objectives identified by Gruppo CAP covered the following five principal areas coherently with its sustainability report's purposes: i) legality, ii)

---

24 For learning more about this innovative tool, all the documents are available at the URL: https://www.comune.milano.it/aree-tematiche/ambiente/aria-e-clima/piano-aria-clima.

25 This implies also being able to guarantee teaching based on innovative methodologies and full usability of the educational environments, also through an enhancement of sports infrastructures.

inclusiveness and gender procurement, iii) innovation, iv) environmental protection, and v) workers' safety.

Looking at the environmental collateral objectives, the collaboration target would be reached if the contractor and/or the supply chain obtained labels attesting compliance with pollution reduction policies or demonstrated the performance of good sustainability practices.[26]

As anticipated, to encourage the contractor, and the entire supply chain, to carry out these non-compulsory activities, reputational,[27] contractual,[28] and economic incentives were provided. The most interesting one was the possibility of entrusting new works to the contractor with a value equal to 2 million euros in case of demonstrated commitment to achieving a substantial number of sustainable objectives.

Finally, it seems fundamental to mention a truly virtuous example provided by Assimpredil ANCE (Association of construction and complementary SMEs of the Provinces of Milan, Lodi, and Monza Brianza), which is promoting 'Cantiere impatto sostenibile', a sustainable development implementation program for its members, with the aim to persuade companies to adopt a voluntary 'code of conduct' to improve sustainability policies on construction sites.

Given that joining the programme is voluntary, if the company decides to participate, the worksite can be awarded the 'Cantiere Impatto Sostenibile' logo. This is granted if the contractor, together with the supply chain, undertakes to adopt and promote the following 8 values/commitments : decarbonisation, environmental protection, legality, contractual regularity in labour relations, worker safety, social support and supply chain involvement.

Each commitment is accompanied by 3 levels of action, characterised by measures of increasing complexity that the company can achieve according to its corporate choices: 1) Silver,[29] 2) Gold, 3) Platinum. By way of example, in the decarbonisation area, the commitment of the worksite is demonstrated through the following steps i) the underwriter promptly appoints a Sustainable Impact Site Implementation Manager, who assumes the task of raising awareness, monitoring and guiding the company towards climate-friendly choices; ii) the governance bodies adopt a resolution that contains the commitment to switch to 100% electricity from renewable sources for the entire worksite or, alternatively, the purchase of certified carbon credits; iii) the commitment to achieve the worksite carbon footprint through a third party that applies the calculation according to ISO 14064 as well as the adoption of a plan to zero emissions from the work site.

---

26 The activities that are rewarded by the contracting authority mainly relate to the achievement of certifications attesting compliance with existing environmental standards (e.g., the achievement of Carbon Footprint Certification UNI EN ISO 14064-1 and Water Footprint UNI EN ISO 14046, which assesses the reduction of CO2 and water consumption in recent years).

27 Precisely, reputational incentives consist of the issuing of certificates in favour of the contractor and/or any members of the supply chain, recognising the achievement of one or more collateral objectives.

28 The contractual incentives were agreed upon by CAP introducing sustainability criteria within the Vendor Rating assessment parameters. The greater the commitment shown, the higher the score earned in the Vendor Rating indexes, and thus the greater the possibility for the contractor and/or supply chain members to obtain further contracts.

29 Mandatory minimum level to obtain the Logo.

Conclusion

Coming to the conclusion of this work, it is clear that we have a very ambitious but, at the same time, complex framework for the transition of the construction market towards net-zero objectives, which is giving rise to some reflections on the topic.

From the described picture, it emerges that the legislator introduced highly complex and rigid rules in an attempt to align with EU requirements, linking the sustainability project exclusively with the application of specific technical guidelines, increasing the risk of conflicts and ambiguity.

Conversely and in parallel, numerous virtuous examples from local contracting authorities and construction company associations emerged. They seem to be the real 'architects' of sustainable empowerment because they drive the achievement of net-zero objectives and companies' professional end economic growth .

Recognizing the strategic use of contracts, particularly collaborative construction contracts, is crucial. In other words, if the construction process is structured to be circular and inclusive (with the involvement of the entire supply chain), the greening of construction is more accessible.

Simplifying the rules, abandoning the excessive bureaucracy that burdens the system and generates distrust in economic operators, beginning to follow the logic of collaboration and incentivising a strategic dialogue among the parties together with the recognition of awards can effectively help the market to respond to the needs required and can nudge the system by also supporting economically the ecological transition.

PART III

KEY CONCEPTS AND DEVELOPMENTS IN COMMON LAW AND CIVIL LAW

CHAPTER 6

Fitness for purpose obligations

Windmills or giants?

Julian Bailey

Introduction

There are few expressions in the construction law field that produce a reaction of anxiety more than the words 'fitness for purpose' (or 'FFP'). For a contractor or designer to be subject to an FFP obligation connotes a requirement of a higher level of performance, or indeed strict liability, when compared with an obligation to act with reasonable skill and care. All construction professionals will accept that should be legally accountable for their own mistakes. But the idea of being legally accountable without having done anything wrong, perhaps in circumstances where a person could not have acted any differently, produces discomfiture to an alarming degree.[1]

FFP obligations may be written into construction contracts and consultants' appointments as express terms. Sometimes, where an admixture of documents and terms are used in a composite contract, there may be ambiguity and disagreement as to whether an FFP obligation applies, as a matter of contractual interpretation. If, however, we step away from the field of express terms, we must ask the question: what, if anything, does English law imply as a term of a construction contract insofar as FFP is concerned? Should we think of FFP obligations as being purely a creature (or monster) of contract? Or do FFP obligations fall part of the underlying contractual framework *even if they are not* expressly written into a contract? If so, should this affect how we conceive of FFP obligations: if they are already there, aside from the written terms of a contract, should they be feared as giants? Or should we view implied FFP obligations as an integral feature of English commercial law, reflective of commercial norms in trade and commerce? Unlike the famous Spanish knight-errant, we should pause and ponder before charging into commercial battle.

Implied FFP obligations

General considerations

In the paradigm of the construction industry, FFP obligations are readily implied into contracts by the common law. The readiness of the common law to imply such a duty is heightened where a contractor undertakes to design and build a particular structure, and it is objectively apparent what purpose the structure is intended to serve.

---

1 This anxiety being compounded by the potential difficulty of actors in the construction industry often being unable to obtain insurance cover in relation to breaches of FFP obligations.

DOI: 10.4324/9781032663975-10

The classic instance of such an implication is in relation to the construction of a home. The law enthusiastically implies an obligation into a contract to design and build a home that it will be fit for human habitation. Numerous statements may be found in the case law confirming the implication of such an obligation. One will suffice here:

> Take the common law position of a house-owner who contracts with a builder to build a house. The builder is obliged to build a house fit for habitation, see *Hancock v Brazier* [1966] 1 WLR 1317, 1332F per Lord Denning MR. If the house is not fit for habitation because it is damp and if the builder comes to rectify the work that he has done but fails to eliminate the damp because he misdiagnoses the cause of the damp he will be liable for that failure.[2]

The language used in these cases is that of 'fitness for habitation', as opposed to 'fitness for purpose'. However, it is self-evident that what is being spoken of is a 'fitness for purpose' obligation. A home is a place for someone to live in. Its sole purpose is that of human habitation. The duty thus implied by the common law in this instance is an FFP obligation.

Residential building provides a neat and easily-understood illustration of the law implying an FFP obligation into a construction contract. The general purpose of a contract to design and build a home will be apparent to employer and contractor alike, as will (in most cases) the employer's reliance upon the contractor to produce a home which the employer is able to live in safely and securely. But if we move beyond this particular situation into, say, the context of commercial building or industrial infrastructure, more general questions of FFP arise.

Those questions include: if an employer indicates to a contractor what it wants the contractor to build, and contractor duly builds what the employer requires of it, has the contractor discharged its contractual obligations, even if the works as performed are not fit for their intended purpose (where that purpose is objectively known)? If so, what role is there (if any) for the law to super-add, by implication, an FFP obligation into this contractual matrix so as to hold the contractor legally responsible for the failure of the works to achieve their intended purpose?

In seeking to answer these questions, one may begin by reflecting on two matters.

The first is what may be called the general indisposition of the common law to imply warranties into contracts between commercial actors who have evidently set out to regulate their relationship by entering into a written agreement. An illustration, which bears certain parallels with our FFP situation, arises in relation to what are known as matters of 'buildability'. Under English law, if an employer provides (either itself, or through its agent) a design to a contractor, and the contractor promises to build what is shown in the design: that the contractor must do. The contractor is bound to build according to the design even if, as a matter of engineering, the design is not 'buildable' – either at all, or in the particular environment in which the project is taking place. The contract contains no implied warranty from the employer as to the possibility of the design being successfully built. This is entirely a matter for the contractor's assessment.[3] If, therefore, an employer does not impliedly warrant that a particular design produced on its behalf will be 'buildable', does it flow – conversely – that a contractor who builds what is shown in such a design will not impliedly warrant that the completed work will be fit for any particular

---

2 *Alderson v Beetham Organisation Ltd* [2003] 1 WLR 1686 [40] (Longmore LJ).

3 *Thorn v The Mayor and Commonalty of London* (1876) LR 1 HL 120. The position in the United States is somewhat different: *United States v Spearin*, 248 U.S. 132 (1918).

purposes (general or specific)? Is the assessment of the functional utility of what is shown in a design not a matter for the designer itself?

Second, competing considerations come into play through the role of sale of goods laws. English statute law, which largely codifies English common law, makes particular provision for the implication of FFP obligations when it comes to contracts for the sale of goods. Thus, section 14(3) of the Sale of Goods Act 1979 (UK) provides relevantly that:

> (3) Where the seller sells goods in the course of a business and the buyer, expressly or by implication, makes known to the seller any particular purpose for which the goods are being bought, there is an implied condition that the goods supplied under the contract are reasonably fit for that purpose, whether or not that is a purpose for which such goods are commonly supplied, except where the circumstances show that the buyer does not rely, or that it is unreasonable for him to rely, on the skill or judgment of the seller.[4]

As is evident from section 14(3), the purpose for which goods are supplied may be expressly stated, and the purpose may be an unusual one. But equally, for the purposes of the section, a purpose may be made known *by implication*, i.e., in the absence of any express statement to the effect that 'I require these goods for purpose X'. Furthermore, the 'purpose' may also be one for which the goods in question are commonly supplied. Indeed, it may be obvious from the objective circumstances what the purpose is of the supply of goods.[5]

What this second consideration will frequently lead to is an outcome whereby goods are purchased, either as a pure sale of goods contract, or under a mixed contract (such as a construction contract)[6] to supply goods and perform services (i.e., to build a structure using the goods supplied). If goods are being provided under a construction contract, and the purpose of their supply is evident to the contractor (as it often will be), the consequence is that the goods provided by the contractor will be subject to an implied term that they are fit for the purpose for which they are being supplied. Different considerations may arise where the purpose of goods being supplied is not a usual one, and the contractor is unaware (and, reasonably, is entitled to be unaware) of the special purpose the goods are to fulfil. But in the majority of cases, where a contractor is engaged directly by an employer for a particular project, and the employer and the contractor engage in communications regarding the employer's requirements, the contractor will usually have a good understanding of the purpose for which it is engaged, and the purpose that the goods it supplies are intended to fulfil.

We must recognise, however, that there is potentially a difference between, on the one hand, the question of whether the goods supplied are fit for their intended purpose, and on the other whether goods when used in construction to implement a design generate an overall *product* (e.g., a house, a road, a hospital) which is fit for purpose. Building materials may be of good quality and otherwise fit for purpose, but even if so it does not follow that the structure built with those goods will necessarily be fit for its desired purpose. A

---

4 An equivalent term is implied under sections 10(1) and 10(3) of the Consumer Rights Act 2015 (UK).

5 *Henry Kendall & Sons v William Lillico & Sons Ltd* [1969] 2 AC 31, 93 (Lord Morris). The 'purpose' of the works is to be ascertained from objective circumstances, and not from a party's subjective understanding of what the 'purpose' is: *Parkview Constructions Pty Ltd v Futuroscop Enterprises Pty Ltd* [2023] NSWSC 178 [195] (Rees J).

6 *Mertens v Home Freeholds Co* [1921] 2 KB 526, 538–539 (Warrington LJ); *Young & Marten Ltd v McManus Childs Ltd* [1969] 1 AC 454, 465 (Lord Reid).

house built with good bricks may not be fit for purpose if the bricks are laid incorrectly, or where the design of the house – when constructed – renders the brick walls liable to crack. Given this, one may well pose the question: will FFP obligations be implied where a contractor is engaged to (a) design and build a particular structure or alternatively (b) build a structure according to a design/specification provided to it?

Design and build

Design and build contracting involves what Lord Denning once described, in compendious language, as a 'package deal'.[7] The 'package deal' is one under which, as the name suggests, the contractor takes responsibility for both designing and building a particular structure.

The nature of the responsibility undertaken by a contractor under a design and build contract may vary. Returning to the paradigm of the design and construction of a new home by a builder, as we have seen the law implies an FFP obligation into the contract between the employer and the contractor, i.e., that the home, when constructed, will be fit for habitation.

It is, though, permissible for this obligation to be watered down by an express contractual term, e.g. to the effect that the contractor will exercise reasonable skill and care in designing and building the home, but (by implication) it does not warrant that the home as constructed will fit for habitation. Such an arrangement may also be said to be a 'package deal', because the contractor takes legal responsibility for the 'package' of design and construction. But the nature of that responsibility is neither absolute nor strict, as it is with FFP obligations. This is because the contractor *will not* be legally responsible, under this arrangement, simply by virtue of the home failing to be fit for purpose (i.e., not fit for habitation). The contractor is only responsible for defects and other shortcomings in the property if and to the extent it failed to act *with reasonable skill and care*.

If, however, a design and build contract is silent as to the existence of any FFP obligation on the contractor's part, that leaves the question of whether the law will imply an FFP obligation in contexts other than those involving home building. That question, early on, was answered in the affirmative by the English Court of Appeal in *Greaves & Co (Contractors) Ltd v Baynham Meikle & Partners*.[8] The case concerned a 'package deal' for the design and construction of a warehouse in Staffordshire in which barrels of oil were to be stored and moved around. As regards the nature of the obligations assumed by the design and build contractor, Lord Denning MR held as follows:

> Now, as between the building owners and the contractors, it is plain that the owners made known to the contractors the purpose for which the building was required, so as to show that they relied on the contractors' skill and judgment. It was, therefore, the duty of the contractors to see that the finished work was reasonably fit for the purpose for which they knew it was required. It was not merely an obligation to use reasonable care. **The contractors were obliged to ensure that the finished work was reasonably fit for the purpose**. That appears from the recent cases in which a man employs a contractor to build a house: *Miller v. Cannon Hill Estates Ltd.* [1931] 2 K.B. 113; *Hancock v. B. W. Brazier (Anerley) Ltd.* [1966] 1 W.L.R. 1317. It is a term implied by law that the builder will do his work in a good and workmanlike

---

7 *Greaves & Co (Contractors) Ltd v Baynham Meikle & Partners* [1975] 1 WLR 1095, 1098.
8 [1975] 1 WLR 1095.

manner; that he will supply good and proper materials; and that it will be reasonably fit for human habitation. Similarly in this case the contractors undertook an obligation towards [the employer] that the warehouse should be reasonably fit for the purpose for which they knew it was required, that is, as a store in which to keep and move barrels of oil.[9] (emphasis added)

What we see in the above passage is a neat transposition, from the residential environment to a wider, commercial environment. Just as a contractor implicitly assumes FFP obligations to the person for whom it is building a home, it will also assume FFP obligations to any other employer for whom it undertakes to design and build any other structure, at least in circumstances where it is apparent what the purpose is of the works, and that the employer is relying upon the contractor to apply its skill and judgment.

The conclusion we may draw from this is a wide one. Contractors who embark upon projects under which they assume 'package deal' obligations of design and construction are likely to assume FFP obligations as regards the 'package' provided to the employer, where it is objectively apparent what the purpose is of the 'package' of works. Those FFP obligations will be assumed unless either qualified or abnegated by the terms of the contract, or if it is evident that the employer does not rely upon the contractor to apply its skill and judgment in relation to the total 'package' of works performed.

This last qualification is particularly pertinent where a contractor's skill and judgment is brought to bear in relation to *part* but not *the whole* of the package of works to be performed, as is the case where a contractor assumes responsibility for *construction* but not also *design*.

Contractor without design responsibility

One of the critical aspects to the existence or negation of an implied FFP obligation is the element of reliance by the employer on the contractor. As we saw from section 14(3) of the Sale of Goods Act, an FFP warranty may be implied in a contract for the sale of goods where the buyer makes known the purpose for which the goods in question are required. However, the potential implication of such a warranty is negatived 'where the circumstances show that the buyer does not rely, or that it is unreasonable for him to rely, on the skill or judgment of the seller'.

Reliance by a buyer on a seller, or equivalently by an employer on a contractor, may be found in instances of 'design and build', where the contractor is providing to the employer a 'package deal' of a completed product. The contractor takes responsibility for everything: designing the structure, and then constructing it in accordance with the design. The structure thus constructed must be of suitable quality, and be fit for its known purpose.

But where, on the other hand, a contractor is engaged to construct a structure according to a design provided to it, and the contractor assumes no contractual (or other) responsibility for the adequacy of the design, the contractor is only providing part of 'the package' which the employer will ultimately receive. If there are errors in the design, the contractor is not responsible for them. The employer is not relying upon the contractor to exercise skill or judgment in relation to the design. The employer will look to its own designer (i.e., an architect or engineer) to apply the appropriate level of 'skill or judgment' in relation

---

9 [1975] 1 WLR 1095, 1098–1099. Geoffrey Lane LJ held to like effect (at 1102–1103).

to the design. The contractor's part of the 'package' is to perform works, which includes providing materials, so as to implement the design provided to it.

One case, from more than a century ago, will be used to illustrate these propositions. The case is *Bowers v Chapel-en-le-Frith RDC*,[10] which concerned a contract for the construction of waterworks in the village of Wormhill, Derbyshire, which included the supply of a windmill to raise the water for the village. In relation to the windmill itself, the contract terms (which were prepared by the employer) provided:

> The contractors will be required to obtain the windmill tower and pump from Messrs. Rickman & Co, windmill engineers, 13 Wallbrook,[11] London E.C., for which a sum of £127 has been included in the quantities ... They must be carefully fixed, and their continuous satisfactory working during the period of maintenance must be guaranteed by the contractors.[12]

In the bill of quantities included in the contract, details of the windmill were laid out, that the windmill was to be a '16 feet diameter Canadian Imperial galvanised steel windmill, complete with vane and governor, back-geared 2.5 to 1, with ball and roller bearings, together with 40 feet high, galvanised steel fourpost tower, complete with all girts',[13] and so on.

Thus, the contract specified what the contractor was to procure (the windmill tower and pump) and from where it was procure it (Rickman & Co). Self-evidently, the employer knew what it wanted, and moreover was in no way relying upon the contractor to select and supply a suitable type of windmill.

The contractor duly obtained the windmill from Rickman & Co, and it was erected on site in Derbyshire. But there was a problem: the windmill did not work. In the words of Lawrance J:[14]

> the windmill ... was unable to perform its duty. It was absolutely useless, and a new mill of a different construction, procured from a different place, was obtained by [the employer].[15]

Turning to the key issues in the case, Lawrance J held thus:

> Then this question arose between the parties, and the [employer] immediately took up the position – there is no doubt about that – and said: 'You [the contractor] are liable for this; you guaranteed the proper working of this mill; you are the persons who are liable for this mill not having performed its duty'. That is the question, and the whole question, to be decided in this case.
>
> The question is: [was the contractor] liable for the inefficient working of the mill, or did their liability cease when they properly erected it under the contract? Another way of putting the question is: was the [contractor's] contract to make the mill answer its purpose; or was it a contract to do the work in accordance with the specification and plans? I need hardly say that in my judgment the answer to each of these questions should be in favour of the [contractor] on the ground that I have already given, namely, that the mill was chosen by the [employer],

---

10 (1910) 9 LGR 339.

11 Which, incidentally, is now the location of the London Mithraeum.

12 (1910) 9 LGR 339.

13 Ibid

14 Lawrance J was evidently somewhat of a polarising figure, both during his lifetime and posthumously. The great arbitration lawyer and judge Sir Frank Mackinnon wrote in no less than the Law Quarterly Review: 'When I was a pupil of TE Scrutton from 1896 to 1897, he told me that the Only Begetter of the Commercial Court was "Long" Lawrance. Mr Justice JC Lawrance was a stupid man, and a bad judge'. See Frank Douglas MacKinnon, 'The Origin of the Commercial Court' (1944) 60 LQR 324.

15 *Bowers* (n 10) 343.

and it was the mill the [contractor was] bound by their contract to erect, and which they did erect, and that the [contractor] had no means or power of objecting to the mill, or altering it, or doing anything to it. It was no part of their contract to guarantee in any way that the mill would be efficient.[16]

The logic of this approach is tolerably clear, and above all sound. The contractor was supplying what it was required to supply, as instructed by the employer. The contractor gave no express warranty as to the suitability of the mill for its purpose. It was not providing a 'package deal'. All of the circumstances negatived the existence of any reliance by the employer on the contractor to select and supply a windmill that was fit for its intended purpose.

Bowers therefore provides a simple and neat illustration of how the absence of any reliance by the employer on the contractor to exercise skill and judgment in selecting goods or materials takes away the imperative to imply an FFP obligation. But we should not see reliance (or the absence thereof) as being necessarily a determinative factor. This is because an FFP obligation may apply, by express agreement between the parties, even if the objective circumstances indicate the absence of reliance by the employer on the contractor's judgment or skill in design or selection of goods or materials.

Express FFP obligations

In commerce, and in our personal lives, knowing where we stand is vital for self-understanding and moreover decision-making. As we have seen, there is certainly scope for ambiguity as to whether a contractor is (or is not) subject to an *implied* FFP obligation. Much depends upon whether the employer is, as a matter of fact, relying upon the contractor to exercise its skill and judgment in selecting and supplying the item or works in question.

Thus, contracting parties may benefit from an express clause (or clauses) which is 'clearly set out to warn' a contractor if it is subject to an FFP obligation, or whether the standard of skill and care it warrants is not absolute in nature. A potential problem, however, even with express contractual obligations, is that they may be presented in contractual form in confusing and apparently contradictory ways.

The paradigm illustration of this concerning FFP obligations arose in the UK Supreme Court case of *MT Højgaard A/S v E.On Climate & Renewables UK Robin Rigg East Ltd*.[17] The case concerned the contractual responsibility for failures to the foundations of wind turbines, being used as part of two offshore wind projects in Scotland.

The contract in *MT Højgaard* was voluminous, and consisted of a number of documents which were evidently prepared by numerous people. One of the key documents was the Employer's Requirements, which included certain Technical Requirements which made express reference to the works being 'Fit for Purpose'.

Another key part of the Technical Requirements included within the contract was a section concerning the 'Design Principles' which the contractor was required to apply. In particular, the Technical Requirements provided that, in designing the foundations for the offshore wind farms, the contractor was to follow a particular international standard

---

16 *Bowers* (n 10) 346.
17 [2017] UKSC 59.

known as J101. J101 was published by Det Norske Veritas ('DNV'), an independent classification and certification agency based in Norway.

These features of the contracting arrangement were in themselves unremarkable, but for a particular issue which only came to light later: J101 contained a major error. The existence of the error was not apparent when the contract was entered into, and only emerged when DNV discovered the error and notified the market of it. The error meant that the faithful application of the standard would lead to the foundations being under-strength by a factor of around 10. The consequence of this error being discovered was that the foundations for each of the offshore wind turbines required major remedial work, at a substantial cost. The economic issue at stake in *MT Højgaard* was therefore: which party should bear the cost of the remedial works – the employer or the contractor?

To answer this question from a layperson's perspective, one could begin by focusing on the matter of fault, as fault is often a strong guide as to where responsibility should lie. But finding fault is an impossibility in a case such as this. The employer had specified the application of a recognized standard published by a renowned international classification society. The contractor had duly applied that standard. Neither employer nor contractor had the slightest reason for suspecting the standard may contain the error in question, let alone asking questions of DNV regarding its standard. The whole purpose of standards is to have a considered, tested, reliable basis for proceeding with design and construction, which does not require the user of the standard (who may, in any case, lack the knowledge or expertise to consider the underlying basis of the standard) to do more than apply it in the situations for which it was developed. Accordingly, there was no 'fault' in any relevant sense on the part of either the employer or the contractor.

From a legal perspective, the answer to the question 'who is to bear the cost of rectifying the foundations?' yields to the contractual risk allocation agreed by the parties.

At a factual level, there was a strong resemblance between the position in the *MT Højgaard* case and that in *Bowers*. Leaving aside the coincidental detail that both projects involved the supply and installation of a windmill or wind turbines, the cases bear close resemblance in that, in each, the contractor's skill and judgment was not relied upon by the employer in relevant respects.

Thus, in *Bowers* the contractor was told to purchase a particular type of windmill from a particular supplier in London. And in *MT Højgaard* the contractor was told to apply a particular international standard in designing the foundations for the wind turbines. In both cases, the contractors did what they were told to do, and therefore fulfilled their contractual promises.

In *Bowers*, as we saw, the contractor was held to have no legal responsibility for the shortcomings in the 'absolutely useless' windmill procured from the London merchant. But in *MT Højgaard* the contractor *was* held responsible for the foundation defects, even though it had faithfully applied the standard (J101) specified by the employer, and had not in any sense acted negligently. So why did the Supreme Court come to this conclusion?

Primarily, because the contract in question contained an express warranty of quality given by the contractor, i.e. an express FFP obligation. As Lord Neuberger PSC held after reviewing case law from the UK and Canada:

> Where a contract contains terms which require an item (i) which is to be produced in accordance with a prescribed design, and (ii) which, when provided, will comply with prescribed

criteria, and literal conformity with the prescribed design will inevitably result in the product falling short of one or more of the prescribed criteria, it by no means follows that the two terms are mutually inconsistent. That may be the right analysis in some cases.... However, in many contracts, the proper analysis may well be that the contractor has to improve on any aspects of the prescribed design which would otherwise lead to the product falling short of the prescribed criteria, and in other contracts, the correct view could be that the requirements of the prescribed criteria only apply to aspects of the design which are not prescribed. While each case must turn on its own facts, the message from decisions and observations of judges in the United Kingdom and Canada is that the courts are generally inclined to give full effect to the requirement that the item as produced complies with the prescribed criteria, on the basis that, even if the customer or employer has specified or approved the design, it is the contractor who can be expected to take the risk if he agreed to work to a design which would render the item incapable of meeting the criteria to which he has agreed.[18]

Thus, where an FFP obligation is made an express term of a construction or engineering contract, it will, unless qualified in some way, operate as an overriding warranty of quality on the contractor's part. It may do so even if the employer has in no way relied upon the contractor to apply its skill or judgment in formulating the relevant article or works, and indeed it may apply even if the employer's specified requirements contain a significant error, so that the intended structure is not in fact 'buildable'.

To some this result may seem unfair, but English law proffers no such assessment. Why? Because capable parties have agreed that the contractor shall build the desired works and warrants that those works will be fit for their intended purpose. It is the role of the courts to uphold that warranty, and the parties' agreed allocation of risk, even if the contractor is wholly devoid of blame or fault, and its contractual performance may in fact have been unimpeachable.

Conclusions

FFP obligations form part of the tapestry of English construction law. As we have seen, they are routinely implied by the common law and statute law into commercial dealings between a purchaser/employer and a supplier/contractor. FFP obligations are a warranty of quality, and liability for breach of this warranty may arise by virtue of what has been supplied not being fit for its known purpose. The 'no fault' nature of this liability could be perceived as burdensome upon a supplier, but on the other hand the absence of such a warranty (and corresponding liability) could place a difficult or even impossible burden on a purchaser to demonstrate fault or negligence as a necessary ingredient of establishing a cause of action.

The position taken by English law may be seen as a pragmatic one. Purchasers of goods or construction works are to be protected contractually against suppliers (or contractors) who can better manage the risks of quality in what they supply. But then again, if a purchaser or employer is evidently not relying upon a supplier or contractor to manage those risks, no FFP obligation will be implied, because no protection is needed in such cases by a purchaser or employer.

---

18 *MT Højgaard A/S* (n 15) [44] (Lord Neuberger PSC); See also Curtis, 'Fitness for purpose obligations' in Julian Bailey (ed), *Construction Law, Costs and Contemporary Developments: Drawing the Threads Together – A Festschrift for Lord Justice Jackson* (Hart Publishing, 2018).

When it comes to express FFP obligations, English law does not interfere with whether, and if so how, such obligations are to be written into the terms of a contract. A number of approaches could be taken by contracting parties, including simply by articulating the FFP obligations that are otherwise implied by law, including by section 14(3) of the Sale of Goods Act. However, if that were to be done there would still be large scope for ambiguity and disagreement, including in relation to the threshold issues of (a) whether the purchaser/employer had indicated a purpose for the goods or works in question; and (b) whether the purchaser/employer was (or was not) relying upon the supplier/contractor to apply its skill and judgment to the selection and provision of the goods or works, so as to ensure that they are fit for the desired purpose.

Contracting parties therefore, not wishing to leave matters to chance, usually go further when it comes to FFP obligations, and will (where agreed) expressly provide that the works in question are to be fit for their particular purpose, irrespective of whether the purchaser/employer is actually relying upon the supplier/contractor to exercise the necessary skill and judgment in relation to the supply of the goods or performance of the works. And as we have seen from the *Højgaard* case, these obligations may have an overriding effect, rendering a contractor 'strictly' or 'absolutely' liable for shortcomings in what has been supplied, even if the contractor has adhered to the employer's directions and specifications as to what and how the contractor is to perform the contract in question.[19]

If we return to the question of whether FFP obligations should be viewed as benign like a windmill, or fearsome like a giant, it is difficult to suggest a strong or adamantine answer. What matters, however, is that parties enter into construction and engineering contracts with open eyes, understanding the risks that they face, and the corresponding rights to which they are entitled. In the end, it is this understanding or perception which matters most. Tilting at windmills or other misunderstood structures ends only in ignominy.

---

19 Cf *Lendlease Construction (Europe) Ltd v AECOM Ltd* [2023] EWHC 2620 (TCC) [137]–[143] (Eyre J).

CHAPTER 7

Performance bonds and bank guarantees

35 years of development

Richard Wilmot-Smith

This paper may be a misnomer since it concludes that the law has not developed much, at least in the areas which it covers. However, it must be said that in the last 20 years there has been a profusion of cases on the law of guarantee and indemnity where old principles are considered and re-considered.

There are three types of development. First the availability of bonds and guarantees on the market, second, statute law, and third case-law.

As to the market, these include the following instruments:[1]

- On-demand bonds.
- Conditional bonds.
- Tender guarantee or bid bonds. This is to insure the risk of a tenderer withdrawing its offer. The period between the selection of a tenderer and the entering into a contract can be a source of great exposure for an employer. A purist would say to the employer 'just accept the tender'; but this is often commercially impracticable. As construction projects became more and more sophisticated and as economic turbulence increases this type of bond will become more and more useful, albeit it is still relatively rare in today's industry.
- Advance payment guarantee bond. In The Mercer's case[2] it was procured to permit an advance payment for tax purposes. However, these instruments are highly popular because an advance payment eases a contractor's cash flow and thus enables site progress where the work intensity and expense is front loaded. This is in contradistinction to a standard construction site where the contractor can front load the prices for foundations. It enables properly measured and valued milestone without loophole tendering being needed by the contractor.
- Refund guarantees being a guarantee of repayment of interim payments made to contractors in the event that the employer under a construction contract or

---

1 Here I am indebted to the Practice Note. See Karen Spencer, Sarah Sabin, Richard White and Holly Howarth, 'Bonds guarantees and standby credits: overview' (*Thomson Reuters Practical Law*) <https://uk .practicallaw.thomsonreuters.com/4-107-3649> accessed 18 October 2023. As a bit of autobiography Richard White and Karen Spenser were my instructing solicitors in *Trafalgar House v General Surety* and as a point of information Richard White subsequently became a long serving and highly successful chief executive of General Surety.

2 *The Wardens and Commonality of the Mystery of Mercers of the City of London v New Hampshire Insurance Company Limited* [1992] 2 Lloyd's LR 365(1992) 60 BLR 26.

DOI: 10.4324/9781032663975-11

101

the buyer under a shipbuilding contract lawfully terminates the contract. In the off-shore construction world in relation to oil rigs termination clauses are often referred to as 'drop dead' clauses. Refund guarantees are more commonly used in the shipbuilding context because the ship is personalty rather than executed work on the employer's realty.

- Retention and maintenance guarantees. This again facilitates cash flow. As opposed to a 5% or 2.5% retention being held by the employer, there is a bond which guarantees the rectification of defects in the defects liability period or maintenance period. This may be no more than a defects guarantee bond (depending on the wording).
- Adjudication Bonds. Because the adjudication award has only temporary finality, there is room in the market for an instrument which allows for an on demand payment of an adjudicator's award and then for an adjustment following the final determination of the Parties' liabilities.

In an era when financial instruments form a large part of the economy of this country, there is room for the continued expansion of their types being available on the market.

The role of statute is limited but historic and important. A guarantee must be evidenced in writing otherwise the Statute of Frauds 1677 and particularly section 4 thereof makes it unenforceable.[3]

The statute provides:

> No action shall be brought whereby to charge the Defendant upon any special promise to answer for the debt default or miscarriage of another person unless the Agreement upon which such Action shall be brought or some Memorandum or Note thereof shall be in Writing and signed by the party to be charged therewith or some other person thereunto by him lawfully authorised.

This is a good example of Parliament, looking to eradicate a mischief, stops one abuse but does not prevent a differently framed but identical obligation from arising. A differently framed obligation would be a contract of indemnity. While section 4 of the 1677 Act made guarantees which were not evidenced in writing unenforceable, the statute does not bite on indemnities.[4]

The 1677 Act is an ancient statute which has survived attempts at its abolition.[5]

The courts will enforce the Statute of Frauds.[6]

The term 'signed by the party to be charged' is widely construed and email is a sufficient memorandum.[7] That case may be taken as no more than re-affirming a generous interpretation of what an acceptable form of signature actually is.[8] Thirty five years ago

---

3 Much of the statute has been repealed or reformed. But the section in relation to guarantees remains.

4 See *Brown-Forman Beverages Europe Ltd v* Bacardi UK Ltd [2021] EWHC 1259 where at paragraphs 10–13 the distinction between the two are spelled out.

5 Law Revision Committee in its Sixth Interim Report, Statute of Frauds and the Doctrine of Consideration (Cmd 5549/1937) paragraph 16.

6 *Actionstrength Ltd v International Glass Engineering SPA* [2003] 2 AC 541, 549.

7 *Golden Ocean Group Ltd v Salgaocar Mining Industries PVT Ltd & Anor* [2012] EWCA Civ 265.

8 Old cases demonstrate the flexibility of the law in relation to signature. See Caton v Caton [1868] LR 2 HL 127; Bluck v Gompertz [1852] 7 Ex 862; Leeman v Stocks [1951] 1 Ch 941.

the internet and email were in embrio. Technology will produce further innovation and *Golden Ocean* illustrates the law's ability to evolve when applying ancient statute.

Looking at modern statute, the Housing Grants, Construction and Regeneration Act 1996, which provides for statutory adjudication and which cannot be opted out of, creates the relatively new concept of 'temporary finality' with regard to the obligations of contractor and employer (and contractor and subcontractor) and this article concludes with the potential effect of the statute on surety obligation and the potential role of adjudication bonds. We conclude with this topic because the law seems to be in its infancy as regards this topic.

As to case-law, we must first look at on-demand and conditional bonds and the difference between them.

Their commercial structure will involve an obligor; an obligee and a guarantor; alternatively a creditor; a debtor and a guarantor. Thus, there is a principal contract (be it a main contract or a subcontract); an employer, a contractor and a guarantor. The employer and contractor will enter into a contract (the underlying contract), the performance of which is guaranteed by the guarantor. The contractor will then have a cross guarantee, under which the contractor indemnifies the guarantor. That latter obligation rarely, if ever, obtrudes into the cases where bonds in the construction industry are considered.

All of these obligations require interpretation. On interpretation, it may be observed that courts tend to be astute to proclaim their view of the 'commercial' purpose of the instruments which they have to construe. It leads to the criticism that they do not understand that commercial purpose is related to the level of premium. The lower the premium the lower the bondsman's risk. Often matters which must be proved and the method of proof are a direct function of the level of premium.

A low premium may mean that there are 'onerous' notice provisions in the guarantee. The presumption in some of the literature that they are obnoxious and are to be got round is not warranted. I suggest that the full 'commercial' nature of any bargain can only be ascertained by reference to the level of risk, quantity of sum payable by the bondsman and the level of premium. The bond sum is known; but, in the cases, the risks undertaken and premiums paid are unknown and do not form part of the ratio. So in the literature and authorities we often have commentary on commercial purpose without all the factors where risk is managed properly in play. I give by way of example *Perar v General Surety*[9] in which the bondsman was held not liable following an analysis of the crystallisation of the obligation of the surety and the provisions for notice. This case was, in my view, correctly decided, although it has come in for academic criticism.[10] One can observe in some of the cases, statements as to the commercial purpose of bonds, but I suggest that the words chosen by the Parties may be the best guide to their construction.

Now to development. The first and most fundamental matter to consider is the distinction between an on-demand bond and a conditional bond.

Given the time-frame this article is concerned with is thirty five years, we should start with *Trafalgar House Construction (Regions) Limited v General Surety and Guarantee*

---

9 (1994) 66 BLR 72.

10 Particularly from my late chambers colleague Ian Duncan Wallace see for example Ian D Wallace, 'Perar Re-visited: when will they ever pay? When will they ever learn?' (1998) 14 *Construction Law Journal* 322.

Company Limited.[11] In that case the first instance judge and the Court of Appeal ignored House of Lords authority[12] to hold that a standard conditional bond was in fact an on-demand bond. It was, to Counsel arguing the case, bewildering at both first instance and in the Court of Appeal.

However, the House of Lords restored sanity and made clear the nature of conditional bonds (namely that there had to be proof of default and loss) and (without over-complication of legal theory) suggested that an overpayment by the bondsman will result in the beneficiary's obligation to account to the bondsman for such overpayment. In the manner of the worst advocates I now write (when this article was a lecture I said), we shall come to that point.

The wording of the instruments of guarantee in *Trade Indemnity Company Limited v. Workington Harbour and Dock Board*[13] and *Trafalgar House Construction (Regions) Limited v General Surety and Guarantee Company Limited*[14] was nearly identical. In both cases the House of Lords held that the guarantee required proof of loss and was not an on-demand bond. An on-demand bond does not require proof of loss but requires payment by the guarantor upon the due and proper demand.

The on-demand bond and its character has been examined in the cases since *Edward Owen Engineering Limited v Barclays Bank.*[15] Lord Diplock referred to them in *United City Merchants (Investments) Limited* v *Royal Bank of Canada,* at page 183D in the following terms:

> Again, it is trite law that in (the contract between the confirming bank and the seller under which the confirming bank undertakes to pay the seller up to the amount of the credit against presentation of the stipulated documents), with which alone the instant appeal is directly concerned, the parties to it, the seller and the confirming bank, 'deal in documents and not in goods,' as article 8 of the Uniform Customs puts it. If, on their face, the documents presented to the confirming bank by the seller conform with the requirements of the credit as notified to him by the confirming bank, that bank is under a contractual obligation to the seller to honour the credit, notwithstanding that the bank has knowledge that the seller at the time of presentation of the conforming documents is alleged by the buyer to have, and in fact has already, committed a breach of his contract with the buyer for the sale of the goods to which the documents appear on their face to relate, that would have entitled the buyer to treat the contract of sale as rescinded and to reject the goods and refuse to pay the seller the purchase price. The whole commercial purpose for which the system of confirmed irrevocable documentary credits has been developed in international trade is to give to the seller an assured right to be paid before he parts with control of the goods that does not permit of any dispute with the buyer as to the performance of the contract of sale being used as a ground for non-payment or reduction or deferment of payment.
>
> To this general statement of principle as to the contractual obligations of the confirming bank to the seller, there is one established exception: that is, where the seller, for the purpose of drawing on the credit, fraudulently presents to the confirming bank documents that contain, expressly or by implication, material representations of fact that to his knowledge are untrue. Although there does not appear among the English authorities any case in which this exception has been applied, it is well established in the American cases of which the leading

---

11 [1995] AC 199. More recent consideration of the principles can be found in *MW High Tech Projects UK Ltd v Biffa Waste Services Ltd* [2015] EWHC 949 (TCC) and *Tetronics (International) Ltd v HSBC Bank PLC* [2018] EWHC 201 (TCC).

12 *Trade Indemnity Company Limited v. Workington Harbour and Dock Board* [1937] AC 1

13 [1937] AC 1.

14 [1995] AC 199.

15 [1978] 1 QB 159.

or 'landmark' case is *Sztejn* v *J Henry Schroder Banking Corporation* (1941) 31 N.Y.S. 2d 631. This judgment of the New York Court of Appeals was referred to with approval by the English Court of Appeal in *Edward Owen Engineering Ltd* v *Barclays Bank International Ltd*, though this was actually a case about a performance bond under which a bank assumes obligations to a buyer analogous to those assumed by a confirming bank to the seller under a documentary credit. The exception for fraud on the part of the beneficiary seeking to avail himself of the credit is a clear application of the maxim *ex turpi causa non oritur actio* or, if plain English is to be preferred, 'fraud unravels all.' The courts will not allow their process to be used by a dishonest person to carry out a fraud.[16]

Note the language used by Lord Diplock. It relates to banking and prior to *Trafalgar House* there was not much discussion of on-demand bonds in the construction context.

To repeat, the difference between an 'on demand bond' and a 'guarantee bond': one is where liability is established through the presentation of documents (usually a demand in a prescribed form) and the other where the guarantee is triggered by default.

One can summarise the development of the law since *Trafalgar House* by giving some history. That is that there have been many cases brought before the courts where the argument has been whether the instrument was an on-demand instrument or a conditional bond where proof of loss is required. This might be thought odd until one uncovers the fact that many bonds have been home-made instruments where ambiguity has seeped through the interstices of the Parties' intentions and commercial objectives where the guarantee is 'Operation Hope Not' and getting the work is the immediate priority.

This led to reliance being placed upon phraseology such as 'first written demand' creating a presumption that it was 'on demand'. However, there would be tension with the use of words such as 'established losses' or other such phrases lurking around the verbiage of the instrument. Somehow the judge would have to resolve the tension.

There was consideration in some cases of the identity of the guarantor. If the bondsman was a bank, then some judges would presume or be pushed into the direction of the bond being of an on-demand nature and equally of the bondsman was a professional bondsman or a parent company then the push would be in the direction of the bond being conditional.

Each case has to be looked at on its own facts and on its own particular contract terms. It would be of no great help to any of you if I was to recite by way of digest all the cases where this distinction has been sought to have been made. One should take an example. The Court of Appeal tried to make sense of it all in *Shanghai Shipyard Co Ltd v Reignwood International Investment (Group) Company Ltd*.[17] Popplewell LJ's explanatory sweep of the law began by reminding practitioners that suretyship can be traced to the Old Testament[18] and from the judgment we can extract the finding that the identity of the bondsman does not affect its construction in the sense of pushing the interpretation into that of on-demand if it came from a bank and a conditional bond if it came from a professional bondsman. See particularly paragraph 32 where he says:

> What this illustrates is that in the present context there ought to be no room for a priori preconceptions or assumptions about the nature of the instrument to be derived from the identity

---

16 [1983] 1 A.C. 168 at 183D.

17 [2021] EWCA Civ 1147.

18 Proverbs Ch 11 v15 *He that is surety for a stranger shall smart for it ...* This is perhaps the first reference to the professional bondsman as opposed to the guaranteeing of the debts of his or her relative for no consideration. Proverbs trace to King Solomon (1015-975 BC) and chapters 10-22 are often referred to as 'Proverbs of Solomon'.

of the guarantor. What matters is the wording in which the parties have chosen to express their bargain, interpreted in accordance with the well-established rules of construction.

The cases show much historic over-citation of authority. In paragraphs 33-35 of the judgment Popplewell LJ concern was expressed at this over-citation:

33. Before turning to the language of the instrument, I wish to say something about the citation of case law on this exercise of construction. Disputes as to whether an instrument is a surety guarantee or a demand guarantee are common, and are fertilised by the tendency to construct them from more than one precedent with negotiated variations. Reliance on decided cases on what are said to be similarly worded instruments is only of assistance in very limited circumstances. An authoritative decision that a form of words bears a particular meaning can legitimately point towards the same construction being placed on the same words if used in another contract in the same context. This is because consistency of judicial approach promotes certainty for businesspeople, and because commercial parties with access to legal advice can reasonably be expected to have intended to achieve the same result as that revealed in the precedent if they use the same form of words in the same context. In *Enterprise Inns Plc v Forest Hill Tavern Public House Ltd* [2010] EWHC 2368 (Ch), Morritt C said of a previous decision at [22]:

'Plainly such a decision cannot be conclusive as to the interpretation of other contracts made at different times, between different parties and in different circumstances even though both are questions of law. But a decision on the interpretation of a contract may be persuasive as to the interpretation of another contract using similar language by parties involved in a similar trade and in similar circumstances, particularly where knowledge of the previous decision may be imputed to the parties.'

34. The availability of this line of argument is, however, rare, at least so far as concerns disputes as to the nature of a guarantee. It is only capable of application if the words used in the document *taken as a whole* are materially identical; and if the contractual context in which they are used is materially identical. Both counsel before us were guilty of identifying a word or phrase in the Guarantee and then pointing to an authority in which such word or phrase was part of the language used and in which the result had been a conclusion of surety guarantee on the one hand or demand guarantee on the other, in order to argue that its inclusion was not fatal to the outcome in the case cited, or that its inclusion supported the conclusion in the case cited. Where there is other language in the instrument being construed in the case cited which means that as a whole it is not materially identical to that before the court in the instant dispute, as there was in all but two of the cases cited to us, that is not an appropriate use of authority or valid process of argument because the nature of any given instrument turns upon its language as a whole in its particular commercial context. I would associate myself with the concern expressed by Longmore LJ in *Wuhan* at [22] at the process adopted in the decisions of the first instance judge in that case, and in *Meritz Fire and Marine Insurance Co Ltd v Jan dee Nul NV* [2011] 1 All ER (Comm) 1049, of analysing over 20 authorities in order to resolve the issue. Citation of authority to argue that the inclusion of a particular phrase in the case cited was not fatal to the outcome achieves no more than is achieved by the well-known principle of

construction that an instrument is to be interpreted according to the whole of its language.

35. There are only two cases which engage the legitimate line of argument in the present appeal, in my view, namely *Wuhan* and S*pliethoff's*, <u>although I will have to refer to some others cited by the parties to explain their irrelevance.</u>[19] Nevertheless the primary focus should be and remain on the words used by the parties and the commercial context in which they are used. I have addressed the commercial context of the Guarantee, which points in neither direction. I turn to its language.

There was then in the judgment an examination of the language which caused the Court to decide that the bond was an on-demand instrument. It involved a process of construction in which the Court differed from the first instance judge. No great principle can be obtained from the process of construction save that the words 'upon receipt by us of your first written demand'; and 'not merely as surety' and 'ABSOLUTELY and UNCONDITIONALLY' and 'immediately' are strong pointers to the instrument being of an on-demand nature.

Therefore, as to development of the law, we can conclude that there has not been much as regards the construction of a bond where the Court has to decide whether it is an on-demand instrument or a conditional bond. In *Shanghai Shipyard* itself one can detect a certain amount of word salad by the draftsman. The instrument included the words cited above which pointed to it being an on-demand instrument, but it also contained pointers against that including a provision permitting the right to withhold payment until an arbitration award was published and a further provision by way of an indulgence clause which is standard in conditional bonds. The Court weighed up the language (words used), deprecated over-citation of authority, debunked the notion that the nature of the obligations provided in the instrument varied according to the identity of the parties to it and executed a standard process of construction.

Some things remain as regards the on-demand bond. Subject to the fraud exception a properly constituted demand triggers payment. This has remained unchanged since *Edward Owen Engineering Limited v Barclays Bank*. There have been many cases where the fraud exception has been prayed in aid in the past 35 years particularly with regard to attempts to obtain injunctive relief either preventing the call being made or preventing payment being made after the call has been made.

In *TTI Telecom International v Hutchison 3G UK Ltd*[20] the first instance judge said (obiter) that a lack of good faith might be added to the fraud exception. On the facts lack of good faith was not shown. The judgment itself is learned and full and gives a good summary of the law in relation to on-demand instruments. But the suggestion of a good faith exception must be doubted.

Simon Carves Ltd v Enus UK Ltd[21] and *Doosan Babcock Energy v Comercializaadara de Equipos*[22] moved towards expanding the fraud exception and granted injunctions. Both cases relied on *Cyanamid* principles[23].

---

19 My emphasis.
20 [2003] EWHC 762 (TCC) [34]–[37].
21 [2011] EWHC 657 (TCC).
22 [2013] EWHC 3201 (TCC).
23 *American Cyanamid Co v Ethicom Ltd* [1975] AC 396.

Additionally, Singapore permits injunctions to restrain a bond call on the ground of unconscionability.[24]

However the fraud exception has been clearly set out by the Privy Council in *Alternative Power Solution Ltd v Central Electricity Board*[25]:

> in interlocutory proceedings the correct test for application of the fraud exception to the strict general rule that the court would not intervene to prevent a banker from making payment under a letter of credit following a compliant presentation of documents was whether it was seriously arguable that on the material available the only realistic inference was that the beneficiary could not honestly have believed in the validity of its demands under the letter of credit and that the bank was aware of such fraud.

That case abjured normal *Cyanamid* criteria for the grant of an injunction.[26] The earlier first instance cases must be read as being modified by this statement of the Privy Council, which dictum has been applied in *Tetronics (International) Ltd v HSBC Bank Plc*[27] and applied again in *Shapoorji Pallonji & Company Private Ltd v Yumn Ltd & Anor*[28].

In summary, additions to the fraud exception have been flirted with at first instance (where much aggrieved innocence and outrage can catch the sympathies of judges) but the law has, since 2014, moved to keeping it alone, despite the pull of Singapore. It is fair to say that had *Solo Industries* (see fn 25) been properly followed, then the flirtation with *Cyanamid* principles in Simon Carves would never have happened.

Next we should look at the special rules of the enforceability and construction of conditional bonds.

Without an 'indulgence clause' if there is a material variation of the underlying contract and the bondsman has not been consulted and given its permission, then the bondsman will be discharged. This is called the rule in *Holme v Brunskill*.[29] This rule can be simply justified. A bondsman will guarantee a specific obligation or set of obligations, but not differing or more onerous ones. However, it is a surprising trap for the unwary. The doctrine itself applies only to guarantee obligations and not indemnities.[30] There are several (but in the circumstances surprisingly few) cases where the doctrine is considered and discussed prior to *Trafalgar House*. There are many cases which follow that case.

---

24 See the decision of the Court of Appeal in *GHL Pte Ltd v Unitrack Building Construction Pte Ltd* [1999] 4 SLR 604.

25 [2014] UKPC 31.

26 ibid [59]: In the view of the Board the expression 'seriously arguable' is intended to be a significantly more stringent test than good arguable case, let alone serious issue to be tried. As Mance LJ put it, a case of established fraud known to the bank, is, by its nature, one which, if it is good at all, must be capable of being established with clarity at the interlocutory stage. In summary, the Board concludes that it must be clearly established at the interlocutory stage that the only realistic inference is (a) that the beneficiary could not honestly have believed in the validity of its demands under the letter of credit and (b) that the bank was aware of the fraud. See also *Solo Industries UK Ltd v Canara Bank* [2001] 1 WLR 1800 and Mance LJ at [31]:

If instruments such as letters of credit and performance bonds are to be treated as cash, they must be paid as cash by banks to beneficiaries. The courts in the Harbottle and *Edward Owen* cases emphasised this, and, in my view, set a higher standard than 'a real prospect of success' in relation to all these situations.

27 [2018] EWHC 201 (TCC).

28 [2021] EWHC 862. See also *Bolivinter Oil SA v Chase Manhattan Bank* [1984] 1 WLR 392; *National Infrastructure Development Company Ltd v Banco Santander S.A.* [2017] EWCA Civ 27. Note however *Salam Air SAOC v Latam Airlines Group SA* [2020] EWHC 2414 (Comm).

29 (1878) 3 QBD 495.

30 *Brown-Forman Beverages Europe Limited v Bacardi UK Ltd* [2021] EWHC (Comm) 1259.

Of those I would particularly recommend *Raffles Offshore (Singapore) Ltd & Anor v Schahin Holding SA*[31] for a discussion of the ambit of the indulgence clause in that particular case; though one should take little from the case itself, being a summary judgment appeal. The same release mechanism can be said to apply to a breach of contract[32]. Indulgence clauses are almost *de rigeur* and will almost always prevent reliance on *Holme v Brunskill.*[33]

The *Holme v Brunskill* rule is not liked by merit-minded judges and in *Aviva Insurance Limited v Hackney Empire Limited*[34] the judge held that additional payments or side agreements were not variations to the contract giving rise to discharge. The rationale of the judge in that case may be thought to push at the edges when one considers that the 'giving of time' to a contractor discharges the bondsman but the giving of money does not. Another early example comes from an 'Advance Payment Bond', which came under the microscope in *The Wardens and Commonality of the Mystery of Mercers of the City of London v New Hampshire Insurance Company Limited.*[35] The facts were that the employer paid the contractor a hefty advance payment for the purpose of avoiding tax. The obligor contractor became insolvent and the oblige employer made a demand on the bond which the courts enforced.[36] There was some tricky discussion as to whether there was a material variation of the underlying contract (which one of the two first instance judges found in accordance with the agreed facts) or whether there was a breach which did not discharge. The Court of Appeal's own investigation of the facts enabled it to find a breach which was not such to discharge the bondsman. In the *Mercer's* case there was no indulgence clause.

In *Re PME Cake Ltd*[37] a *Holme v Brunskill* argument was summarily dismissed when it was submitted that a Tomlin order varied the terms of a lease and the companies judge stated that the Tomlin order did not vary the terms of the lease but rather settled the secondary liability for damages arising from a breach of its terms. I am not altogether sure that the variation of a secondary liability is any less a variation of an underlying contract than the variation of a primary liability for the purposes of the rule in *Holme v Brunskill.*[38] The case illustrates the distaste for discharging professional bondsmen by applying *Holme v Brunskill.*

In relation to parent company guarantees where a director of the primary obligor is also a director of the guarantor, then a court will, most likely, hold that the consent of the guarantor to the variation of the underlying contract has been given if the common director signs the variation to the underlying contract even if his or her signature is as director of the contractor and not the guarantor company. This will be because the consent of the guarantor to the material variation will be inferred.[39]

---

31 [2013] EWCA Civ 644.

32 See *National Westminster Bank plc v Riley* [1986] FLR 213. See also *Mercers* case.

33 See e.g. *Samuels Finance Group plc v Beechmanor Ltd* [1993] 67 P&CR 282 and *Oceanfill Ltd v Nuffield Health Wellbeing Ltd & Anor* [2022] EWHC 2178 (Ch) [35]–[37].

34 [2012] EWCA Civ 1716.

35 [1992] 2 Lloyd's LR 365(1992) 60 BLR 26.

36 I think to this day wrongly, but an explanation as to why this is the case is outside the purview of this talk. Suffice it to say that the decision of Phillips J which was set aside by Hobhouse J and the Court of Appeal is to be preferred. The case is a classic merits decision.

37 [2022] EWHC 1783 (Ch).

38 (1878) LR 3 QBD 495.

39 See *Geoquip Marine Operations AG v Tower Resources Cameroon SA & Anor* [2022] EWHC 531 (Comm) [155]–[165].

What has the past 35 years told us about *Holme v Brunskill*? It is looked at with some distaste but it is a rule which prevails. Quite why the Mercers did not insist on an indulgence clause is hard to credit. No doubt its absence reduced the premium, but discharge was avoided. One can only conclude that the cases demonstrate that what is perceived as merit will often prevail and *Holme v Brunskill* may be more honoured in the breach. All the same, beneficiaries can insist on an indulgence clause; usually they do, so perhaps *Holme v Brunskill* is only relevant to that rare breed of case where there is no indulgence clause which must mean a minority of cases.

Finally, as promised, I come to adjudication bonds.

As to their necessity and the place of temporary finality, the law as it stands does not speak with one voice. Here we should note the first instance decision of Fraser J in *Yuanda (UK) Company Ltd v Multiplex Construction Europe Ltd & Anor*[40] in which it was held *per incuriam* that what the judge described as an 'Adjudication Decision Demand' made under a standard conditional bond (not an on-demand bond) which made no provision for an adjudicator's decision required payment by the guarantor on the adjudicator's decision.

See particularly paragraph 109.2 of the judgment. This decision might be explained by the presence of the surety at the hearing (where the principal argument was whether the bond was on demand or conditional). It does not appear that Counsel for the bondsman took the point that established and uncontested law meant that it was loss from default which triggered a payment on a conditional bond, not a decision of an adjudicator. No doubt this was for good commercial reasons. Often bondsmen will agree to pay on a judgment of a court or an arbitration award. But the law does not require them to without an express term saying so.

The better view is that the judge was wrong. Robert Goff J's decision in *Bruns v Colcotronis*[41] was not cited. Neither was *Re Kitchin*[42] nor Ramsey J's decision in *Beck Interiors*.[43] If an arbitrator's award is not binding on the surety, there is no logic in an adjudicator's decision being so binding.[44] The applicability of this line of authority has been underlined by Popplewell LJ's judgment in in *Shanghai Shipyard Co Ltd v Reignwood International Investment (Group) Company Ltd*[45]:

> The Guarantor is not party to the arbitration agreement in the Shipbuilding Contract, and but for this proviso would not be bound by any award in an arbitration between the Builder and the Buyer. The award might go by default against the Buyer, without any detailed consideration of the merits, but if the document were a surety guarantee Reignwood would be entitled to challenge whether the Buyer was indeed liable notwithstanding that the tribunal had so held, absent the agreement in the proviso to abide by the award. The proviso therefore binds Reignwood to pay what may not be an underlying liability; it involves payment against a document, namely an award. Another indication that it involves payment against a document, not a liability, is that the obligation arises the moment an award is made, irrespective of any subsequent challenge, for example for procedural irregularity under s 68 Arbitration Act 1979 (clause 17 of the Shipbuilding Contract contains an express agreement that there would be no right of appeal, but this would only preclude a s 69 challenge). In other words the proviso

---

40 [2020] EWHC 468 (TCC).
41 [1979] 2 Lloyd's Rep 412.
42 (1881) 17 Ch D 668.
43 [2010] BLR 37, [2009] EWHC 3861 (TCC).
44 See also *Grant v Easton* (183) 13 QBD 302 and *Clarington Developments Ltd v HCC International Insurance* [2019] IEHC 630 (High Court of Ireland).
45 [2021] EWCA Civ 1147 [37.6].

to clause 4, if triggered, does not introduce a surety obligation. It is true that it introduces an obligation to pay against a different event from a demand, namely an award, and to that extent, if and when the proviso is triggered, the obligation is converted into that which I have termed a conditional bond (of which a demand guarantee is but a subset). But I accept Mr Berry's submission that this is all of a piece with the first part of clause 4 being a demand guarantee unless and until the proviso is triggered. It is not consistent with the document being a surety guarantee unless and until the proviso is triggered because it is improbable that such a guarantee based upon secondary liability would include a provision for it to become a guarantee which did not depend upon a secondary liability.

The dictum of Foxton J. in *SK Shipping Europe PLC v Capital VLCC Corp and Anor* is helpful:

> An issue arose as to whether the guarantee extended to the costs of an arbitration brought by the owner against the charterer to recover outstanding hire. In addition to the express reference to the arbitration award, Mocatta J held that it was an implied term of the charterparty that the parties would agree to honour any award made pursuant to the arbitration clause in the charterparty (applying *Bremer Poelstransport GmbH v Drewry* [1933] 1 KB 753), and that the guarantee extended to that obligation.
>
> The suggestion that a choice of dispute resolution clause in the principal contract can enlarge the scope of liability of a guarantee to include the costs of enforcement is not a particularly attractive one, and I note that the decision in *The Rosarino* has been criticised on this point (*Ards Broigh Council v Northern Bank Ltd* [1994] NI 121). Taken to its logical conclusion, it would make the determination of the principal debtor's liabilities in an arbitration award binding on the guarantor under the guise of the argument that it had guaranteed performance of the principal debtor's implied promise to honour the award, whereas it has long been clear that, absent an express term, the guarantor is not so bound (*Bruns v Colocotronis (The Vasso)* [1979] 2 Lloyd's Rep 412, 418).[46]

A fuller explanation of this position comes in Ramsey J's decision in *Beck Interiors Ltd v Russo*:

> 46. Ms Andrews submits that Dr Russo, as guarantor, is not bound by the Adjudicator's decision against the company. She relies on *Re Kitchin* [1881] 17 ChD 668 and *Bruns v Colocotronis (the Vasso)* [1979] 2 Lloyd's Rep 412 which were applied recently by Christopher Clarke J in *Sabah Shipyard v Government of Pakistan* [2008] 1 Lloyd's Rep 210.
>
> 47. In *Re Kitchin* James LJ said this at page 671:
>
> > 'It is contended that it is liable to pay any sum which an arbitrator shall say is the amount of the damages. The guarantee must be expressed in very clear words indeed before I could assent to the construction which might lead to the grossest injustice ... If a surety chooses to make himself liable to pay what any person may say is the loss which the creditor has sustained, of course he can do so, and if he has entered into such a contract he must abide by it. But it would be a strong thing to say that he had done so unless you find that he has said so, in so many words. The arbitration is a proceeding to which he is no party; it is a proceeding between the creditor and the person who is alleged to have broken his contract and if the surety is bound by it, any letter which the principal debtor had written, any expression he had used, or any step he had taken in the arbitration, would be binding upon the surety. The principal debtor might entirely neglect to defend the surety properly in the arbitration; he might make admissions of various things which would be binding as against him, but which would not, in the absence of agreement, be binding as against the surety. It would be monstrous that a man, who is not bound by any

---

46 [2020] EWHC 3448 (Comm) [359]–[360].

admission of the principal debtor, should be bound by an agreement between the creditor and the principal debtor as to the mode in which the liability should be ascertained.'

48. Lush LJ said this at page 674:

'You must find explicit words to make a person liable to pay any amount which may be awarded against a third person, whether it be a jury, a judge or an arbitrator.'

49. In *The Vasso* Goff J (as he then was) said this, at page 418–419:

'It is well-established that general words in a guarantee, guaranteeing the due performance of all the obligations of the principal debtor do not, of themselves, have the effect of the surety as bound by an arbitration award in an arbitration between the principal debtor and the creditor, even where the arbitration award arises out of an arbitration clause in the contract containing the obligations of the principal debtor guaranteed by the surety. That is established by the case of *Re Kitchin* [1881] 17 ChD 668, a decision of the Court of Appeal which had stood unchallenged for nearly 100 years and is still cited in leading text books as good authority today. As was pointed out in that case, if the law was otherwise, serious injustice might occur. For example an arbitration award might result from an admission made by the principal debtor in the course of the arbitration without the authority of the surety. Again to take a more extreme example, the principal debtor might take no part in the arbitration whatsoever; he might not even appoint an arbitrator in which event, pursuant to Section 7 of the Arbitration Act of 1950, the creditor's arbitrator would act as sole arbitrator and the case, although it could not go by default, would simply proceed on the basis of the creditor proving his case before the sole arbitrator. It cannot be right that a surety, by general words such as those in the Defendant's guarantee in the present case, should be bound by such an award. In truth, an arbitration clause which provides the machinery for resolving disputes arising between the parties to the contract and special characteristics which distinguishes it from the main obligations of the contract, as can be seen from the leading case of *Heyman v Darwin* [1942] AC 356. The short answer is that, as a matter of construction, a guarantee containing general words, as in the case of the guarantee of the Defendant, although applicable generally to obligations of the principal debtor arising under the relevant agreement, does not apply to an obligation to honour an arbitration award.'

50. Whilst Mr Mort sought to draw a distinction between a temporarily binding adjudication decision and an arbitration award, I consider that the principle derived from the cases concerned with arbitration awards is equally applicable to any dispute resolution method which involve a decision on what sum is due or what damages are payable. This is made clear by Lush LJ in the passage from Re Kitchin cited above. The underlying rationale for that principle is that a party might neglect to defend itself properly; might make admissions or might otherwise conduct the case in the dispute resolution differently from the guarantor. Therefore, to overcome that difficulty, what is required is an agreement by the guarantor to be bound by the decision of an adjudicator, arbitrator or the court as between the parties to the contract or other means under which underlying dispute arises.[47]

The obvious point is that if a judgment or award does not bind a bondsman then neither should an adjudicator's decision. Ramsey J's decision is to be preferred. Thus, there is the need in the market for an adjudicator's bond. Perhaps these, not featuring in the past 35 years of jurisprudence, will come forward for decision as temporary finality is worked

---

47 [2010] BLR 37 [46]–[50].

through. Perhaps not though, given that 97% of adjudicator's decisions are accepted by the Parties and go no further.

The conclusions we can draw from the above is that, as presaged at the beginning of this article the law has remained steady even if its application has zig zagged and been uncertain where what are thought of as 'merits' hove into view.

For construction lawyers this is not new. The 'General Surety' cases cited above demonstrate that sometimes it takes a court of final appeal to re-assert the application of trite law in individual cases.

The real development comes with new legal landscapes (such as the arrival of adjudication) and the financial instrument industry's ability to create new instruments to satisfy the new demands of the construction industry.

CHAPTER 8

English residential building law – from *Anns* to Grenfell and beyond

Philip Britton

Introduction

Her Honour Frances Kirkham CBE has said that '[t]here is a serious gap between the expectations of reasonable people as to the remedies which should be available for shoddy building and design and the reality, namely failure by policymakers to provide a robust regulatory regime and inability of the courts to provide the remedies people need'.[1]

How has English law evolved over the last half-century in imposing civil liability for housing defects, particularly where the claimant has no contractual link with any potential defendant?[2] To offer an answer, this chapter channels one of theatre's more tiresome and superannuated bit-players – the ghost of Hamlet's father.[3] Like the (traditionally) whiskery and helmeted Dane, it brings a warning of ill deeds needing retribution: homeowners – both freeholders and long leaseholders – suffer construction defects caused by others, yet regularly have no judicial remedy.[4] It is a gloomy and unoriginal message, but worth repeating in the hope of reform.

For non-specialists, '*Anns*' means *Anns v Merton LBC*, decided in 1977 by the House of Lords, then the UK's highest civil court of appeal.[5] 'Grenfell' means the fire at Grenfell Tower in London W11 on the night of 13–14 June 2017; as a result, 72 died (including 15 disabled people). In insiders' memories, *Anns* is central in a trio of cases considering

---

1 From the Foreword to Philip Britton & Matthew Bell, *Residential Construction Law* (Oxford, Hart Publishing, 2021), which explores in greater depth all the topics discussed here in relation to the UK, Ireland and Australasia. HH Frances Kirkham CBE was a TCC judge in Birmingham (2000–2011) and Coroner in the inquest into deaths in the 2009 cladding related Lakanal House fire in London.

2 'English law' means the law of both England & Wales (unless otherwise explained). In Scotland, 'the common law' of delict and quasi-delict appears identical in our field, but no part of the Defective Premises Act 1972 applies; it also has its own statutory regime for prescription and limitation of actions, as well as for construction. Northern Ireland has a version of the original DPA but its own building control system.

3 William Shakespeare, *Hamlet* (first published 1599, Penguin 2015); Father may also have been named Hamlet, hence sometimes 'Old Hamlet' or 'King Hamlet'.

4 As above, 'owner' or 'homeowner' here covers both freeholders and long leaseholders. 'Builder' is meant generically; 'remediation' and 'rectification' are used interchangeably. The Defective Premises Act 1972, s 1 (now joined by s 2A) protects a holder of any legal or equitable interest in a building or dwelling, theoretically including short-term periodic tenants, though such occupiers have no stake in the capital value of their home: see also n 49. But the DPA, s 1 can also protect a developer: *URS Corporation Ltd v BDW Trading Ltd* [2023] EWCA Civ 772, following [2021] EWHC 2796 (TCC), [2022] EWHC 2966 (TCC) and [2023] EWCA Civ 189 (now before the UKSC). The new 'construction products liability' provisions in the Building Safety Act 2022, ss 146–150 similarly protect freeholders, long leaseholders and short-term tenants via the definition of 'a relevant interest': see the main text to n 97.

5 *Anns v Merton LBC* [1978] AC 728. The Court of Appeal judgment (on the limitation issue alone) is reported at [1976] QB 882; Judge Fay's similarly narrow ruling in the QBD (OR) appears unreported.

114

DOI: 10.4324/9781032663975-12

a local authority's liability in tort for negligent supervision of a residential construction project. Its prequel six years earlier is *Dutton v Bognor Regis UDC* in the Court of Appeal, with Lord Denning MR in robust form.[6] Fourteen years later, the House of Lords emphatically and expressly overrules both *Dutton* and *Anns* in *Murphy v Brentwood DC*.[7] Nevertheless, *Anns* has more than historical interest: it offers a principled route to the enforceability of basic building standards in the civil courts, at the initiative of the party primarily hurt by their non-observance.[8]

Judgments from the higher courts of England are thus centre stage; but we include contrasts from Australasia, notably an illuminating coda to *Anns* and *Murphy* from Aotearoa New Zealand in 1996: *Invercargill City Council v Hamlin*.[9] In England & Wales there has of course been statutory intervention along the way – most recently the Building Safety Act 2022 (BSA) and specific fire-related measures.[10]

A post-Grenfell view, exemplified by the BSA, holds that we have done the essential if we respond adequately to the risk of danger from buildings – prevention as well as cure (but this chapter really addresses only cure). However, minimising danger is just one (key) aspect of a broader goal: quality in general. In construction, it cannot always be abstractly defined (like its obverse: 'defect'), often including subjective elements.[11] But in our field it surely includes compliance with:

- The relevant mandatory external standards at the time (for example, 'the building code').
- Whatever goals, specifications, or functional requirements are or were contractually in place for that project (including via terms included in a relevant contract, or implied into it by statute or case law).[12]

---

6 *Dutton v Bognor Regis UDC* [1972] 1 QB 373. Other House of Lords' cases in the same sequence include *Governors of the Peabody Donation Fund v Sir Lindsey Parkinson & Co Ltd* [1985] AC 210 and *D&F Estates v Church Commissioners for England* [1989] AC 177.

7 *Murphy v Brentwood DC* [1991] 1 AC 398 (CA and HL): the fourteenth use by the HL of its 1966 Practice Direction to depart from its own case law.

8 For analysis of the law's evolution in our field, see Peter Coulson, 'Keating Flagship Lecture: From Ronan Point to Grenfell: The Decline and Fall of Building Safety' (*Keating Chambers*, 28 March 2023) <https://www.keatingchambers.com/wp-content/uploads/2023/07/Keating-Chambers-Flagship-Lecture-Paper-From-Ronan-Point-to-Grenfell.pdf> accessed 20 November 2023.

9 *Invercargill City Council v Hamlin* [1996] AC 624, 78 BLR 78, 50 Con LR 105 (PC).

10 For the new fire safety regime, see the Fire Safety (England) Regulations 2022 (SI 2022/547), under the Regulatory Reform (Fire Safety) Order 2005 (SI 2005/1541), as modified by the Fire Safety Act 2021 and the BSA 2022, s 156 (both intended to apply also in Wales).

11 Even a construction employer's intended high standards may not translate into remedies for all perceived defects. In relation to a multi-million-pound Jersey mansion for Ian McGlinn (who made a fortune financing The Body Shop), Coulson J commented that the designers were to produce a 'high quality finished building (...) not (...) a perfect building', because 'a perfect standard of interior fitting and finish could only be provided by boat-fitting specialists, not construction contractors': *McGlinn v Waltham Contractors Ltd (No 3)* [2007] EWHC 149 (TCC), 111 Con LR 1 [192]. The 'reasonableness' test for damages in contract may similarly exclude compensation for 'defects' which do not constitute non-compliance with external standards: *Goodman-Jones v Hughey* [2023] NZHC 180.

12 The Consumer Rights Act 2015 imposes obligations on a trader entering a contract for services (in an off-plan home sale by a developer, construction services as the prelude to transfer of ownership) with an individual acting on their own account and not by way of trade, business, craft or profession (a consumer, in effect): Consumer Rights Act 2015 (CRA 2015), ss 2 and 49–52. The CRA 2015 offers specific remedies for breach of these B2C obligations: CRA 2015, ss 54–56. For B2B combustible cladding cases in England and Wales where

- Any other rules to which 'the builder' is committed: English examples would include standards in an industry-wide Code (the title of the most recent makes its aim clear: 'The New Homes Quality Code');[13] or technical standards adopted by a third-party warranty provider (insurer) with whom 'the builder' is registered.[14]

The background to *Anns*

The starting-point is utterly unremarkable – routine, even, in what look like hidden short cuts and cost savings. All this long before the phrases 'Value Management' and 'Value Engineering' were invented, then devalued in projects like the Grenfell Tower refurbishment.[15] The claimants – then still called plaintiffs, but respondents in the Lords – are a group of current long lessees of individual dwellings in a 1960s block of two-storey maisonettes in London SW19. A mixture of first and later purchasers are asserting that the block's foundations are not as deep as the plans indicated.[16] When internal damage appears in individual dwellings – note that word 'damage' – inspections must have pinpointed its probable source in the foundations, leading to the litigation. The homeowners' primary aim is an award of damages for the cost of rectification (not yet quantified). They are aiming at two defendants: the developer as builder (still owning the freehold, but not an active party in the Lords); and the current local authority, responsible for 'building control'.[17]

Time-travelling forwards, the Grenfell Tower fire shifts everyone's focus from structural inadequacy to combustible external cladding (or insulation). *Martlet Homes v Mulalley* is the first such case to reach judgment in the Technology and Construction Court (TCC).[18] It concerns a series of design-and-build refurbishment contracts under-

---

the contractual duty to comply with 'Statutory Requirements' led to liability for non-compliance with 'the building code', see (n 20).

13 On the NHQC, see the main text to (n 107). A developer who signs up to a sectoral Consumer Code may be required to incorporate the Code's build quality and other obligations into their contract with each buyer (off-plan or not), but not all Codes require formal incorporation. Public acknowledgment of membership of the Code, and a copy of the Code given to the buyer, may be enough contractually, as well as giving the consumer potential remedies under the EU-derived Consumer Protection from Unfair Trading Regulations 2008 (SI 2008/1277) (UK), whose para 5 (under conditions) treats failure to abide by a code of practice acknowledged by the trader as binding as a 'misleading action', hence unfair.

14 See e.g. the NHBC Standards (current edition valid from 1 January 2024): www.nhbc.co.uk.

15 David Churcher, 'RICS professional standards and guidance, UK. Value management and value engineering. 1st edition, January 2017' (*RICS*, 30 January 2017) <https://www.rics.org/profession-standards/rics -standards-and-guidance/sector-standards/construction-standards/black-book/value-management-and-value -engineering-1st-edition#:~:text=This%201st%20edition%20guidance%20note,manage%20value%20across %20the%20project> accessed 20 November 2023, contains a useful bibliography. See also the play text Richard Norton and Nicholas Kent, *Value Engineering: Scenes from the Grenfell Inquiry* (Methuen Drama, 2021). Their second play drawn from the Inquiry transcripts, *Grenfell: System Failure*, opened in London in 2023. See David Jays, 'Grenfell: System Failure review – sobering unpicking of a tragedy' (*The Guardian*, 24 February 2023) <https://www.theguardian.com/stage/2023/feb/24/grenfell-system-failure-review-sobering -unpicking-of-a-tragedy> accessed 20 November 2023. A third play, Gillian Slovo's *Grenfell: In the Words of Survivors*, ran at the Royal National Theatre in July–August 2023. See 'Grenfell: in the words of survivors' (*National Theatre*) <https://www.nationaltheatre.org.uk/productions/grenfell-in-the-words-of-survivors/> accessed 20 November 2023.

16 Second or later purchasers are, technically, assignees of the lease entered into by the first purchaser.

17 Following local government reorganisation, Merton by statute took on all the liabilities of Mitcham Borough Council, the local authority when the maisonettes were built.

18 *Martlet Homes Ltd v Mulalley & Co Ltd* [2022] EWHC 1813 (TCC).

taken in 2005–2008 by the defendant builder on 1960s residential blocks in Gosport. Alerted to the possible fire risk created by the blocks' exterior, the current owner is housing association Martlet Homes (part of Hyde Housing), successor to the original construction employer. It evidently has the resources (perhaps via insurance) to solve the problem 'on the ground' without needing court success first: a temporary 'Waking Watch' scheme, then rectification.[19]

In after-the-event litigation, Martlet Homes sues the builder in contract; the residents (many merely periodic tenants) must rely on their social landlord to protect them, as they have no legal link with any project party. The defects are initially described as resulting from inadequate installation; added mid-way – with the agreement of the Court of Appeal – is a claim that the cladding reflected specifications failing, as at Grenfell Tower, to meet the then current mandatory standards.[20] In 2022, Judge Stephen Davies holds the specifications non-compliant, awarding damages of about £8m (and costs on top) against Mulalley, for the 'Waking Watch' expenses, as well as for new cladding.[21]

Issue 1 in Anns: starting legal action in time?

Liability in *Anns* – if it can be reached – derives from what happened during the block's original construction, more than a decade before, so a key issue concerns the law of limitation. The homeowners in SW19 survive a challenge on this basis in the Lords;[22] however, later case law rethinks the English rules which define when a cause of action 'accrues', denying any role for the claimant's state of knowledge.[23] Combined with statutory rules defining fixed periods after 'accrual' – within which legal proceedings must be formally started – the result very effectively protects potential defendants (and the courts too) against 'stale claims'. It thus erects barriers against potential claimants who, long after construction occurred, discover facts which might justify a claim ('latent defects'),

---

19 For the Waking Watch Replacement Fund 2023 – £18.6m of Government funding for installing alarm systems in residential buildings which already have 'Waking Watch' in place – and a summary of earlier schemes, see Departmet for Levelling Up, Housing and Communities, 'Guidance. Waking Watch Replacement Fund 2023' (*GOV.UK*, 25 May 2023) <www.gov.uk/guidance/waking-watch-replacement-fund-2023> accessed 20 November 2023.

20 *Mulalley & Co Ltd v Martlet Homes Ltd* [2022] EWCA Civ 32, upholding Pepperall J at [2021] EWHC 296 (TCC). For a similar contract-based outcome against a specialist subcontractor, see *LDC (Portfolio One) Ltd v George Downing Construction Ltd* [2022] EWHC 3356 (TCC) at [40]ff (Veronique Buehrlen KC).

21 Had the judge upheld only the 'installation' head of claim, the damages awarded would have reflected the cost only of repairing, not replacing, the affected cladding, though the difference in money may have been small (final figures were not before the court); 'Waking Watch' costs would then have been excluded.

22 Their success comes from the Law Lords following *Sparham-Souter v Town & Country Developments (Essex) Ltd* [1976] 1 QB 858 (CA), where the court took a different approach to limitation from that in *Dutton* (n 6), later overruled by *Pirelli* (n 23).

23 On 'accrual', discoverability and latent defects, see *Pirelli General Cable Works Ltd v Oscar Faber & Partners* [1983] 2 AC 1 (HL); not followed by *Hamlin* (n 9), but re-examined by *URS v BDW* (n 4) at [68]ff. The main relevant statutory rules in our field are the current text of the Limitation Act 1980, ss 2, 5, 8 and 14A–B. On ss 14A–B, see (n 24); for the BSA changes to claims under the DPA, see (n 29) and its main text. 'Accrual' is also the normal point from which interest on the sum eventually awarded as damages will be calculated: see *Carton-Kelly v Darty Holdings SAS* [2022] EWHC 3234 (Ch). Where the parties are in a contractual relationship, it will often be in the claimant's interest to claim a concurrent duty of care in tort owed by the defendant, as a claim on this basis may be in time when one in contract would not, but the law is complex and not fully settled: see *Robinson v PE Jones (Contractors) Ltd* [2011] EWCA Civ 9, [2011] BLR 206, 134 Con LR 26, now *Sheffield Teaching Hospital Foundation Trust v Hadfield Healthcare Partnerships Ltd* [2023] EWHC 644 (TCC) [54]ff (O'Farrell J).

even where delay is in no way their fault. *Anns* takes place almost a decade before the Latent Damage Act 1986 (E&W) attempts to redress the balance, not in the long run doing much good.[24]

Time-limit issues can arise not just in relation to litigation but also for claim under a third-party (insurance-backed) warranty. Most policies in our field follow the UK market leader *Buildmark* from the National House-Building Council (NHBC), scaling down the level of protection dramatically at the end of Year 2 since construction work was completed. No third-party warranty offers redress in Years 3–10 equivalent to a usable right of action in court; and cover beyond the end of Year 10 is exceptional.[25] Claiming on insurance should be less onerous, costly and time-consuming than litigation. However, if a claim cannot be resolved amicably (or via the statutory free-to-access Financial Ombudsman Service), an insurer can prove a tenacious and well-resourced defendant.[26]

Limitation issues have inevitably been part of post-Grenfell legal manoeuvrings, under the pre-BSA law often meeting a procedural roadblock.[27] Even the successful cladding-related litigation in *Martlet v Mulalley* related to only four of the five blocks in Gosport: a claim deriving from the earliest refurbishment contract was timed out, though each contract took the form of a deed, enjoying a double-length 12-year limitation period.[28] The BSA introduces a 15-year limitation period for future defects-related claims under the Defective Premises Act (DPA) 1972 section 1; for such claims still potentially in existence when the Act came into force (28 June 2022), the period now extends backwards 30 years.[29] Individual homeowners may not easily benefit, continuing to suffer all the heavy disincentives against becoming a claimant in civil litigation. Even a commercial

---

24 The main provisions now are the Limitation Act 1980, s 14A–B and the Latent Damage Act 1986, s 3, on which see *Broster v Galliard Docklands Ltd* [2011] EWHC 1722 (TCC), [2011] BLR 569, 137 Con LR 26, applying *Payne v John Setchell Ltd* [2001] EWHC 457 (TCC), [2002] BLR 489, (2001) 3 TCLR 26. Coulson LJ in *URS v BDW* (n 4) summarised these changes at [108]: 'the Latent Damage Act did not reverse the decision in *Pirelli* [n 23] as to when the cause of action accrued; instead, the Act was based on the correctness of the decision in law, but sought to ameliorate its effect by extending the limitation period in certain circumstances.' For a post-Grenfell attempt to rely on s 14A, see *Vinci Construction UK Ltd v Eastwood and Partners (Consulting Engineers) Ltd* [2023] EWHC 1899 (TCC) at [54]ff (O'Farrell J). In 2001 the Law Commission made radical proposals for a shorter basic limitation period in contract and tort, moderated by a knowledge-based test: see n 114.

25 For more detail, see Britton and Bell (n 2) section 7.2. Since 2020, policies from Premier Guarantee include cover for inherent defects in machinery (e.g. water and space heating systems, but not for resulting fire or water damage) up to the end of Year 5. See 'Machinery Inherent Defects Insurance' (*Premier Guarantee*) <www.premierguarantee.com/midi> accessed 20 November 2023.

26 See e.g. the litigation against Zurich and its Approved Inspector subsidiary about the defects in New Lawrence House in Manchester: *Zagora Management Ltd v Zurich Insurance Plc* [2019] EWHC 140 (TCC), 182 Con LR 180; then *Manchikalapati v Zurich Insurance Plc* [2019] EWCA Civ 2163, [2020] BLR 1, discussed as Case Study 11 in Britton and Bell (n 2). The insurer asked the Supreme Court for permission to appeal, but the UKSC refused. Even when an insurer is not the named defendant, it can in effect take over the defence of its insured by exercising subrogation rights.

27 E.g. *Sportcity 4 Management Ltd v Countrywide Properties (UK) Ltd* [2020] EWHC 1591 (TCC), 192 Con LR 131.

28 *Martlet Homes Ltd v Mulalley & Co Ltd* (n 18). The 12-year period for deeds in English law comes from the Limitation Act 1980, s 8; the 2001 Law Commission proposals (n 114) would have abolished this rule, though allowing parties to a contract to choose a longer-than-normal limitation period. For a B2B construction project which had a contractual 12-year limitation period, without being executed as a deed, see *Children's Ark Partnerships Ltd v Kajima Construction Europe (UK) Ltd* [2022] EWHC 1595 (TCC).

29 BSA 2022, ss 135 and 151 (Scots law); on s 135 and the possibility of adding fresh claims under the Defective Premises Act 1972, s 1 to litigation already under way when retrospective changes in the limitation rules came into effect, see *URS v BDW* (n 4). For obligations under the DPA s 1, see n 95 and its main text.

or professional party may find difficulty assembling evidence about work completed long ago. The first case to be reported on the retrospective extension of the limitation period, *URS v BDW*, was about structural defects in over 500 flats and had four outings to court (including the Court of Appeal) on preliminary issues alone.[30] Negatively, these limitation changes may increase the future premiums those in construction must pay for PI cover.[31]

Issue 2 in Anns: a right of action?

In *Anns*, the main substantive law issue for the Law Lords concerns the claimants' assertion (challenged by the London Borough of Merton) that the local authority is responsible in law for its predecessor's potential negligence in operating the statutory system of building control when the block was built, which the current claimants had no realistic possibility of checking:

- 'Potential': Merton (as appellant) is asking the Lords to strike out this part of the claim as unsustainable in law, even if the plaintiffs can prove every fact they allege. This procedural context is identical to the case which launched the modern law of negligence more than 40 years earlier, *Donoghue v Stevenson* in the Lords.[32] Here too the key legal question was determined on assumed facts: that the bottle of ginger beer Mrs Donoghue drank in the Wellmeadow Café in Paisley contained parts of a decomposed snail, making her ill.
- 'Statutory system': at the time, the Public Health Act 1936 gives each local authority a power – but not a duty – to adopt its own byelaws regulating construction in its area. The statute does not expressly require, if the local authority adopts such byelaws, that they be enforced. This Act, like many others, also says nothing either positive or negative about the liability consequences of exercising such powers.
- 'No realistic possibility of checking': a would-be off-plan buyer who wants to inspect 'work in progress' would normally have no right to do so, ahead of completing on the purchase.[33] Once foundations are 'encapsulated', checking already becomes physically difficult: even first buyers may arrive on scene too late, and almost every second or later buyer would. So 'intermediate inspection' by any potential claimant may never be reasonable – perhaps impossible, just as the opaque glass bottle (crucially) prevented Mrs Donoghue from seeing its contents. For a new home, just as for such a drink, the ultimate consumer of the outcome of a technical process must rely on the competence of the maker, as well as of any organisation responsible for inspection.

---

30 *URS v BDW* (n 4).

31 The scope of available cover may now exclude future cladding-related claims, even for rectification work see David Stocks, 'News & Insights. Securing Professional Indemnity Cover for Cladding and Fire Safety' (*Gallagher*, 22 January 2021) <www.ajg.com/uk/news-and-insights/2021/january/professional-indemnity -cover-for-cladding> accessed 20 November 2023.

32 Donoghue v Stevenson [1932] AC 562.

33 A developer's power to refuse a request for a pre-completion inspection now has a modest exception, for developers signed up to the New Homes Quality Code (n 106). Its section 2.8 authorises a committed buyer to carry out a pre-completion inspection via an appointed representative, but only after the developer has given notice to complete on the purchase. Inspection under any other conditions still requires the developer's consent.

Anns: the significance of the context

The relevant legal framework, leading to 'the answer', comes from principles developed by judges, properly labelled 'the common law' – thus capable of evolution, even revolution, from time to time. The substantive issue is: how can one get from activities empowered by statute to the possibility of tort liability, if carried out negligently? The DPA 1972, implementing Law Commission proposals to impose minimum build quality obligations in relation to dwellings, was adopted only after the flats in *Anns* were completed, coming into force in 1974 with no retrospective effect.[34] In any event, in 2019 the Court of Appeal held that its key provision does not impose liability on building control bodies (either public or private), so could never have helped the homeowners in *Anns* against the local authority.[35]

Consider the claimants' options: none were ever construction employers in any real sense, having rights in contract – at best – only against the developer. Its failings could be the basis for a claim, but only by first buyers – breaches of its own standard-form sale contract, and then perhaps only for maisonettes sold off-plan, where caveat emptor ('let the buyer beware') would not operate. The claimant housing association in *Martlet v Mulalley* was not a construction employer either; but its predecessor seems to have assigned it the benefit of its construction contracts, on selling the blocks to Martlet Homes.[36]

Back in *Anns*, a first buyer could in theory have assigned their rights against the developer to those buying as second owner (and so on to third or later owners); but such assignments are rare in practice. The developer – still owning the freehold of the whole development in SW19, now as the landlord of each separate unit sold off – should arguably be the primary (perhaps only) defendant.[37] Even if enough homeowners are able to mount a claim in contract against a developer, the target defendant may be not worth suing or no longer exist (a Special Purpose Vehicle, liquidated on selling the freehold to a ground rent investor); or a contract claim may already be 'timed out'.[38] The local authority may therefore represent 'the last person standing': the only remaining chance, in fact as well as law, for a claim by all maisonette owners. None of them have any relevant contractual link with those operating building control, at the time of construction or after, and no statutory right of action against anyone, so the only claim they can make must be in tort.

In Australia, distinguished judges have said that in order to persuade the court to find a duty of care in tort against the perpetrator or enabler of defective building work, a

---

34 Law Commission, *Civil Liability of Vendors and Lessors for Defective Premises* (Law Com No 40, 1970) (not all the report's proposals were legislated); on the DPA coming into force, see DPA, s 7(2).

35 *The Lessees and Management Company of Herons Court v Heronslea Ltd* [2019] EWCA Civ 1423, [2019] 1 WLR 5849, upholding Waksman J at [2018] EWHC 3309 (TCC); but see also David Sawtell and Samantha Jones, 'Opening the Floodgates? Potential Parties to Claims under the Building Safety Act 2022' (*Society of Construction Law*, May 2023) <https://www.scl.org.uk/papers/opening-floodgates-potential-parties-claims-under-building-safety-act-2022> accessed 20 November 2023.

36 *Martlet Homes Ltd v Mulalley & Co Ltd* (n 18). In court, Mulalley (or perhaps its insurer) did not challenge Martlet Homes' right to bring legal proceedings.

37 Under the DPA 1972, s 3, the developer retains liability – if relevant – under s 1 (presumably also the new s 2A) after parting with ownership of the building; see also n 59.

38 The Insolvency Service reports that 4,160 companies active in construction (not all are developers, of course) went out of business in the UK in the calendar year 2022, the highest figure since 2008–2009. See The Insolvency Service, 'Insolvency Service Official Statistics' (*GOV.UK*, 14 July 2014) <www.gov.uk/government/collections/insolvency-service-official-statistics> accessed 20 November 2023. For new powers to 'pierce the corporate veil' under the BSA, aiming at SPVs, see the main text to n 104.

claimant may have to convince the court of their own vulnerability – meaning their inability to protect themselves by other routes, notably through contract (including insurance).[39] Such an approach has ideological purity and conceptual tidiness on its side, but a claimant may have no judicial remedy at all, if judges consider that meaningful alternative forms of protection were (or would have been) available.

How would this Australian 'vulnerability' test apply to the standard B2C English home purchase?

- Few developers will accept a buyer of a new home changing any of the clauses in their own (unpublished) standard form sale contract or long lease.
- No developer would normally agree to assign to an individual home buyer the benefit of any of the developer's own B2B construction contracts with a main contractor, designer or other original project parties (or equivalent collateral warranties).[40]
- A developer is not (yet) legally required to offer a third-party warranty with each new home sale (and the standard scope of cover for Years 3–10 is far narrower than their contractual obligations).[41]
- On selling an existing home, its current owner will normally refuse to warrant its build quality to a buyer, relying on caveat emptor ('let the buyer beware').

To refuse to recognise a tort claim where contract claims are so limited in scope is simply to narrow the scope of the law of negligence, directly limiting the pool of those who can recover for defects. Thankfully, English law has not adopted the Australian concern with 'vulnerability'.

Note that the claimants in *Anns* are targeting what we could label a secondary defendant. Their beef with the local authority is for an omission: that it culpably failed to protect them against what they say was the developer's inadequate execution of a structural part of the project.[42] They are in effect saying: 'To limit the risk of such problems, in the interests of society in general, we have statutory building control and entrust it to bodies

---

39 In *Woolcock Street Investments Pty Ltd v CDG Pty Ltd* [2004] HCA 16, 216 CLR 515, the High Court of Australia moved firmly away from *Anns*-type proximity towards the vulnerability of the plaintiff as potentially justifying imposing a duty of care in tort in relation to pure economic loss caused by construction defects. But at [94], the judgment of the plurality of the Justices holds: 'in all cases – not merely building cases (...) the capacity of a person to protect him or herself from damage by means of contractual obligations is merely one – although often a decisive – reason for rejecting the existence of a duty of care in tort in cases of pure economic loss'. Continuing at [96]: 'The first owners and subsequent purchasers of commercial premises are usually sophisticated and often wealthy investors who are advised by competent solicitors, accountants, architects, engineers and valuers. In the absence of evidence, this Court must assume that the first owner of commercial premises is able to bargain for contractual remedies against the builder. It must also assume that a subsequent purchaser is able to bargain for contractual warranties from the vendor of such premises'. These issues are revisited in *Brookfield Multiplex Ltd v Owners Corporation Strata Plan 61288* [2014] HCA 36 (2014) 254 CLR 185 and *Mallonland Pty Ltd v Advanta Seeds Pty Ltd* [2023] QCA 24. For a critique of the assumption that contractual protection is readily available, see Matthew Bell and Wayne Jocic, 'Negligence Claims by Subsequent Building Owners: Did the Life of Bryan End too Soon?' (2017) 41 *Melbourne University Law Review* 1, 21–23.

40 Unusually, collateral warranties directly with first purchasers or tenants featured in *URS v BDW* (n 4) at [6]–[7].

41 For the future possibility of such a requirement, see n 112 and its main text.

42 In *Dutton* (n 6), Lord Denning MR seemed to believe that a local authority would only rarely have to pick up part or all of the liability in a building defect case, as 'the builder' would be first in line: but the case itself, and Anns and Murphy in due course, together suggest otherwise.

independent of "the builder". It is meant to be an effective, though necessarily selective, last-chance safety-net; here, it failed.'

Liability, if imposed on the local authority, is for its own negligence in carrying out its statutory functions (we do not know what inspections, if any, it undertook during construction of the block). It cannot be vicariously liable for the developer's negligence (assuming this could be established), as there is no employment relationship (or equivalent) between them.

Housing defect claimants: other ways forward

At the limit, potential claimants may have three other possibilities, all in the news, in England and beyond, following Grenfell Tower:

1. An insurance claim – on the homeowner's own buildings insurance; or on a third-party warranty, which protects the current owner against defined categories of defects, on and after completion. In 2019 the NHBC changed its standard Buildmark wording, eliminating from future new policies the category of cover which would have responded to physical danger to inhabitants resulting from regulatory non-compliance.[43]
2. Government initiatives – offering cash, or mobilising developers and manufacturers of dangerous products to rectify or pay up. The first threats of legal proceedings against developers for failure to progress remediation on buildings in England were made in 2022. In Rt Hon Michael Gove's first period as Secretary of State, he boldly said: 'it is clearly unjust that innocent leaseholders should be landed with bills to remove cladding products from their buildings they had no reason to suspect were dangerous'.[44] This led to measures attempting to ensure that long leaseholders in residential blocks with combustible cladding or insulation are not left with the lion's share of costs, either for temporary protection or rectification. Hence forms of finance to assist with 'Waking Watch' schemes;[45] and with the costs of rectification (e.g. the Building Safety Fund, and a new Cladding Safety Scheme, opened for applications in July 2023). These taxpayer-funded initiatives will in future be reimbursed by a Building Safety Levy on developers, likely to be paid indirectly by new homebuyers. Alongside is Governmental pressure on developers to fund rectification work, in England but also in the other 'home nations'.[46] By November 2023, 56 developers had made

---

43 For an example where this category of cover, from a different insurer, was crucial in the success of the homeowners' claim, see n 26. For the possibility of a statutory requirement to offer a warranty, see n 112 and its main text.

44 Michael Gove, 'Letter from the DLUHC Secretary of State to the Construction Products Association' (*GOV.UK*, 23 January 2023) <https://www.gov.uk/government/publications/letter-from-the-dluhc-secretary-of -state-to-the-construction-products-association> accessed 20 November 2023.

45 See n 19.

46 In August 2023, the Northern Ireland Executive launched a £33m safety net fund for cladding remediation or mitigation in residential buildings of more than 11m tall; this appears to be close enough to the Cladding Safety Scheme to be administered by Homes England as part of the English scheme. Comparable but distinctly different initiatives are being pursued in Cardiff and Edinburgh for Wales and Scotland respectively. For Wales, see Mark Palmer, 'Plan to fix building fire safety defects in Wales announced' (*BBC News*, 21 March 2023) <https://www.bbc.co.uk/news/uk-wales-politics-64968810> accessed 20 November 2023. A Scottish Safer Buildings Accord is under development by the Scottish Government, where developers will give effect to

pledges exceeding £2bn, each taking effect via the 'Deed of Bilateral Contract' from the Department of Levelling Up, Communities and Housing (DLUHC). The 112 pages of non-negotiable remediation obligations cover more than cladding and potentially reach back 30 years from 4 April 2022; there are real sanctions.[47] No Ministerial finger has yet been publicly pointed at any building control bodies or warranty providers involved in the same projects.

3. Statutory intervention: its most recent form is the BSA 2022 (discussed elsewhere in this chapter), which imposes and regulates liability for past and future defects. It specially concerns residential buildings higher than our flats in SW19 and defects compromising safety, notably by posing a fire risk.[48] An *Anns*-type structural defect scenario, and liability for it, is not its central focus.

Grenfell Tower may have triggered all these changes, but with important factual differences from most case law discussed here:

- The tower was a local authority block, let mostly to periodic tenants (no stake in the capital value of their flat, or the block).[49]
- It was on any test a high-rise building.
- The project was one only of refurbishment, not new-build or extension.
- The central harm was the actualisation of the danger of fire.

As in *Anns*, or *Martlet v Mulalley*, Grenfell residents were in no sense construction employers, in fact or law. Evidence to the Grenfell Tower Inquiry shows how little input they had to the project's design, specifications, and implementation.[50] The result was not an unwelcome and unaffordable bill for rectification; instead, loss of possessions, injury and death of loved ones. The law (both criminal and civil) is more obviously on their side for such forms of harm than if they were now facing a rectification project and claiming

---

remediation needs identified via the Single Building Assessment programme, but a detailed contract is not yet in place. See Caroline Maciver and Lynda Ross, 'Burness Paull: Developers commit to Scottish Safer Building Accord' (*Scottish Housing News*, 8 June 2023) <www.scottishhousingnews.com/articles/burness-paull-developers-commit-to-scottish-safer-buildings-accord> accessed 20 November 2023.

47 If developers targeted by the DLUHC to join the Responsible Actors Scheme fail to commit to the Government's non-negotiable remediation contract, or to carry out the obligations they undertake, they will be excluded from essential legal steps under the building control and planning regimes for future projects in England: see the Building Safety (Responsible Actors Scheme and Prohibitions) Regulations 2023 (SI 2023/753), adopted under the BSA 2022, in force from 4 July 2023. By 11 August 2023, 14 developers or their holding companies were on the DLUHC list as members of the Scheme.

48 See e.g. the BSA 2022, Part 5 and its definitions of 'relevant building' in s 117 and 'relevant defect' in s 120 for the purposes of 'remediation'. For building control purposes, the definition of a 'higher-risk building' in the Building Act 1984, s 120D (inserted by the BSA, s 31) is expanded in the Higher-Risk Buildings (Descriptions and Supplementary Provisions) Regulations 2023 (SI 2023/275), in force in England & Wales from 6 April 2023.

49 Improving quality in social housing and the private rented sector in England – beyond the scope of this chapter – is equally on the DLUHC agenda, with the relationship between regulation, complaints handling and building quality subject to reform, notably via the Social Housing Regulation Bill (before Parliament in 2023).

50 *Value Engineering* (n 15) summarises the poor relations between residents and their direct landlord (the TMO), as well as with contractors during the refurbishment project, at 115ff. For a similar story see Peter Apps, *Show Me The Bodies: How We Let Grenfell Happen* (London, Oneworld, 2022) 173–188. The BSA 2022 newly mandates residents' involvement in building safety issues. See BSA 2022, ss 91–97.

its cost as damages.[51] Case law makes it easier to show a duty of care in relation to negligent construction, or supervision of construction, in relation to danger – more so, where physical injury or death have already occurred – than just in relation to defects without such consequences.[52]

To attach sources of mortal danger to the façade of a tower block surely prevents each flat meeting any standard of habitability; a landlord of a tower block also owes statutory duties under the Occupiers Liability Act 1957, which looks directly to safety. Successful claims by Grenfell Tower survivors against the Royal Borough of Kensington & Chelsea and its former Tenant Management Organisation illustrate the protective impact of these rules, with the refurbishment main contractor also in the frame.[53]

The legal issues in Anns

To get to the liability of the local authority in negligence, the claimants in *Anns* must surmount the 'duty of care' hurdle: a question of law embodying a concept which is 'exceptionally vague and blunt'.[54] A duty of care never exists in the abstract, but in relation to one or more categories of harm. If the judges find such a duty to exist, their definition of its scope must be broad enough to include the primary harm in the claim before them. If the claimants go on to show that the original local authority was at fault, Merton will be liable for any damages validly claimed. English law's principle of joint and several liability – shared with the law in New Zealand, though not Australia – will make Merton shoulder the risk that it cannot in practice shift any damages awarded against it to another party concurrently liable, by way of a claim for contribution.[55] Further, a judgment against any local authority is almost certain to be satisfied – not reliably so for any original project

---

51 For a construction-related claim arising out of personal injury or death, more generous limitation rules apply than for harm consisting only of property damage, drop in the capital value of a building or the cost of rectification. The Limitation Act 1980, s 11 lays down alternative start points, either accrual of the cause of action or (if later) the claimant's 'date of knowledge' (as defined), a three-year standard period applying. In such cases, but not generally, s 33 also gives the court a discretion to disregard the expiry of the limitation period: see cases summarised in *Chief Constable of Greater Manchester v Carroll* [2017] EWCA Civ 1992, [2018] 4 WLR 32, then *Gregory v HJ Haynes Ltd* [2020] EWHC 911 (Ch), *SKX v Manchester City Council* [2021] EWHC 782 (QB) and *Tyers v Aegis Defence Services* (BVI) Ltd [2023] EWHC 896 (KB).

52 Jackson LJ in *Robinson v PE Jones (Contractors) Ltd* (n 23) at [43] quotes Lord Bridge in *Murphy* (n 7) at 475E: 'If a builder erects a structure containing a latent defect which renders it dangerous to persons or property, he will be liable in tort for injury to persons or damage to property resulting from that dangerous defect. But if the defect becomes apparent before any injury or damage has been caused, the loss sustained by the building owner is purely economic. If the defect can be repaired at economic cost, that is the measure of the loss. If the building cannot be repaired, it may have to be abandoned as unfit for occupation and therefore valueless. These economic losses are recoverable if they flow from breach of a relevant contractual duty, but, here again, in the absence of a special relationship of proximity they are not recoverable in tort'.

53 *Abdel-Kader v Royal Borough of Kensington and Chelsea* [2022] EWHC 2006 (QB). 900 civil claims against a range of defendants were settled via ADR in 2023, details not being disclosed: see Ian Weinfass, 'Grenfell contractor contributes to £150m settlement' (*Construction News*, 14 April 2023) <https://www.con-structionnews.co.uk/health-and-safety/grenfell-contractor-and-cladding-firms-contribute-to-150m-settlement-14-04-2023/> accessed 20 November 2023; Neil Gerrard, 'Contractor [Rydon] pays out millions to settle civil claim after Grenfell Tower disaster' (*Construction Europe*, 6 July 2023) <https://www.construction-europe.com/news/contractor-pays-out-millions-to-settle-civil-claim-after-grenfell-tower-disaster/8030102.article> accessed 20 November 2023.

54 Basil S Markesinis and others, *Tortious Liability of Statutory Bodies* (Oxford, Hart Publishing, 1999) 44.

55 In a jurisdiction with a statutory proportionate liability regime, like all in Australia (but not NZ), the risk on the primary target defendant is automatically and intentionally reduced: for a cladding example from Victoria, see n 88.

party. But a 'deep pocket' never leads automatically to liability, though in *Dutton* Lord Denning was clearly tempted by this idea.[56]

So *Anns* raises two questions the Law Lords must resolve:

- Q1: What are the criteria for imposing a duty of care?
- Q2: Are the criteria satisfied in relation to this claim, about the statutory supervision of construction work?

This involves following, or not, the outcome and reasoning in *Dutton*. Here Saidee Dutton, second owner of a recently built new home on the south coast, shows that its internal walls do not comply with the local authority's byelaws; she argues that the authority negligently failed to notice this during construction. The Court of Appeal agrees, imposing liability on Bognor Regis council for the cost of rectification, minus the small amount Mrs Dutton had accepted from the original builder.[57]

Anns: the Law Lords' response

The first part of the test the Law Lords define as the answer to Q1 comes directly from *Donoghue v Stevenson*: is there proximity between the local authority and the respondents? Are they its neighbours, in law?[58] With this in mind, Q2 involves a more precise question: if the local authority fails to exercise an appropriate level of care, is it reasonably foreseeable that the building will not comply with the plans or the regulations, the cost of restoring it to its intended condition then falling on the leaseholders?[59] Answer: it clearly is – the statutory background defines and explains the local authority's role in the project. This leads to a finding of its proximity in law with anyone now owning one of the maisonettes.

English law has no general principle that proximity, plus negligence, equals liability. However, *Anns* elevates this almost into a presumption (sometimes called a 'prima facie' duty of care), adding an escape route as the second part of its answer to Q1: are there any factors here arguing against a duty of care, or in favour of a more limited duty?

In the case itself, one such factor might have been that the original developer owes no comparable duty of care: if so, how could or should the local authority incur tort liability? In line with *Dutton*, if we classify the defect as damage to the claimants' maisonettes, in turn creating a risk of injury, then the developer certainly does owe such a duty of care,

---

56 *Dutton* (n 6) 398A: 'They [the local authority] were entrusted by Parliament with the task of seeing that houses were properly built. They received public funds for the purpose. The very object was to protect purchasers and occupiers of houses. Yet they failed to protect them. Their shoulders are broad enough to bear the loss.'

57 Anecdotal evidence in 2011 from a Lord Justice of Appeal (now retired) suggests that Mrs Dutton did not use her damages to repair the foundations – which a winner in such a case is never required to do. However, when a Council inspector later saw the state of the house, he offered to pay for repairs, which were then done (in effect compensating her twice for the same loss).

58 *Donoghue v Stevenson* (n 32).

59 We do not know from the House of Lords speeches whether those individual unit owners who are first buyers are suing the developer-landlord in contract; nor whether any claimants are relying on the terms of their leases. It would be very rare for a lease of a unit in a block – usually drafted by or on behalf of the landlord in common form, and hence with little scope for negotiation by a would-be lessee – to impose any responsibility on the landlord for the state of the building, at the start or later. Usually, leases contain elaborate mechanisms (via a variable service charge) attempting to impose all rectification and maintenance costs on the lessees.

independent of contract and sounding in damages for the cost of rectification. That is how Lord Wilberforce defines its scope in the main speech in the Lords. No escape route here, then: we are in what Jackson LJ has labelled 'the heroic age of the law of negligence'.[60]

Following this success, the actual outcome for the claimants in *Anns* is not a matter of public record. Unless they settle with Merton (or perhaps its insurer), they must go to back to their first instance court – Judge Edgar Fay QC, one of the Queen's Bench Division's Official Referees (the TCC's predecessors)[61] – and prove the shortcomings in the building's foundations, the local authority's negligence, the cost of rectification and any other claimable heads of damages. We also do not know the fate of their parallel claim against the developer/freeholder.

A significant issue on remedies, which Judge Stephen Davies must resolve in *Martlet v Mulalley*, relates to the quantification of damages, once liability is established: what level and specification of rectification work is necessary (or perhaps reasonable), to deal with the defects as revealed? Within that head of damages, is temporary protection ('Waking Watch') against the demonstrable threat of fire properly claimable?[62] Even a claimant like Martlet Homes, urgently undertaking work to protect residents' safety, may later be faced in court with an argument that the scheme undertaken (or proposed) is unreasonable;[63] or that the original builder should have a chance to return and sort the problem: cheaper than now paying for a new construction team to do the same work.[64]

The defendant may also argue that the claimant has culpably 'failed to mitigate' their loss: if delay has unjustifiably inflated the cost of the work, the damages awarded may be less than those claimed.[65] The case law is exclusively contract-related, but comparable arguments could in theory also be made in a tort context. The claimants in *Anns* may face such issues after they win in the Lords, though delay caused by the defendants' preliminary legal issues (and the claimants' response) ought not to work against either party.

But the block of maisonettes is still there in SW19; and we do know what happened, in later litigation and critical commentary, to the principles Lord Wilberforce laid down: a counterblast of epic proportions.

---

60 *Robinson v PE Jones (Contractors) Ltd* (n 23) [72].

61 For background on Judge Fay, see Peter Coulson and David Sawtell, 'The Later Official Referees and Judges of the Technology and Construction Court' in Peter Coulson and David Sawtell (eds), *The History of the Technology and Construction Court on its 150th Anniversary* (Oxford, Hart, 2023) 98–99.

62 *Martlet v Mulalley* (n 18) [420]ff.

63 Joanna Smith J in *St James's Oncology SPC Ltd v Lendlease Construction (Europe) Ltd* [2022] EWHC 2504 (TCC) [315]: 'It is not an answer to a claimed remedial scheme to demonstrate that the defects could have been rectified through an alternative scheme at a lower cost (see *Struthers v Davies* [2022] EWHC 333 (TCC) at [29]). [The builder] must demonstrate that [the employer's] Proposed Remedial Works are unreasonable'. For further discussion, making the point that judges will not be overly critical of a claimant's choices when properly acting urgently or having to act on incomplete information, see Veronique Buehrlen KC in another cladding case, *LDC (Portfolio One) Ltd v George Downing Construction Ltd* (n 20) [82]ff.

64 *Woodlands Oak Ltd v Conwell* [2011] EWCA Civ 254, [2011] BLR 365 and *Mul v Hutton Construction Ltd* [2014] EWHC 1797 (TCC), [2014] BLR 529 [25] (Akenhead J); from Australia, see also *The Owners – Strata Plan 89041 v Galyan Pty Ltd* [2019] NSWSC 619 [21] (Stevenson J).

65 See Britton and Bell (n 1) section [4.12.2]. Similar rules about delay apply to claims under third-party warranties (*Buildmark* etc) for new homes.

The case law retreat

The setting for a reverse shift is a close reiteration of the facts in *Anns*, but about a free-hold home in leafy Essex; it too started before an Official Referee, this time Judge Esyr Lewis QC.[66] The statute is still the Public Health Act 1936, now joined by the DPA 1972. Does Brentwood District Council owe a duty of care to the purchaser (second owner) of a house with concrete slab foundations which were – allegedly – under-designed, producing a crack in the slab and movement of the house itself, with consequential damage? This happens thanks to the original negligence of the developer's designers, not picked up by the engineers to whom the Council subcontracted the reviewing of the plans. The claimant, Thomas Murphy, reduces the price he expects on selling the house: can he claim this difference from the Council?

In *Murphy v Brentwood*, an unusually large bench of seven Law Lords – all different from *Anns* – hear Brentwood's appeal against liability.[67] The judges reclassify the harm for which the claimants in *Anns* wanted compensation as 'pure economic loss' (a want of quality in the construction work, causing a need to spend on rectification, or a drop in the building's value, rather than damage to individual maisonettes).[68] As a result, with no parallel contractual link between claimant and defendant, the case at best fits in the special category of potential tort liability first recognised at House of Lords level in the 1960s by *Hedley Byrne v Heller & Partners*.[69]

The test for a duty of care in such a 'pure economic loss' situation still requires reasonable foreseeability of that type of harm; crucially, though, the defendant also needs to be in a 'special relationship' with the claimant(s) and those in a similar position, or to have (voluntarily) 'assumed responsibility' for the sequence of events which has led to the loss now claimed. Applied in *Murphy*, this treats the physical construction of buildings (actions or omissions) and the impact of defects on the value of such tangible things in the same way as providing information or advice (words) causing loss.[70] Does this really make sense?[71] Some scholars treat the outcome as necessarily correcting the *Anns* 'mistake'.[72] Others consider the Law Lords' fear of uncontrollably expanding circles of

---

66 *Murphy v Brentwood* (1988) 13 Con LR 96. For background on Judge Lewis, see Coulson & Sawtell (n 61) 103.

67 The Court of Appeal judgment is reported at [1990] 2 WLR 944. For further analysis of the litigation, see Coulson and Sawtell (n 61) 335–338.

68 *Murphy v Brentwood* (n 7). For an extract from Lord Bridge's speech in the case, see n 52.

69 *Hedley Byrne v Heller & Partners* [1964] AC 465.

70 Later 'apex court' cases in this 'information and advice' stream include *Caparo Industries Plc v Dickman* [1990] 2 AC 605 (an influential but not decisive 'three-stage test'); *X v Bedfordshire County Council* [1995] 2 AC 633; *Marc Rich & Co AG v Bishop Rock Marine Co Ltd* [1996] AC 211; and *Barrett v London Borough of Enfield* [2001] 2 AC 550, with *Steel v NRAM Ltd* [2018] UKSC 13, [2018] 1 WLR 1190 as the most recent instalment.

71 Green and Davies (n 1) argue at 53: 'the common law should recognise a dichotomy between (i) genuine pure economic loss cases, such as those in the *Hedley Byrne* line, in which no physical thing has been affected, and (ii) physical defect cases, which are concerned with tangible things, the value of which has been reduced by a defendant's negligence.'

72 See e.g. Robert Stevens, 'Torts' in Louis Blom-Cooper, Brice Dickson and Gavin Drewry (eds), *The Judicial House of Lords 1876–2009* (Oxford, OUP, 2009). In *Robinson v Jones* (n 52) [92], Stanley Burnton LJ described *Anns* in the light of *Murphy* as 'aberrant, indeed as heretical'.

liability simply inappropriate in our field, leading as it does to circumscribing tightly the acknowledgment and extent of a duty of care.[73]

This redefinition process crystallises in a question: did Mr Murphy, the current claimant, reasonably rely on Brentwood not to be negligent?[74] Certainly not, say the Law Lords, eagerly overruling both *Dutton* and *Anns* but hardly engaging with the policy consequences of depriving such claimants of any right of action. In turn, cases in other fields based on the *Anns* 'two-stage test' become unreliable, a more cautious 'incremental approach' to duties of care starting to dominate.[75] The conclusion in *Murphy* is supported by the limited 'dwellings' scope of the DPA, not relied on as an independent head of claim but in effect relieving the judges from attempting to find a common law route to redress.[76] The 1972 Act does not justify the courts in recognising a wider principle of liability, applicable to all buildings and their owners. Counsel for Mr Murphy would have accepted a duty of care owed only 'where there is an occupier of a dwelling house who is a successor in title to the developer or building owner'.[77] That too the Law Lords reject, so *Murphy* closes the door firmly against almost all claims in negligence by homeowners against building control bodies, for the cost of rectification or the drop in value caused by the home's non-compliance with mandatory construction standards.[78]

In the thirty-plus years since *Murphy*, there has been no serious head-on challenge in court to this new orthodoxy. There is copious recent case law at appeal court level on how to get from a statutory scheme to a common law duty of care, but in relation to other categories of harm.[79] No cases directly concern rectifying defects in homes or other buildings, or redress for the resulting drop in their capital value.

In 1996 comes *Invercargill v Hamlin*.[80] Here the Judicial Committee of the Privy Council offers support for those who always preferred the outcome and reasoning in *Anns* to that of *Murphy*, or who thought it ought to be easier for claimants to satisfy the *Hedley Byrne* tests. It upholds the judgment of the NZ Court of Appeal in Wellington, which has awarded damages to Noel Hamlin against the City of Invercargill for the cost of rebuilding his bungalow's foundations.[81] The municipal building inspectors culpably failed to notice the actual depth – only about half what the plans and byelaws required. Later on, in a flood of 'leaky building' litigation, the NZ Supreme Court holds – more broadly – that statutory

---

73 Green and Davies (n 1) at 57: 'there is no danger of a floodgates problem arising where loss is related (howsoever it is classified) to physical property'.

74 In *Hedley Byrne* itself, reliance was not reasonable, nor had responsibility had been assumed, as the advice came with a disclaimer of liability: the Lords held that no duty came into existence. For a comparable Australian case in relation to a product, see *Mallonland Pty Ltd v Advanta Seeds Pty Ltd* (n 39).

75 For analysis of these case law shifts of direction in relation to duties of care, see *Royal Bank of Scotland International Ltd v JP SPC 4* [2022] UKPC 18, [2022] 3 WLR 261 [50]ff (the judgment of the Court), following *Robinson v Chief Constable of West Yorkshire Police* [2018] UKSC 4 [21]ff (Lord Reed).

76 See further *The Lessees and Management Company of Herons Court v Heronslea Ltd* (n 35).

77 *Murphy v Brentwood DC* (n 7) 450A.

78 But not necessarily in deceit, if the facts support such a claim: see the New Lawrence House litigation (n 26).

79 See e.g. *Poole BC v GN* [2019] UKSC 25, [2020] AC 780 [25]ff (Lord Reed) and *HXA v Surrey CC* [2022] EWCA Civ 1196 [33]ff (Baker LJ). For a comparable discussion in Australia, in the context of physical damage caused by fire, see *Electricity Networks Corporation v Herridge Parties* [2022] HCA 37 [19]ff.

80 *Hamlin* (n 9).

81 *Invercargill City Council v Hamlin* [1994] 3 NZLR 513, 72 BLR 39; upholding the finding of liability in *Hamlin v Bruce Stirling Ltd* [1993] 1 NZLR 374 and reaffirming *Bowen v Paramount Builders (Hamilton) Ltd* [1977] 1 NZLR 394 (NZCA).

building control is for the benefit of (all) building owners and users.[82] Where negligence results in a building being non-compliant, the person or body responsible owes a duty of care, measured by the cost of making the building compliant or the drop in its value.[83] The continuing attachment in the Land of the Long White Cloud to *Anns v Merton* trumps any judicial anxiety about indeterminate circles of liability.

Balance sheet: English law

The evidence strongly suggests that the current English (and Scots) version of the common law fails many homeowners. It impacts most clearly on those who have – for whatever reason – no right of action in contract and whose homes when first sold would have been in breach of the terms of any developer's construct-and-transfer off-plan sale contract, or remain in breach of the mandatory external standards at the time of construction. We acknowledge the intellectual and analytical force of the post-*Murphy* judicial rethink; but the result is an unfilled legal gap, making any promise to consumers of enforceable basic construction standards a hollow boast, even as the new Building Safety Regulator arrives on the scene. The BSR and the linked new fire safety regime are intended to transform the landscape of prevention, not just at the time of construction but also during the life of most multi-unit domestic buildings.[84] The BSA adds new possibilities for cure if – or rather when – prevention fails, but in very specific and narrowly focussed ways, discussed below.

The inadequacy of English law becomes clearer on looking at kinder and more protective ('liberal') regimes Down Under. As noted, the common law in New Zealand has a generous concept of duties of care in tort in construction.[85] By contrast, Australian law adopts a narrow view of construction situations giving rise to a duty of care in relation to defects, close to post-*Murphy* English law.[86] But this matters less than it might, because all states and territories impose a set of mandatory contractual obligations on 'the builder' in residential situations, most also controlling in detail the form and substance of those contracts (and all jurisdictions except Western Australia include baseline 'statutory warranties' as to quality), as well as imposing elaborate occupational licensing regimes on most construction activities.[87]

---

82 'A temperate, rain-prone nation which hitherto had done well by building gabled, weatherboard houses, turned misguidedly instead to Mediterranean-style dwellings, made with a "monolithic construction" method involving plastered walls, flat or curved roofs and no eaves to speak of. The result was a sprouting of mould, litigation funders and lawsuits.' Stephen Kós and Dina Qiu, 'Parallel Universes: The Curious Dearth of Trans-Tasman Citation' [2023] NZLRev 61, 75.

83 *North Shore City Council v Body Corporate 188529 (Sunset Terraces) and Body Corporate 189855 (Byron Avenue)* [2010] NZSC 158, [2011] 2 NZLR 289; also *Body Corporate 207624 v North Shore City Council (Spencer on Byron)* [2012] NZSC 83, [2013] 2 NZLR 297.

84 On the BSR, see the BSA 2022, Part 2; for the new fire safety regime, see n 10.

85 For *Invercargill v Hamlin*, see the main text to n 80.

86 The Law Lords in *Murphy* referred approvingly to *Council of the Shire of Sutherland v Heyman* (1985) 157 CLR 424, where the High Court of Australia (Brennan J giving the single judgment) refused to follow the *Anns* two-stage approach to identify situations where a duty of care was owed in a statutory context. On the Australian approach, see also n 39 and n 79.

87 The main statutory sources for the contractual obligations imposed on those undertaking residential construction are: (ACT) Building Act 2004 and Building (General) Regulation 2008; (NSW) Home Building Act 1989; (NT) Building Act 1993 and Building Regulations 1993; (Qld) Queensland Building and Construction Commission Act 1991; (SA) Building Work Contractors Act 1995; (Tas) Residential Building Work Contracts

Further, every Australian jurisdiction (except WA) transmits by law the benefit of these 'statutory warranties' (in a contractual, not insurance, sense) to the current building owner(s), who can rely on them to start legal action within a special limitation period (often a fixed 10 years). The litigation following Melbourne's 2014 Lacrosse tower cladding fire illustrates how straightforwardly, under such a regime, a homeowner can recover what English tort law would class as 'pure economic loss'. A proportion of the total recoverable damages was awarded against the developer's private sector building inspector, exercising statutory inspection and certification powers by reference to 'the building code' during construction.[88] It is no accident that the Law Lords in *Murphy* thought the prospect of a 'transmissible warranty of quality' a compelling reason against recognising a duty of care in tort between builder and homeowner in relation to defects which are no longer (if ever) latent and which cause no personal injury, nor any damage to personal or real property other than the building itself.[89] To impose liability on a building control body in such a situation was self-evidently unjustified.

Does statutory intervention help?[90] Most recently, the BSA 2022 has extended the scope of the DPA 1972, whose main obligations originally applied only to anyone who takes on 'work for or in connection with the provision of a dwelling' (i.e., a complete dwelling) in England & Wales, by construction or conversion.[91] Who might 'take on work', and with what functions, is not defined anywhere in the statute.[92] For work not yet completed once the main provisions of the BSA came into force (28 June 2022), the new section 2A applies the same obligations to any person who by way of business takes on 'work in relation to any part of a relevant building' (i.e., containing one or more dwellings, with no

---

and Dispute Resolution Act 2016 and Residential Building Work Contracts and Dispute Resolution Regulations 2016; (Vic) Domestic Building Contracts Act 1995 and Domestic Building Contracts Regulations 2017; (WA) Home Building Contracts Act 1991 and Home Building Contracts Regulations 1992. NSW is part-way through a significant process of upgrading the regulation of construction, including significantly retrospectively extending by statute the obligations and liability of those involved, with interventionist figurehead Building Commissioner David Chandler OAM.

88 *Owners Corporation No 1 of PS613436T v LU Simon Builders Pty Ltd* [2019] VCAT 286, appealed as *Tanah Merah Vic Pty v Owners Corporation No 1 of PS613436T* [2021] VSCA 72 and 122. Aotearoa New Zealand adopted a different but comparable statutory regime for residential construction contracts (as defined) in 2015, though without Victoria's proportional liability provisions: Building Amendment Act 2015, inserting Part 4A into the Building Act 2004.

89 Lord Keith in *Murphy* at 469A: 'if such a duty [as accepted in Anns] is incumbent upon the local authority, a similar duty must necessarily be incumbent also upon the builder of the house. If the builder of the house is to be so subject, there can be no grounds in logic or in principle for not extending liability upon like grounds to the manufacturer of a chattel. That would open up an exceedingly wide field of claims, involving the introduction of something in the nature of a transmissible warranty of quality'. Or like Lord Buckmaster, dissenting in *Donoghue v Stevenson* (n 32) at 577: 'If such a duty [of care towards the ultimate consumer of goods which cause injury] exists, it seems to me it must cover the construction of every article, and I cannot see any reason why it should not apply to the construction of a house. If one step, why not fifty? Yet if a house be, as it sometimes is, negligently built, and in consequence of that negligence the ceiling falls and injures the occupier or any one else, no action against the builder exists according to the English law' (probably no longer true, even after *Murphy*).

90 For detailed analysis of the liability changes in the BSA 2022, see Sawtell and Jones (n 35).

91 DPA 1972, s 1(1), but a developer who merely organises work to be done by others is caught by s 1(4); see also n 35 and its main text. On who can claim under the DPA s 1, see n 4.

92 But the Court of Appeal in *The Lessees and Management Company of Herons Court* (n 35) apparently approved Waksman J's view at first instance that 'taking on work' in the context of s 1(1) covers only those who are part of the project team, contributing to the physical coming into being of a new dwelling; *URS v BDW* (n 4) confirms that it includes professionals carrying out design functions, perhaps also those who supervise (other than independent building control bodies exercising statutory powers).

height threshold).[93] Works of extension, refurbishment and perhaps even routine building maintenance are now captured, including to 'the common parts' of multi-unit residential developments.[94]

On the positive side, this 'DPA+' regime moves closer towards Australia's transmissible statutory warranties, similarly benefitting the owner for the time being of a dwelling. Unlike some Australian regimes, a project does not have to meet a minimum cost or price test. However, the threefold obligations which these sections of the DPA impose on anyone caught within its net by 'taking on work' are more open-textured and more limited, as currently interpreted by the judges, than any Australian statute.[95] The DPA may well catch safety-critical defects, at least where created by project parties; but it may often be difficult to show non-compliance with 'the building code', given its ambiguity and the status of its linked 'guidance'. Like the original DPA rules, the new provisions use neither contract nor tort terminology. As the case law shows, a duty so defined makes possible awards of damages for what in tort terms would be 'pure economic loss'.[96]

Further statutory innovations

Two key elements in the updated DPA regime discussed above reappear in the BSA as ingredients of a completely new right of action, imposing civil liability in both English and Scots law for construction products, in favour of the dwelling's owner, or the building's owner if it contains two or more dwellings.[97] The shape of this widely drawn section 148, followed by an almost identically worded section 149 specifically about past defaults relating to cladding, clearly targets events like those leading to the Grenfell Tower fire. Each looks to failure to comply with the requirements linked to a relevant construction product via regulations; making a misleading statement when marketing or supplying such a product, then 'installed in, or applied or attached to a relevant building';[98] or manufacturing an inherently defective such product, causing 'a relevant building' to be 'unfit for habitation'. The statute expressly clarifies that a successful claim under either head can lead to damages for 'personal injury, damage to property or economic loss' (the first time that 'economic loss' has appeared in a UK statute?);[99] neither right of action can be

---

93 The wording of the new s 2A seems to permit an argument that these duties are broad enough to encompass building control bodies as 'taking on work' in a residential refurbishment project, in contrast to their role in new build under the DPA, s 1(1) and to the reasoning in *Lessees and Management Company of Herons Court v Heronslea Ltd* (n 35). However, it would be very odd if a project under s 2A could impose liability, when one under s 1 does not.

94 BSA 2022, s 134, inserting s 2A into the DPA; s 2A(7) expressly extends the new duty to subcontractors, but s 2 cannot be relied on if s 1 applies, so a claimant must decide whether the work is 'provision' under s 1, or just 'work' under s 2A. A 15-year limitation period applies, though with no retrospective effect.

95 'to see that the work which he takes on is done in a workmanlike or, as the case may be, professional manner, with proper materials and so that as regards that work the dwelling will be fit for habitation when completed'. In the new s 2A, 'which he takes on' is omitted and 'will be' is replaced by 'is'. The judges have treated lack of habitability as having to be shown in every case; but for a generous approach to this part of the test in relation to a recently completed multi-unit residential development and the liability of the design and build main contractor, see *Rendlesham Estates Plc v Barr Ltd* [2014] EWHC 3968 (TCC).

96 See e.g. *Rendlesham Estates v Barr* (n 95).

97 BSA 2022, ss 147–150. Sawtell and Jones (n 35) note how little explanation accompanied the insertion of many of the new liability rules in the BSA 2022, at a late stage in the Parliamentary process.

98 BSA 2022, s 148(3). The equivalent cladding definition in s 149(3) is 'attached to, or included in, the external wall of a relevant building'.

99 BSA 2022, s 148(6).

bargained away by contract.[100] Special retrospective limitation rules potentially authorise legal action under these sections against actions or omissions up to 30 years ago, as under aspects of the DPA.[101]

The Government has undertaken to activate the Building Act 1984 section 38 (presumably for the future only), the BSA in advance extending this provision's standard limitation period to 15 years forwards (as for the DPA).[102] This appears a positive move: the section applies to construction in general, giving a right of action in situations where a 'breach of a duty imposed by building regulations' has caused harm. The duties the new Building Safety Regulator will impose on project participants (and residents) relating to building safety and the building control process may give this section extra 'bite', but the BSA itself does not go so far. It is unclear whether duties imposed directly by the BSA itself or by – rather than under – the now heavily modified Building Act 1984 will count as 'imposed by building regulations'.[103] This leaves the position of those operating building control uncertain; other unresolved issues include what categories of harm fit within this section: its own definition of 'damage' includes physical injury and death, but what about damage to property or 'pure economic loss'? And can section 38 be used to ask for an injunction to prevent anticipated 'damage' being suffered which would give rise to a claim under the same provisions? There are no definitive answers yet.

The liability of a body corporate under the DPA or the Building Act 1984 section 38 now potentially extends to other bodies corporate (like companies linked to the Special Purpose Vehicle which was the nominal developer). The BSA gives the High Court a discretion to 'pierce the corporate veil' and make a building liability order, shifting liability in relation to building safety risks (as defined) to that 'associate' company (even if already dissolved) or limited liability partnership.[104]

Even in this transformed legal landscape, many homeowners seeking judicial remedies for defects in UK homes will remain the poor relations of their equivalents Down Under, as well as of most other consumers of construction. Commercial players as building owners more reliably have contractual rights of action against project parties: directly or via assignment from the original employer (*Martlet v Mulalley* again); via third-party rights (expressly or by implication); or in some cases by project participants giving assignable collateral warranties, which usually in turn require PI cover for the potential liability undertaken.[105] Such players may also have retentions or rights of recourse under bonds or parent company guarantees. Together, these devices fill most of the gap left by *Murphy v Brentwood* (though seldom against a negligent building control body). Anyone in a position to use them is likely to be supported by established routes to professional and legal advice.

Even if homeowners had, or could use, additional rights of action in relation to defects, many would still be first-time litigants, taking aim at well-resourced 'repeat players'.

---

100 BSA 2022, s 148(7). Regulations are expected to clarify how claims can be brought and the meaning of key definitions.

101 BSA 2022, ss 150 (England & Wales) and 151 (Scotland); for the limitation of actions under the DPA, see the main text to (n 29).

102 Although the BSA, s 135 suggests that s 38 is already in force, this is not yet so (at the time of writing). Early versions of the Building Safety Bill would have repealed s 38!

103 The 1984 Act defines 'building regulations' in s 1(2).

104 BSA 2022, s 130; 'associate' is defined by s 131, as is a wide timeframe in which 'association' may have taken place. For more details, see Sawtell and Jones (n 35) 13ff.

105 *Martlet Homes Ltd v Mulalley & Co Ltd* (n 18).

Transcending their own vulnerability would remain for many – as now – too great a struggle, notably to find skilled and affordable professional assistance and representation. In multi-unit developments, the task first requires a residents' action group capable of mobilising effectively, ready organisationally and financially – if necessary – to engage lawyers and at least to threaten litigation.

Possible futures: rights

What of the 'and beyond' in our title? The BSA, once fully in operation, ought to raise construction quality generally, notably by improving the impact, quality and reliability of the building control function nationally, in both private and public sector contexts. Proof of success – if coupled with changes in culture in the industry – would be that the sorts of residential problems that led to the situations discussed above occur less often.

Part 5 of the 2022 Act also includes two sets of provisions looking specifically to reform of future new home sales:[106]

1. The BSA permits a set of enforceable obligations to be imposed on all developers of new homes via a registration requirement and a Code of Practice in relation to the sales process, build quality and remedies offered, with free access to a new ombudsman service for the first two years (only) after a home's first sale, if a complaint to the developer does not resolve the problem.[107] In 2021, Government encouraged the formation of the New Homes Quality Board (NHQB), which in turn has registered more than 200 developers; they are signing up to the New Homes Quality Code (NHQC), publicly launched in London, Edinburgh and Cardiff in November 2022 with support from the then Housing Minister. The New Homes Ombudsman Service (NHOS) is already open for business, resolving complaints by homeowners against developers under the new Code.[108]

   But all this quasi-official activity has (so far) no statutory backing, operating on a contractual (voluntary) basis only, in competition with existing sectoral Consumer Codes, each sponsored by one or more third-party warranty providers and including its own independent dispute resolution service.[109] Of these,

---

106 Philip Britton, 'New Home Sales, Defects and Insurance in the UK: The Building Safety Act 2022 and after' (2022) 38 Const LJ 355; a revised and updated version of that article is available on LinkedIn.

107 BSA 2022, ss 136–143 and schs 9–10. The proposals give effect to many of the key ideas in All Party Parliamentary Group for Excellence in the Built Environment, 'Better redress for homebuyers. How a New Homes Ombudsman could help drive up standards in housebuilding and improve consumer rights' (*CIC*, June 2018) <https://www.cic.org.uk/uploads/files/old/appg-ebenew-homes-ombudsman-report-2018.pdf> accessed 20 November 2023.

108 Its first decision (anonymised) was published in July 2023; regrettably, only summaries of future decisions will be published on its website: www.nhos.org.uk. The full text of decisions will be communicated only to developers registered with the NHQB.

109 The CCHB scheme offers an Independent Dispute Resolution Scheme run by the Centre for Effective Dispute Resolution (CEDR). The 2021 Annual Report from CEDR records that 307 cases were referred to it, with 46% resolved fully or partly in favour of the home buyer; 13% settled before being formally referred to a scheme adjudicator. The substance of those complaints going to adjudication was overwhelmingly about the sales process and a developer's system for handling complaints, rather than about unresolved defects as such (though failure to respond adequately to build quality complaints may be counted as a problem with the complaints system). Complainants overall claimed more than ten times in compensation than the scheme in the end awarded them. Of all cases decided by an adjudicator, under half of all awards were formally accepted by the complainant (binding the complainant and putting an obligation on the builder to give effect to the award, backed by potential sanctions

the Consumer Code for Home Builders (CCHB) has operated for more than ten years, going through five editions; a revised Code entered force in January 2024. It is supported by the NHBC with its *Buildmark* policy, which explains the CCHB claim to cover 95% of all new home sales.[110] Like other warranty providers, the NHBC now permits its registered developers to shift to the NHQC and NHOS, as equivalent in obligations and consumer protection.[111]

2. Other powers in the BSA could be used to require every future new home to have the benefit of a qualifying 15-year insurance-backed warranty, during its construction and on first sale.[112] But the present Government has made no commitment to activate this possibility. It is not certain that all current UK warranty providers could obtain insurance (or re-insurance) beyond the current 10-year norm. To impose such a requirement – for a period half as long again, potentially also requiring a higher minimum level of cover – raises fears of destabilising the whole market.

Moving forward under the BSA may be delayed by responses to the market study into housebuilding by the Competition and Markets Authority, published in 2024.[113] But the ideal regime for residential construction would go further:

- Adequately defining quality obligations, protecting every homeowner for at least ten years since the completion of construction work, but providing access to redress for late-revealed latent defects, provided the homeowner has acted reasonably.[114]
- Introducing accessible methods of enforcing these obligations (not initially requiring litigation or significant upfront expense) against those responsible.
- Enforcement including reliable and effective remedies, available to the current homeowner.

---

from its warranty provider); not to accept an award leaves the complainant free to pursue other avenues of redress. For summaries of each case, see 'What is the Code and why is it important to me?' (*Consumer Code for Home Builders*) <www.consumercode.co.uk/home-buyers> accessed 20 November 2023.

110 The CCHB is supported by three other warranty providers: Premier Guarantee, LABC Warranty and Checkmate.

111 See e.g. 'Codes of Practice: Rules of Registration Update' (*Premier Guarantee*, 24 November 2022) <https://www.premierguarantee.com/insite/codes-of-practice-rules-of-registration-update/> accessed 20 November 2023; 'Changes to new-build consumer codes that may affect you' (*LABC*, 30 November 2022) <https://www.labcwarranty.co.uk/news-blog/changes-to-new-build-consumer-codes-that-may-affect-you> accessed 20 November 2023. The NHBC website includes links to both the CCHB and the new Code. See 'Consumer Codes' (*NHBC*) <https://www.nhbc.co.uk/homeowners/consumer-code> accessed 20 November 2023.

112 BSA 2022, ss 144–145 (added to the Bill at a late stage, with no warning), in force from 6 April 2023: the Building Safety Act 2022 (Commencement No 4 and Transitional Provisions) Regulations 2023 (SI 2023/362). These provisions echo All Party Parliamentary Group for Excellence in the Built Environment, 'More homes, fewer complains. Report from the Commission of Inquiry into the quality and workmanship of new housing in England' (*CIC*, July 2016) <https://www.cic.org.uk/uploads/files/old/more-homes.-fewer-complaints.pdf> accessed 20 November 2023, Recommendation 6.

113 Competition and Markets Authority, 'Housebuilding Market Study: Final Report' (GOV.UK, 26 February 2024) <https://assets.publishing.service.gov.uk/media/65d8baed6efa83001ddcc5cd/Housebuilding_market_study_final_report.pdf> accessed 12 April 2024.

114 The Law Commission proposed as the normal start point for time running 'the date of knowledge of the relevant facts', including 'constructive knowledge', which the claimant would acquire, for example, if they unreasonably failed to consult an expert. For the period within which proceedings must be started, all actions for damages in contract or tort would have a three-year basic period from this newly defined start date, with a 10-year longstop from the date the cause of action accrued and some closely defined exceptions and extensions. See Law Commission, *Limitation of Actions* (Law Com No 270, 2001). These proposals have never been close to implementation.

- Guaranteeing by law – at least in most situations, but perhaps with financial minima and maxima – the ability of a target defendant to satisfy an Ombudsman award or court judgment, or to pay for rectification (greater protection than under any current third-party warranty).

A simple redrafting of section 1 (and now 2A as well) of the DPA could achieve the first key objective above: imposing wider and more specific obligations, closer to those in the Australian regimes, looking to compliance with 'the building code'. These would apply specifically to those with statutory building control responsibilities; the newly extended limitation periods would of course be preserved.[115]

Any reform must make proper provision for multi-unit developments using long lease-hold structures. It must recognise the special difficulties of long leaseholders in multi-unit developments mobilising in relation to 'building safety risks' – especially in 'the common parts' of the building.[116] Any response must solve the Grenfell-type difficulty of reconciling the fair funding of such repairs by landlords and third parties with each lease's text. The BSA contains elaborate provisions attempting to address this, an 'interested person' having power to apply to the First-Tier Tribunal for a remediation order (against a landlord) and a remediation contribution order (against a landlord, developer or linked entity), as well as restricting service charges. The detail is beyond our scope, but leaseholders are starting to use these new possibilities.[117]

Curtailing long leasehold in favour of a relaunched and improved version of commonhold tenure for new multi-unit developments – as the Law Commission proposed in 2020 – would also assist significantly, especially if on handover the law imposed continuing liability on original project parties for original construction defects.[118] Any reform should also include easier and cheaper ways for existing unit owners to buy out their landlord interest collectively, transitioning to commonhold: Law Commission proposals for this are on the table too, but the DLUHC's initial championing of such changes seems much diluted.[119]

---

115 See the main text to (n 29).

116 'Building safety risk' is part of the definition of 'a relevant defect' in the BSA 2022, s 120. For the buildings covered, see s 117 (a wider definition than for other provisions of the Act, which apply only to residential buildings of more than 18m in height).

117 BSA 2022, ss 121–124 and sch 8, discussed by Sawtell and Jones (n 90) 16ff; see also the Building Safety (Leaseholder Protections) (England) Regulations 2022 (SI 2022/711), amended by the Building Safety (Leaseholder Protections) (England) (Amendment) Regulations 2023 (SI 2023/126) and by a second set of Regulations with the same title (in draft form in July 2023); and the Building Safety (Leaseholder Protections) (Information etc) (England) Regulations 2022 (SI 2022/859). The first reported decision on s 124 appears to be *Batish v Inspired Sutton Ltd* in January 2023 from the First-Tier Tribunal Property Chamber (Residential Property) (LON/00BF/HYI/2022/0002). Leaseholders who had to pay part of the costs of the fire-related remediation work on their development via service charges were granted orders against their freeholder for these costs. Other leaseholder groups are claiming under s 123. See 'Leaseholders take legal action against building owners over fire safety issues' (*FPA*, 2 March 2023) <https://www.thefpa.co.uk/news/leaseholders-take-legal-action-against-building-owners-over-fire-safety-issues#:~:text=Leaseholders%20filed%20the%20legal%20action,the%20issues%20at%20the%20building> accessed 20 November 2023.

118 Wendy Wilson and Cassie Barton, 'Leasehold and commonhold reform' (*House of Commons Library*, 22 September 2023) <https://commonslibrary.parliament.uk/research-briefings/cbp-8047/> accessed 20 November 2023. This summarises the proposals up to that date and Governments' reactions.

119 Law Commission, *Leasehold home ownership: buying your freehold or extending your lease* (Law Com No 392, 2020); Law Commission, *Leasehold home ownership: buying your freehold or extending your lease: Report on options to reduce the price payable* (Law Com No 387, 2020). On 20 February 2023 Rt Hon Michael Gove MP, Secretary of State, said: 'We need to end this feudal form of tenure and ensure individuals

Possible futures: remedies

Making effective remedies properly available is a harder nut to crack – already better achieved (but not always ideally) in those Australian jurisdictions which allocate 'residential construction' disputes to mandatory forms of State-run mediation or to specialist statutory tribunals.[120] In the UK context, Part II of the Housing Grants, Construction and Regeneration Act 1996 makes 'quick and dirty' statutory adjudication available as of right where there is a 'dispute or difference' between parties to a construction contract (as defined), with tight timescales and the resulting decision presumptively enforceable.[121] But the HGCRA contains a 'residential occupier exception', where statutory adjudication is unavailable as of right.[122]

Suggestions surface regularly to scrap this exception.[123] Some consumers might like being able to insist on this form of ADR against a 'builder', but the exception primarily protects them against adjudications by 'builders'; this risk would increase if the exception were removed. Where at present a situation falls within the 'residential occupier exception', nothing stops an individual consumer agreeing an adjudication clause in the contract with their 'builder', though they could in theory argue that such a term is unfair (unlikely to succeed).[124] Nor is a consumer protected against finding themselves the responding party in an *ad hoc* adjudication launched by the builder, unaware that they could resist this form of ADR (and challenge the jurisdiction of the adjudicator) as neither within the statute, nor contractually agreed.[125] When they fail to object to the adjudication and do not pay the amount the adjudicator awards the builder, they next find themselves in the TCC with a judgment against them for the same sum, additionally owing the builder's litigation costs, usually on the indemnity basis.[126] No comfort to learn that they can separately start litigation to get back what they must now pay.

An alternative would require every referring party or Adjudicator Nominating Body to send a prescribed notice to each responding party, explaining the scope and timescales of statutory adjudication and warning them of the need to protect their position before the adjudicator, including taking legal advice if necessary. There are models for such a

---

have the right to enjoy their own property fully'. But on 10 May 2023, Kiran Stacey reported in The Guardian: 'Plans to abolish 'feudal' leasehold system in England and Wales dropped'. On 24 July 2023, the Secretary of State said: 'We want to ensure that those who have paid for their home by acquiring a leasehold can finally truly own their own home by becoming free of an outdated feudal regime which has been holding them back. So we will continue action on exploitative ground rents, expand leaseholder' ability to enfranchise – and to take back control from distant freeholders. We will reduce punitive legal service charges, reduce insurance costs – and improve transparency. Some of these changes are in the Leasehold and Freehold Reform Bill.

120 On the use of both approaches in Victoria, see Britton and Bell (n 1) section [9.9].

121 For the key definitions, see the HGCRA 1996, ss 104–105 and 108(1).

122 HGCRA 1996, s 106. S 106(3) allows the Secretary of State to modify the definition of 'a construction contract with a residential occupier' in s 106(2), but s 106A (added in 2011) gives power to disapply any of the provisions of Part II to any description of construction contract (but seemingly not to repeal the whole of s 106).

123 See e.g., Renato Nazzini and Aleksander Kalisz, *2022 Construction Adjudication in the UK: Tracing Trends and Guiding Reform* (*King's College London*, 3 November 2022) <https://doi.org/10.18742/pub01-160> accessed 20 November 2022.

124 For a Scottish example, see *AGB Scotland Ltd v McDermott* [2023] CSOH 31. No challenges to the fairness of a contractual adjudication clause in a B2C construction contract fitting within the 'residential occupier exception' appear to have reached the courts. For the relevant law, see Britton and Bell (n 1) sections [4.10] and [9.7].

125 As in *ICCT Ltd v Pinto* [2019] EWHC 2134 (TCC).

126 Philip Britton, 'Adjudication and the "Residential Occupier Exception": Time for a Rethink?' (*The Society of Construction Law*, May 2015) <https://www.scl.org.uk/papers/adjudication-and-%25E2%2580 %2598residential-occupier-exclusion%25E2%2580%2599-time-rethink> accessed 20 November 2023. For costs in an adjudication enforcement application, see *J&B Hopkins Ltd v A&V Building Solution Ltd* [2023] EWHC 1483 (TCC).

statutory notice, notably in New Zealand, whose adjudication regime as a result no longer contains special procedural protections for residential occupiers.[127]

Far better in our view to activate Part 5 of the BSA: impose a Code and Ombudsman by law, free to access by the homeowner, determinations by the NHOS becoming enforceable as judgments. But real progress would go further:

- Extend the ambit of the Code to all those undertaking significant works of residential construction (not just new home sales or builds, but perhaps with a minimum job value threshold).
- Give the Ombudsman a realistic upper limit for its compensation awards (higher than the £75,000 with which the NHOS is starting out).
- Offer a generous maximum time between completion of the work and the homeowner making a complaint, with flexibility about latent defects.
- Make this form of redress linked to solvency requirements (or PI cover obligations) on all those – registered developers and other 'builders' – included within the Ombudsman scheme.

However, neither the HGCRA nor any of these proposals will help a homebuyer procedurally, if they have no claim in contract, under a third-party warranty or under a statutory Code, against their target defendant. Here litigation remains the default.

And finally...

It seems unrealistic to imagine a version of *Anns* ever rising again out of oblivion; or the related ideas in *Hamlin* gaining traction in English law. However, our judges might one day conclude that the ultimate consumers of building control services are in a 'special relationship' with those supplying those services, reasonably relying on all of them not to be negligent. Grenfell Tower survivors already feel in an unwantedly close relationship with all those (including the Royal Borough's building control service) who had a hand in enabling the disaster. But could the key common law part of *Murphy* be overturned without reimposing the possibility of tort liability for any construction activities which have led to a defective building?

The recent legislative response in the BSA will discourage judicial activism, looking as it does to fill gaps left by the common law. These are primarily in relation to safety, except for the changes to the more wide-ranging DPA. It is to further initiatives in Parliament, as well as the implementation of provisions already adopted, that we should look to arm homeowners with comprehensive rights and remedies in relation to construction quality more generally.

As Shakespeare shows in 'Hamlet', when dawn approaches, ghosts melt away, taking their unwelcome messages with them. However, bear in mind that, on stage, the part of Hamlet's father in Acts I and III is often doubled with the cynical and sardonic First

---

127 Construction Contracts Act 2002 (NZ), s 28(3), added by the Construction Contracts Amendment Act 2015 (NZ). The text of the information is Form 2, as laid down in the Construction Contracts Regulations 2003, reg 5 (as amended). Failure to include this makes the notice of adjudication of no effect, though the claimant may start again, if they then follow the correct procedure. See Construction Contracts Act 2002 (NZ), s 31A(3).

Gravedigger in Act V: he is no more likely than Old Hamlet to look positively on the current state of English law in our field.

Acknowledgments

Thanks go to Dr Matthew Bell, Associate Professor and Co-Director of Studies, Construction Law, Melbourne Law School, for reviewing an early draft. For insightful analysis of the tort topics in this chapter, see Sarah Green and Paul S Davies, '"Pure Economic Loss" and Defective Buildings' in Andrew Robertson and Michael Tilbury (eds), *Divergences in Private Law* (Oxford, Hart Publishing 2016).

CHAPTER 9

Building regulations in England

A history of lurching from crisis to crisis

Abdul-Lateef Jinadu and Sam Grimley

In England, local government responsibility for building control stretches back to the twelf12th century.[1] The earliest building regulations are associated with Henry Fitz-Ailwyn, the first mayor of London:[2]

Fitz-Ailwyn's Assize of Buildings of Allaying Contentions as to Assizes of Buildings

> In the year of our Lord 1189, in the first year, namely, of the reign of the illustrious King Richard, Henry Fitz-Ailwyn being then Mayor, it was by the more discreet men of the city thus provided and ordained for the allaying of the contentions that at times arise between neighbours in the city touching boundaries made, or to be made, between the lands and other things; to the end that, according to the provisions they made and ordained, such contentions might be allayed.

It seems that, as long ago as the 12th century, neighbours have been arguing about whose responsibility it is to fix the garden fence!

However, the impetus for building regulation has not always been so mundane. At 52 minutes past midnight, on 14 June 2017, a fire broke out on the fourth floor of Grenfell Tower in Kensington, West London. The fire was started by an electrical fault in a refrigerator. It spread rapidly, and soon engulfed the 24-story building. Seventy-two people died, and 70 people were injured. It was the worst residential fire in the UK since World War II.

Earlier this year, the Building Safety Act 2022 was enacted. It represents the most radical shakeup of building regulations for almost 40 years. But for the residents of Grenfell, the Building Safety Act came too late. In the history of building regulation, this story is all-too-familiar. The foundation stone of modern building regulation is tragedy; and not just its foundation, but its four walls; its stairwells and ceilings. Tragedy has shaped, and continues to shape, the buildings we live, work, and congregate in.

Tragedy, however, has not been the only force bearing down on building regulation. Two other factors have played a hand in its development: cost and control. Who gets to say what happens; and who has to pay for it?

This paper will trace three broad eras in the history of building regulation. First, it will examine the very earliest history of building regulation. It will be argued that, from

---

1 Anthony J Ley, 'Building Control UK – An Historical Review' (CIB T5 Performance Based Buildings and Regulatory Systems) <https://www.irbnet.de/daten/iconda/CIB9498.pdf> accessed 20 November 2023.

2 Clifford C Knowles and PH Pitt, *The History of Building Regulation in London 1189 – 1972* (London: Architectural Press 1972) 6.

DOI: 10.4324/9781032663975-13

the outset, the impetus for change has been disaster, followed by piecemeal legislation. Second, this paper will consider the seismic shift in building regulation under Thatcher's government in the mid 1980s. It will uncover a pattern of continual deregulation – giving priority to cost reduction and autonomy over safety protections. Finally, it will survey the recent changes brought in by the Building Safety Act 2022. It will ask whether these changes properly address the shortcomings in the preceding regime highlighted by the tragedy at Grenfell Tower.

The Great Fire of London

Modern building regulation began in the aftermath of the Great Fire of London. The fire started in the early hours of the morning on Sunday, 2 September 1666. It was hot, dry, and windy – ideal conditions for fire to spread.[3] A spark shot out from the oven of the King's Baker, Thomas Farriner, and ignited fuel lying nearby. The fire burned for almost five days. It incinerated 13,000 wooden houses, 87 churches and St Paul's Cathedral. 85% of London was destroyed. Many Londoners sought refuge in the fields beyond the city's boundaries, remaining there for extended periods – often for months or even years – until they felt the danger had receded.[4]

If the Great Fire of London was caused by a spark, it was spread by chaos. London at that time was a sprawl of tightly packed wooden buildings. Once the fire started, it was unstoppable.

The London Building Act 1667

Parliament decided to act. In 1667, it passed the London Building Act. The Act required all houses to be built from brick or stone; it meticulously specified the number of stories, and the width of the walls. Streets had to be widened. The Act set guidelines for the construction of load-bearing walls, the establishment of foundations, the use of timber in shared walls, spacing of joists, support of beams, roofing materials, and the installation of gutters and down-pipes. The Act provided for surveyors to enforce the regulations. Anyone erecting a building in contravention of the regulations was guilty of a criminal offence – the building would be condemned and destroyed.[5]

Ultimately, however, the provisions of the Act proved to be weak. When the three surveyors, tasked with overseeing the implementation, died, or resigned, they were not replaced. Eventually, the 1667 Act was replaced by the Acts of 1772 and 1774. The legislature had learned a key lesson: if building regulations were to be effective, they had to be adequately enforced.[6]

---

3 'The Great Fire of London' (*The Monument*) <https://www.themonument.org.uk/great-fire-london-faqs> accessed 20 November 2023.

4 ibid.

5 Helen Carr 'Grenfell Tower and the failure of building and fire safety regulations' (2017) 20(5) JHL 2017 110, 110.

6 Ley (n 1).

Regional Acts

Following the London Building Acts, building regulations started to spring up around the country. In 1788, the City of Bristol introduced a Building Act, modelled on the provisions of the London Acts. In 1825, the City of Liverpool introduced 'An Act for the better regulation of Buildings in the Town of Liverpool'. The target of the Act, however, was not fire, but disease. Between 1801 and 1830, Liverpool had doubled in size to accommodate an influx of Irish immigrants. The congested residential developments were thought to have contributed to outbreaks of typhoid, typhus, and tuberculosis. The Act regulated drainage, the building of chimneys, party walls, and provided for surveyors 'skilled in the art of buildings'.[7]

By the mid 19th century, a patchwork of local byelaws had emerged across England and Wales. However, provision was inconsistent – many local authorities made no attempt to regulate building safety. Two factors held back the introduction of building regulations: cost (they were too expensive to comply with), and control (they stifled autonomy).

Cholera – the first attempt to secure a national regulatory scheme

In October 1831, a ship carrying cargo and sailors from Bengal docked in Sunderland. Shortly afterwards, William Sproat, a keelman, died of cholera. From Sunderland, cholera rapidly made its way north to Scotland, and south to London. The disease knew no boundaries. It affected towns and rural communities; rich and poor alike. By the time it had run its course, it had claimed over 52,000 lives. A report by the Poor Law Commissioners recommended sanitary measures to control the spread of disease in the form of building regulations.[8]

Many now considered building regulation a national problem demanding a national solution. In 1841, a Bill was placed before Parliament designed to replicate the provisions of the London and Bristol Building Acts on a national scale. The Act's provisions would be available for adoption by all urban districts and major towns.[9]

But the Bill failed. Two countervailing forces appear to have led to its demise: cost and control. On the one hand, it was resisted by builders, who saw it as a threat to their profits. On the other hand, it was viewed as unwelcome interference with regional autonomy by local authorities. The complex patchwork of local byelaws was retained, and by 1936 as many as 60 local authorities still had no building regulation at all.[10]

Public Health Act 1936

A further attempt to introduce a nationwide system of building regulation was attempted by the Public Health Act of 1936. The Act required all local authorities to adopt building byelaws by 1939. However, when 1939 finally arrived, the British Government had become preoccupied with another, far more ominous, threat. After the war, many feared that the introduction of building regulations would impede urgent rebuilding and

---

7 ibid.
8 ibid.
9 ibid.
10 ibid.

re-housing programs. The scheme was revisited in 1953, but its adoption by local authorities remained discretionary.[11]

More tragedy leading to piecemeal legislation

During the 20th century, some nationwide building safety legislation was introduced. However, these regulations affected only particular types of buildings, or guarded against specific dangers. In each case, tragedy provided the impetus for change.

Factories

The Factories Act 1937 required fire escape routes for workplaces with over 40 employees. However, a tragic 1956 fire at Eastwood Mills, Keighley, which killed eight, prompted an expansive review. The 1961 Factories Act, which followed, included rules governing the installation of fire alarms, and enhanced requirements for the provision of adequate means of escape.[12]

Shops and offices

In June 1960, a fire devastated the William Henderson & Sons store in Liverpool. Despite the prompt arrival of the fire brigade, ten people died after becoming trapped on the fourth floor. Another man perished while trying to rescue those trapped in the blaze. A subsequent report concluded that the rapid spread of the fire was caused by suspended ceilings and un-enclosed escalators. In the wake of this tragedy, the 1963 Offices, Shops and Railway Premises Act was amended to include new fire safety measures. The clauses drew heavily on the wording of the 1961 Factories Act.[13]

The Fire Precautions Act 1971

On Boxing Day 1969, a fire at the Rose and Crown Hotel in Saffron Walden resulted in 11 fatalities. The hotel lacked alarms, fire doors, or emergency exits – the fire brigade used ladders to rescue 17 people. The blaze at the Rose and Crown was one of several hotel fires that lead to the passing of the 1971 Fire Precautions Act. Beginning in 1972, hotels and boarding houses became subject to stringent certification requirements.[14]

The Public Health Act of 1961

The Public Health Act of 1961, for the first time, gave the Minister for Housing and Local Government the power to make national regulations. The Act repealed the power of local authorities to make local building byelaws. The first national Building Regulations were issued in 1965. The Regulations were highly prescriptive – they contained rules and standards that had to be followed. However, this approach was to last less than 20 years. The

---

11 ibid.

12 'History of Fire Safety Legislation' (*Fire Safety Advice Centre*) <https://www.firesafe.org.uk/history-of-fire-safety-legislation/> accessed 20 November 2023.

13 ibid.

14 ibid; Daniela Nadj, 'Deregulation, the Absence of the Law and the Grenfell Tower Fire' (2019) 5(2) QMHRR 1.

Building Act of 1984, passed during Margaret Thatcher's deregulatory drive, introduced a radically different approach to building regulation.

The 1984 Building Act

In December 1979, Michael Heseltine, who was the Secretary of State for the Environment at the time, delivered a speech to the National House Building Council. He began:

> I want to speak to you about a field in which we can take constructive action. It is important for this industry, and it needs attention. I am speaking about the system of Building Control; does it serve us well enough; does it address itself to the right objectives, and if not, how can it be improved?[15]

Heseltine argued that a new system of building regulation was required. One that was characterised by 'maximum self-regulation, minimum government interference'. The new regulation, Heseltine proposed, should be totally self-financing, and simple in operation. The new scheme should have two main consequences: slashing cost to government, and decentralising control.

The speech was to mark a watershed in the history of building regulation. The changes that followed were radical and far-reaching. In 1981, Heseltine introduced a white paper to Parliament titled 'The Future of Building Control in England and Wales'. Subsequently, he proposed legislation that partly transitioned building control to private certifiers. The Building Act, enacted in 1984, was the first comprehensive primary legislation for building regulations in England and Wales.[16]

The Building Regulations 1985 were introduced under the Act in the following year. The updated rules adopted a 'performance-based' approach. Instead of providing specific directives or enumerating prohibited materials (as the 1965 Building Regulations had done), these rules specified the general results that buildings should meet. It was left to industry to work out how these standards were to be met. Existing regulatory guidance was cut down from 306 pages to just 24.[17] Importantly, the monitoring and implementation of building safety standards was taken out of the hands of local government and given over to private certifiers.

Approved Document B

The story of Approved Document B is one of progressive deregulation, decentralisation, and, ultimately, disaster. The story of Approved Document B is the story of Grenfell.

In the new regulatory scheme, building requirements were set out in 'Approved Documents'. If these standards were met, no one could be held legally liable for problems

---

15 Michael Heseltine, Speech at the Annual Dinner of the National House Building Council (December 1979).

16 'The Grenfell Tower Fire: A Crime Caused by Profit and Deregulation' (*Fire Brigades Union*, 23 September 2019) <https://www.fbu.org.uk/publications/grenfell-tower-fire-crime-caused-profit-and-deregulation> accessed 20 November 2023, p 16.

17 Peter Apps, 'The Paper Trail: the Failure of Building Regulations' (*Inside Housing*, 23 March 2018) <https://www.insidehousing.co.uk/news/news/the-paper-trail-the-failure-of-building-regulations-55445> accessed 20 November 2023.

that might ensue. But these standards were not technical, they were 'performance-based'. Performance-based regulations created uncertainty.

A paragraph at the beginning of each of the Approved Documents explains their purpose:

> The Approved Documents are intended to provide guidance for some of the more common building situations. However, there may well be alternative ways of achieving compliance with the requirements. Thus *there is no obligation to adopt any particular solution contained in an Approved Document if you prefer to meet the relevant requirement in some other way.*[18] (Emphasis added)

Approved Document B set out standards relating to fire safety. It was revised in 1992, 2000, and 2006. With each iteration, the safety standards governing external fire spread became progressively weaker.

ADB 1985 – Class 0

ADB 1985 stipulated that external cladding products should be of 'limited combustibility'. Section A13 and table A6 of Schedule A provided that 'Class 0' materials met this standard. However, according to the Fire Brigade's Union:

> Class 0 material is not equivalent to a material of limited combustibility. A material of limited combustibility is usually a material that is either totally non-combustible or one that contains a small amount of combustible material. Combustible materials, such as plastics, are not materials of limited combustibility. They can achieve Class 0 performance by adding fire retardants or covering them with metal foil. A combustible material can therefore achieve a Class 0 rating as defined by the regulations, yet still be added to a building while being a fire hazard.[19]

ABD 1992

In 1992, the 'limited combustibility' standard was also applied to insulation.

ABD 2000

Astonishingly, after a deadly blaze at Garnock Court in Irvine, Scotland, in 1999, there was a marked weakening of the 'limited combustibility' standard. The fire at Garnock Court should have served as a warning about the risks associated with flammable cladding. It did not. The blaze ravaged apartments across nine of the building's 14 levels, leading to the death of a 55-year-old disabled man, and injuries to five others, one of whom was 15 months old. Flammable composite window panels had allowed the fire to spread – the building was engulfed in roughly 10 minutes.[20]

The multi-party Environment, Transport, and Regional Affairs Committee conducted a parliamentary inquiry into the fire. The Inquiry heard evidence from the Building Research Establishment ('BRE'), the body responsible for designing and implementing fire safety tests. However, a few years earlier, the BRE had been privatised. It was now charging manufacturers £15,000 to carry out fire safety tests at its laboratory in Watford – the only suitably equipped facilities in the UK. Arguably, this created a conflict of interest

---

18 E.g., HM Government, *The Building Regulations 2010 Fire Safety: Approved Document B* (Crown Copyright 2022).
19 'The Grenfell Tower Fire: A Crime Caused by Profit and Deregulation' (n 16) p 17.
20 Apps (n 17).

for the BRE: it was under a duty to offer guidance to ministers, but also had a commercial interest in testing materials for manufacturers.[21]

The BRE had developed a new test: one that allowed large-scale testing of external cladding products. The Garnock Court Inquiry conducted a review of Approved Document B, and adopted the BRE's new large-scale test – Fire Note 9 (later BS 8414) – as an alternative path to compliance. The test consisted of constructing a nine-meter-tall wall in a 'burn hall' and igniting a fire below it. BRE treated the results of these tests as 'commercially confidential', disclosing them only if the manufacturer consented. Thus, it was the manufacturer – not BRE – that decided whether to release test results.[22]

As well as introducing a new route for compliance, the ADB 2000 introduced further changes to the 'limited combustibility' standard for insulation, requiring it only for ventilated cavities.[23] Following Garnock Court, Scotland took a different approach. From 2005 onwards, Scottish building regulations mandated that cladding and insulation on high-rise residential structures either be completely non-flammable or undergo a comprehensive fire assessment. Following the Grenfell incident, 300 residential high-rises in England were identified as covered with potentially hazardous cladding, whereas in Scotland, no such buildings were found.[24]

ADB 2006

By 2003, talks had already began about revising the 2000 Approved Document B. Environmental issues, particularly climate change, had started to dominate the political agenda. In 1997, the UK had signed up to the Kyoto Agreement, pledging to cut carbon emissions;[25] and in 2002, the EU issued a new European Directive of Energy Performance of Buildings. Under the Directive, member states were obliged to enhance the energy efficiency of old and new buildings, principally by improving standards of insulation. However, flame retardant insulation materials were prohibitively expensive – millions of buildings needed to be insulated. Subsequently, the building regulations were relaxed to allow cost-effective combustible insulation to be used.[26]

ADB 2006 made two key changes. First, it expanded the use of the alternative 'test route' to compliance for insulation as well as external surfaces. Limited combustibility was no longer a requirement even for insulation in ventilated cavities. Second, it made a subtle change to the wording of the test route requirement: 'large-scale test' was replaced with 'full-scale test data'. This change appears to have opened the door to the use of 'desktop study' tests.[27]

What are desktop studies and why are they controversial?

The idea of desktop studies emerged from a private consultation conducted by the BRE. Representatives from combustible cladding and insulation sectors had argued that it would

---

21 ibid.
22 ibid.
23 'The Grenfell Tower Fire: A Crime Caused by Profit and Deregulation' (n 16) p 17.
24 Apps (n 17).
25 ibid.
26 Nadj (n 14).
27 Apps (n 17).

not be practical to require all material combinations to be tested. Consequently, desktop studies were proposed as a cost-effective solution: materials that had already passed BRE tests could be subject to a theoretical analysis in order to ascertain whether a new combination of materials would pass if they were tested.[28]

In 2014, the use of desktop studies was approved by the Building Control Alliance (BCA) – an industry group representing organisations involved in building control. Initially, the BCA recommended that only UKAS-accredited laboratories carry out desktop studies; however, this requirement was rapidly downgraded to a recommendation that 'a suitably qualified fire specialist' conduct them. No definition of 'suitable qualifications' was provided by the BCA.[29] At present, there is no restriction on who can carry out desktop studies, and no requirement that the reports or methodology are made public.[30]

In the same year, Celotex's RS5000, the insulation used on Grenfell Tower, was approved in a desktop study. However, RS5000 was analysed when combined with cement fibre cladding – a much less combustible type of cladding than that used on Grenfell. Strikingly, the manufacturer, Celotex, revealed in January 2018 that it had 'inaccurately described' the result of the desk top study in its marketing. The precise details of the misrepresentation remain unclear.[31]

ADB 2010

At 4:20pm on 3 July 2009 a fire broke out at Lakanal House in Camberwell, south London. It should have precipitated a radical reappraisal of fire safety regulation. It did not. The fire was started by an electrical fault in a television. Within minutes, a cladding panel on the exterior of the building caught fire. The blaze rapidly engulfed the tower block. Ultimately, six people died, including two children and a three-week-old baby. The rapid spread of the fire was facilitated, in part, by window panels that failed to meet the Class 0 standard.[32]

Her Honour Judge Frances Kirkham, the Coroner overseeing the Lakanal House Inquest, recommended a review of Approved Document B. She described it as 'a most difficult document to use'. Further, an All-Party Parliamentary Group on Fire Safety sent numerous letters to ministers calling for a review. The Committee requested a return to regulations which required one hour fire resistance for the external walls of buildings, and for clarification of Approved Document B. However, more than three years after the Coroner's report, no attempt had been made to review ADB. The housing minister at the time, Gavin Barwell, explained to Parliament that: '[w]e have not set out any formal plans to review the building regulations as a whole, but we have publicly committed ourselves to reviewing Part B following the Lakanal House fire'.[33] The review never took place.

---

28 ibid.
29 Nadj (n 14).
30 Apps (n 17).
31 ibid.
32 ibid.
33 ibid.

Other deregulation

The weak enforcement of building standards under the Building Act 1984, and subsequent regulations, has been part of a broader trend towards deregulation. The drive to deregulate began under the Conservative governments of the 1980s and continued apace under New Labour in the late 1990s and 2000s. Tony Blair founded the Better Regulation Task Force; giving it a mandate to 'reduce unnecessary regulatory and administrative burdens' on businesses. Government departments were tasked with simplifying or abolishing regulation in their areas of competence.[34]

The Regulatory Reform (Fire Safety) Order 2005

A key innovation, introduced by New Labour, was The Regulatory Reform (Fire Safety) Order 2005. The primary goal of the Order was to unify the current fire safety laws into one comprehensive piece of legislation. The Order brought about two key changes. First, fire certificates – which had enabled fire authorities to raise safety standards – were scrapped. A new risk-assessment approach was adopted. Second, the responsibility for ensuring these risk-assessments took place was left in the hands of a 'responsible person' – usually the person in control of the premises. The risk assessment had to be carried out by a 'competent person' with 'sufficient training and experience or knowledge and other qualities' to conduct it. In effect, the requirement for oversight by a trained fire safety professional was abandoned, and fire safety assessments became poorly monitored.[35]

The 2010s

The Cutting Red Tape initiative was launched by the Cabinet Office soon after the Coalition Government came to power in 2010. The business secretary at the time, Vince Cable, chaired the Committee. He proclaimed: '[t]his coalition has a clear new year's resolution: to kill off the health and safety culture for good'.

The coalition introduced a 'one in, one out' rule – which required a regulation to be removed whenever a new one was introduced. In 2016, soon after David Cameron's Conservative majority government came to power, this target was increased to 'one in, three out'.[36]

The Hackitt Report

In 2017, Dame Judith Hackitt, in her interim report into the Grenfell Tower disaster, lamented:

> I have been shocked by some of the practices I have heard about and I am convinced of the need for a new intelligent system of regulation and enforcement for high-rise and complex buildings which will encourage everyone to do the right thing and will hold to account those who try to cut corners.... it has become clear that the whole system of regulation, covering what is written down and the way in which it is enacted in practice, is not fit for purpose, leaving room for those who want to take shortcuts to do so.

---

34 ibid.
35 Nadj (n 14).
36 Apps (n 17).

A Government consultation followed the Hackitt Report in 2019, and a further response in 2020. Finally, a new Building Safety Bill was introduced to Parliament in July 2021. The Bill received Royal Assent in April 2022.

The Building Safety Act 2022

So, what changes have been brought in by the new Building Safety Act (BSA)? Will they address the problems discussed so far?

Three broad categories of changes will be considered:

1. Causes of action.
2. Oversight.
3. New regulations.

1(a) Building Liability Orders

The High Court can now make a building liability order if it considers it just and equitable to do so.[37] These can apply to corporate bodies and associated corporate bodies. A corporate body is 'associated' with another if one controls the other, or both are controlled by a third party.[38] Corporate bodies can be both jointly and severally liable.[39]

Building Liability Orders relate to liability arising under the Defective Premises Act 1972 or section 38 of the Building Act 1984,[40] or as a result of a building safety risk;[41] that is, a risk to the safety of people from the spread of fire or structural failure.[42]

1(b) Section 38 Building Act

Section 38 of the Building Act 1984 provides a right of action to any person who has suffered damage caused by a breach of a duty imposed by building regulations.[43] The idea is to allow compensation claims for physical damage or injury caused by a breach of the regulations. While Section 38 has not yet been brought into force, the Government has indicated that it intends to do so.[44] The advantage of bringing a claim under s38 would be that, unlike the Defective Premises Act 1972, it applies to all breaches of the building regulations, not just dwellings.

---

37 Building Safety Act 2022 (BSA 2022), s130(1).

38 Department for Levelling Up, Housing & Communities and Ministry of Housing, Communities & Local Government, 'Guidance. Redress: factsheet' (*GOV.UK*, 5 April 2022) <https://www.gov.uk/government/publications/building-safety-bill-factsheets/redress-factsheet> accessed 20 November 2023 (DLUHC Guidance).

39 BSA 2022, s130(2)(b).

40 BSA 2022, s130(3)(a).

41 BSA 2022, s130(3)(b).

42 BSA 2022, s130(6).

43 The Building Act 1984, s38(1)(a).

44 DLUHC Guidance (n 37.

1(c) Liability relating to construction products

The BSA introduces a new cause of action that will enable claims to be brought against persons involved in the manufacture, supply and marketing of construction products.
  This applies where:

1. A person fails to comply with a construction product requirement in relation to a construction product.
2. A misleading statement is made in relation to a construction product in the process of marketing or supply.
3. The process of manufacture results in a construction product that is inherently defective.[45]

If this causes, or contributes to, a dwelling becoming 'unfit for habitation'[46] then a civil claim can be brought through the courts.

1(d) Extension of limitation periods

This is a major change introduced by the Act. Limitation periods will be extended to 15 years for breaches of:

1. Section 1 or 2A of the Defective Premises Act 1972.
2. Section 38 of the Building Act 1984.[47]

Very significant (and unusual) is the inclusion of retrospective claims.
  If a person had the right to initiate a claim based on section 1 of the Defective Premises Act 1972 before 28 June 2022, they now have a 30-year window to do so. For claims that reached the 30-year mark between 28 June 2022 and 28 June 2023, the deadline was 28 June 2023.

2(a) New Building Safety Regulator

Part 2 creates a new Building Safety Regulator, who will be responsible for protecting against building safety risks and improving the standard of buildings generally.[48] They will also be subject to specific duties relating to the safety of higher-risk buildings.[49]
  The Health and Safety Executive ('HSE') will act as the Building Safety Regulator in England.[50] HSE will therefore become the building control authority for high-rise buildings, overseeing decision points during the planning, design, building and occupation of higher-risk buildings. It will also provide advice on fire safety matters.[51]

---

45 BSA 2022, s148(2).
46 BSA 2022, s148(5).
47 BSA 2022, s135(1).
48 BSA 2022, s3(1).
49 BSA 2022, s4.
50 'Building Safety Regulator' (*Health and Safety Executive*) <https://www.hse.gov.uk/building-safety/regulator.htm> accessed 20 November 2023.
51 ibid.

2(b) New Home Ombudsman

The New Homes Ombudsman Scheme provides an avenue for owners of new build homes to have complaints against developers investigated and determined.[52] The BSA empowers the Secretary of State to enact regulations that require developers to become and remain members of the scheme.[53]

2(c) The 'Golden Thread' of vital building information

A key change is an obligation to create and maintain a 'golden thread' of building information throughout the lifecycle of a higher-risk building (over 18 m, containing at least one dwelling).[54] Duty holders and Accountable Persons (discussed below) will be required to demonstrate that the building was compliant with building regulations during its construction, and to manage building safety risks in relation to fire spread and structural collapse.[55] Government guidance states that the 'golden thread' information must be kept up to date, and stored as structured digital information.[56]

2(d) Accountable Person

All high-rise residential buildings must have one or more Accountable Persons, including a Principal Accountable Person, to manage fire and structural safety risks.[57]

This is not quite the same as a 'Responsible Person' under the previous regime. The Accountable Person is defined under the Bill as the person who either has:

1. Legal estate in possession of common parts of the building.
2. Or is under a relevant repairing obligation – such as where there is a lease which sets out repair and maintenance obligations on that management body.

The Accountable Person may be an individual, partnership or corporate body and there may be more than one Accountable Person for a building.

A Responsible Person is a person who has control of the premises, which could include leaseholders, owners of the building, or managers.

New duty-holder regulations to ensure compliance with Building Regulations

During the Bill's passage through Parliament, the UK Government published numerous factsheets relating to the Bill. However, in July 2022 those factsheets were withdrawn, although they remain available online for the time being.

---

52 BSA 2022, s137.

53 BSA 2022, s140(1)(a)-(b).

54 Building Regulations Advisory Committee and Ministry of Housing Communities & Local Government, Policy paper. Building Regulations Advisory Committee: golden thread report' (*GOV.UK*, 21 July 2021) <https://www.gov.uk/government/publications/building-regulations-advisory-committee-golden -thread-report/building-regulations-advisory-committee-golden-thread-report#golden-thread-definition> accessed 20 November 2023.

55 ibid.

56 ibid.

57 Health and Safety Executive, 'Guidance. Safety in high rise residential buildings: Accountable persons' (*GOV.UK*, 5 April 2023) <https://www.gov.uk/guidance/safety-in-high-rise-residential-buildings-accountable -persons> accessed 20 November 2023.

One of those factsheets set out the purpose of proposed secondary legislation governing duty holders. It states that:

Duty holders will be:

- Client.
- Principal Designer.
- Designers.
- Principal Contractor.
- Contractors.

Duty holders will need to:

- Work together to plan, manage and monitor the design work and the building work.
- Ensure they cooperate and communicate with each other.
- Coordinate their work and have systems in place to ensure that building work, including design work, complies with all relevant building regulations.[58]

The status of this guidance is currently unclear.

Higher-risk buildings

The Act creates a stricter regime for higher-risk buildings; that is, residential buildings over 18m in height, or over six storeys.[59]

Approved Document B 2022

Concerningly, perhaps, section 12.3 still allows for compliance to be achieved by way of 'full-scale test *data*' and test BS-8414 (the successor to Fire Note 9). This means that, for many buildings, the Desktop Studies may still provide a path for compliance. However, the use of such tests has been limited. Under Regulation 7(4) 'higher-risk' buildings have been exempted from this compliance route. 'Relevant buildings' are at least 18 metres above ground level, containing:

i. One or more dwellings.
ii. An institution.
iii. Or a room for residential purposes.

Such buildings must meet Class A2-s1, d0 standards or better. In England and Wales, this means materials of limited combustibility that produce little or no smoke and no flaming droplets. In Scotland, the materials must be non-combustible.

---

58 Department for Levelling Up, Housing & Communities and Ministry of Housing Communities & Local Government, 'Guidance. Duty Holders: factsheet' (*GOV.UK*, 5 April 2022) <https://www.gov.uk/government/publications/building-safety-bill-factsheets/dutyholders-factsheet> accessed 20 November 2023.

59 BSA 2022, pt 4.

Further, metal composite materials that contain a layer of high-calorie material are prohibited in the external walls of buildings of any height.

Conclusion

Once again, disaster has precipitated legislative change. It is likely that the new regime – with its thorough oversight, increased accountability, and more stringent regulations – will make a tragedy like Grenfell less likely occur in the future. It is regrettable, however, that it has taken this long. Previous warnings – such as Garnock Court and Lakanal House – were not heeded.

Undoubtedly the other priorities relevant to Building Safety Regulations – the need for cost savings, and a desire for greater autonomy in the selection of materials and building technology – will continue to be championed by some. However, if those priorities are allowed to weaken the protections afforded by the new Building Safety Regime, then more disasters will occur.

CHAPTER 10

Quantifying prolongation costs

Ronan Champion

Introduction

When delays occur on construction projects questions quickly arise, whether on the part of the employer, architect, or engineer, or contractor, as to what additional costs might be incurred due to those delays. It may be a matter for which no provision has been made in the agreement between the parties, in which case one is concerned with the common law position, measuring damages if caused by an employer breach. Alternatively, one can turn to the provisions agreed between the parties, typically via a standard form of construction contract, which may or may not assist.

One might well ask whether much, or anything, of substance has changed over the past 35 years[1] to merit consideration of claims by contractors to recover 'prolongation costs', as they are termed here. Some long-established principles of evaluation survive but much has changed. There are new and revised standard forms, new categories of cost to grapple with, and an old question has re-emerged: should we revert to an easier price-based approach to evaluation, dispensing with long claims and disputes?

The main theme developed in this paper is that when considering how to quantify contractor's delay-related losses, 35-odd years ago the response would have been a simple one that looks to additional costs incurred. Today the response is rather more complex, with a move toward price-based evaluation mechanisms, within the context of collaborative working and rapid dispute resolution. Further, construction processes have developed with work carried out working from home, via off-site assembly, or via Joint Venture entities. The approaches to evaluation of loss need reconsideration to respond to those changes. The approach to teaching construction law in this field may have to adapt too.

Classification and approaches to quantification

The traditional treatment by authors of quantification of prolongation costs has followed one of two broad approaches. One is to address quantification under different cost categories: labour, plant, site overheads (staff etc), head office overheads,[2] etc. The difficulty

---

1 An outline of this paper was presented to the 35th Anniversary Conference hosted by the Centre of Construction Law and Dispute Resolution, part of the Dickson Poon School of Law at King's College London, on 18 November 2022. That presentation was titled: 'Quantifying Prolongation costs: after 35 years, new solutions and new challenges'.

2 See e.g., Franco Mastrandrea, 'Preliminaries in Construction Prolongation Claims' [2009] ICLR 428; Franco Mastrandrea, 'The Evaluation of Contractors' Overheads Claims in Construction' [2010] ICLR 299;

DOI: 10.4324/9781032663975-14

153

with that classification of the subject is that it is cost-based and hence does not include other available approaches to quantification. A second approach is one that considers approaches under particular standard forms of contract, but the risk there is of missing some underlying principles or comparative analysis with other forms. Little is written about the historical origins of the subject, or of its inter-disciplinary nature. Some texts and guides have been produced from a quantify surveyor or Quantum Expert's perspective.[3] Legal textbooks and articles risk approaching the subject as being one shaped predominantly by judgments, missing the underlying surveying and accounting threads.

It will be tempting for lawyers to look to sources of law – cases, standard forms, statutes, or textbooks – as primary sources when considering changes in this field. Evaluation of losses on construction projects sits at the conflux of several disciplines, primarily construction management, quantity surveying, contract administration, and construction law, with touchstones in contact drafting policy, dispute resolution, and accounting. Some underlying policy drives toward collaboration are relevant here too. Clearly, some inter-disciplinary discourse remains as valuable now as ever, whether as part of LLM or MSc courses, or within institutions like the Society of Construction Law or informally through social networks. Although this paper has been prepared from a UK perspective, the principles will likely be familiar across common law jurisdictions and beyond.

A new classification of the subject is used here to help capture the breadth of the subject as currently apparent from an English perspective. This paper considers four different approaches to quantification or evaluation of prolongation cost claims which variously arise under the JCT, NEC, and FIDIC forms:

- Valuation based on costs.
- Valuation based on contract rates and prices.
- Valuation by agreement, perhaps on a fair basis or derived by mutual cooperation.
- Valuation by formula, whether involving percentages or contract data.[4]

Under most standard forms of construction contract the employer will only be required to reimburse the contractor those additional costs or losses where the delays were caused by certain prescribed causes or matters for which the employer has taken the delay risk, and where the contractor has fulfilled the relevant claims notification requirement. Beyond that remains the question: how much is due? How is that amount to be calculated? It is these points that are addressed in this paper.

A claim made by a contractor to recover prolongation costs, put simply, is a claim to recover additional costs incurred or losses incurred as a consequence of delay. In this context, delay ordinarily means delay to the entire project. When an event delays an entire project, the number of work activities affected might be very limited or might be

---

Franco Mastrandrea, 'The Evaluation of Plant Claims in Construction' [2011] ICLR 295; Ronan Champion, 'A consideration of recovery of prolongation costs in a construction context' (2011) 3(3) *International Journal of Law in the Built Environment* 237; Ronan Champion, 'The Hudson Formula, Death by Footnote' (*Society of Construction Law,* September 2021) <https://www.scl.org.uk/papers/hudson-formula-death-footnote> accessed 19 November 2023.

3 Mark Hackett and Geoffrey Trickey, *The Presentation and Settlement of Contractors' Claims* (2nd edn, 2001); John Mullen and Peter Davison, *Evaluating Contract Claims* (3rd edn, Wiley-Blackwell 2019).

4 For a similar classification in respect of variations, see Will Hughes, Ronan Champion and John Murdoch, *Construction Contracts: Law and Management* (5th edn, Routledge 2015), para 15.3.5.

widespread across the project. Much work may be deferred to start later than planned. For any particular type or cause of delay, one cannot easily predict whether the impact will be felt on the main contractor alone or additionally by some subcontractors, suppliers, designers or others working on the project.

With a delay to the project's total duration, the site overheads – supervisors, managers, site offices, and some plant – will be committed to the project for a longer period, and typically cannot be reallocated quickly to other projects at the time the delay occurs to offset delay-related losses. It is these overhead-type losses that typically form the bedrock of a prolongation costs claim. The categories of costs or losses seen in prolongation cost claims is not strictly defined but might also include some consequential matters like loss of opportunity to earn a contribution to overheads, or even a claim for additional costs incurred in carrying out specific works later in a programme or in more adverse weather than planned[5] because the project as a whole was delayed into an adverse weather season. A prolongation costs claim, traditionally at least, does not include claims arising from variations, instructions or changed conditions as those are valued separately under most forms.[6] It will not include claims were work elements have been carried out less efficiently than planned, often labelled as disruption claims.

Traditionally at least, consideration of prolongation cost claims within textbooks or cases has been in the context of employer and main contractor disputes. The same principles ought to apply to subcontracts, so relevant particularly to those subcontractors with a continuous site overhead which is necessarily detained on the site for longer due to the delays. We also see quantification issues arise in professional negligence claims. A good example arises where, under a design and build contract, delays are incurred and the main contractor seeks to recover a contribution from its own design consultant towards delay-related losses incurred.[7] In that circumstance of a claim against a design professional, the principles for calculation of loss under the consultancy agreement may differ from those prescribed under the main contract where the losses were incurred in the first place, either because of the terms of the consultancy contract or because the claim against the professional is one for common law damages where different principles may arise.

There are two points to note at this point. One is that the context in which prolongation cost claims can arise is far from uniform. Second, there is no one-size fits all solution. Some standard forms of contract and practices still follow the same approaches of 35 years ago; others are breaking new ground.

Valuation based on costs

It is useful to commence with a consideration of quantification of damages at common law. The principles are of widespread relevance, not least because many compensation provisions within standard forms are directed at cost-based compensation and hence mirror the common law position. The principles for quantification are well known: damages

---

5 Often termed a 'winter working' claim, based on the premise that work done carried out in winter proceeds more slowly than in summer due to shorter working daylight hours and prevalence of colder, windy weather.

6 cf NEC4 where valuation of variations and delay costs is addressed together as Compensation Events: Clause 60.1.

7 See e.g. *Costain Ltd v Charles Haswell & Partners* [2009] EWHC B25 (TCC).

are a matter of fact, based on costs incurred or losses provided they are not too remote; and assessment is made at the time of the breach.

Under the standard forms, before 2021, the term 'prolongation costs' has not appeared within the commonly used standard forms of contract at all. A fleeting review of the history behind development of these claims is helpful, not least in understanding terminology and some anachronistic provisions still with us today.

Take building forms first. Before 1955, the RIBA form contained a number of separate provisions for recovery of additional amounts whether due to variations, changes, and so on. Some of those clauses contained, almost incidentally, additional provisions for the contractor to claim additional costs. By 1963 there was a new and separate clause in the RIBA forms to the effect that where regular progress of the works was materially affected due to one of the qualifying delay events the contractor could make a claim to recover of 'direct loss and/or expense' incurred. This was a nod to the reality that, when delayed, additional overhead costs were incurred that had not been picked up as part of the valuation of variations, and contractors sought to recover those additional overhead costs from the employer. The clause was qualified to note this permitted claims for amounts 'not already recovered under other provisions', acknowledging in effect the reality that part of the loss might already have been recovered as part of the value of variations. Those provisions for recovery of loss and expense remain today in the JCT 2016 form at Clause 4.23, largely in the same form as 60 years ago. Under that Clause, the contractor makes an application 'if in the execution of this Contract the Contractor incurs or is likely to incur direct loss and/or expense for which he would not be reimbursed by a payment under any other conditions'. Those qualifying words, referring to payment under any other conditions, were required because the contractor might recover some overhead costs as part of the value of a variation. Once the application is made, it is the architect or contract administrator, or quantity surveyor on his behalf, who ascertains the amount of loss and/ or expense incurred.

As to engineering forms, the early ICE and FIDIC forms contained a number of separate provisions throughout each form for recovery of additional costs. Unlike the RIBA or JCT forms, those separate provisions were never consolidated in later editions. The ICE fourth edition contained, under a section titled Alterations Additions and Omissions, clause 51 covering Variations and clause 52 Valuation of Variations. At the end of clause 52 was a short clause titled 'Claims' which noted:

> (4) The contractor shall send to the Engineer once in every month an account giving full and detailed particulars of all claims for any additional expense to which the Contractor may consider himself entitled and of all extra or additional work ordered by the Engineer which he as executed during the preceding month and no claim for payment for any such work will be considered which has not been included in such particulars.[8]

An identical provision was included in the FIDIC first edition published in August 1957, under the same clause number. The clause was expanded in the ICE 5th edition in 1973, again with FIDIC following suit, with the revised clause addressing notification and submission of claims. The present FIDIC clause 20.1 is, of course, just a further development of that clause. But that provision relates to process: when and how to submit a claim. It

---

8 ICE fourth edition, Clause 52.

does not set out the grounds or basis for making a claim for additional costs, as those appear in a multitude of separate clauses within the form.

What is striking about the early JCT, ICE, and FIDIC clauses, and the provisions right up to the present day, is how little is said about quantification. Other than a statement that the contractor can claim additional costs, how those costs are calculated is left unsaid. A solution of sorts to that difficulty was presented in *Wraight v PHT Holdings.*[9] This was a case involving termination. The contractor had claimed losses under clause 26(2)(b)(vi) of the RIBA 1963 form which provided for recovery of '[a]ny direct loss and/or damage' and, in the amounts claimed, had included a loss of profit. The employer sought to argue that loss of profit was consequential, not a direct loss, and therefore irrecoverable under the clause. In a case stated from the arbitration to the High Court, Megaw J (as he then was) rejected the argument, deciding there were no grounds for giving the words in the clause any other meaning than that which they have in the case of a breach of contract. As the authors of BLR noted, this meant in effect that all losses and expenses that could fairly be said to arise naturally in the ordinary course of things were ordinarily recoverable. Put another way, the approach to evaluation of claims based on additional costs or losses would match that used under the common law for measure of damages for breach of contract.

So how is a costs-based evaluation made? Contractors' accounting systems record costs incurred each month. As a matter of principle, one ought to be able to review the accounts, identify the costs incurred during the period when the delay was incurred and use that data as a base for evaluation of additional costs incurred.

In practice when making a costs-based assessment there are many problems to be addressed:

(a) Were the claimed costs incurred at all? An invoice is no more than a request for payment. Even if paid, it may have been reversed at a later date or subject to an overall account settlement. In practice a pragmatic approach taken is for the claimant contractor to provide an excel export of the project cost ledger. One can then check a small sample of claimed costs against the claimant's cost ledger for the project and overall subcontractor or supplier accounts for the project.

(b) Were the costs claimed additional? In practice, a two-part test is required. First, if one has a copy of the contractor's cost ledger, one can simply identify costs within the months when the delays occurred and adjust to match the precise delay period. Second, within those, one can identify the categories of cost that are additional solely due to the project taking longer. So, large plant like a tower crane will invariably be detained on the site for longer but task-based plant or labour would not be, so not part of the prolongation costs. Identifying which staff and which plant are time-related is not easy and often contentious. A 'winter working' claim for additional costs is more difficult, involving proof of both costs incurred and as originally planned.

(c) On a large project with multiple areas of work proceeding concurrently, across how many parts of the project does liability extend? This is a challenging point: a subcontractor or design professional who causes delay to a main contractor

---

9 13 BLR 26. The case was decided in 1968 but reported later when BLR reports were published.

affecting a small area of the project can find (somewhat unexpectedly) that the one area of the project was critical (causing critical delay) to the entire project. On one view, the subcontractor or contractor may seek to argue their liability ought to be limited to the discrete part of the project with which they were involved, in that they should not be taken to have assumed responsibility to a wider extent: see *The Achilleas*.[10] The safer position for defendants will be to limit the scope and extent of liability expressly within their appointment.

(d) Of the contractor's future or consequential losses, how far does liability extend? The question whether the defendant is liable for loss of a future contract (or more precisely the contribution that future fixture would have provided to cover head office overheads and profit) is largely settled. Claims of this nature are accepted in principle at least: it is part of what is ordinarily expected if a project runs late. Evaluation is typically addressed via a Hudson or Emden-type formula. These are not without contention, requiring access to the contractor's accounts.

(e) Where the claim is against a professional arising from a failing pre-contract, credit may need to be made for the position had no negligence arisen. Hence, if an engineer designs a foundation structure without piles and the piles are later found to be required meaning in turn the project takes longer to complete than anticipated, the delay-related loss is not measured as being that in the period of delay. Account also has to be taken for the period that would have been required had the project's design included piling in the first place and the impact that would have had on the tender and contract price.

In practice, the process of identifying additional costs due to delays, involving working through accounting and other documents, can be laborious, expensive, and contentious. It can involve specialist quantum expert expertise and is unlikely to be prompt. Yet this is the approach anticipated by the JCT and FIDIC forms, traditionally at least.

Valuation based on agreement

A more recent development, evident within JCT and FIDIC forms, is to permit valuation of variations by agreement, during the works. The contractor raises a quotation which might or might not be accepted. Significantly, where the variation or change had resulted in delays, it is open to the parties to agree to a valuation of the variation on an all-inclusive basis so including the additional cost of the works and perhaps allowances for site overheads or other matters. That is, of course, sensible. But it also means that if a separate and overarching project-wide prolongation claim is made by the contractor, account needs to be taken for the amounts already recovered through agreements in respect of variations.

Separately, there is a well-known practice in some countries for parties to simply ignore the detailed contract machinery altogether and to mid-project agree an adjustment to the contract sum in respect of a collection of variations and delay claims – the so-called 'Supplemental Agreement'. Standard forms do not refer to these, because these are

---

10 *Transfield Shipping Inc v Mercator Shipping Inc (The Achilleas)* [2008] UKHL 48; [2009] 1 AC 61.

supplemental to the agreement itself. Where there are multiple Supplemental Agreements on a single project and subsequent delays and claims arise, this can give rise to considerable debate as to what disputes are already compromised. The use of such wide-ranging agreements to vary agreements mid-project has increased in UK in the past 20-odd years, a product of mid-project adjudications.

Within standard forms there is no guidance as to how that additional cost might be calculated, but that perhaps is the point of the provision; it allows parties to come to an accommodation that would therefore avoid protracted or exacting calculations.

Valuation based on prices: an 'extended preliminaries' claim

There is a long-held practice held by construction professionals of calculating amounts for additional periods on site based on contract rates and prices. As noted in more detail below, it is an approach that has the merit of convenience and simplicity, even if the approach is not one anticipated by most contract forms. Strictly speaking, this approach does not aim to calculate exactly the additional cost incurred per week, but an approximation of that additional cost based on the available contract prices. It has the merit of transparency, using the agreed contract prices. It also has the merit of some level of sense: if the contract rates and prices can be used to calculate the amount for variations, why not use them also for additional time periods?

Using Preliminaries to price claims

It is useful to recall first the principles, practices, and terminology used in quantification of variations and prolongation claims as they stood in UK in mid-1980s. That period is informative for four reasons. First, some of the most prolific and considered writing on quantification of prolongation claims was prepared then.[11] Second, the influence and reach of the JCT 1963 and 1980 forms is far and wide. Standard forms of contract in Ireland, Hong Kong, Malaysia, and a collection of African states, are based on the wording of those forms and many remain in use today. Third, the quantification practices used then are still widely used today. Fourth, an appreciation of claims in that era helps understand why new approaches to quantification are being developed today, in a complete departure to that earlier era.

As to terminology, origins lie in the use of bills of quantities and standard methods of measurement. Although today one is more likely in UK to see parties use a contract sum analysis, compiled in a more summary form, some terminology survives. The BQ was, first, a pricing document. It showed the price for each work element, all of which was measured in accordance with a standard method of measurement. From the BQ, the value of work done each month could be calculated using the contract rates and measuring what was done. The pricing of each work element provided a basis for valuation of variations. Under the Standard Method,[12] each BQ was to contain a section for overhead type

---

11 See Ian Duncan Wallace Construction Contracts: Principles and Policies in Tort and Contract (1986), chapter 8, for example.

12 For Building works: SMM6 was published by RICS and NFBTE in 1979. SMM7 was published by RICS in 1988, revised 1998 and superseded by NRM2 (New Rules of Measurement volume 2) currently in 2nd Edition, 2021. For Civil works, see CESMM published 1976, now CESMM4, all by ICE, for example.

elements that were not included under particular trades. It was headed 'Preliminaries', covering what were listed as Preliminary and General items. From this, the terms 'Prelims costs' or 'Ps & Gs' are variously used across the globe to cover notionally those overhead costs. There was no explicit practice as to where in the BQ, or how, allowances for head office overheads and profit were made. Some contractors just included an allowance for overheads and profit within rates and prices; others made a separate percentage-based additional allowance for head office overheads and profit at the end of the BQ, signalling a percentage that might be used in valuing variations or in making claims. Critically, as the BQ was a collection of prices, one never knew what anything cost to the contractor. When variations arose, the value of those variations could be determined by working from the BQ rates and prices as a starting point if any relevant BQ items were available. If paid additional sums for variations based on those rates, or based on a quotation, it was always possible those prices included allowances for overheads or profit. Inevitably, pricing variations often involved a mix of BQ pricing plus additional cost allowances for matters the contractor claimed were involved.

A claim for 'additional preliminaries' or 'Prelims costs' is a shorthand term for a claim to recover some additional preliminaries-type, or site overhead, costs. Viewed at their simplest, these might take one of two forms.

(a)   The claim for additional overhead costs arising from delays to the project might be based on the contract *prices* using priced preliminaries items within the contract BQ. If the BQ had shown a tower crane priced at £50,000 for 10 weeks, it is not difficult to surmise that if the project was delayed, the tower crane might cost in the order of an extra £5,000 per week. Similarly, a pro-rata approach could be taken with the total of the entire preliminaries section of the BQ (representing notionally all site overheads) to derive a cost per week. Any such approach had, at least, the merit of administrative convenience, although there was never any guarantee that particular contract rates and prices might reflect underlying costs to the contractor at all.

(b)   The second approach was to quantify the additional cost per week based on the additional costs incurred by the contractor in those delayed weeks. This was what was envisaged by the JCT and ICE and FIDIC forms, by their reference to a contractor making a claim for loss or expense, or additional cost. But this was administratively inconvenient. It meant compiling tables of costs, and discussions as to which of the costs were additional and consequent upon the delays.

In practice, one might guess the contractor and the employer's quantity surveyor charged with valuing the delay-related loss would concur based on the answer easily reached, using the BQ priced allowances. In practice this rarely occurred for several reasons. First, a calculation of amounts per week based on BQ allowances was often seen to be excessive because it included set-up costs that ought to be excluded. Hence, a BQ showing a tower crane allowance of £50,000 might include fixed installation costs of £10,000 and removal costs of £10,000, leaving a weekly amount of £3,000 for each weeks delay, an amount might consider inadequate if claimed on a cost incurred and proved basis. Clearly, the shorthand approach using the BQ price that might suggest the higher amount of £5,000/wk was preferable. Second, as often as not, the amounts in fact incurred per week by the contractor were vastly in excess of contract allowances, begging the question whether the contractor ought to be permitted to recover large amounts per week when, it might be argued, amounts ought to be lower.

A further source of tension was that in claims made by contractors further heads of claim emerged that were notoriously contentious. These included claims to recover financing costs, interest and claims preparation costs. Using compound interest, the amounts involved often beggared belief. Most contentious of all were claims to recover head office overheads and profit on a loss of opportunity basis based on the notion that, had the present project not been delayed, the contractor could and would have moved on to another project, earning a contribution to overheads and profit that alas, due to current delays, could not be recovered at all. To advance claims of this nature based on a simple Hudson or Emden-type formula claim, potentially recovering large sums, was seen as opportunistic claims making, an afront to many.

The account above of quantification based on contract 'preliminaries' reflects the common practice of valuing claims, particularly for short delays, using contract price data as a shorthand in lieu of the costs based approach anticipated by the JCT and FIDIC forms. As noted in below, approach to quantification of claims under the NEC forms marked a radical departure from past practice because, in effect, it formalised and adopted the old practice of using contract rates and prices (where they had been provided) to calculate the amount of compensation due.

Valuation based on a formula

A long standing question within construction law was whether it might be easier for the contractor to provide a fixed amount per week and for that rate to be used as the basis to quantify the amount in respect of whatever delay period was involved. It would have the merit, after all, of administrative convenience, much like liquidated damages amounts are used in respect of employers' delay costs. There were two objections to use of an agreed amount in respect of contractors' delay costs. First, a delay at the start of a project may mean additional costs incurred were remarkably low compared to costs incurred mid-project per week of delay. That point is addressed in different ways under NEC and the new FIDIC Green Book 2nd Edition provisions, as noted below. Second, a flat rate of compensation risked over or under compensating the contractor. That variability could potentially be used to argue that a fixed amount was *in terrorem*, a penalty. That difficulty appears to have fallen away following the UK Supreme Court's decision in *Makdessi*[13] setting out a revised test based on commerciality.

The NEC form, introduced in 1995 and currently in its fourth edition as NEC4, was revolutionary in three respects in its approach to quantification of prolongation claims.

(a) NEC4 provides an explicit method of valuation of delay claims: if the contract form is price-based, say Option A, then additional costs are at contract rates and prices, if provided within the agreement. That, in effect, mirrors the old-style use of preliminaries to calculate an amount per week of delay. If prices for

---

13 *Cavendish Square Holding BV v Talal El Makdessi* [2015] UKSC 67.

cost components are not provided, the Schedule of Cost Components or Shorter Schedule provides a detailed list as to what costs will be included.

(b) NEC4 does not distinguish between prolongation claims and, say, claims for the cost of variations. All are treated together under the same rules, all priced as Compensation Events. That has the merit of avoiding a situation under JCT and FIDIC forms which can result in variations and delay claims being valued on different basis with credits required to avoid duplication.

(c) The cost categories used to calculate additional costs under NEC4 do not include head office costs. Those are calculated simply by adding a pre-priced percentage, called the Fee. The use of the Fee, at a stroke, eliminates the need to refer to companies accounts to glean overhead percentages.

The NEC does not provide a flat rate for compensation of delay. It allows for compensation based on the staff and plant on site at the time of the delay. Hence, compensation will be low when little work is underway. That avoids risk of over or under compensation on a large scale.

The approach adopted in the NEC forms is not perfect. A difficulty is that a contractor might provide contract rates and prices that are exceedingly high, knowing they will be used in calculating the amount due under Compensation Events. That can be alleviated by use of a matrix-based tender evaluation model.[14] Further, one might quibble that it cannot be right to estimate the head office overheads loss based on a percentage of the additional costs incurred.

The approach introduced in the FIDIC Green Book, 2nd edition, is of particular note. In simple terms it provides a flat rate of compensation to the contractor per week of delay, but does so with an interesting adjustment. It uses a default rate of 20% of the contract sum, from which a rate per week is calculated. If the delays arise in the first or last third of the project by value spent, the contractor is paid at 60% of that weekly rate. If the delays occur in the middle third by value, the contractor is paid at 125% of that weekly rate: see sub-clause 1.1.35 Part A, Contract Data. That helps overcome the risk noted above of over or under compensation, and use of the contract sum to calculate the weekly rate helps overcome the risk of distorted pricing of that weekly rate.

What is particularly striking about this FIDIC provision, other than it being entirely new when published in early 2022, is that the rationale for its introduction is set out in the form as being to ease contract administration. Indeed, FIDIC says in the Forward to the 2nd edition that it might act as an alternative to the Red and Yellow Books. It is directed at projects who may not be able to benefit from the same legal support typically available for projects covered by the Red and Yellow Books. As FIDIC notes in the Guidance to the form

> The mechanism has the merit of providing a quick remedy (...) where the Contractor will not have to provide/substantiate such loss, and the Parties will not have to enter into possible lengthy discussions about what is the fair and reasonable amount of prolongation cost to consider, which could result in a dispute and require expert evidence, with the knock-on time and cost impacts on the Parties that this mechanism is aiming at avoiding.[15]

---

14 See Ireland's Public Works Contract (PW-CF1 version 2.6 published January 2022), clause 10.7 which explicitly provides for use of rates within the contract sum, which aims to address this risk.

15 At page 26.

It is expressly aimed at avoiding reliance on expert quantum evidence. One might go as far to say this mechanism signals the merits of price-based contract administration at the expense of more traditional approaches. The new provision risks some entanglement with disruptions claims and recovery under variation claims, but is nevertheless a commendable initiative.

Modern complexities

Some 40 years ago, discussion of approaches to quantification was made in the context of a traditional employer/main contractor dispute. Much has changed since then in the way buildings and structures are assembled. New technologies and techniques add new challenges to assessment of the additional costs arising from a delay to a project. Listed here are some examples:

Staff costs have traditionally been based on staff costs allocated to a project, often with the staff member based on site. Post-pandemic, many staff will work remotely. This raises questions as to the basis upon which staff costs are allocated when they might have been working on multiple projects concurrently. In February 2023 NEC4 Amendments were issued specifically to address costs relating to staff working from home and other locations outside the defined work areas.

Of plant costs, where the plant is hired the identification of costs in an additional month is comparatively simple. Yet today plant use may be arranged through structured finance leases. If a tower crane is leased at £10,000/month on a 5-year purchase lease, its retention on a project for an extra month does not increase the cost to the lessor. Some projects involve complex systems of working and complex plant particular to that one project. A good example is tunnelling involving a tunnel boring machine and a range of support plant, some of which may have a life limited to that one project only. Then, the loss due to delays cannot be calculated absent market rates if the plant is unique. The better characterisation may be one of loss of opportunity, in the period of delay, to profitably use the plant elsewhere. An excellent example of this arose in *Bernard Sunley*.[16] Sunley won a contract to build a new airstrip in Guernsey. They imported an excavator from US, one of a few of its kind in England, for £4,500. The defendants were to ship it from Doncaster to the site, but it arrived a week late. The claim was for a week's loss. The Court of Appeal decided that in the absence of proof of special damage, they could recover the loss based on depreciation, but not at the high rate claimed which was based on writing off the cost of the machine in 3 years. Instead, they could recover at a lower rate, reflecting the fact the machine had been idle for a week. In effect, the claimant was deprived recovery of the profits they might have earned from working on the project in that week. But the better view may be that if writing off the plant on one project only, no loss arises at all.

Where off-site manufacturing is delayed, whether due to late designs required for manufacturing or due to delayed works on site that pushes back the planned installation date, the loss can be difficult to predict or assess. A feature of modern projects is that many components are manufactured, stored off-site and brought to site for rapid installation. Manufacturing bespoke components involves having a completed design and then

---

16 *B Sunley & Co Ltd v Cunard White Star Ltd* [1940] 2 All ER 97.

assembly in a factory during an assigned assembly time-slot. If the slot is lost because of a design-led delay, the next available time slot within the factory may be months later as factories typically have carefully planned schedules. Large additional payments may have to be made for queue-jumping within the factory, if that is possible. Or alternative more expensive factory options methods may have to be explored. The simple point here is that a small delay in resolution of design, or a delay in the dates for installation on site, can cause large loss when manufacturing processes have to be changed. Assessment of loss will be fact-specific.

The identity of the contracting party may be relevant to whether the claiming contractor has suffered some categories of loss. If works are carried out by a Joint-Venture contracting group, some consideration of the intra-group structure may be required to establish who suffered the loss. Loss of opportunity type claims are not easy to establish if the JV is to be dissolved on completion of the project, or if staff were hired specifically for the project or might not have been easily redeployed elsewhere. Alternatively, where the claim is made by a contractor's subsidiary it may be difficult to establish losses relating to other group subsidiaries. The case of *Fluor*,[17] for example, provides a salutary reminder that the Court might conclude there is insufficient evidence to prove overhead losses were incurred by the project-specific entity.

Finally, where a contractor is engaged on a design and build basis, part of the loss claimed as a result of delays may include design costs or overheads that include design resources. Whether any delay is incurred by the design team is likely to be a moot point. Quantifying loss in respect of prolonged design involves some understanding of design processes specific to the trade or specialism affected.

Some concluding thoughts

In quantification of prolongation cost claims, there are a number of basic and long-standing principles reflecting older contract forms and practices.

a) Distinguish local works from project-wide matters. A delay to excavation in one corner of a project will not necessarily delay the project as a whole, and vice versa. The term prolongation costs tends to be reserved for costs arising from delay to the project overall.

b) As with the works, above, consider costs as falling into a number of discrete parts: the cost of carrying out work in a local area; off-site component costs; the wider project overheads; and head office costs.

c) Understand the particular mechanisms under which the contract form provides for recovery of delay related costs, and how that fits in with other provisions. Traditionally the value of the works including variations to it was considered first under one discrete set of rules, with the wider project delay costs considered separately. Today, that division may not be so clearcut, particularly if valuing variations on a quotation basis or if valuing compensation events under the NEC4 form.

---

17 *Fluor Ltd v Shanghai Zhenhua Heavy Industry Co Ltd* [2018] EWHC 490 (TCC).

The NEC forms and the new edition of the FIDIC Green Book provide good examples of a newer, different, approach to quantification of contactor's delay costs: a price-based calculation. The reality, as this paper relates, is one of shifting sands with evidence of change of many fronts: changes to how construction work is carried out; changes in pricing and accounting practices; and changes in the ways construction is managed. It remains important to understand that quantification should not be seen to simply follow provisions in standard forms, but will at times require understanding of the underlying principles and various approaches available.

CHAPTER 11

Liquidated damages

A common law perspective

Nicholas Gould and Katherine Butler

Introduction

The classic rules relating to liquidated damages arise from the case of *Dunlop Pneumatic Tyre Co v New Garage & Motor Co Ltd.*[1] That case concerned the ability for a party to pre-fix (liquidate) damages in relation to a particular breach by the other party. The construction industry mostly associates this rule with a pre-agreed amount of liquidated damage for each day or week for a delay that occurs to a project. The mechanism has been widely used in the standard forms and bespoke construction contracts. Liquidated damages could be used in a wider variety of situations, beyond simply the fixing of a pre-agreed amount over time arising from delay. For example, it could be used in relation to a failure to perform to a particular standard ('performance damages'). Indeed, the forfeiture of a deposit in circumstances where the contract is not to proceed, the ascertained level of the deposit retained is a form of liquidated damage to compensate the other party for opportunity cost.

Much of the legal analysis, discussion and debate on this topic focuses on whether specific liquidated damages provisions are enforceable, most usually in respect of whether it can be said to be a penalty. Questions as to whether liquidated damages are enforceable in a particular contract should not be limited to whether the amount can be said to be a penalty. Many commentators and claims focus on this point; however, it is clear from the *Dunlop* test that the construction of the clause and its operation need to be considered in addition to whether the pre-estimation of the amount is 'extravagant and unconscionable'.

In reality, few cases have held that an amount of liquidated damages is a penalty. The position was carefully reviewed by Mr Justice Jackson (as he then was) in *Alfred McAlpine Capital Projects Ltd v Tilebox Ltd,*[2] and this case is considered in more detail below. However, more recent case law has identified the importance of liquidated damages as a contractual mechanism, which the court have become increasingly more willing to uphold. Further case law has shown a departure from, or expansion of, the *Dunlop* test, and this chapter explores those cases in order to analyse and arrive at the current legal position.

---

1 [1915] AC 79 HL.
2 [2005] EWHC 281 (TCC), (2005) 21 Const LJ 539.

166

DOI: 10.4324/9781032663975-15

The classic liquidated damages/penalty rules

The *Dunlop* test was germinated in the cases of *Clydebank Engineering and Shipbuilding Co v Don Jose Ramos Yzquierdo y Castaneda*[3] and *Commissioner of Public Works v Hills*[4] at the turn of the 20th century. In the latter case, Lord Dunedin (sitting on the Privy Council) grappled with the difficult balance required between upholding freedom of contract and potentially unfair outcomes. Here, a contract for railway works directed that the retention would be forfeited by the contractor in the event that the works were delayed. Taking the view that such damages are intended to be ascertained and yet compensatory, the provision was struck down as a penalty. This was on the basis that the amount of retention was a percentage sum relative to the value of the works done. It was, therefore, not a static figure and, accordingly, could not be a pre-estimation of the potential losses. In making this determination, his Lordship stressed that the 'indicia' of whether a liquidated sum is truly a penalty 'will vary according to the circumstances'.[5] However, Lord Woolf also noted '[e]normous disparity of the sum to any conceivable loss will point one way, while the fact of the payment being in terms proportionate to the loss will point the other. But the circumstances must be taken as a whole, and must be viewed at the time the bargain was made'.[6]

Not long thereafter, Lord Dunedin had the opportunity to go further in codifying his principled approach to the rule against penalties. In *Dunlop*, the Respondents ('New Garage') entered into a dealership agreement whereby it would receive a discount on motor tyres and accessories in exchange for complying with various stipulations insisted upon by the Appellants ('Dunlop') as the primary supplier. Such stipulations limited the basis on which New Garage would be able to treat the products, their pricing and to whom they could be sold. In the event that any of these stipulations were compromised, Dunlop would be able to recover liquidated damages of £5 for each tyre sold in breach of the agreement. In modern terms, that may seem like a very small fee to pay in the face of potentially much greater commercial advantage. However, taking inflation into account, £5 in 1915 is the equivalent of over £400 today.[7]

One of the primary stipulations that Dunlop required its dealers and sub-dealers to comply with was the covenant not to sell any of its products to private customers (or co-operative societies) at less than the listed sale price. Notwithstanding the terms of the agreement, New Garage sold a tyre cover to the Motorists' Manual Cooperative for 9 shillings and 1 pence less than the list price (a circa £30 discount in today's money). Upon learning of this, Dunlop launched proceedings against New Garage for £5 in damages. The question for the Courts was whether the charge of £5 was an enforceable remedy in the face of the breach, or whether it was a penalty.

Taking the matter all the way to the House of Lords, the argument from Dunlop was consistently that the value of the discount was not the factor against which the agreed liquidated sum was to be judged. Rather, it was the effect that underselling had on its wider business model which Dunlop was seeking to guard against. The sale of Dunlop

---

3 [1905] AC 6.

4 [1906] AC 368.

5 ibid 375.

6 ibid 376.

7 'Inflation Calculator' (*Bank of England*, 18 October 2023) <https://www.bankofengland.co.uk/monetary-policy/inflation/inflation-calculator> accessed 3 November 2023.

tyres was largely done through a network of dealers and sub-dealers. This meant that the undercutting of retail prices by one of these dealers would upset the wider market amongst Dunlop's various agents. Ultimately, a local supplier may choose to stock a competitor's product which it can sell at the expected margin, without fear of losing custom to an undercutting rival. In the face of such market distortion, there was no way to calculate the damage that Dunlop would suffer as a result of what might be considered a minor infringement of the supply agreement.

New Garage's arguments that the provision was indeed a penalty and, therefore, not enforceable centred on the fact that the sum of £5 was specified regardless of the provision breached by the dealer. Whilst it may be that undercutting was the main mischief concerning Dunlop, the sum to be paid for other infringements, having much less significant consequences, was the same. Given this disparity, the sum of damages cannot possibly be a genuine pre-estimate of losses and, therefore, the clause must be considered penal.

In the Judgment, Lord Dunedin helpfully set out the established parameters of 'penalty' clauses that were void and otherwise enforceable "liquidated damages" provisions. In summary, these are as follows:

1. Whether the terms 'penalty' or 'liquidated damages' are used in the contract is informative but not determinative;
2. A penalty is a sum payable 'in terrorem' (i.e. under threat) whereas liquidated damages relate to a genuine pre-estimate of the damage flowing from breach;
3. Each provision has to be judged on its own circumstances but with consideration given to various tests:
   a. Sums in damages that are 'extravagant and unconscionable' in amount in comparison to the greatest loss that could conceivably be proved will be penal;
   b. Sums payable following breaches of covenants for the payment of money for an amount greater that the primary obligation will be penal;
   c. It is a penalty to require the payment of a lump sum on the occurrence of different events, some of which cause serious damage whereas others have 'but trifling' impact;
   d. Parties can impose 'liquidated damages' in instances where it is very difficult, if not impossible, to make a precise pre-estimation of the potential losses.

Their Lordships ultimately found that, in all the circumstances, the sum stipulated was not 'unreasonable, unconscionable or extravagant', but evidenced a genuine attempt to pre-estimate losses in terms of Dunlop's wider commercial interests. Therefore, it was rightly a liquidated damages provision and not a penalty.

The classic test applied

It is clear from the formulation of the *Dunlop* test that it was very much a set of parameters to be applied to the specific facts, on a case-by-case basis. Taking account of what would be 'extravagant and unconscionable' would evidently differ widely depending on the scale of the claimed 'penalty', the overall value of the contract and the relative profiles of the contracting parties. As the case law that followed over the next century shows, the *Dunlop* test was applied relatively restrictively. This is perhaps best demonstrated by the decision in *Philips Hong Kong v Attorney General of Hong Kong*.[8] In this case, the Privy Council determined that a (less than clear) liquidated damages clause was not a penalty. In doing so, Lord Woolf (giving the leading judgment) directed that the penalty rule was not to be readily engaged in negotiated contract between two equally sophisticated parties. More specifically, his Lordship recognised that the party claiming that the provision is penal 'has to surmount the strong inference to the contrary resulting from its agreement to make the payments as liquidated damages'.[9] This sentiment clearly endorsing the wider ethos of English law that judicial interference into the application of freely agreed contractual terms should be minimal.

Lord Woolf was also keen to lay down a clear position as regards to what is indeed meant by a 'genuine pre-estimate of loss' in all the circumstances. His Lordship noted that, whilst there must be thought given to the potential ranges of losses, the agreed sum of liquidated damages must not be slavishly judged against such ranges. This is clear from the following passage which, again, highlights the importance given to party autonomy:

> Except possibly in the case of situations where one of the parties to the contract is able to dominate the other as to the choice of the terms of a contract, it will normally be insufficient to establish that a provision is objectionably penal to identify situations where the application of the provision could result in a larger sum being recovered by the injured party than his actual loss.[10]

In the more recent decision in *Tilebox*, Mr Justice Jackson (as he then was) took the opportunity to explore the authorities related to the rule against penalties. In this case, pursuant to a Development Funding Agreement, Tilebox engaged Alfred McAlpine to carry out significant rebuilding works at an office block in Guildford. Under a JCT 1998 Standard Building Contract with Contractor's Design, the parties agreed for liquidated damages to accrue at £45,000 for every week (or part thereof) for delays beyond the Completion Date. The original Completion Date was 12 July 2002 but the works remained incomplete in February 2005, by which time £5.4m had accrued in liquidated damages. In the face of such a sum, McAlpine sought a declaration from the Courts that the provision was void for being a penalty.

In finding that the provision was an entirely valid requirement to pay the ascertained sum in liquidated damages, Jackson MJ made the following observations regarding the application of the *Dunlop* test:

1. A party's pre-estimation of loss that informs the contractual rate of liquidated damages does not have to be accurate in order to be considered reasonable. Such a provision would only be considered a penalty if there were a 'substantial discrepancy between the level of damages stipulated in the contract and the level of damages which is likely to be suffered'.[11]
2. The test is not applied by reference to the actual pre-estimations made by the parties at the time the contract was formed. Rather, it is an objective test to be

---

8 (1993) 9 Const LJ 202

9 ibid 210.

10 ibid 209.

11 *Tilebox* (n 2) [48].

applied by the Courts, albeit having 'some regard to the thought processes of the parties at the time of contracting'.[12]

3. The rule against penalties is an 'anomaly within the law of contract' and, as such, the presumption is that the parties' agreement is to be enforced, especially when made between those 'of comparable bargaining power'.[13]

4. The weight of the case law on this subject supports the presumption that, unless there is a significant discrepancy between the potential losses and the agreed level of damages, the Courts will not, and should not, interfere.

Lord Woolf's final observation exemplifies the restrictive approach of the *Dunlop* test and very few claims seeking to rely on the rule against penalties have actually succeeded. More specifically, cases where clauses were struck down as penalties can objectively be seen as relatively extreme. By way of examples:

1. In *Bridge v Campbell Discount Co Ltd*,[14] the House of Lords determined that a payment to be made on termination of a hire purchase agreement, which decreased over the term, was a penalty. This was on the basis that the charge was intended to compensate the owner for depreciation and, therefore, the sum should increase over the term, not decrease. Accordingly, it could not possibly be a genuine pre-estimate of loss.

2. In *Workers Trust & Merchant Bank Ltd v Dojap Investments Ltd*,[15] the Privy Council held that the requirement to forfeit 25% of the purchase price for non-completion of a property sale was a penalty. Instead, the defaulting party would forfeit the prevailing average non-refundable deposit of 10% of the purchase price.

3. In *Jeancharm Ltd (t/a Beaver International) v Barnet Football Club Ltd*,[16] the Court of Appeal struck down a clause requiring interest on late payments at a rate of 5% per week as a penalty and unenforceable. This was on the basis that this rate of weekly interest equated to 260% interest per annum and, therefore, was not a genuine pre-estimate of the supplier's loss flowing from late payment.

Liquidated damages as a secondary obligation

The *Dunlop* test for establishing a penalty prevailed until the Supreme Court had the opportunity to revisit the subject in *Cavendish Square Holding BV v Makdessi* and *ParkingEye Ltd v Beavis*.[17]

This decision concerned two linked, but markedly different, cases. The common link was that both called for a decision on whether a clause requiring the payment of an ascertained sum upon breach was a penalty and, therefore, unenforceable. On their facts, *Makdessi* related to a complicated commercial contract regarding the sale of shares in an

---

12 ibid.
13 ibid.
14 [1962] AC 600.
15 [1993] AC 573.
16 [2003] EWCA Civ 58.
17 [2016] AC 1172.

advertising and marketing agency whereas *ParkingEye* concerned the stipulated payment for overstaying in a privately owned car park.

In *Makdessi*, the terms of the sale agreement included strict non-competition clauses. If Mr Makdessi fell afoul of these covenants, he would not be entitled to further instalments of the purchase price. Further, at Cavendish's option, breach could result in Mr Makdessi having to sell his remaining shares for their Net Asset Value ('NAV') less a sum representing the 'goodwill' value of the same.[18] The Court of Appeal had found that, whilst the rule against penalties constituted an interference with broader freedoms of contract, these provisions were, none the less, penalties. This was on the basis that they did not relate to a 'genuine pre-estimate' of Cavendish's losses and that they did not fulfil any 'justifiable commercial or economic function'.[19]

In *ParkingEye,* Mr Beavis was charged £85 for overstaying the permitted 'free parking' period at a private car park in Chelmsford by approximately half an hour. This late stay fee could have been reduced to £50 if payment were made within 14 days. Mr Beavis argued that the sum at issue was far greater (so as to be extravagant or unconscionable) than the ostensible losses that would be suffered by the innocent party. Further, the underlying purpose of the fee was not to encourage compliance but to punish breach. The Court of Appeal here found that the requirement to pay a fee for overstaying the permitted period was not a penalty.[20] In upholding the Trial Judge's decision, their Lordships held that, whilst the tangible direct losses by ParkingEye for individual overstays were minimal (if not non-existent), the term was 'commercially justifiable because it was neither improper in its purpose nor manifestly excessive in its amount'.

At the Supreme Court, Cavendish's arguments, militating for the provisions to be enforced, invoked English Law's commitment to freedom of contract. Relying on the maxim of 'pacta sunt servanda',[21] the principle follows that judicial interference with a lawful contract entered into between two commercially sophisticated parties of equal bargaining power should be extremely limited. In considering the application of the rule in *Dunlop*, Counsel for Cavendish vehemently contended that it was time for change. Specifically, stating that:

> the law of penalties is plainly deficient and out of step: it is uncertain when and how it applies; it leads to arbitrary and capricious differences in treatment; it undermines the freely agreed bargains of sophisticated commercial parties; and it lacks any coherent rationale by which those results can be explained to commercial parties in a satisfactory manner.[22]

This being their primary case that the rule should, in fact, be abolished or, at the very least, restricted in application only to consumer cases.

Representatives for Mr Makdessi, unsurprisingly, took a more traditional stance. Such being that penalty clauses should rightly be struck down where their aim is 'the impermissible goal of punishment as opposed to compensation'.[23] Further, questions as to the enforceability of contracts between parties of equal bargaining power should not arise given the broader commercial protections available. The proper question, more

---

18 It is notable that the majority of the shares' NAV was comprised of consideration for 'goodwill'.

19 *Talal El Makdessi v Cavendish Square Holdings BV and another* [2013] EWCA Civ 1539, 121.

20 *Parkingeye Limited v Barry Beavis v The Consumers' Association* [2015] EWCA Civ 402.

21 Legal principle directing that the terms of a binding contract are to be adhered to.

22 *Cavendish* (n 18) 1179G.

23 ibid 1184E.

fundamentally, relates to whether the compensation is in line with the breach and/or exorbitantly exceeds what the innocent party could have recovered by way of general damages.

Counsel for Mr Beavis likewise focused on the 'extravagant and unconscionable' fee to be paid for overstaying in the car park, even for one minute, as against the greatest possible loss flowing therefrom that *ParkingEye* could demonstrate. Such a provision could only be for the purpose of deterrence and, therefore, offended public policy, particularly in circumstances where Mr Beavis had no opportunity to negotiate the terms imposed. Opposing Counsel countered that deterrence was not a death knell for provisions which aimed to prevent specified behaviours (i.e. staying longer than two hours on private property). In addition to which, Mr Beavis was informed of these terms upon entering the car park and had freely chosen to accept them by parking his car.

Taking these arguments on board, their Lordships Neuberger and Sumption (giving the leading judgment) did consider that the century-old approach to the penalty rule may be in need of revitalisation. Specifically, if not unflatteringly, describing the rule as 'an ancient, haphazardly constructed edifice which has not weathered well'.[24] The principle, not having had the benefit of ventilation in the highest Court for several generations, was set out in considerable detail by their Lordships. Focus ranged from the roots of the rule in equity to the application of the same in complex modern finance arrangements. The considerations, however, boiled down to the critical questions regarding freedom of contract, what terms are to be considered penal as opposed to compensatory, and what factors impact on whether the ascertained sum is extravagant, exorbitant or unconscionable.

Their Lordships could not see their way to agreeing with Cavendish that the principle should be abandoned or severely restricted, and instead asserted that it very much still had a place in common law in order to 'restrain exorbitant or unconscionable consequences following from breach'.[25] Notwithstanding, the Supreme Court were also minded to ensure that the penalty rule would only apply in the narrowest of circumstances. To this end, the Judgment offers a reformulation of the basis to determine whether a provision, such as for liquidated damages, should be struck down as a penalty. In doing so, it breaks contractual obligations into two categories – primary and secondary.[26] A primary obligation is one that supports the overall objective of the contract, and a secondary obligation arises as a consequence to the performance of the primary obligation. Using the example of a liquidated damages provision relating to delay, the primary objective is for the works to be completed on time. Insofar as the works are delayed (and where there is no entitlement to an extension of time), the requirement to pay a designated sum in liquidated damages is the secondary obligation.

As per the majority decision, the new test to be applied, rather than considerations of 'genuine pre-estimates' of loss, is whether it is 'a secondary obligation which [imposes] a detriment on the contract-breaker out of all proportion to any legitimate interest of the innocent party in the enforcement of the primary obligation'.[27]

As regards the facts in *Makdessi,* Cavendish had a legitimate interest in the noncomplete clauses being observed and that, where they were not observed, would have an impact on the value of the goodwill in the shares. Accordingly, and specifically taking

---

24 ibid 1192B.
25 ibid 1251G.
26 Albeit noting that their Lordships were not in full accord as to these categorisations.
27 *Cavendish* (n 18) 1173C.

account of the equal bargaining power between the parties, the clauses could not be considered penalties. The fee to be paid in *ParkingEye* for overstaying at the car park was, likewise, not a penalty. Notwithstanding that £85 was indeed disproportionate to the tangible losses that the owners would suffer for the breach, they had a legitimate interest in ensuring that the parking spaces would be available to be used by others. Accordingly, the imposition of the fee was a deterrent to commit the breach, but such deterrence was valid in the circumstances.

The new formulation to establish a penalty is arguably now more restrictive than the previous test under Dunlop. This is on the basis that the innocent party no longer has to establish that the liquidated damages specified were indeed a genuine pre-estimate of losses. Whilst this requirement was tempered by the condition that the same was not 'exorbitant' or 'unconscionable', evidence was still required to show that there had been attempts to quantify the potential losses in the event of breach. It is now sufficient to demonstrate that the agreed sum is proportionate to the innocent party's 'legitimate interest' in the relevant obligations being performed. However, when taken to the granular level, showing proportionality will, to a degree, require prior thought as to how this interest might be quantified. What constitutes a 'legitimate interest' is broad and goes beyond considerations of purely financial losses. As was seen in *ParkingEye*, the actual loss arising from one person overstaying the free parking period was arguably negligible. On such a basis, how could any requirement to pay a fee be a 'genuine pre-estimate' of a non-existent loss.

Partial possession

Whilst the Courts have taken a demonstrably restrictive approach, Judges have also been alive to the potential for damages to far outstrip the potential losses where the Employer takes partial possession and the Contract does not provide for sectional completion. Such issues were seen in the case of *Bramall & Ogden Ltd v Sheffield City Council*.[28] This case concerned the building of a housing estate comprising 123 new dwellings and the associated works. Whilst it had been the intention of the Council (as the Employer) to include Sectional Completion dates in the contract, this was not done. The contract included a liquidated damages provision which stated that £20 per week was recoverable for each incomplete dwelling. The (extended) contractual date for completion was 4 May 1977 and the final dwelling was handed over on 29 November 1977. As the works progressed, the Council took partial possession of the houses as they were completed. However, given that there was no provision for Sectional Completion, the Council argued that it was entitled to £2,460 in damages per week, comprising £20 per each of the 123 houses, irrespective of whether the dwelling had already been handed over. It is, however, notable that the Council did not actually levy this sum for the period of delay.

In the initial arbitral award, the Council succeeded and was granted damages totalling £26,150 (10.6 weeks of delay at £2,460 per week). Bramall appealed the decision to the Official Referees where his Honour Judge Howser QC upheld the appeal. Notwithstanding that the Council had arguably applied the liquidated damages provisions reasonably, the unavoidable fact was that the provision itself was inconsistent with a wider mechanism

---

28 (1983) 29 BLR 73.

that did not allow for Sectional Completion. Accordingly, the liquidated damages provision fell away because it was inoperable. Whilst not part of the ratio, the Judge was evidently moved by the arguments that the extent of damages claimed could be penal as the rate of damages would far outweigh the actual losses sustained where the employer had the benefit of the completed houses. In remitting the award back to the arbitrator, the Judge made it clear that the Council was not without remedy and would be able to claim general damages. It simply could not claim the liquidated sum where it had had the opportunity to make appropriate provision in the contract to cover circumstances where the employer had significant partial possession.

This was the position before the decision in *Makdessi*. By the time the TCC came to consider comparable facts in *Eco World – Ballymore Embassy Gardens Co Ltd v Dobler UK Ltd*[29] in 2021, the landscape had evidently changed.

In *Eco World*, the contract was for the design, supply and installation of the façade (including glazing works) for residential blocks (A, B and C), forming part of the regeneration of Nine Elms, near Vauxhall in London. The works were undertaken pursuant to a JCT 2011 Construction Management Trade Contract which did not include Sectional Completion Dates. The Contract did, however, direct that liquidated damages, at a rate of £25,000 per week (prorated for part of a week) were payable up to a cap of 7% of the final Trade Contract Sum.[30] As in *Bramall*, the Employer was permitted, with the Contractor's consent, to take partial possession of the works as and when they were complete. The (extended) contractual Completion Date was 30 April 2018. Ultimately, Eco World took possession of Blocks B and C on or around 15 June 2018. Practical Completion for the whole of the works, including Block A, was certified on 20 December 2018.

Dobler sought a declaration from the Court that the liquidated damages provision was unenforceable as a penalty. It argued that, because the rate of liquidated damages applied to the 'Works' as a whole, there was no opportunity to reduce that rate unless, and until, the whole scope was completed. It was, therefore, not possible to reduce the rate of liquidated damages in circumstances where the losses incurred reduced because the Employer had the benefit of Partial Possession. Accordingly, the provision could not be considered compensatory and was, therefore, a penalty. Mrs Justice O'Farrell disagreed. In this very clear judgment, her Ladyship made the following comments and determinations:

1. Notwithstanding that the rate of liquidated damages applied regardless of the beneficial use that the Employer had of Blocks B and C, the provision was not a penalty. This was because Eco World had a legitimate interest in the completion of the whole works and the fact that one block remained incomplete would impact the overall development.
2. In any event, the rate of weekly liquidated damages and the overall cap was not extravagant, exorbitant or unconscionable in the circumstances. Rather, it was, 'a secondary obligation which imposes a detriment on *Dobler* which is proportionate to the legitimate interest of [Eco-World] in the enforcement of the primary obligation of completion of the Works in accordance with the terms of the Contract'.[31]

---

29 [2021] EWHC 2207 (TCC).
30 Subject to a four-week grace period immediately following the contractual Completion Date.
31 *Eco World* (n 28) [83].

3. In situations where it is necessarily difficult to quantify the extent of losses, liquidated damages provisions are to be upheld wherever possible. The quantification of losses was especially difficult in this case given the variable combinations of possible possession scenarios. The liquidated damages clause had also been negotiated by the parties' lawyers and the Court should 'be cautious about any interference in the freedom of the parties to agree commercial terms and allocation of risk in their business dealings'.[32]
4. Both parties were able to benefit from the application of a liquidated damages provision. The Contractor was not exposed to 'unknown and open-ended liability' and the Employer had certainty regarding the sums it was entitled to in order to compensate for losses. Accordingly, '[e]ach party is, therefore, better able to manage the risk of delay in the completion of the project'.[33]

By reference to their individual ratios, *Bramall* and *Eco-World* are distinguishable in one key regard. Whilst His Honour Judge Howser QC was concerned that the weekly rate of liquidated damages was rather high in circumstances where the Employer had beneficial use of many of the dwellings, this was not the reason the overall provision was struck down. Rather than the rate being 'extravagant, exorbitant or unconscionable' (as described by O'Farrell MJ), the provision itself could not be properly applied where the wider contract did not permit Sectional Completion. The two decisions are, therefore, not direct comparators, but the earlier decision would indicate a more lenient approach of the Courts when considering the potential unfairness to a Contractor who has completed most, but not all, of its works.

Do liquidated damages survive termination?

Between August 2017 and July 2021, construction law commentators were treated to the judicial saga surrounding the case of *Triple Point Technology Inc v PTT Public Co Ltd*.[34] This case concerned a contract for the delivery, by Triple Point, of a new trading and management system, over two phases (Phase 1 – replacing PTT's existing trading system and Phase 2 – system enhancements to accommodate new types of trade). The contract provided for staged, milestone payments and included a liquidated damages clause requiring Triple Point to pay 0.1% of the undelivered work for each day of delay up until 'PTT accepts such work'.[35] The project suffered delays and, at the point where Triple Point had delivered some aspects of Phase 1 but no elements of Phase 2, PTT terminated the contract.

Triple Point commenced proceedings to claim outstanding payments and PTT counterclaimed for losses flowing from the termination and payments due under the liquidated damages provision. Triple Point resisted the payment of liquidated damages on the basis that the operative provision described the same as a 'penalty'. The Judge at First Instance, Mrs Justice Jefford, clearly explained that the use of the word "penalty" was not determinative of the nature of the obligation and whether or not it was enforceable. Triple

---

32 ibid [79].
33 ibid.
34 [2018] EWHC 45 (TCC), [2019] EWCA Civ 230 and [2021] UKSC 29.
35 ibid [39] (detailing Article 5 of the Contract).

Point also argued, relying on *Makdessi*, that the rate of liquidated damages was 'out of all proportion to the legitimate interest' PTT had in enforcing the primary obligation. This argument was, again, succinctly dismissed by her Ladyship.

The more difficult aspects to be determined concerned the inter-relationship between damages payable following delay and the termination of a contract at the point it was in delay. On this subject, Triple Point argued that, by virtue of the wording of Article 5 (regarding liquidated damages), this obligation did not survive termination. As detailed above, damages were detailed to be payable at a daily rate in respect of 'undelivered work' for each day of delay 'from the due date for delivery up to the date PTT accepts such work'.[36] It was Triple Point's case that, given the termination, PTT could no longer 'accept' any further work, necessarily making this obligation open ended and, therefore, inoperable. Mrs Justice Jefford disagreed and held that liquidated damages, at the agreed rate, accrued from the date the relevant milestone date was missed up until the contract was terminated.

Triple Point appealed to the Court of Appeal and their Lord Justices Floyd, Lewison and Jackson overturned the decision at First Instance. In tracking back the relevant authorities to 1913, their Lordships relied on the House of Lords' decision in *British Glanzstoff Manufacturing Co Ltd v General Accident Fire & Life Assurance Corp Ltd*.[37] In *Glanzstoff*, it was held that, in the event that works were late but could not be completed because the contract was terminated, the remedy should be general damages rather than contractual liquidated damages. In finding that this decision should be followed, Lord Justice Jackson, in his leading judgment, determined that Article 5 'has no application in a situation where the contractor never hands over completed work to the employer'.[38] His Lordship was also keen to point out that *Glanzstoff* was a judgment of the highest court that, whilst being over a century old, had never been disapproved.[39] The overall finding, therefore, was that the liquidated damages obligation (focusing on delays prior to the 'completion' of the works) fell away in circumstances where the contract was terminated during the period of delay.

There followed more than two years of uncertainty pending PTT's appeal to the Supreme Court. During this time, many employers had to carefully consider the opportunity cost of terminating a non-performing contractor as against foregoing the liquidated damages that would otherwise accrue until the works were complete. Thankfully, in July 2021, the Supreme Court offered much needed clarity. Overturning the Court of Appeal decision, the Supreme Court held that the liquidated damages provision falls away at the point of termination but not before. Therefore, damages that had accrued in line with that obligation up until that point were payable in the normal way and the employer would not need to resort to claiming general damages. Lady Arden, strongly rejecting the Court of Appeal's finding, described the inferior Court's reasoning as a 'radical re-interpretation of the case law on liquidated damages clauses'.[40] Her Ladyship also commented that the

---

36 ibid.
37 [1913] AC 143.
38 [2019] EWCA Civ 230 [112].
39 ibid [109].
40 [2021] UKSC 29 [42].

Court of Appeal's approach was 'inconsistent with commercial reality and the accepted function of liquidated damages'.[41]

Lord Leggatt, likewise rejecting the Court of Appeal's decision, considered that there were, in addition, policy arguments to support the enforceability of liquidated damages up until a contract was terminated. Were it to be otherwise, his Lordship noted that such a position 'would give a contractor who badly overruns the time specified for completion an incentive not to complete the work in order to avoid paying liquidated damages for the delay which its breach of contract has caused. It makes no sense to create such an incentive'.[42] The overall tenor of the decision was that forcing an employer to the time and exertion of proving its losses in general damages undermined the guiding principle of liquidated damages. Namely, that such obligations should 'provide a remedy that is predictable and certain for a particular event (here, as often, that event is a delay in completion)'.[43] Once again, the Supreme Court underlined the critical importance of non-interference by the English Courts in agreements freely negotiated and entered into by equally sophisticated commercial parties.

Post-termination and caps of liability

Another issue which the Supreme Court was called to consider in *Triple Point* was whether the Court of Appeal had erred in its findings regarding the proper construction of the contractual cap on liability.

The contract between PTT and Triple Point included the following provision within the limit of liability clause (Article 12.3):

> The total liability of [Triple Point] to PTT under the Contract shall be limited to the Contract Price received by [Triple Point] with respect to the services or deliverables involved under this Contract. Except for the specific remedies expressly identified as such in this Contract, PTT's exclusive remedy for any claim arising out of this Contract will be for [Triple Point], upon written notice, to use best endeavours to cure the breach at its expense, or failing that, to return the fees paid to [Triple Point] for the Services or Deliverables related to the breach. This limitation of liability shall not apply to [Triple Point's] liability resulting from fraud, negligence, gross negligence or wilful misconduct of [Triple Point] or any of its officers, employees or agents.

In establishing the overall damages due following the termination of Triple Point's employment, PTT sought to rely on the carve out of 'negligence' under the limit on liability. It asserted that Triple Point had failed to exercise 'reasonable skill, care and diligence' (as was contractually required) in its performance of the contract and this had led to delay and the termination. On this basis, PTT claimed that this constituted 'negligence' within the meaning of Article 12.3 and sought damages over and above the specified cap. Triple Point rejected these claims and asserted that the limit of liability would be practically meaningless if 'negligence' were given such a wide definition in a contract for services. Both the Judge at First Instance and the Court of Appeal preferred Triple Point's interpretation of the provision and determined that, in the context within which the word

---

41 ibid [35].
42 ibid [81].
43 ibid [35] (Lady Arden).

'negligence' was used, it had to describe 'unusual or extreme conduct'.[44] Accordingly, the lower Courts held that the limit on liability should apply, save in circumstances where the tort of Negligence was engaged rather than in respect of breaches of the contractual duties of reasonable skill and care.

The Supreme Court took a different view. By a majority decision, it was held that importing the application of negligence in only a tortious sense was beyond what the words in the Contract could, and should, mean. Lord Leggatt specifically noted that Triple Point's construction of the limitation clause was 'not merely contrary to the ordinary legal meaning of the word 'negligence' but is not a meaning which the term can reasonably bear'.[45] On the basis that the liquidated damages arose because of delays caused by Triple Point's failure to exercise the requisite level of skill and care (i.e. by its negligence), the sums payable were not subject to the cap on liability. Such a stance, again, demonstrates the strict adherence under English law to the ordinary natural meaning of the text to be interpreted. As clearly set out by Lord Neuberger in *Arnold v Britton*:

> While commercial common sense is a very important factor to take into account when interpreting a contract, a court should be very slow to reject the natural meaning of a provision as correct simply because it appears to be a very imprudent term for one of the parties to have agreed, even ignoring the benefit of wisdom of hindsight. The purpose of interpretation is to identify what the parties have agreed, not what the court thinks that they should have agreed.[46]

Void for uncertainty seems unlikely

As one of the keystones of contract formation, it is trite law that contractual terms must be 'certain' if they are to be enforceable. Whilst there have been many cases where the English Courts have struck down clauses and/or entire agreements on the basis that they are too vague to stand, such determinations are not made lightly. In the face of potential uncertainty, Judges will often take significant measures to ensure that, despite imprecise wording, the matter can be rendered certain where at all possible. As Lord Justice Rix eloquently explained in his decision in *Scammell v Dicker*:

> it is simply a non sequitur to argue from a disagreement about the meaning and effect of a contract to its legal uncertainty (...) For that to occur – and it very rarely occurs – it has to be legally or practically impossible to give to the parties' agreement any sensible content.[47]

In the context of liquidated damages, the matter of uncertainty came up in the 2022 case of *Buckingham Group Contracting Ltd v Peel L&P Investments and Property Ltd*.[48] Buckingham was employed under an amended JCT Design and Build Contract 2016 for the construction of a new manufacturing facility. The Contract included the standard wording regarding the payment of liquidated damages in the event of contractor delay (clause 2.29). However, the Contract also referred to a bespoke clause 2.29A detailing a milestone date regime and an additional Schedule dealing with the periods of delay and the rates at which liquidated damages would accrue. The provisions included drafting errors in respect of

---

44 [2019] EWCA Civ 230 [119].
45 [2021] UKSC 29 [115].
46 [2015] UKSC 36 [20].
47 [2005] EWCA Civ 405 [30].
48 [2022] EWHC 1842 (TCC).

the completion date, the applicable rates for liquidated damages and the basis on which liquidated damages would be calculated. The liquidated damages provisions also failed to provide a workable scheme in respect of partial possession. The works ultimately suffered severe delays and *Buckingham* brought proceedings for a declaration that the liquidated damages mechanism was void for uncertainty and, therefore, unenforceable.

Alexander Nissen KC, sitting as a Deputy High Court Judge, detailed previous authorities which emphasised the high threshold that Buckingham would need to reach in order to get the remedy it sought. In unpicking each of Buckingham's arguments, the Judge was able to find an interpretation of the relevant provisions 'which gives clear effect to the intention of the parties'.[49] Such an intention was that there would be defined consequences and routes to compensation in the event that the works were not delivered in line with the specified dates. The fact that the determination of those dates and the levels of liquidated damages to be recovered were not straightforward did not render the overall provisions void.

More broadly, the Judge noted that

> the court is reluctant to hold a provision in a contract is void for uncertainty and, if it is open to the court to find an interpretation which gives effect to the parties' intentions, then it will do so. It is only if the court cannot reach any conclusion as to what was in the minds of the parties or where it is unsafe to prefer one possible meaning to other equally possible meanings that the provision would be void.[50]

This decision, therefore, offers yet another example where the English Court's non-interventionalist approach is brought to the fore.

Conclusion

Liquidated damages as a mechanism for managing breaches between contracting parties is commercially convenient and avoids uncertainty in relation to the amount of any unliquidated damages that might arise from a breach. It is also a powerful and helpful mechanism for quantifying delay in construction contracts (and potentially other breaches). On the one hand, the employer is saved from attempting to ascertain its actual loss, whilst, on the other hand, a contractor knows the pre-determined loss that will arise for any delay. In this respect, a liquidated damages provision is not just a legal mechanism in a contract, but also a commercial risk management tool between the parties in relation to the project.

The rule against penalties does not regulate remedies for the primary obligation between the parties. A liquidated damages mechanism only applies to the secondary obligation. In other words, the rule against penalties does not relate to the breach of the primary obligation, but, instead, to the balancing act set out by the liquidated damage clause and, in particular, the liquidated amount as a secondary obligation.

The most recent case law points to a test that requires, first, one to ask whether the amount is out of all proportion to the legitimate interest of the other party. This is a higher test than the original *Dunlop* formulation of a genuine pre-estimate of loss. Second, one should also consider whether the term was negotiated and therefore subject to debate between the parties. Third, the Courts will consider the balance of power between the

---

49 ibid [51].
50 ibid [39].

parties, perhaps taking into account any legal representation of both parties. A negotiated term, especially with the assistance of lawyers, will point to a mechanism and amount that will be difficult to challenge.

The question as to how difficult it is to calculate loss suffered due to a breach of the primary obligation now seems to be a question that falls very much in favour of supporting most attempts at pre-estimating the amount. The amount need not represent the actual loss and, indeed, partial possession seems now to favour payment of the entire liquidated damages rather than a finding that the mechanism has broken down and cannot be operated.

The question as to whether an amount could be said to be a penalty is more likely to be answered by consideration of whether the liquidated damages amount is 'extravagant, exorbitant, or unconscionable'. The application of the Supreme Court's approach in *Makdessi* points very much to supporting the legitimate interest ensuring compliance with the terms of the Contract, particularly where the ascertainment of actual loss is potentially vague, or, indeed, entirely uncertain.

Clear drafting is also important, but the Courts now seems less likely to find a term void for uncertainty. The purposive approach to enforcement has become more prevalent over the years, and is, no doubt, welcomed by project sponsors. The supply side of the industry must assess carefully whether it can complete a project or manage the liquidated damages arising from delay. There is, of course, the question of waiver and caps of liability, and it perhaps remains to be seen how they will impact liquidated damages provisions. A waiver could, of course, change the express situation between the parties depending on the circumstance, but it seems likely (and this depends on the drafting) that caps of liability specifically for liquidated damages will be effective.

CHAPTER 12

Liquidated damages in the Middle East

A UAE perspective[1]

Gordon Blanke[2]

Introduction

The award of liquidated damages features as a common form of relief in construction disputes in the Middle East, including, more specifically, in the United Arab Emirates (UAE).[3] Construction projects in the UAE are routinely governed by the FIDIC conditions of contract,[4] which allow for the employer to recover liquidated damages for a contractor-caused delay to the time for completion.[5] For the avoidance of doubt, for present purposes, *liquidated damages* are understood to be a contractual pre-estimate of monetary compensation payable to the employer for a contractor-caused delay to the time for completion.

Construction contracts for projects carried out in the UAE tend to be subject to UAE law on the merits. As a result, any contractual provision for liquidated damages must be interpreted and as such produces legal effects under UAE law as the governing law on the merits. This requires contracting and/ or disputing parties to investigate the position on liquidated damages under UAE law in order fully to understand their contractual rights and obligations. This, in turn, is assisted by guidance from the *jurisprudence constante*[6]

---

1 As a note of caution, the reader is advised that this chapter does not aim to be exhaustive but, given prevailing constraints of space, aims to provide some initial guidance only.

2 Founding Principal, Blanke Arbitration, Dubai/London/Paris.

3 For further guidance on the availability of liquidated damages in construction disputes in the UAE and the wider Middle East, see Joseph A. Chedrawe, 'Liquidated Damages for Delay in the Middle East: Not Etched in Stone' 4(1) BCDR International Arbitration Review (2017) 99–112; Ahmed F. Waly, 'Legal Rules Commonly Applied to Contract Breaches in Constructions Arbitrations in Egypt and the United Arab Emirates' 4(1) BCDR International Arbitration Review (2017) 135–152, in particular at section 4.2; and Mohammed S. Abdel Wahab, 'The Nuts and Bolts of Construction Arbitration in the MENA: Principles and Practice' in Stavros Brekoulakis and David Brynmor Thomas (eds), *The Guide to Construction Arbitration* (GAR 2017) 230–249, 244–246. See also, with a focus on the UAE and the Gulf countries, Michael Grose, *Construction Law in the United Arab Emirates and the Gulf* (Wiley/Blackwell 2016) 137 *et seq.* Finally, with a focus on the UAE, see Richard Harding, 'Making and Defending Claims for Liquidated Damages in the United Arab Emirates', a paper given at a meeting of the Society of Construction Law (UAE) in Dubai on 30 May 2006; Richard Harding, 'Damages under UAE Law: The Jane Lemon QC Memorial Lecture', a paper given at a meeting of the Society of Construction Law (Gulf) in Dubai on 6 October 2019; and Nicolas Bremer, 'Liquidated Damages under the Law of the United Arab Emirates and its Interpretation by UAE Courts' (October 2015) 199–212.

4 Usually the FIDIC 1987, 4th edition.

5 See Cl. 47(1), FIDIC 1987 4th edition.

6 Which, albeit not strictly binding, establishes a body of rulings of the courts of cassation that are commonly accepted to provide persuasive guidance on the interpretation of UAE law to the lower courts, i.e., the courts of appeal and the courts of first instance, and are recognised for their consistency in the courts'

DOI: 10.4324/9781032663975-16

of the onshore UAE Courts.[7] UAE law is codified, following the Egyptian and French law tradition. Of particular importance for present purposes is the UAE Civil Code,[8] which, *inter alia*, contains specific provisions on works or building contracts, the so-called *muqawala*.[9] For an accurate construction of its provisions, the UAE Civil Code does not only rely upon the *jurisprudence constante* of the UAE Courts but also on the commentary issued by the UAE Ministry of Justice on the UAE Civil Code.[10,11]

In the alternative, to govern their contractual relationship, parties may contract into the application of the substantive body of law of one of the judicial free zones specific to the UAE. To that end, the contracting parties have a choice between the laws of the Abu Dhabi Global Market (ADGM) and the laws of the Dubai International Financial Centre (DIFC). The ADGM and the DIFC are common law jurisdictions, equipped with their own, autonomous common law courts, the DIFC and ADGM Courts respectively, which, in turn, are modeled on the English legal system. Both the DIFC and the ADGM dispense their own, standalone body of laws: Albeit adopted autonomously,[12] DIFC law is inspired by English law[13] whereas ADGM law incorporates English common law and statute wholesale by reference.[14] Both the DIFC and the ADGM Courts abide by the doctrine of *stare decisis* and further develop the law in a piecemeal fashion through binding case law precedent on a case-by-case basis.

In the following, this chapter briefly explores the UAE law position on liquidated damages, both onshore and offshore. In doing so, it will show that the UAE Courts take a fairly unique approach to the concept of liquidated damages. In particular, the onshore courts, sensitive to the requirements of the Shari'ah,[15,16] retain the power to adjust an employer's

---

decision-making. In a construction context more specifically, this also stands confirmed by Grose in Michael Grose, *Construction Law in the United Arab Emirates and the Gulf* (Wiley/Blackwell 2016) 8–9.

7 In the following, this chapter relies upon the established jurisprudence of the Dubai and Abu Dhabi Courts in particular. For the avoidance of doubt, Emirati courts follow the civilian legal tradition and are as such – unlike common law courts – not bound by judicial case law precedent.

8 Which codifies Law No. 5 of 1985, the UAE Civil Transactions Law, as amended by Federal Law No. 1 of 1987 and Federal Law No. 30/2020.

9 See Articles 872–896 of the UAE Civil Code.

10 For an English translation, see James Whelan, *UAE Civil Code and Ministry of Justice Commentary – 2010* (Thomson Reuters 2011), hereinafter referred to in shorthand as the 'Commentary'.

11 As confirmed by the Preface of the Commentary: 'The Commentary is a substantial and scholarly work published by the Ministry of Justice in 1987, which provides an analysis of the historical, jurisprudential and comparative background of each of the various parts of the [UAE] Civil Code and, in most cases, of individual articles. It also provides numerous examples of how many of the provisions work in practice. Although the Commentary does not have statutory authority, it is nevertheless so important, so profuse in its guidance, and held in such respect by the Courts of the United Arab Emirates, that it can properly be said that it is an essential tool for the correct interpretation of the statutory provisions of the Code, and that it is often unsafe to rely on the words of the Code alone in determining their meaning and effect.' James Whelan, *UAE Civil Code and Ministry of Justice Commentary – 2010* (Thomson Reuters 2011), 'Preface', at xiii.

12 See, e.g., DIFC Law No. 6 of 2004 on Contract Law; DIFC Law No. 6 of 2005 on Implied Terms in Contracts and Unfair Terms; DIFC Law No. 7 of 2005 on Damages and Remedies; and DIFC Law No. 5 of 2005, the DIFC Law of Obligations.

13 And the DIFC Courts rely upon English law by See Article 8(1) DIFC Law No. 3 of 2004, the Law on the Application of Civil and Commercial Laws in the DIFC.

14 See the Application of English Law Regulations 2015.

15 Which forms a source of UAE law (see Article 7 of the UAE Constitution 1971) and is fully incorporated into the provisions of the UAE codes, including the UAE Civil Code.

16 For further background on the role played by the Islamic Shari'ah in Middle Eastern legal systems, including the UAE, see Faisal Kutty, 'The Shari'a Factor in International Commercial Arbitration' 4 J. of Arab Arb. (2009) 63–112.

contractual entitlement to liquidated damages to actual loss suffered. By contrast, albeit that the DIFC and the ADGM Courts are likely to follow a more common law-inspired approach to liquidated damages, recent case law precedent of the DIFC Courts suggests that the DIFC Courts remain open to consider the adjustment of liquidated damages to actual loss suffered if requested to do so by the parties.

For the avoidance of doubt, the considerations in this chapter are of relevance to the lawful articulation of claims for liquidated damages in any contentious proceedings under UAE law on the merits, whether litigation or arbitration.[17] As a note of caution, the international composition of an arbitral tribunal cannot and must not be mistaken for an opportunity to import common law-style or other internationalist reasoning on the application of liquidated damages[18] into an arbitral process that is governed by UAE law on the merits.[19,20] With that in mind, the provisions of the UAE Civil Code (and by extension those of the DIFC and ADGM laws) that follow must be read from the perspective of a judge and an arbitrator or an arbitral tribunal alike. As Harding, quite rightly, cautions: 'Many in the UAE approach questions of liquidated damages with preconceptions based on English Law. However the law of the UAE is entirely different. All ideas of "time at large", "prevention" and "penalties" should be forgotten.'[21] 'Arbitrators must therefore be careful not to determine disputes relying on foreign legal concepts.'[22]

For the avoidance of doubt, given prevailing constraints of space, this chapter does not discuss the potential defenses that are available to a contractor that faces a claim for liquidated damages by an employer under UAE law. For further guidance, the reader is referred to complementary literature on the subject.[23]

The position under the UAE Civil Code

Article 390 of the UAE Civil Code provides the legal framework for liquidated damages under UAE law. Article 390 is comprised of two limbs, sub-paragraph (1) and sub-paragraph (2), with which we shall deal under separate headings below.

---

17 This includes arbitration on- and offshore: For arbitration onshore, see Gordon Blanke, *Blanke on UAE Arbitration Legislation and Rules: A Multi-Volume Article-by-Article Commentary* (Sweet & Maxwell Volume I 2021). For free zone arbitration, see Gordon Blanke, 'Free Zone Arbitration in the MENA: The UAE Example' in Gordon Blanke and Soraya Corm-Bakhos (eds), *The MENA Leading Arbitrators' Guide to International Arbitration* (Juris 2023) 471–513.

18 See, e.g., Joseph A. Chedrawe, 'Liquidated Damages for Delay in the Middle East: Not Etched in Stone' 4(1) BCDR International Arbitration Review (2017) 99–112, 111: 'Looking beyond the courts, it is the author's experience that international arbitral tribunals may be less likely to adjust contractually-agreed amounts and will consider a range of additional factors, including sanctity of contract, industry practice, party sophistication and possibly the difficulty of establishing loss in construction projects.'

19 An arbitral tribunal being commonly mandated to apply the governing law to the facts of the case before it, hence exercising a judicial decision-making function.

20 Albeit that the limits of this cautionary note are readily acknowledged, as the *bona fide* misapplication of the governing law does usually not qualify as a valid ground for challenge of a resultant arbitral award.

21 Richard Harding, 'Damages under UAE Law: The Jane Lemon QC Memorial Lecture', a paper given at a meeting of the Society of Construction Law (Gulf) in Dubai on 6 October 2019, 3.

22 Richard Harding, 'Making and Defending Claims for Liquidated Damages in the United Arab Emirates', a paper given at a meeting of the Society of Construction Law (UAE) in Dubai on 30 May 2006, at footnote 6.

23 See, e.g., Richard Harding, 'Making and Defending Claims for Liquidated Damages in the United Arab Emirates', a paper given at a meeting of the Society of Construction Law (UAE) in Dubai on 30 May 2006, 21 *et seq.*, where Harding lists both contractual defenses and defenses at law.

For context, Article 390 follows on from Article 389 of the UAE Civil Code, which provides that '[i]f the amount of compensation is not fixed by a provision of law or of the contract, the judge shall assess it in an amount equivalent to the harm in fact suffered at the time of the occurrence thereof.' Article 389 clarifies that absent any contractual pre-estimate of loss, the default position under UAE law is for the judge (and by extension an arbitral tribunal) to assess compensation for a contractual breach on the basis of actual loss suffered. Pursuant to the Commentary, '[t]he rule in positive laws is that if compensation is not assessed in the contract or by a provision of the law, then it is the judge who assesses it.' The Commentary further explains as follows:

> Compensation includes all damage and loss of earnings sustained by the obligee, provided that that is a natural result of non-performance or delay in performance of the obligation. Damage is regarded as being a natural result if it was not within the power of the obligee by making reasonable efforts to avert it. In general, in case of obligations that have their origins in contracts, the obligor who has not committed any fraud or gross error is obliged to pay compensation only for the damage that could have been ordinarily foreseen at the time the contract was made.[24]

The Commentary then continues to highlight the rationale of the default position under Article 389 in the following terms, rooting it firmly in the Islamic Shari'ah:

> It has been seen that this [A]rticle adopts the approach of the Islamic shari'a and follows the way it expresses it, on the basis that if the amount of the liability or compensation is not laid down in the law or by contract, it will be assessed by the judge in an amount equal to the damage in fact caused, subject to any specific legal provision.[25]

In the light of the foregoing, it is evident that absent party agreement or the law stating otherwise, Article 389 of the UAE Civil Code confers upon the judge and by extension an arbitrator the power to award compensation for actual loss suffered by a breach of contract, including for the late performance of a contractual obligation, such as a contractor-caused delay to the time for completion.

It is against this background that the two limbs of Article 390 of the UAE Civil Code operate and that their operation must be construed.

Article 390(1) of the UAE Civil Code

Article 390(1) of the UAE Civil Code confirms that under UAE law, parties are allowed to contract into a fixed or pre-agreed amount of compensation for a future breach of contract, whether by a provision in the main contract or subsequently by a submission agreement.[26] For that purpose, the UAE Courts – unlike the English or common law courts

---

24 Commentary, 2-0575.

25 *Ibid.*

26 For the avoidance of doubt, the judge's or the arbitral tribunal's powers under Article 390(2) of the UAE Civil Code do not engage if the contracting parties agree to liquidated damages after the breach of contract has occurred or, in the construction context more specifically, after the contractor-caused delay to the time for completion: See Case No. 205/2002, ruling of the Dubai Court of Cassation of 23 June 2002: 'The judge may however in the circumstances and upon the request of either party, modify such agreement [to liquidated damages within the meaning of Art. 390(1) of the UAE Civil Code] in such a manner as necessary to make the estimated compensation equivalent to the damage sustained. If the parties agree, following the obligor's breach, to the amount of compensation payable to the aggrieved party, the judge would not interfere with their agreement which he may only do if an estimate was made in advance of the breach.'

more generally – do not draw any distinction between liquidated damages and penalty clauses.[27] In the terms of the first limb of Article 390, '[t]he contracting parties may fix the amount of compensation in advance by making a provision therefor in the contract or in a subsequent agreement.' As the Commentary notes, '[t]his [A]rticle deals with the question of a prior agreement determining the amount of compensation for loss.'[28] To mark its importance, the Commentary further explains that '[t]his is a different case from compensation for damage after it has occurred, because in the case of the assessment by the parties of damage after it has occurred there is not the same fear of error or quasi-coercion that may be present in a prior assessment, which requires a special regulating provision.'[29] Unsurprisingly, therefore, this provision is expressly stated to be 'subject to the provisions of the law', which, for present purposes, invites a direct reference to the second limb of Article 390, i.e., Article 390(2) of the UAE Civil Code.

Before taking a closer look at Article 390(2), it is important to emphasise that 390(1) of the UAE Civil Code only operates if compensation has been shown to be in fact due. In other words, taking Cl. 47.1 FIDIC for an example, the payment of liquidated damages under that Clause depends on a prior demonstration by the employer that the contractor's failure to meet the time for completion caused the employer *some actual* loss.[30] To the extent that the employer is unable to establish that it incurred some actual loss as a result of the contractor's failure to complete, the contractor's obligation to pay liquidated damages under Clause 47.1 fails to engage. This is supported by the Commentary in the following terms:

> In order for this rule [i.e., the rule under Art. 390] to apply, compensation must in fact be due, and if there is no compensation due then there will be no scope for the application of this article. If compensation is due and the amount assessed by the parties is equivalent to the damage, then [such compensation shall be payable].[31]

This also stands confirmed by authoritative, third-party commentary on the subject. As explained by Attia:

> It should be noted, from the outset, that liquidated damages clauses are deemed to be ancillary contractual obligations, in the sense that they will not apply unless an obligation for payment of damages (i.e. the primary obligation) has been established in the first place. In other words, liquidated damages are not, per se, a cause of action for a claim for damages. Rather, they can only be invoked for establishing the amount of damages claimed.
>
> For instance, there are two distinct obligations arising out of a liquidated damages clause (concerning delays) in a construction contract. Firstly, the contractor's obligation to complete the works within a specified time limit (i.e. the primary obligation). Secondly, the contractor's

---

27 To this effect, see Michael Grose, *Construction Law in the United Arab Emirates and the Gulf* (Wiley/Blackwell 2016) 139: 'the courts have emphasised that provisions in construction contracts possessing the characteristics of an agreement as to the amount of delay damages are subject to judicial scrutiny. No distinction is drawn or recognised between a damages and a penalty clause for this or any other purpose.'

28 Commentary, 2-0577.

29 *Ibid.*

30 In support, see also Bremer, who, in reliance on Case No. 222/2005, ruling of the Dubai Court of Cassation of 19 June 2006, concludes: 'The Dubai Court of Cassation appears to hold that the compensation owed under a liquidated damages clause may be adjusted wherever there is a discrepancy between the compensation agreed upon in the liquidated damage clause and the losses actually suffered by the party invoking it.' See Nicolas Bremer, 'Liquidated Damages under the Law of the United Arab Emirates and its Interpretation by UAE Courts' (October 2015) 199–212, 208.

31 *Ibid.*

obligation to pay liquidated damages (i.e. the ancillary obligation), provided that the contractor is in breach of the primary obligation and the employer has sustained actual loss as a result of this breach.[32]

In reliance on the commentary provided on Article 390 of the UAE Civil Code in the Commentary, Bremer echoes this view, noting that no liquidated damages are payable where no actual damages have been incurred by the employer:

> As per the Commentary to the UAE Civil Code issued by the UAE Ministry of Justice (Commentary on the Civil Code) [i.e., the Commentary] an agreement on liquidated damages may only oblige the party in breach to pay the pre-agreed compensation where loss was in fact incurred. Hence, while a party seeking compensation under a liquidated damage clause does not have to substantiate the actual amount of loss it incurred – unless either of the parties requests the court to adjust the compensation owed pursuant to Article 390(2) [UAE] Civil Code – the fact that loss was in fact sustained by the party invoking the liquidated damage clause has to be proven.[33]

Further, for a claim for liquidated damages to succeed under UAE law, it must comply with the *tripartite* test that generally applies to the assessment of damages under UAE law.[34] As Attia helpfully confirms:

> Under the UAE law, in order for liquidated damages to be awarded, the following requirements must be satisfied (failing which, no liquidated damages would be awarded):
> A) A breach committed by the party who agreed to pay the liquidated damages;
> B) Actual damage sustained by the party who invokes the liquidated damages clause; and
> C) A causative link between the fault and the damage suffered.
> The UAE high courts have confirmed, in several occasions, that this tripartite test must be satisfied. The Dubai Court of Cassation held that the inclusion of a liquidated damages clause into a contract does not supersede this tripartite test for awarding damages.[35] The Federal Supreme Court has also concluded that the liquidated damages are subject to this tripartite test.[36,37]

Bremer further explains the position of the UAE courts authoritatively as follows:

> A review of judicial practice of UAE courts shows that UAE courts generally recognize the validity of liquidated damage clauses provided that 1) the party who agreed to pay the liquidated damages is legally responsible for committing a specific breach of contract, 2) the party invoking the liquidated damage clause actually sustained losses and 3) a causative link exists between the specific breach and the damage suffered.[38,39]

---

32 Faisal Attia, 'Liquidated Damages – The Bigger Picture', Al Tamimi Law Update (March 2012).

33 Nicolas Bremer, 'Liquidated Damages under the Law of the United Arab Emirates and its Interpretation by UAE Courts' (October 2015) 199–212, 205. Internal footnote omitted.

34 Tellingly, one of the fundamental principles upon which Harding bases his analysis of an employer's entitlement to liquidated damages reads as follows: 'First, liquidated damages are precisely that – damages which have been liquidated (that is, defined in amount). The law relating to liquidated damages therefore starts with the law relating to damages. If a party is not entitled to damages, he cannot be entitled to liquidated damages.' See Richard Harding, 'Making and Defending Claims for Liquidated Damages in the United Arab Emirates', a paper given at a meeting of the Society of Construction Law (UAE) in Dubai on 30 May 2006, 4.

35 Petition no. 494/2003, the hearing of 24 April 2004. [Footnote 4 in the original.]

36 Petition no. 344/19, the hearing of 23 January 1999. [Footnote 5 in the original.]

37 Faisal Attia, 'Liquidated Damages – The Bigger Picture', Al Tamimi Law Update (March 2012).

38 See Supreme Court, Case No. 103 of Judicial Year 24, Judgement rendered 21 March 2004; Supreme Court, Case No. 782 of Judicial Year 22, Judgement rendered 7 April 2002. [Footnote 25 in the original.]

39 Nicolas Bremer, 'Liquidated Damages under the Law of the United Arab Emirates and its Interpretation by UAE Courts' (October 2015) 199–212, 206.

On that basis, Bremer provides further guidance on the application of the tripartite test in the following terms:

a) Specific Breach

Liquidated damages may be awarded where the party agreeing to the liquidated damage clause is legally responsible for the specific breach defined in the clause. Specific breach can be any active infringement of or default in performance of the obligations under the relevant contract. A common event of default that triggers compensation under a liquidated damage clause is delay in performance.[40] For the party invoking the liquidated damage clause to be entitled to compensation, the party in breach has to be legally responsible for such breach.[41]

b) Loss Sustained

Compensation under a liquidated damage clause will only be awarded where the party invoking the clause actually sustained losses due to the breach of contract. The UAE Union Supreme Court (المحكمة الإتحادية العليا) (Supreme Court) for instance dis- missed a claim brought by the main-contractor against its sub-contractor based on the liquidated damage clause of the sub-contracting agreement whereby the main- contractor sought compensation for delay in completion of the sub-contracted works, because in the opinion of the court the main-contractor did not suffer any losses due to the late performance of the sub-contractor. The client – despite the late performance of the contracted works – did not claim damages from the main- contractor. Therefore, the court found that, since the client did not invoke the liquidated damage clause under the main-contracting agreement or seek compensation due to late performance from the main-contractor in any other way, the main-contractor had suffered no loss. Accordingly the court refused to award compensation under the liquidated damage clause of the sub-contracting agreement to the main-contractor. The court stated that: establishing fault on the part of the respondent [the sub-contractor] is not by itself sufficient for awarding liquidated damages. The claimant [the main-contractor] has to actually have sustained loss as a result of this fault.[42]

c) Causative Link

Damages may only be awarded where the underlying act of the obligated party is causal for the loss suffered by the injured party; thus, a causative link must exist between the two. In respect to liquidated damages this means that a causative link has to exist between the specific breach by the party against which the liquidated damage clause is invoked and the losses sustained by the party invoking the clause.[43]

---

40 See Supreme Court, Case No. 103 of Judicial Year 24, Judgement rendered 21 March 2004. [Footnote 26 in the original.]

41 See Supreme Court, Petition No. 26 of Judicial Year 24, Judgement rendered 1 June 2004. [Footnote 27 in the original.]

42 See Supreme Court, Petition No. 26 of Judicial Year 24, Judgement rendered 1 June 2004. [Footnote 29 in the original.]

43 Nicolas Bremer, 'Liquidated Damages under the Law of the United Arab Emirates and its Interpretation by UAE Courts' (October 2015) 199-212, 206-207 (bold in the original).

The rulings of the UAE Federal Supreme Court consistently confirm the application of the tripartite test to the entitlement and assessment of liquidated damages under UAE law as follows:

a) Case No. 103/24, ruling of the UAE Federal Supreme Court of 21 March 2004:

Article 390 of the Civil Code, as applied by this Court, provides that a delay penalty may only be applied if the obligor is proved to have been at fault but also that the obligee should be proved to have sustained damage. If the obligor disproves damage on part of the obligee, the penalty clause shall be inapplicable. The judge may reduce a delay penalty provided by contracts if he finds that it is not pro rata to the damage because damage should be proportionate to the compensation.[44]

b) Case No. 742/23, ruling of the UAE Federal Supreme Court of 16 May 2004:

It is settled law that a penalty for delay in private muqawala contracts is in essence no more than a consensual assessment of the compensation payable in the event that the contractor fails to fulfil his obligation. In order for it to be payable, the same conditions required for a judgment for compensation must be made out, namely the default, the damage, and the causal connection between them, which is the criterion for the assessment of compensation.[45]

c) Case No. 782/22, ruling of the UAE Federal Supreme Court of 7 April 2002:

In order to establish whether compensation is payable, the court must examine the conditions giving rise to it, namely a default, the damage, and the causal relationship between the default and the damage, which is the criterion for the assessment of compensation payable.[46]

d) Case No. 344/19, ruling of the UAE Federal Supreme Court of 23 January 1999:

The delay penalty included in the special contracting agreements – as per the rulings of this court – is, in essence, merely a contractual estimation for compensation that is payable where the contractor fails to perform its obligation or is late in performing the same beyond the date scheduled in the agreement, and for eligibility thereof, the conditions required for a compensation-awarding judgment must be met; namely, the fault, causal relation between the fault and damage which constitutes the basis of estimating the compensation payable.[47]

For completeness, it also bears mentioning that some UAE Courts have failed to condition the award of liquidated damages on an employer's compliance with the tripartite test. More specifically, similar to the approach taken by common law courts, those courts have found in favour of an employer's *automatic* entitlement to liquidated damages upon a contractor-caused delay to the time for completion, there being no need on part of the employer to prove *any* actual loss. This, in our view, raises concerns of proper compliance with the Islamic Shari'ah, there being a tangible risk that such awards may unjustly enrich the employer in circumstances where the employer has suffered no loss as a result

---

44 Case No. 103/24, ruling of the UAE Federal Supreme Court of 21 March 2004.
45 Case No. 742/23, ruling of the UAE Federal Supreme Court of 16 May 2004, at para. 2.
46 Case No. 782/22, ruling of the UAE Federal Supreme Court of 7 April 2002, at para. 6.
47 Case No. 344/19, ruling of the UAE Federal Supreme Court of 23 January 1999, at para. 1.

of a contractor-caused delay to the time for completion or where the contractual amount of liquidated damages by far exceeds the amount of loss actually suffered by the employer.[48] With that consideration in mind, some UAE Courts have consciously adopted a compromise solution or a middle way, refusing to award liquidated damages only where these prove excessive[49] or where there is no evidence of any actual loss at all.[50,51]

---

48 By analogy, see Case No. 706/26 (Sharia): 'Whereas, this interpretation is valid and does not deviate from the prima-facie meaning of the statements of the contract, the Judgment subject of the Cassation Appeal is not reproachable insofar as it adopted the principle that the Claimant recovers the value of this equipment in response to its case, as its deprivation of both the equipment and its value involves undue enrichment on the part of the Cassation Appellant at the expense of the Cassation Appellee, which is not permissible by sharia and law, and therefore, the subject-matter court has the right to intervene in order to amend the two Parties' agreement provided for in the penalty clause so that the compensation becomes commensurate with the amount of damage that the Cassation Appellant sustained.'

49 Adjusting the entitlement to liquidated damages accordingly under Article 390(2) of the UAE Civil Code. See Harding, who adduces the example of minor repair works outstanding, which, in turn, allows the employer to take over the works and fully benefit from them, in which case the contractor is likely only liable for actual, quantifiable loss (which is likely to be 'trivial'): See Richard Harding, 'Making and Defending Claims for Liquidated Damages in the United Arab Emirates', a paper given at a meeting of the Society of Construction Law (UAE) in Dubai on 30 May 2006, 46. See also Case No. 941/2009, ruling of the Abu Dhabi Court of Appeal: '[t]here is an assumption that the assessment of compensation agreed corresponds with the loss sustained by the party invoking the liquidated damage clause. The judge has to abide by the agreement of the parties and give effect to it unless the party against which the clause is invoked proves that the agreed compensation is excessive.' In addition, see Case No. 494/2003, ruling of the Dubai Court of Cassation of 24 April 2004, which requires the exercise of the judge's or arbitral tribunal's discretion under Article 390(2) to be based on sound reasoning and capable of sustaining his or her decision: 'This Court has held that a clause embodied in a contract specifying a sum payable for each period of delay in performance is a penalty clause (liquidated damages) which, on breach, creates a presumption of damage relieving the creditor from having to prove the occurrence of damage, the resulting loss and its amount. With liquidated damages the parties agree to an amount of damages ascertained by estimation such that damage is acknowledged on breach without prejudice to the other party's (debtor's) right to prove that the amount of damages stipulated in the penalty clause exceeds the damage actually incurred by the creditor or that the creditor never incurred any damage to begin with. It is further settled in this Court that damages, in all cases, must be assessed according to the loss the aggrieved party has incurred and the gain he has foregone provided that the alleged damage was the direct result of a fault and has or will actually occur. Contingent damages that have not occurred would only be recoverable if they actually occur and the burden lies with the aggrieved party to prove such damage. While parties may agree (in their contract) a pre-determined amount to be paid as damages, Article 390 of the Civil Transactions Code would allow the judge, upon request of either party, to vary such agreement commensurate with the actual damage and to determine the amount of damages to be awarded provided his decision is based on sound reasoning and evidence capable of sustaining his decision.'

50 See, e.g., Case No. 414/21 (Civil), ruling of the UAE Federal Supreme Court of 27 March 2001, reported in Joseph A. Chedrawe, 'Liquidated Damages for Delay in the Middle East: Not Etched in Stone' 4(1) BCDR International Arbitration Review (2017) 99–112, 110. *Contra*, however, see Case No. 138/1994, ruling of the Dubai Court of Cassation of 13 November 1994, reported in Michael Grose, *Construction Law in the United Arab Emirates and the Gulf* (Wiley/Blackwell 2016) 143, in which the Dubai Court of Cassation reversed the lower court's decision to accept a common 10% cap on liquidated damages in building contracts, enforcing the parties' agreement to a higher amount of liquidated damages over and above local custom and usage. In support, see also Ricahrd Harding, according to whom '[t]he general law is that if there is 'no loss' there is no damage and so one of the essential elements of a claim is missing.' See Richard Harding, 'Damages under UAE Law: The Jane Lemon QC Memorial Lecture', a paper given at a meeting of the Society of Construction Law (Gulf) in Dubai on 6 October 2019, 42. By way of further illustration, Harding adduces the example of an employer who, despite the purported delay, has taken over 100% of the works and derives the full benefit from the works: See Richard Harding, 'Making and Defending Claims for Liquidated Damages in the United Arab Emirates', a paper given at a meeting of the Society of Construction Law (UAE) in Dubai on 30 May 2006, 45.

51 To seemingly the same effect, see also Case No. 941/2009, ruling of the Abu Dhabi Court of Cassation of 29 September 2009: 'since pursuant to Article (390) of the Civil Transactions Law, [...], which means – as per the ruling of the present court – that stipulating a penalty clause reflects the estimation of occurrence of the damage in the minds of the contracting parties, thus the creditor shall be exempted from the burden of proving its occurrence; while the debtor shall bear the burden of proving that the damage hasn't occurred. Further, the

Finally, it bears mentioning that the UAE Courts have found that a liquidated damages provision will lapse in the event that the underlying construction contract is terminated[52] unless that provision is expressly agreed by the contracting parties to survive termination, in which case the employer's entitlement to the pre-agreed contractual amount of damages for a contractor-caused delay endures beyond termination.[53]

Article 390(2) of the UAE Civil Code

The second limb of Article 390 of the UAE Civil Code, i.e., Article 390(2), flows on naturally from the first limb of that Article, i.e., Article 390(1). It does so by linking up directly with the proviso to which the application of the first limb is subject, to wit the reference to 'the provisions of the law', of which the second limb of Article 390 is one. In other words, the operation of Article 390(1) must be read as subject to the application of Article 390(2).

Article 390(2) of the UAE Civil Code more specifically empowers a judge and by extension an arbitral tribunal to adjust any pre-agreed compensation within the meaning of Art. 390(1) of the UAE Civil Code to actual loss suffered. Accordingly, in the terms of Article 390(2), '[t]he judge may in all cases, upon the application of either of the parties, vary such agreement [i.e., as referred to under Article 390(1)] so as to make the compensation equal to the harm.'

Importantly, the powers conferred upon the judge or an arbitrator under Art. 390(2) of the UAE Civil Code are strictly subject to a request for adjustment being made by a disputing party ('upon the application of either of the parties') and are discretionary ('may').[54] They may be invoked by both the contractor and the employer. This implies that the power to 'vary' the contractual amount of liquidated damages may serve either to increase or to decrease that amount provided that the pre-agreed amount of damages is not equal to the extent of loss actually suffered: In other words, in circumstances where the contractual amount of liquidated damages exceeds the extent of loss actually suffered

---

agreed-upon estimation of the compensation shall be commensurate with the damage incurred by the creditor, hence the judge shall abide by said condition and apply same unless the debtor proves that the agreed-upon compensation is overestimated or that no damage has occurred.'

52 Given that a liquidated damages provision qualifies as a subsidiary obligation, ancillary to the contractor's obligation to complete by the time for completion: See Case No. 302/21, ruling of the UAE Federal Supreme Court of 17 June 2001, reported in Michael Grose, *Construction Law in the United Arab Emirates and the Gulf* (Wiley/Blackwell 2016) 139. On the qualification of liquidated damages as a subsidiary or an ancillary obligation, see also the quote from Faisal Attia, 'Liquidated Damages – The Bigger Picture' Al Tamimi Law Update (March 2012) at section 2.1 above. See also Case No. 402/2004, ruling of the Dubai Court of Cassation: 'Whereas this objection is valid, since the contract agreement is a contract that may be annulled as it is a contract of mutual commitments between the two parties and the agreement therein or thereafter is one of the party's entitlement of the delay penalty against the other party is a penal condition makes the damage in the estimation of the two parties, the debtor only shall prove the non-achievement of the damage. If the contract agreement is annulled, the included penal condition shall be null, following to the fall of the original commitment of the contract nullification, therefore the agreed upon compensation shall not be considered.'

53 See Case No. 790/2013, ruling of the Abu Dhabi Court of Cassation of 22 October 2014, reported in El-Amir Noor and Ahmad Ghoneim, 'Abu Dhabi Court of Cassation Judgment on Liquidated Damages Clauses after Termination', E-Journal (LexisNexis 30 March 2016).

54 To the same effect, see also Richard Harding, 'Damages under UAE Law: The Jane Lemon QC Memorial Lecture', a paper given at a meeting of the Society of Construction Law (Gulf) in Dubai on 6 October 2019, 43(3)(a): 'The court or tribunal "may" adjust the rate for liquidated damages. This is therefore a discretionary remedy, and not one that the contractor can insist on as of right.' Albeit that in our view, the judge or arbitrator will need to bear in mind the need to comply with the Islamic Shari'ah, which qualifies as of public policy and therefore needs to be raised *ex officio*, in the exercise of these powers.

by the employer, the contractor is free to apply to the judge or an arbitral tribunal for a reduction in the liquidated damages to the actual amount suffered, and in the reverse scenario, i.e., where the contractual amount of liquidated damages is lower than the extent of loss actually suffered by the employer, the employer may apply for an increase in the amount of damages to the extent of actual loss suffered by the employer. As much stands confirmed by the Commentary, which provides that 'if the previously assessed amount [i.e., the contractual amount of liquidated damages] is greater or less, then the judge may increase or reduce it on the application of either of the parties, as the basic rule of jurisprudence is that compensation must be equivalent to the damage in fact suffered.'[55] By way of reminder, that 'basic rule of jurisprudence' referred to in the afore-quoted portion of the Commentary is the one laid down at Article 389 of the UAE Civil Code in the terms further explained above[56] and ensures compliance of the operation of Article 390 with the requirements of the Islamic Shari'ah. As confirmed by Bremer:

> In a liquidated damage clause the parties commit to a pre-defined amount of compensation due for a future breach of contract. Thus, the amount of compensation is determined before the loss sustained due to such breach being quantifiable. Liquidated damage clauses, therefore, bear the risk that the compensation agreed upon by the parties deviates from the loss actually sustained due to the actual breach of contract. Hence, the pre-defined amount may exceed or fall short of the losses actually incurred by the party invoking the liquidated damage clause. Consequently liquidated clauses conflict with the principle of *garar*. Pursuant to the principle of *garar* an agreement that comprises the risk of one party benefiting or sustaining loss due to unknown circumstances is not permissible.[57]

As such, the power accorded to the judge or an arbitrator under Art. 390)(2) of the UAE Civil Code qualifies as of public policy and may not be contracted out of by the parties: This stands confirmed by the express terms of Article 390(2), which states that 'any agreement to the contrary shall be void.' In other words, any agreement by the contracting or disputing parties that has the effect of depriving a party of the right to apply to the judge or an arbitral tribunal to adjust a contractual amount of damages to loss actually suffered or to deprive the judge or an arbitral tribunal of the power to make such an adjustment is met by absolute nullity, i.e., is considered null and void *ab initio*. According to Harding, '[t]his means that issues such as notices and conditions precedent cannot prevent the contractor from applying to the court [or an arbitral tribunal] for an adjustment.'[58] As a result, liquidated damages provisions in construction contracts governed by UAE law are subject to judicial control. As affirmed by the UAE Federal Supreme Court,

> [i]t is established that delay fines in construction contracts are a financial penalty that project owners resort to when the contractor is in breach of its obligations in executing the work on time. However, these penalties are subject to control by law to protect a party from any unjustified actions and from any contravention of the law.[59]

---

55 Commentary, 2-0577.

56 See the introductory wording to section 2 above.

57 Nicolas Bremer, 'Liquidated Damages under the Law of the United Arab Emirates and its Interpretation by UAE Courts' (October 2015) 199–212d, 204.

58 Richard Harding, 'Damages under UAE Law: The Jane Lemon QC Memorial Lecture', a paper given at a meeting of the Society of Construction Law (Gulf) in Dubai on 6 October 2019, 43(3)(e).

59 Case No. 595/18, ruling of the UAE Federal Supreme Court of 26 April 1998. In Grose's analysis of the case, '[t]he court accepted the subcontractor's submission that all aspects of levying a penalty are subject to scrutiny by the courts and their overriding power to intervene to prevent injustice.' See Michael Grose, *Construction Law in the United Arab Emirates and the Gulf* (Wiley/Blackwell 2016) 140.

Turning to the practice of the UAE Courts, on a number of occasions, by virtue of the power vested in them by Article 390(2) of the UAE Civil Code, the UAE Courts have adjusted pre-agreed amounts of contractual compensation to actual amounts of loss suffered.[60] In those cases, unlike the UAE Federal Supreme Court,[61,62] the Dubai Court of Cassation imposed the burden of proof on the subcontractor or contractor to demonstrate the lack of entitlement to the contractual amount of liquidated damages on part of the contractor or employer respectively. As confirmed by Grose, 'it is possible to discern a difference of approach as between the Federal Supreme Court and the Dubai Court of Cassation.'[63]

Further, it has been reported that there are so far no examples, at least in a construction context, that show that the court's power under Article 390(2) of the UAE Civil Code has ever been exercised to *increase* a contractual amount of damages in favour of an employer.[64] In this sense, it might be arguable that the UAE Courts have exhibited some reluctance to use their powers under Article 390(2) against the contractor.[65]

Finally, it has been held that absent any agreement to the contrary, an employer will not be entitled to enforce a liquidated damages provision against a contractor for delays caused by a *nominated* subcontractor.[66]

The Position under the Free Zone Laws

The position on liquidated damages under the laws of the UAE judicial free zones, i.e., the DIFC and the ADGM, presently remains in its infancy as it has been little tested by the free zone courts.

---

60 See, e.g., Case No. 138/1994, ruling of the Dubai Court of Cassation of 13 November 1994; Case No. 177/1998, ruling of the Dubai Court of Cassation of 12 July 1998; Case No. 494/2003, ruling of the Dubai Court of Cassation of 24 April 2004; and Case No. 48/2005, ruling of the Dubai Court of Cassation of 29 May 2005. All reported in Michael Grose, *Construction Law in the United Arab Emirates and the Gulf* (Wiley/Blackwell 2016) 140.

61 On which see Article 390(1) of the UAE Civil Code above.

62 Bar a potential outlier: See UAE Federal Supreme Court No. 356/23 dated 19 October 2004, reported in Michael Grose, *Construction Law in the United Arab Emirates and the Gulf* (Wiley/Blackwell 2016) 140.

63 Michael Grose, *Construction Law in the United Arab Emirates and the Gulf* (Wiley/Blackwell 2016) 141, footnote 15.

64 To this effect, see Michael Grose, *Construction Law in the United Arab Emirates and the Gulf* (Wiley/Blackwell 2016) 142: 'the application for adjustment may be made by 'either of the parties', and an employer can, in principle therefore, obtain an upward adjustment to the pre-agreed level of compensation to ensure that this is equal to the loss. There do not appear to be any reported cases in which the UAE courts have reached this conclusion or addressed this issue.'

65 Albeit that one cannot be certain as employers might simply not have been able to prove that the actual extent of the loss suffered by them as a result of a contractor-caused delay to the time for completion in fact exceeded the contractual amount of liquidated damages, e.g., where they contributed to their own loss or where the contractor was able to make out a valid defense, e.g., under Article 291 of the UAE Civil Code.

66 See Case No. 266/2008, ruling of the Dubai Court of Cassation of 17 March 2009: 'it is established by the jurisprudence of this court that the basis for the liability of the main contractor shall be for the delay caused by the subcontractors that the original contractor has selected or appointed; however, if they have been selected by the employer or his consultant, then any delay in completion caused by them shall be the liability of the employer and not the main contractor who shall not be liable for the delay fine if the contractor can prove that his failure towards his obligation in delivering the building on the date specified by the contract is due to causes beyond his control.'

DIFC law

DIFC law makes provision for payments agreed by the contracting parties for a party's failure to perform. More specifically, Section 21 of the DIFC Law of Damages and Remedies[67] (the **'DIFC Damages Law'**), which deals with 'agreed payment for non-performance', provides in longhand as follows:

(1) Where the contract provides that a party who does not perform is to pay a specified sum to the aggrieved party for such non-performance, the aggrieved party is entitled to that sum irrespective of its actual loss.

(2) However, notwithstanding any agreement to the contrary the specified sum may be reduced to a reasonable amount where it is manifestly disproportionate to the loss envisaged as capable of resulting in relation to the loss resulting from the non-performance and to the other circumstances.

In slightly different, yet substantively similar terms, Section 122 of the DIFC Law of Contract[68] (the **'DIFC Contract Law'**) states *verbatim* as follows:

(1) Where the contract provides that a party who does not perform is to pay a specified sum to the aggrieved party for such non-performance, the aggrieved party is entitled to that sum irrespective of its actual harm.

(2) However, notwithstanding any agreement to the contrary, the specified sum may be reduced to a reasonable amount where it is grossly excessive in relation to the harm resulting from the non-performance and to the other circumstances.

The wording of both Section 21 of the DIFC Damages Law and Section 122 of the DIFC Contract Law applies to the payment of a 'specified sum',[69] i.e., a pre-agreed amount of damages for contractual 'non-performance',[70] i.e., a breach of contract and, as such, is sufficiently wide to extend, within a construction context more specifically, to the award of liquidated damages for a contractor-caused delay to the time for completion.

That said, it is evident from the wording of the above-quoted DIFC laws that the test that applies to the award of liquidated damages in the DIFC stands in marked contrast to the provisions of Art. 390 of the UAE Civil Code and closely resembles the position under English common law. Most strikingly, both the DIFC Damages Law and the DIFC Contract Law codify an *automatic* entitlement by the aggrieved party, e.g., the employer, to liquidated damages in the event of a contractual breach by the other party. In that sense, in the terms of Section 21(1) of the DIFC Damages Law and Section 122(1) of the DIFC Contract Law, payment of the contractually-agreed amount of liquidated damages to the aggrieved party falls due upon the other party's failure to perform. To that end, DIFC law does not require any consideration to be given to the 'actual loss'[71] or 'harm'[72] caused to the aggrieved party, the employer's entitlement being triggered 'irrespective of'[73] *any such loss or harm.*

---

67 DIFC Law No. 7 of 2005.
68 DIFC Law No. 6 of 2004.
69 Section 21(1) of the DIFC Damages Law; and Section 122(1) of the DIFC Contract Law.
70 *Ibid.*
71 Section 21(1) of the DIFC Damages Law.
72 Section 122(1) of the DIFC Contract Law.
73 Section 21(1) of the DIFC Damages Law and Section 122(1) of the DIFC Contract Law.

Notwithstanding, both the DIFC Damages Law and the DIFC Contract Law provide for an exception to the rule articulated above, to wit where the contractually-agreed amount of liquidated damages is 'manifestly disproportionate to the loss envisaged as capable of resulting in relation to the loss resulting from the non-performance and to the other circumstances'[74] or 'grossly excessive in relation to the harm resulting from the non-performance and to the other circumstances'.[75] In both instances, the contractually-agreed amount of liquidated damages is to be 'reduced to a reasonable amount'.[76] Unlike the position under Article 390 of the UAE Civil Code,[77] DIFC law does not contemplate any increase in the contractually-agreed amount of liquidated damages under any circumstances. Further, any reduction is to be to a 'reasonable' sum, a clear reference to the concept of reasonableness under English law. Further, the power to reduce applies 'notwithstanding any agreement to the contrary'[78] and can, therefore, not be contracted out of by the parties. According to Brödermann, '[t]he reduction of the sum itself is not mandatory ("may") while the power of reduction is mandatory ("notwithstanding any agreement to the contrary") and, as an expression of the Unidroit Principles' commitment to supporting 'fair dealing' in international trade.'[79] Brödermann further clarifies that '[t]he reduction will be made to "a reasonable amount" which leaves again wide discretion to the court (and which by no means needs to be identical with the actual harm)'[80] and that '[i]n (very) extreme cases a reduction of the amount to zero may be possible.'[81]

For further guidance, the DIFC Contract Law typically relies on the International Institute for the Unification of Private Law (UNIDROIT) Principles of International Commercial Contracts (PICC) 1994, upon which the majority of the DIFC Contract Law is based.[82] Section 122 of the DIFC Contract Law more specifically is modeled on Article 7.4.13 PICC.[83] The commentary of the PICC 2014 confirms the automatic engagement of an employer's entitlement to liquidated damages in the event of a breach, advising that '[t]he non-performing party may not allege that the aggrieved party sustained less harm or none at all.'[84] The commentary of the PICC 2014 further confirms that the amount of liquidated damages may only be reduced, as opposed to increased,[85] but only if it is '"grossly excessive", i.e. that it would clearly appear to be so to any reasonable person',[86] having '[r]egard [...] in particular [...] to the relationship between the sum agreed and the harm actually sustained.'[87] The commentary of the PICC 2014 further insists that '[t]he

---

74 Section 21(2) of the DIFC Damages Law.
75 Section 122(2) of the DIFC Contract Law.
76 Section 21(2) of the DIFC Damages Law; and Section 122(2) of the DIFC Contract Law.
77 On which see Article 390(2) of the UAE Civil Code above.
78 Section 21(1) of the DIFC Damages Law and Section 122(1) of the DIFC Contract Law.
79 Eckart Brödermann, *UNIDROIT Principles of International Commercial Contracts: An Article-by-Article Commentary* (Kluwer Law International 2nd edition 2023) 325–452, comments on Article 7.4.13 PICC, C.4. Internal footnote omitted.
80 *Ibid.* Internal footnote omitted.
81 *Ibid.* Internal footnote omitted.
82 For confirmation, see *Laws of the DIFC*, Volume 2 (LexisNexis 2017) 1.2.
83 See *Laws of the DIFC*, Volume 2 (LexisNexis, 2017) 1.124.
84 PICC 2014, at p. 253.
85 *Ibid.*, 253–254.
86 PICC 2014, 254.
87 *Ibid.* Further helpful guidance is provided by Brödermann: 'An amount will be found "grossly excessive" if (i) it "would clearly appear to be so to any reasonable person", and this (ii) "in relation to the harm resulting from the non-performance and to the other circumstances", which, it has been argued, means the

same paragraph makes it clear that the parties may under no circumstances exclude such a possibility of reduction.'[88] This, in our view, mirrors the public policy nature of Article 390(2) of the UAE Civil Code[89] and to some extent accommodates the binding nature of the Islamic Shari'ah, which forms an integral part of UAE public policy, in the DIFC.

The DIFC Damages Law, by contrast, receives guidance from English law 'as the [DIFC] Damages Law [...] in general reflects English common law principles in relation to damages.'[90] It has been confirmed that the contracting parties' right to agree liquidated damages under Article 21(1) of the DIFC Damages Law 'is subject always to the Court's discretion to reduce the amount of damages (i.e. to an amount less than the amount agreed upon in the contract) based on considerations of reasonableness and proportionality.'[91] It further stands confirmed that the tests for liquidated damages under Section 21(2) of the DIFC Damages Law ('manifestly disproportionate') and under Section 122(2) of the DIFC Contract Law ('grossly excessive') have so far remained untested and there is hence no reported judgment that would clarify whether there is any difference in their application.[92] That said, given the general guidance taken from English law, it would be save to conclude that the threshold of either test is high and likely to follow the one that prevails under English law.[93] For completeness, for further guidance on the English law position, the interested reader is referred to Chapter 11.

Turning to some case law precedent, the DIFC Courts have awarded liquidated damages in a case where it was found that the defendant had no answer to the claim for liquidated damages.[94] In another, more recent case,[95] the Small Claims Tribunal of the DIFC Courts awarded a security deposit by way of liquidated damages. More relevantly for present purposes, in Panther v. MESC,[96] the DIFC Court of Appeal rejected a claim for liquidated damages in circumstances in which the contractor had mischaracterised its challenge of the employer's claim for liquidated damages against it on the basis of Section 122(2) of the DIFC Contract Law:

> So far as concerns Article 122 of the DIFC Contract Law, this begins by emphasising that in general a liquidated damages clause will be enforced 'irrespective' of the actual loss suffered by the aggrieved party. It then goes on, in Article 122(2) to provide that the amount of liquidated damages may be reduced to a reasonable amount 'where it is grossly excessive in relation to the harm resulting from the non-performance' of the contract. The Contractor's

---

"actual" harm and needs not be "foreseeable" at the time of contract. It is argued here that, like in Art. 7.4.3 (3), there should be wide discretion to the court to assess the facts and circumstances of the case. In light of the possible and foreseeable harm at contract conclusion which did not substantiate for various reasons, a high amount may still not be grossly excessive, while the circumstances of the case – including e.g. the position and bargaining power of the parties – may indicate otherwise.' See Eckart Brödermann, *UNIDROIT Principles of International Commercial Contracts: An Article-by-Article Commentary* (Kluwer Law International 2nd edition 2023) 325–452, comments on Article 7.4.13 PICC, C.3. Internal footnotes omitted.

88 PICC 2014, 253.

89 On which see Article 390(2) of the UAE Civil Code above.

90 See *Laws of the DIFC*, Volume 1 (LexisNexis 2016) 5.4. To this effect, see also Sir A. Colman in DIFC Case No. 008/2007 – *Ithmar Capital v. 8 Investments Inc and 8 Investment Group FZE*, ruling of the DIFC Court of First Instance.

91 See *Laws of the DIFC*, Volume 1 (LexisNexis 2016) 5.28(3).

92 To this effect, see *Laws of the DIFC*, Volume 1 (LexisNexis 2016) 5.28(4).

93 For confirmation, see *Laws of the DIFC*, Volume 1 (LexisNexis 2016) 5.28(5).

94 *Arabtec Construction LLC v. Ultra Fuji International LLC* [2007] DIFC CFI 0004.

95 DIFC 046/2022 – *Lanakila v (1) Lang (2) Lancelot (3) Laneetees*, ruling of 13 May 2022.

96 *Panther Real Estate Development LLC v. Modern Executive Systems Contracting LLC* [2022] DIFC CA 016.

argument appears to assume that the relevant 'non-performance' is its own failure to give the required notices under Sub-Clause 21. If that were the case, there would be a respectable argument for saying that the obligation to pay up to 10% of the contract price as liquidated damages for that failure would be grossly excessive. But this would be to mischaracterise the position. The liquidated damages are payable not for the failure to serve the required notices within the required time but for failing to complete by the contractually agreed completion date. There has been no attack on the amount of liquidated damages payable for that failure, nor could there be without detailed investigation into and evidence of the cost of that delay to the Employer.[97]

This has invited speculation to the effect that 'the DIFC Court of Appeal appears to have left open the door to arguments of the type that are common in disputes governed by UAE law and other laws in the Gulf jurisdictions against application of liquidated damages, though precisely how Article 122 [of the DIFC Contract Law] will ultimately be applied by the DIFC Courts remains to be seen.'[98] It is arguable, therefore, that DIFC law, as it currently evolves, is able to accommodate the requirements of the Islamic Shari'ah without losing sight of the common law notion of liquidated damages from an English law perspective.

ADGM law

As regards the position on liquidated damages under ADGM law, there is little case law precedent on the subject. That said, given that, as mentioned previously,[99] ADGM law is based on a wholesale incorporation of English common law and statute by reference, the position on liquidated damages under ADGM law will be closely aligned, not to say the same as, under English law. With reference to the position under English law more specifically, the interested reader is referred to Chapter 11 for some initial guidance.

This approach stands confirmed by the ADGM Court's ruling in *Rosewood v. Skelmore*,[100] in which the ADGM Court of Appeal affirmed the ADGM Court of First Instance's award of liquidated damages in favour of Rosewood on the basis of a liquidated damages clause in the underlying contract, applying the English law on liquidated damages. As a point of interest, the ADGM Court of Appeal also accepted that claims in liquidated damages did not attract the usual rules on mitigation under English law, noting that 'McGregor, 20th Ed. para 16–122 stated in terms that the concept of a duty to mitigate is entirely foreign to a claim for liquidated damages.'[101]

Conclusion

It has been seen that the UAE onshore position on liquidated damages under Article 390 of the UAE Civil Code is markedly different from the position commonly adopted in common law. It affords the judge and by extension the arbitrator an opportunity to adjust

---

97 *Ibid.*, 62.

98 D. Hume, 'Claim notices and liquidated damages – The DIFC Court of Appeal provides useful guidance', Perspectives (Shearman & Sterling 17 May 2023).

99 See Introduction above.

100 ADGM 0009/2019 – *Rosewood Hotel Abu Dhabi LLC v Skelmore Hospitality Group Ltd*, ruling of the ADGM Court of Appeal of 16 December 2019.

101 *Ibid.*

a contractually pre-agreed amount of liquidated damages to the extent of actual loss suffered by the employer. This is a requirement that is imported into the application of the UAE Civil Code by the requirements of the Islamic Shari'ah, which qualifies as of public policy, and as such may not be contracted out of by the parties.

Albeit that, by contrast, the DIFC and the ADGM law position on liquidated damages is strongly influenced by the common law position prevailing under English law, DIFC law in particular appears to be capable of accommodating onshore Shari'ah law requirements that reach into the UAE's judicial free zones by dint of UAE public policy that is binding in both the DIFC and the ADGM. More recent case law precedent of the DIFC Courts signals the DIFC Courts' ability to construe DIFC law on liquidated damages in accordance with the requirements of the Islamic Shari'ah.

Interesting times lie ahead in an area of construction law that is key to construction disputes both on- and offshore. In particular, it will be interesting to see to what extent the civil and common law positions on liquidated damages in the UAE will converge over time.

CHAPTER 13

Liquidated damages in civil law jurisdictions

Cecilia Carrara

Introduction

When a breach of a contractual obligation arises, a party may seek relief through several remedies. These can have the form of specific performance, avoidance and/or a condemnation to pay damages. The latter appears to be the most frequently sought remedy in international trade.

In order to avoid the uncertainty which comes with every decision-making process on the quantum of damages, be it in court or in front of an arbitral tribunal, or in case of an expert determination, the parties to a contract may decide to predefine the damages upfront, with a contractual liquidation of damages.

Whereas in the civil law tradition such kind of clause is defined by reference to the notion of penalty ('clause pénale', 'clausola penale', 'Vertragsstrafe', etc) common law systems prefer the concepts of 'lump sum damage' or 'liquidated damages'. The divergence between common law and civil law countries regarding the function and, most of all, the enforcement of these clauses is still extremely debated in comparative law.

Despite the differences, there are common features and advantages that derive from the stipulation of 'clauses pénales' and/or liquidated damages clauses.[1] First, as mentioned, they both regulate in advance the assessment of damages in the event of a breach of a contractual obligation. As a consequence, they constitute an element of deterrence,[2] since the foreseeability and the certainty of the amount of damages to be paid may discourage a party from breaching the contract. Second, from a procedural prospective, if it is not possible to avoid the dispute, the party claiming damages will not need to prove the actual damages. This leads to greater efficiency in the conduct of the dispute both in terms of time and costs.

Due to the mentioned advantages, penalty clauses are very frequent in practice, as they are fit for different kinds of contracts, and can be tailored for different types of breached obligations, such as delay, failure to supply, inadequate performance and breach of contract or of a specific obligation.

This is also one of the reasons why the studies conducted on the drafting techniques of penalty clauses show different practices,[3] and often the nature of the contractual provi-

---

1 Robert Ribeiro, *Damages and other remedies for breach of commercial contracts* (Thorogood, 2002) 48.

2 Ugo Mattei, 'The Comparative Law and Economics of Penalty Clauses in Contracts' (1995) 43(3) *American Journal of Comparative Law* 427, 430.

3 In this sense, see the two reports of UNCITRAL on liquidated damages and penalty clauses UNCITRAL, 'Report of the Secretary-General: liquidated damages and penalty clauses (A/CN.9/161)' (1979) 10 *Yearbook*

198   DOI: 10.4324/9781032663975-17

sions remains ambiguous, in particular as to their compensatory or punitive function.[4] Thus, parties that decide to include penalty clauses in their contracts should carefully ponder key aspects of penalty clauses, such as the fixing of a maximum amount, the possible reduction of penalties, the provision of a grace period, but also establish whether the clause constitutes the sole remedy for damages, whether it can be cumulated with additional damages or whether the party seeking relief can opt to seek a judicial quantification of the damages in lieu of enforcing the clause.[5]

Further, if the clause has a punitive function, enforcement may be prevented if the amount of the penalty is excessive (a punitive clause may be considered null in common law countries and be subject to reduction, if disproportionate, in civil law countries).

In sum, parties who wish to include in their contracts a penalty or liquidated damages clauses should carefully consider their enforceability and their relationship with the other remedies, either under the contract or at law, that are available to them. Further, depending on the law applicable to the contract, the interpretation of the clause may vary.

Clauses pénales and liquidated damages

In penalty clauses there is usually a convergence of two elements: on the one hand, a contractual mechanism to regulate reparation in case of breach; on the other hand, if the clause is punitive, a contractual sanction.[6] This explains the reluctance of certain legal systems to consider the punitive function subject to the parties' autonomy, for it is normally administered by the courts.[7] In this sense, the German and French scholars of the previous century have often defined the idea of contractual punishment as a 'foreign body' to private law.[8]

Nowadays, the cautious approach that united both civil law and common law scholars of the previous century has been gradually superseded by a broader acceptance of penalty clauses, though with some differences between the two systems.

Whilst penalty clauses are regulated in most of the European civil codes and considered permissible, subject to the power of the judge to reduce the penalty, in English law and,

---

of the United Nations Commission on International Trade Law 40; UNCITRAL, 'Report of the Secretary-General: liquidated damages and penalty clauses (II) (A/CN.9/WG.2/WP.33)' (1981) 12 *Yearbook of the United Nations Commission on International Trade Law* 30. See also Marcel Fontaine and Filip De Ly, *Drafting International Contracts* (Transnational Publishers 2006), ch 6.

4 Antonias Dimolitsa, 'Contractual Remedies: Clauses Pénales and Liquidated Damages Clauses' in Filip De Ly and Laurent Lévy (eds), *Interest, Auxiliary & Alternative Remedies in International Arbitration – Dossier V of the ICC Institute of World Business Law* (2008) 2, refers to clauses such as withdrawal payments (clauses de dédit), price adjustment clauses and, especially, clauses limiting liability.

5 ICC, *The ICC Guide on Penalty and Liquidated Damages Clauses* (ICC Publishing 1990) represents a valid tool to guide parties interested in the drafting of penalty clauses.

6 Ermanno Calzolaio, 'Il nuovo volto della clausola penale nel diritto inglese' (2016) 8-9 *I Contratti* 817; Andrea Zoppini, *La pena contrattuale* (Giuffrè 1991) 1.

7 Mattei (n 2) 443.

8 Werner Flume, *Allgemeiner Teil des bürgerlichen Rechts* (Springer 1979) 390; Marcel Crémieux, 'Réflexions sur la peine privée moderne' in *Études offertes à Pierre Kayser* (PUAM 1979) 261; Henri Mazeaud, *Traité théorique et pratique de la responsabilité civile délictuelle et contractuelle* (1935), which, however, will have a softer approach to penalty clauses in the subsequent editions of its manual. A similar approach is historically found in common law systems; see e.g. Oliver Wendell Holmes, 'The Path of the Law' (1897) 10 *Harvard Law Review* 457 stating that 'The duty to keep a contract at common law means a prediction that you must pay damages if you do not keep it – and nothing else'.

in general, in common law countries,[9] a penalty clause is considered null and void if its purpose is punitive, i.e., meant to exert pressure on the debtor's will or to economically punish it for its failure, even in a way that is not excessive. The only legitimate purpose of such clauses shall be the early liquidation of future damages,[10] without the possibility for courts to intervene to reduce or increase the amount (so-called 'rule against penalties').[11] It follows that the term 'penalty' is usually avoided by common law practitioners, since such wording might imply a punitive purpose of the clause, which, in turn, might lead to its invalidity.

In 2015, the UK Supreme Court found that, although the well-established rule against penalty was not in discussion, the 'genuine pre-estimate of loss' test did not fit more complex cases.[12] As a consequence, the Supreme Court found that a liquidated damages clause is unenforceable if it consists in 'a secondary obligation which imposes a detriment on the contract-breaker out of all proportion to any legitimate interest of the innocent party in the enforcement of the primary obligation'. This new test considerably reduces the scope of application of the rule against penalties.[13] Indeed, while the principle according to which the judge cannot intervene to rebalance the position of the parties in the case where the penalty is found to be excessive or disproportionate remains firm the validity of the clause is not questioned if it is anchored to the performance of the main obligation of the contract. Moreover, even if the clause refers to a secondary obligation, the court may still find it valid, if it considers it to be supported by a legitimate commercial interest.[14]

The new course set by the UK Supreme Court opens to a less drastic approach to penalty clauses. However, the general rule against penalties remains firm. Such factor has to be carefully considered by the parties that stipulate a liquidated damages clause with a punitive/extra-compensatory element in their contract under common law. In fact, a common law court that qualifies a clause as a penalty, will not simply reduce its amount as in civil law countries, but may find that the clause is invalid altogether.[15]

---

9 One notable exception in the common law countries is India, where penalty clauses are usually enforced. Indeed, Indian Contracts Act's § 74 permit liquidated damages clause even if the intent of the clause is punitive; see Jay Frank McKenna, 'Liquidated Damages and Penalty Clauses: A Civil Law versus Common Law Comparison', in *The Critical Path*, (Reed Smith 2008) 3.

10 *Dunlop Pneumatic Tyre Co Ltd v New Garage & Motor Co Ltd* [1915] AC 79, 86: 'The essence of a penalty is a payment of money stipulated as in terrorem of the offending party; the essence of liquidated damages is a genuine covenanted pre-estimate of damage'.

11 *Lordsvale Finance Plc v Bank of Zambia* [1996] QB 752. On this point, see the extensive analysis offered in Andrew Burrows, *Remedies for Torts and Breach of Contracts* (Oxford 2004). From a comparative perspective see also Antonio Pinto-Monteiro, 'La clause pénale en Europe' in *Études offertes à Jacques Ghestin – Le contrat au début du XXIe siècle* (LGDJ 2001).

12 *Cavendish Square Holding BV v Talal El Makdessi* [2015] UKSC 67.

13 Calzolaio (n 6) 821. Indeed according to the UK approach, the discretion of courts to deem invalid liquidated amages clause is significantly reduced after such decision; in this sense, see Jonathan Morgan, 'The Penalty Clause Doctrine: Unlovable but Untouchable (2016) 75(1) CLJ 2016 11, 11.

14 *ZCCM Investments Holdings Plc v Konkola Copper Mines Plc* [2017] EWHC 3288 (Comm);

England and Wales High Court in *ZCCM Investments Holdings Plc v. Konkola Copper Mines Plc*, 2017; *GPP Big Field LLP v Solar EPC Solutions SL (Formerly Prosolua Siglio XXI)* [2018] EWHC 2866 (Comm), subsequently applied the new approach.

15 Paul Gélinas, 'General Characteristics of Recoverable Damages in International Arbitration' in Yves Derains and Richard H Kreindler (eds), *Evaluation of Damages in International Arbitration – Dossier IV of the ICC Instiute of World Business Law* (2006) 6.

In contrast, civil law courts may reduce the amount of the penalty, but the clause remains valid and enforceable.[16] The rule that grants the power to courts to reduce the amount of the penalty if it is grossly excessive, is mandatory in most civil national laws.

For example, in Italy the academic literature and jurisprudence have extensively discussed the nature and the regime of application of penalty clauses. Article 1382, first sentence, of the Italian Civil Code stipulates that:

A clause by which it is agreed that in case of non-performance or delay of performance one of the contracting parties is liable for a specified penalty, has the effect of limiting the compensation to the promised penalty, unless compensation was agreed on for additional damages.[17]

Italian scholars are still debating as to the function of such clauses: some Authors sustain that it is compensatory,[18] others that it is punitive,[19] or both.

The courts often found that penalty clauses have an implied coercive/deterrence function.[20] Furthermore, Italian courts embrace a restrictive interpretation of the penalty clauses, by considering that the penalties are applicable only to those obligations which the clauses specifically mention in their wording.[21]

Pursuant to Article 1382, second sentence, of the Italian Civil Code: '[t]he penalty is due regardless of proof of damage'.[22] The provision leaves some uncertainties as to whether the defaulting-party may be exempted from paying liquidated damages if it shows that the other party has not suffered an economic prejudice from the non-performance/delay. In any event, the defaulting-party may seek reduction of the clause by virtue of Article 1384 of the Italian Civil Code.

In addition, under Article 1383 of the Italian Civil Code: '[t]he creditor [of the penalty] cannot demand the main performance and the penalty together if the latter was not stipulated for the mere delay'.

Nonetheless, if the penalty refers only to a specific obligation and the defaulting party has breached other obligations, the penalty and the request of performance of the latter obligations may coexist.[23] Italian law grants judges the power to reduce the penalty. Article 1384 of the Italian Civil Code states:

The penalty can be diminished equitably by the judge, if the main obligation was executed in part or if the amount of the penalty was apparently excessive, having always regard to the interests that the creditor had in the performance.[24]

---

16 ICC Award No 3267 (1979), available in Pieter Sanders, *Yearbook of Commercial Arbitration. Volume VII – 1982* (1982) 96 and Dimolitsa (n 4) 12.

17 It is undisputed that parties may agree upon liquidated damages both for delay and non-performance and that they may be requested cumulatively; in this sense, Italian Corte di Cassazione, 19/22050, 03/8813 and 18/27994.

18 Cesare Massimo Bianca, *Diritto civile 5. Le responsabilità* (Giuffrè 2020) 242.

19 Andrea Zoppini, 'Clausola penale e caparra', in Giovanna Visintini, *Trattato della responsabilità contrattuale* (CEDAM 2009) 1013.

20 Italian Corte di Cassazione, case 98/11204, 91/6561 and 93/96660.

21 Italian Corte di Cassazione, case 46/910.

22 However, if the parties agree that the penalty will be without prejudice of additional damages, the party requesting compensation shall demonstrate such additional damages. See Italian Corte di Cassazione, 16/12956 and 05/15371. In this case, the liquidated damages under the clause are absorbed by the damages awarded when upholding the claim for additional damage. See Italian Corte di Cassazione, 21/21398.

23 Italian Corte di Cassazione, 63/1807.

24 Reference to the creditor's interest is made because if the partial performance is of scarce benefit to the creditor, the penalty is due in its entirety.

The ratio behind the rule is to avoid that the party seeking compensation receives more than the actual damages suffered due to the non-performance. Whereas the traditional view required the party in default to expressly demand such reduction to the judge,[25] the Italian Supreme Court now considers judges empowered to reduce the amount of the penalty on their own initiative (ex officio).[26] A similar solution applies under French law. Different considerations may apply if the parties refer their disputes to arbitral tribunals, for arbitrators are bound to issue their decision only based on the requests for relief formulated by the parties.

Moving now to the French legal system, Article 1231-5 of the French Civil Code recognizes that:

> Where a contract stipulates that the person who fails to perform shall pay a certain sum of money by way of damages, the other party may be awarded neither a higher nor a lower sum.
>
> Nevertheless, a court may, even of its own initiative, moderate or increase the penalty so agreed if it is manifestly excessive or derisory.
>
> Where an undertaking has been performed in part, the agreed penalty may be reduced by a court, even of its own initiative, in proportion to the advantage which partial performance has procured for the creditor, without prejudice to the application of the preceding paragraph.
>
> Any stipulation contrary to the preceding two paragraphs is deemed unwritten.
>
> Except where non-performance is permanent, a penalty is not incurred unless the debtor was put on notice to perform.

The traditional interpretation is that the aim of the provision is to guarantee that a certain amount of compensation will be paid, independently of the proof of the damage and the occurrence of an actual loss.[27] The prevailing view in the literature is that the penalty clause has a hybrid nature, both compensatory and punitive.[28]

The parties are not allowed to exclude the courts' power of supervision over the penalty.[29] In fact, French courts may, also on their own initiative, reduce or increase the penalty if they deem it manifestly excessive or derisory.[30] In line with Italian law, Article 1231-5 of the French Civil Code also specifies that when the obligation has been partially performed, the penalty may be reduced by a court, in proportion to the advantage which the partial performance has procured to the creditor. Along the years, the French Cour de Cassation has created some guidelines to partially limit the discretion that courts have to reduce or increase penalty clauses. These guidelines include the assessment of the amount provided in the clause and the damage actually suffered, the bargaining powers of both parties, the economic situation of the debtor and its good faith.[31]

---

25 Italian Corte di Cassazione, 98/10439, 95/3549 and 94/7859.

26 Italian Corte di Cassazione, 19/34021, 16/21646 and 15/2491.

27 French Cour de Cassation, Chambre civile 1, 22 February 1977 and Chambre civile 3, 12 January 1994. John A Trenor (ed), *The Guide to Damages in International Arbitration* (Global Arbitration Review 2022) 36.

28 Lucinda Miller, *Penalty Clause In England and France: A Comparative Study* (2004) 53(1) ICLQ 79, 85.

29 Any stipulation excluding or reducing such power is deemed unwritten.

30 French Cour de Cassation, Chambre commercial, 11 February 1997.

31 The broad nature of these factors has been considered to lead to unpredictability in the courts' assessment; Miler (n 28) 91.

In addition, Article 1231-5, last sentence, of the French Civil Code clarifies that, contrary to Italian law,[32] except where non-performance is permanent, a penalty is not due unless the debtor was put on notice to perform.

Germany is another country that has historically permitted the provision of penalty clauses. The discipline may be found in the German Civil Code from § 339 onwards. According to § 339 of the German Civil Code:

> Where the obligor promises the obligee, in the event of their failing to perform their obligation or failing to do so properly, payment of an amount of money as a penalty, the penalty is payable upon the obligor being in default. If the performance owed consists of forbearance, the penalty is payable on breach.

The German discipline differs from the French and Italian ones by providing different regimes for penalties for non-performance and misperformance. As to non-performance, § 340 of the German Civil Code stipulates that:

(1) If the obligor has promised the penalty in the event of their failing to perform their obligation, then the obligee may demand the penalty that is payable in lieu of fulfilment. Where the obligee declares to the obligor that they are demanding the penalty, the claim for performance is excluded.

(2) If the obligee is entitled to a claim for damages for non-performance, then they may demand the penalty payable as the minimum amount of the damage. Assertion of additional damage is not excluded.

Therefore, German law is in line with the French and Italian ones in establishing both that the request of payment of the penalty and the request of performance of the contract cannot be cumulated and that, in any case, the creditor may demonstrate – and the court may evaluate – whether additional damages were also suffered by the creditor.

The regime of the penalty differs in that under German law the creditor may demand the penalty in addition to the performance. Indeed, § 341 of the German Civil Code states:

(1) If the obligor has promised the penalty in the event of their failing to perform their obligation properly, including performance at the specified time, the obligee may demand the payable penalty in addition to performance.

(2) If the obligee has a claim for damages for the improper performance, the provisions of section 340 (2) apply.

(3) If the obligee accepts performance, they may demand the penalty only if they reserved the right to do so on acceptance.

In addition, § 343 of the German Civil Code establishes that:

(1) If a payable penalty is disproportionately high, it may be reduced, on application by the obligor, to a reasonable amount by judicial decision. In judging the appropriateness, regard is to be had to every legitimate interest of the obligee, not merely their property interests. Once the penalty is paid, reduction is excluded.

---

32 Under Italian law it is debated whether it is necessary for the creditor to put the debtor on notice (costituzione in mora) for the penalty to become due. In favor, Italian Corte di Cassazione 76/4664; contra, Italian Corte di Cassazione, 99/10511.

(2) The same also applies, except in the cases governed by sections 339 and 342, if someone promises a penalty in the event of their taking or failing to take an action.

Thus, also under German law, upon application of the party in default, the courts may reduce the penalty that is deemed disproportionately high. In order to evaluate the reasonableness of the penalty, the courts shall consider 'every legitimate interest of the creditor'.

In case of contestation of the enforceability of the penalty, the German Civil Code is also very clear in the allocation of the burden of proof. §345 states that: 'If the obligor contests the payability of the penalty on the basis of its performance of its obligation, it shall prove performance, unless the performance owed consisted in forbearance'.

Penalty clauses are also admissible under Swiss law. In comparison with the previous systems analysed, the Swiss Code of Obligations presents a particular approach to the possible coexistence of performance and penalties. Article 160 of the Swiss Code of Obligations states that: '(1) Where a penalty is promised for non-performance or defective performance of a contract, unless otherwise agreed, the creditor may only compel performance or claim the penalty'.

However, the same provision sets some exceptions to the prohibition to cumulate performance and penalty:

(2) Where the penalty is promised for failure to comply with the stipulated time or place of performance, the creditor may claim the penalty in addition to performance provided he has not expressly waived such right or accepted performance without reservation.

(3) The foregoing does not apply if the debtor can prove that he has the right to withdraw from the contract by paying the penalty.

In addition, Article 161 of the Swiss Code of Obligations provides that:

(1) The penalty is payable even if the creditor has not suffered any damage.

(2) Where the damage suffered exceeds the penalty amount, the creditor may claim further compensation only if he can prove that the debtor was at fault.

Therefore, consistently with the other systems previously analysed, the penalty is payable even if the creditor has not suffered any damage. In any case, if the damage suffered exceeds the penalty amount, the creditor is allowed to claim additional compensation if it is able to prove that the debtor was at fault.

Finally, Article 163 of the Swiss Code of Obligations states:

(1) The parties are free to determine the amount of the contractual penalty.

(2) The penalty may not be claimed where its purpose is to reinforce an unlawful or immoral undertaking or, unless otherwise agreed, where performance has been prevented by circumstances beyond the debtor's control.

(3) At its discretion, the court may reduce penalties that it considers excessive.

The second sentence of Article 163 introduces some specific limitations to the enforceability of the penalty, which 'may not be claimed' if the purpose of the clause if to provide a private sanction for obligations that are contra legem; the third sentence grants to the courts a broad and unfettered discretion in reducing penalty clauses as compared to the other legal systems previously analyzed.

International principles

Except for a couple of relevant exceptions, there are no transnational rules that regulate penalties in international commercial contracts.[33] The reason for this is the divergence between the civil and the common law approaches to penalty and liquidated damages clauses.[34]

In the absence of binding transnational rules regulating liquidated damages, parties may rely on non-binding instruments by designating them as applicable to the contract. The possible principles that could be applicable are (i) the 1983 UNCITRAL Uniform Rules on Contract Clauses for an Agreed Sum Due upon Failure of Performance, (ii) the UNIDROIT Principles of International Commercial Contracts, (iii) the Principles of European Contract Law (PECL), and (iv) the Draft Common Frame of Reference (DCFR).

All the above principles adopt solutions which are closer to the civil law countries' approach to penalty clauses rather than to common law ones.[35] Indeed, they favor the conservation of the validity of the penalty, by reducing it in case of excessive/disproportionate amount, rather than annulling the clause whenever it has a punitive character.

The 1983 UNCITRAL Uniform Rules on Contract Clauses for an Agreed Sum Due upon Failure of Performance[36] were redacted with the aim to unify the treatment of penalty clauses in international commercial transactions. Indeed, UNCITRAL wanted to find a worldwide standard to balance the civil law enforceability of penalty clauses, unless manifestly excessive, and the common law rule of unenforceability.[37] Under the UNCITRAL Uniform Rules, contractual clauses for an agreed amount due upon failure of performance are presumptively valid and the courts' intervention may consist only in the reduction of the agreed amount if 'substantially disproportionate' with respect to the actual harm. In fact, Article 8 of UNCITRAL Uniform Rules provides that: '[t]he agreed sum shall not be reduced by a court or arbitral tribunal unless the agreed sum is substantially disproportionate in relation to the loss that has been suffered by the oblige'.

In addition, Article 7 of UNCITRAL Uniform Rules states that:

> If the obligee is entitled to the agreed sum, he may not claim damages to the extent of the loss covered by the agreed sum. Nevertheless, he may claim damages to the extent of the loss not covered by the agreed sum if the loss substantially exceeds the agreed sum.
>
> Although the purpose of the UNCITRAL Uniform Rules was to create a balance between civil and common law approaches, the content of the provisions above

---

33 Edward Allan Farnsworth, *Contracts* (Aspen Publishers 2004); Bruno Zeller, *CISG and the Unification of International Trade Law*, (Routledge-Cavendish 2007), which refers to the United Nations Convention on Contracts for the International Sale of Goods (CISG) as a lost occasion for regulating the topic: 'Because of the wide gulf between common law systems and other legal systems, the Vienna Convention contains no provision on the important subject of stipulated damages'.

34 Ignacio Marín García, 'Enforcement of Penalty Clauses in Civil and Common Law: A Puzzle to Be Solved by the Contracting Parties' (2012) 5(1) *European Journal of Legal Studies* 95, 115.

35 Dimolitsa (n 4) 16.

36 UNCITRAL, Unifrom Rules on Contract Clauses for an Agreed Sum Due upon Failure of Performance (A/38/17, annex I) (A/CN.9/243, annex I) (UNCITRAL Unifrom Rules).

37 The intent is clear from UNCITRAL Uniform Rules, art 1: 'These Rules apply to international contracts in which the parties have agreed that, upon a failure of performance by one party (the obligor), the other party (the obligee) is entitled to an agreed sum from the obligor, whether as a penalty or as compensation'.

is clearly closer to the civil law one.[38] This result was not appreciated by the common law countries participating in the project and the aim of providing a uniform approach to penalty and liquidated damages clauses failed.[39]

The UNIDROIT Principles of International Commercial Contracts (UPICC),[40] one of the main tools of soft law in the field of international commercial contracts, also follow the approach of the civil law legal systems, based on the principle of enforcement of penalties subject to reduction.

Article 7.4.13 UNIDROIT Principles ('Agreed payment for non-performance') states that:

> (1) Where the contract provides that a party who does not perform is to pay a specified sum to the aggrieved party for such non-performance, the aggrieved party is entitled to that sum irrespective of its actual harm.
>
> (2) However, notwithstanding any agreement to the contrary the specified sum may be reduced to a reasonable amount where it is grossly excessive in relation to the harm resulting from the non-performance and to the other circumstances.

Despite the broad definition of 'agreed payment for non-performance' under Article 7.4.13, which meant to include both liquidated damages and penalties, the general rule is the recoverability of liquidated damages regardless of the actual harm. In line with most civil law countries, courts may in any event reduce penalties that are deemed 'grossly excessive'.

The Principles of European Contract Law (PECL)[41] and the Draft Common Frame of Reference (DCFR)[42] also address liquidated damages clauses. Article 9:509 of the PECL ('Agreed payment for non-performance') states that:

> (1) Where the contract provides that a party who fails to perform is to pay a specified sum to the aggrieved party for such non-performance, the aggrieved party shall be awarded that sum irrespective of its actual loss.
>
> (2) However, despite any agreement to the contrary the specified sum may be reduced to a reasonable amount where it is grossly excessive in relation to the loss resulting from the non-performance and the other circumstances.

Article III-3:712 of the DCFR ('Stipulated payment for non-performance') states that:

---

38 Larry A DiMatteo, 'Enforcement of Penalty Clauses: A Civil-Common Law Comparison' (2010) 10(5), *Internationales Handelsrecht* 193.

39 Jonathan S Solórzano, 'An Uncertain Penalty: A Look at the International Community's Inability to Harmonize the Law of Liquidated Damages and Penalty Clauses' (2009) 15(4) *Law and Business Review of the Americas*, 2009 813.

40 'UNIDROIT Principles of International Commercial Contracts' (*UNIDROIT*, 2016) <https://www.unidroit.org/instruments/commercial-contracts/unidroit-principles-2016/> accessed 20 November 2023.

41 The first part of the PECL was published in 1995, the second part in 1999 and the third and last part was completed in 2002. For full text see Commission, 'Communication from the Commissio to the Council and the European Parliament on European Contract Law' COM (2001) 398 final.

42 Study Group on European Civil Code and Research Group on EC Private Law (Acquis Group), *Principle, Definitions, and Model Rules of European Private Law. Draft Common Frame of Reference (DCFR). Outline Edition* (Christian von Bar and others (eds), Sellier 2009) (DCFR).

(1) Where the terms regulating an obligation provide that a debtor who fails to perform the obligation is to pay a specified sum to the creditor for such non-performance, the creditor is entitled to that sum irrespective of the actual loss.

(2) However, despite any provision to the contrary, the sum so specified in a contract or other juridical act may be reduced to a reasonable amount where it is grossly excessive in relation to the loss resulting from the non-performance and the other circumstances.

For the sake of balancing civil law and common law approaches, liquidated damages are named 'agreed payment for non-performance' in the PECL, and 'stipulated payment for non-performance' in the DCFR. In both texts the civil law approach prevails, since the governing principle in the two sets of principles is the recoverability of the sum irrespective of the actual harm, unless courts find it to be 'grossly excessive' and, therefore, subject to possible reductions.

In sum, all of the above mentioned principles of soft law are quite similar, their definitions of liquidates damages are broad and cover both penalty clauses, as intended in civil countries, and liquidated damages, as applicable under common law countries. In addition, they all provide that liquidated damages agreed under the contract may be reduced by courts, if they are 'grossly excessive' or 'substantially disproportionate'. However, it is only the UNCITRAL Uniform Rules that expressly provides that the aggrieved party may claim additional damages 'if the loss substantially exceeds the agreed sum'.

In addition to the mentioned international instruments, there have been discussions whether the Convention on Contracts for the International Sale of Goods (CISG) regulates the matter of liquidated damages.[43] Indeed, the CISG does not take position regarding the recoverability of damages agreed by the parties in a penalty clause or a liquidated damages clause.[44] In cases where the CISG does not expressly regulate a matter, this has to be decided by virtue of the principles on which the CISG is based or by applying the applicable law to the contract.[45] Tribunals have tried to fill the gap accordingly and suggested that penalty and liquidated damages clauses would respect and enhance the principles which the CISG is based on, i.e., to preserve business continuity.[46] Indeed, penalty and liquidated damages clauses may encourage performance of the contract and deter a breach. In addition, in case of a breach of contract, penalty and liquidated damages clauses may

---

43 Petra Butler, 'Damages Principles under the Convention on Contracts for the International Sale of Goods' in John A Trenor (ed) *The Guide to Damages in International Arbitration* (Global Arbitration Review 2022) 71ff.

44 United Nations Convention on Contracts for the International Sale of Goods (adopted 11 April 1980, entered into force 1 January 1988) 1489 UNTS 3 (CISG) art 4: 'This Convention governs only the formation of the contract of sale and the rights and obligations of the seller and the buyer arising from such a contract. In particular, except as otherwise expressly provided in this Convention, it is not concerned with: (a) the validity of the contract or of any of its provisions or of any usage.'.

45 CISG art 7: '(1) In the interpretation of this Convention, regard is to be had to its international character and to the need to promote uniformity in its application and the observance of good faith in international trade. (2) Questions concerning matters governed by this Convention which are not expressly settled in it are to be settled in conformity with the general principles on which it is based or, in the absence of such principles, in conformity with the law applicable by virtue of the rules of private international law.'.

46 See in regard to the application CLOUT case No 133 [Oberlandsgericht München, Germany, 8 February 1995); Hof Arnhem, 22 August 1995; CLOUT case No 104 [ICC Court of Arbitration, Arbitral Award No 7197/1992]; CISG AC Opinion No. 10, *Agreed Sums Payable upon Breach of an Obligation in CISG Contracts*, Rapporteur Pascal Hachem.

also encourage the parties to settle their differences and avoid the costs of legal proceedings.[47] In any case, as will be assessed in the paragraph dedicated to arbitration cases (see 4. infra), practice shows that the issue of penalty and liquidated damages clauses under the CISG has been resolved on a case by case basis with the application of the rules of the national law applicable to the contract.

In light of the above, it is clear that transnational instruments have preferred the approach of the civil law legal systems, based on the principle of enforcement of penalties subject to reduction. This means that also under such instruments, parties providing a penalty/extra-compensatory element will not risk to face a nullity of the clause, but, in the worst scenario, they will see the amount of the clause appropriately reduced.

Securing the enforceability of penalty clauses

For the reasons mentioned above, the enforceability of contractual penalties will depend on the law applicable to the contract and on the choice of courts or arbitration clauses included in the contract. As explained, civil laws are generally more favorable to the enforceability of penalty clauses, and some courts have a broader discretion that others to reduce the penalties. Some courts may only reduce penalties upon initiative of the party in default and in some regimes the penalty becomes due only if the debtor has been previously put on notice. Arbitrators, as opposed to courts, will consider themselves usually restricted to reduce penalties or find them to be invalid ex officio.

Thus, parties increase their chances to enforce their penalty clauses by providing, in order of preference: a pro-penalty choice of law and arbitration in a civil law country; a pro-penalty choice of law in conjunction with the selection of a civil law forum; only a pro-penalty choice of law.[48] Indeed, in those regimes where the rule against penalties is still in force, an excessive extra-compensatory element will likely lead to the nullity of the clause.

In addition, parties are free to agree upon contractual mechanisms to secure the application of the penalty clause. For example, they may agree upon a guarantee and/or a bond to secure the payment of the penalty, provide for an escrow account, provide for a third party determination of the penalty, etc.

Parties should nevertheless be careful not to exaggerate in the determination of the extra-compensatory amount, ie the penalty element. In the latter case, even if the courts/ arbitral tribunals were not to reduce the amount of the penalty, still there might be obstacles in the enforcement and/or recognition phase of the decision. Indeed, the punitive element of the penalty clause may be assimilated to punitive damages, that are still not recognized in many legal systems.[49]

---

47 Micheal Bridge, 'Remedies and damages' I n Larry DiMatteo and others (eds), *International Sales Law: Contract, Principles & Practice* (Hart-Beck-Nomos 2021), para 72.

48 DiMatteo (n 38) 200.

49 The Italian Corte di Cassazione (16601/17) has expressly recognized the validity of punitive damages within the Italian legal framework in 2007; however, the Corte di Cassazione has also stated that this does not mean that foreign judgments disposing of punitive damages can be recognized without any limits: the fundamental principles of due process and the principles of legality and proportionality of the sanction must remain guaranteed. The review of whether the foreign judgment meets these criteria will have to be conducted by the judges of the deliberation on the basis of the applicable foreign system through the lens of the fundamental rights of the Italian system. See in this sense Cecilia Carrara, 'Danni Punitivi, un'apertura alla nuova

Also in case of arbitral awards, punitive damages may be seen to contrast with the notion of public order under the 1958 Convention on the Recognition and Enforcement of Foreign Arbitral Awards. Notably, the New York Convention allows a court to refuse the recognition or enforcement of an award, if such acts would be contrary to the public policy of the country of that court.[50] Being public policy a concept that is not uniform in every legal system, it remains uncertain whether a common law court would accept recognition and enforcement of a foreign award ordering the payment of a penalty clause with a punitive element,[51] or indeed a civil law court of a penalty which substantially equates punitive damages. However, the notion of public order should and is usually interpreted narrowly, and even common law courts requested to reject the enforcement of awards ordering payment of penalty clauses tend not to accept public policy exceptions.[52]

From an international private law perspective, one may question if some rules have substantive or procedural nature.[53] In general terms, if judges are granted specific powers, this is a matter which pertains to the procedure and to the lex fori. To the contrary, whether or not there are specific cases of invalidity or nullity will be an issue that depends on the lex contractus. When it comes to the rules on the burden of proof, these are usually qualified as pertaining to the substantive law, unless they pertain to specific procedural remedies or instruments of proof.

Finally, some legal systems may consider the rules which provide for limitations to the validity and enforceability of penalty clauses as mandatory provisions that cannot be derogated from by the parties, ie overriding mandatory provisions ('norme di applicazione necessaria' – 'dispositions impératives').[54]

---

responsabilità civile' (*Intermedia Channel*, 10 July 2017) <https://www.intermediachannel.it/2017/07/10/danni-punitivi-unapertura-alla-nuova-responsabilita-civile/> accessed 20 November 2023.

50 Convention on the Recognition and Enforcement of Foreign Arbitral Awards (adopted 10 June 1958, entered into force 7 June 1959) 330 UNTS 3 (New York Convention) art V(2)(b): 'Recognition and enforcement of an arbitral award may also be refused if the competent authority in the country where recognition and enforcement is sought finds that (...) the recognition or enforcement of the award would be contrary to the public policy of that country'.

51 *A v R* [2009] HKCFI 342 ruling that the Danish arbitration award providing for over- compensatory liquidated damages does not violate public policy; conversely, DiMatteo (n 38) 200, sustains that a similar award is likely to be questioned by American courts.

52 However, if the penalty amount is considered grossly excessive this might change the courts' assessment. See

Mastrobuono v Shearson Lehman Hutton Inc, 514 US 52 (1995); Order of the United States District Court for the Southern District of Florida Recognizing and Enforcing International Arbitration Award CAS 2008/A/1644. See *Chelsea Football Club v Mutu* 849 FSupp2d 1341. If enforcement of punitive damages awarded in arbitration is not contrary to US public policy, the same must hold true, all the more so, for penalty clauses. The position of English courts apparently does not differ.

53 Marín García (n 34) 120.

54 Regulation (EC) No 593/2008 of the European Parliament and of the Council of 17 June 2008 on the law applicable to contractual obligations (Rome I) [2008] OJ L177/6, art 9: '1. Overriding mandatory provisions are provisions the respect for which is regarded as crucial by a country for safeguarding its public interests, such as its political, social or economic organisation, to such an extent that they are applicable to any situation falling within their scope, irrespective of the law otherwise applicable to the contract under this Regulation.

2. Nothing in this Regulation shall restrict the application of the overriding mandatory provisions of the law of the forum.

3. Effect may be given to the overriding mandatory provisions of the law of the country where the obligations arising out of the contract have to be or have been performed, in so far as those overriding mandatory provisions render the performance of the contract unlawful. In considering whether to give effect to those provisions, regard shall be had to their nature and purpose and to the consequences of their application or non-application.'.

Liquidated damages in arbitration

In light of the uncertainties created by the different approaches of civil law and common law systems, as well as by the lack of binding transnational instruments, it is of interest to see in which way international arbitral tribunals assess the issue of liquidated damages.

Unsurprisingly, from the available public information it seems that the arbitrators' analysis is mainly based on the interpretation of the relevant contractual clauses and on specific provisions of the applicable national laws.[55]

Arbitral tribunals seated in common law countries and/or deciding on the basis of common law, focus their analysis on the reasonableness of liquidated damages in order to assess whether the clause included in the contract is of punitive nature, and therefore null, or represents an estimate in advance of the damages.[56] The standard to determine the reasonableness is most of the time the difference between the liquidated damages contractually agreed and the actual damage.[57]

Similarly, when the seat of arbitration is in a civil law country, arbitral tribunals focus on contract interpretation and the relevant provisions of the law applicable to the contract. Therefore, the principle of enforcement of penalties subject to reduction applies.[58]

Whilst references in arbitral awards to international instruments are very scarce, in some cases the arbitral tribunals relied on the UPICC provisions on liquidated damages.[59] Indeed, Article 7.4.13 of the UPICC has been directly applied in proceedings where the UPICC were contractually agreed upon by the parties or because they were considered applicable in the absence of an explicit choice of law in the contract.[60] In addition, the

---

55 Antonias Dimolitsa reports that only one of awards analysed involved a direct discussion of the purposes of the clause (ie the nature of penalty or of liquidated damages), concluding with its validation as a reasonable estimate of the expected loss (ICC Case No 9839/1999). Looking at more recent cases, the trend seems not to have changed: arbitral tribunals applying common law rules, tend to deem null a liquidated damages clause only if it is unreasonable, but they do not increase/decrease the amount set out in the clause. On the other hand, arbitral tribunal applying civil law rules do not assess the validity of the liquidated damages clause, but may decide to lower or increase the amount established by such clause.

56 *Natural Brands Inc v Beaumont Juice Inc D/B/A Perricone Juicees*, American Arbitration Association, Case No.= 01-20-0000-4293; *Elvia Besil Sampieri and Haffan Properties LLC v Belfiore Developers LLC, Pierpoint Capital Company LLC, TIC Belfiore LLC, Joseph J Lopez, Giorgio Borlenghi and Inter-Pier LLC*, American Arbitration Association, Case No 01-16-0001-3080.

57 *Oceltip Aviation 1 Pty Ltd v Gulfstream Aerospace Corporation*, ICDR Case No 01-14-0001-3711.

58 *Winterthur Gas & Diesel AG v Nuclebrás Equipamentos Pesados S.A*, Ad Hoc Arbitration, 2014; ICC Case No 10302.

59 See Cecilia Carrara, 'The multiple usages of the UNIDROIT Principles and the rules governing limitation', in Galizzi, Rojas Elgueta and Veneziano (eds), *The multiples uses of the UNIDROIT Principles of International Commercial Contracts: theory and practice* (Giuffrè 2020). In general, the UPICC shall be applied when they are elected as the lex contractus by the parties; on the other hand, they may be applied when, failing an express choice by the parties: (i) the parties referred to the general principles of law or the lex mercatoria, (ii) the governing law needs to be interpreted or supplemented, (iii) the contract does not provide an express choice of applicable law. Practice shows that arbitrators tend to refer to the UPICC also to reinforce their reasoning.

60 ICC Case No 8261/1996; Arbitral Award in Case No A-1795/51 of December 1, 1996 of the Camera Arbitrale di Milano; ICC Case No 9797/2000, as reported in Dimolitsa, (n 4) 14; Arbitral Award of November 30, 2006 of the Centro de Arbitraje de México.

UPICC have also been applied when the applicable law referred to international trade usages,[61] or used to confirm the validity of the applicable national rules.[62]

As previously noted, the CISG does not regulate the issue of penalty and liquidated damages clauses. When arbitral tribunals face the task of interpreting and applying such clauses in contracts governed by the CISG, they may either resort to the general principles on which the CISG is based or choose to apply a national law. In the first case, the general principles of the CISG, such as the freedom of the parties (Articles 6 and 45(2) CISG) and the full compensation of damages (Article 74 CISG), may suggest the application of a principle similar to the one included in Article 7.4.13 of the UPICC. Nonetheless, case law shows that most of the awards applying the CISG have referred to domestic principles when addressing the issue of clauses pénales/liquidated damages clauses rather than opting for a CISG-oriented interpretation.[63]

Whether arbitral tribunals have the power to reduce or increase the amount of penalty or liquidated damages will depend on the applicable law, as well as on the applicable rules of procedure and on the requested reliefs as formulated by the parties. Therefore, the parties should be mindful to formulate their claims and/or defenses by making reference to the contractual provisions, to the law applicable to the substance, as well as to the rules governing the procedure (ie, both the lex arbitri as well as the special rules that may be contained in the applicable institutional rules or terms of reference and the like).

Liquidated damages in construction arbitration

Notably, the quantification of damages in construction disputes is often very complex. Disruptions occur very frequently in large construction projects and typically affect the determination of the quantum: changes to the work, project delays, instructions of the owner/contractor, change in law, third party liabilities, etc.[64]

Thus, liquidated damages clauses, both for non-performance and delay, are widely used in construction contracts.[65]

Penalties are frequently used in relation to the timely achievement of key milestone dates prior to the expiry of the overall time for completion and work as incentives for the contractor to constantly keep up the works' progress.

In the event of contractor-caused delay, most construction contracts contain provisions for liquidated damages as the exclusive damages remedy to the employer.[66] Liquidated damages avoid the need for the employer to prove the actual loss caused by the con-

---

61 Arbitral Award in Case No 229/1996 of June 5, 1997 of the International Arbitration Court of the Chamber of Commerce and Industry of the Russian Federation.

62 Arbitral Award of January 28, 1998, Ad hoc Arbitration, Helsinki; Arbitral Award in Case No 134/2002 of April 4, 2003 of the International Arbitration Court of the Chamber of Commerce and Industry of the Russian Federation.

63 *Petro-Chem Development Co Inc v Pangang Group International Economic & Trading Co Ltd, and Pangang Group Chongqing Titanium Industry Co Ltd*, ICC Case No 19574/GFG; *Hoshine Silicon Industry Co Ltd v AB Speciality Silicones LLC*, CIETAC Case No ZJR20190012.

64 Conrad Bromley and Terry Hawkins, 'Damages in Construction Arbitrations' in A Trenor (ed), *The Guide to Damages in International Arbitration* (Global Arbitration Review 2022) 1.

65 Herfried Wöss and others, *Damages in International Arbitration under Complex Long-term Contracts* (Oxford, 2014) 48; Jane Jenkins, *International Construction Arbitration Law* (Wolters Kluwer, 2021) 38 stresses that is commonplace in civil law countries to include penalty clauses in construction contracts.

66 ibid 58.

tractor's delay and they grant certainty to contractors as to their exposure, especially if damages are capped.

A per day or per week rate is often applied for delays measured at the contractual milestone dates, subject to adjustment or exclusion at final termination of the works.[67] On larger projects, liquidated damages are typically capped at a percentage of the contract price, usually 5 or 10 per cent.[68] With specific reference to turnkey construction contracts, the liquidated damages for delay will usually be deducted from the final price. In addition, contracts often specify that payment of liquidated damages for delay does not relieve the contractor from its obligation to complete or perform any of its other obligations.[69] However, under some applicable laws, the employer must expressly reserve its rights and claims in respect of penalties upon acceptance of the works, as it will otherwise be considered to have waived them.

Parties to construction contracts often provide liquidated damages not only with regard to delay but also in respect of failure to achieve the specified performance standards. Liquidated damages for failure to meet performance standards will vary with the degree of the failure. These clauses may be unclear in their application and might be difficult to enforce, depending on the way they are drafted and on the discretion that may be applied by the experts and/or arbitrators in determining whether or not there is a failure and whether there was grave or simple negligence.

These kinds of damages may be measured with reference to the difference between the contractual agreed targets (e.g. capacity, production) and the actual capacity demonstrated in testing. By way of example, in the case of a factory built and equipped to produce certain products, liquidated damages may apply to guarantee the gross output contractually agreed. In the case of an energy plant, there may be a failure to achieve a pre-agreed energy production, testified by the failure to pass the tests on completion.

In case of non-performance, the enforcement risk of the liquidated damages clause is commonly secured through a performance bond, a bank guarantee, a standby letter of credit and the like.[70]

The Fédération Internationale des Ingénieurs Conseils (FIDIC)[71] contributes to the process of harmonization of contractual conditions in the construction sector with the publication of international standard forms of contract. The 2017 FIDIC Yellow Book, which contains guidelines for drafting conditions of Plant and Design-Build Contract, expressly provides a liquidated damages clause for delay at Clause 8.7:

If the Contractor fails to comply with Sub-Clause 8.2 [Time for Completion], the Contractor shall subject to Sub-Clause 2.5 [Employer's Claims] pay delay damages to the

---

67 Indeed, it is often provided that the contractor may be released from any such liability if it finally achieves overall completion in time; see Bromley and Hawkins (n 64).

68 *OGI Group Corporation v Oil Projects Company of the Ministry of Oil, Baghdad, Iraq (SCOP)*, ICC Case No 20994/ZF/AYZ; *Natura Furniture, UAB v GE Power Sweden AB*, ICC Case No 21983/MHM; other legal instruments, especially with regard to other types of contracts, such as sale of goods ones, have similar approaches: e.g. the 2020 ICC Model Contract – International Sale (Manufactured Goods) provides at art 10.2: 'When there is delay in delivery of any goods, the Buyer is entitled to claim performance and liquidated damages equal to <u>0.5% or such other percentage</u> as may be agreed of the price of those goods <u>for each commenced week of delay. Liquidated damages for delay shall not exceed 5% of the price</u> of the delayed goods or such maximum amount as may be agreed in Box A-10 (underline added)'.

69 Jenkins (n 65) 38.

70 Wöss and others (n 65) 53–54.

71 The official website of FIDIC may be found at: https://fidic.org/.

Employer for this default. These delay damages shall be the sum stated in the Appendix to Tender, which shall be paid for every day which shall elapse between the relevant Time for Completion and the date stated in the Taking-Over Certificate. However, the total amount due under this Sub-Clause shall not exceed the maximum amount of delay damages (if any) stated in the Appendix to Tender.

These delay damages shall be the only damages due from the Contractor for such default, other than in the event of termination under Sub-Clause 15.2 [Termination by Employer] prior to completion of the works. These damages shall not relieve the contractor from his obligation to complete the works, or from any other duties, obligations or responsibilities which he may have under the Contract.[72]

The International Chamber of Commerce (ICC) Commission on Commercial Law has released in 2020 the ICC Model Contract – Major Turnkey Projects,[73] which offers some guidelines on how to structure a performance-related liquidated damages clause.

The ICC Model Contract provides that 'if the works fail to achieve the Guaranteed Performance during the Performance Test, and/or the Retest, but do exceed the Minimum Performance, then Performance-related liquidated damages (if any) as set out in the Contract shall be payable'.[74] Indeed, for major projects, the provision of a guaranteed and a minimum performance as standards to measure liquidated damages represents a valid suggestion.

Furthermore, the ICC Model Contract underlines that the payment of any such liquidated damages shall not affect the employer's rights to terminate the contract, if such right has been expressly agreed. In any case, it is suggested that the parties provide that as long 'as the performance of the Works is equal to or better than the Minimum Performance, the agreed liquidated damages shall in respect of the relevant performance parameters be the Employer's sole and exclusive remedy for the Works' failure to achieve the Guaranteed Performance'.[75]

The United Nations Industrial Development Organization (UNIDO) has issued in 1996 the UNIDO Guidelines for Infrastructure Development through Build-Operate-Transfer (BOT) Projects.[76] The Guidelines recommend including lump-sum payments in case of a substantial breach of contract or of force majeure situations exceeding a reasonable period, supplemented by liquidated damages specified in the delay and penalty clauses of the project agreement. In addition, cases not covered by liquidated damages and contract penalties should be expressly dealt with in the contract by providing: terms and conditions

---

72 As to liquidated damages clauses, the FIDIC Construction Contract Red Book's Clause 8.8 and the FIDIC EPC/Turnkey Contract Silver Book's Clause 8.7 also contain a similar provisions.

73 The ICC Commission on Commercial Law and Practice, *ICC Model Contract – Major Turnkey Projects* (2020) was drafted with the aim to ensure successful completion and delivery of such projects and providing a legal framework for a more collaborative approach to turnkey projects.

74 The ICC Commission on Commercial Law and Practice, ICC Model Contract – Major Turnkey Projects, 2020, art 46.10.

75 ibid art 46.13.

76 A build-operate-transfer (BOT) contract is a model used to finance large projects, typically infrastructure projects developed through public-private partnerships. BOT projects are normally large-scale, greenfield infrastructure projects that would otherwise be financed, built, and operated solely by the government. The UNIDO Manual covers the entire spectrum of financial and legal issues faced by government authorities and project managers in the development of BOT projects, while offering developing countries the basic orientation needed to design effective BOT strategies. See UNIDO, 'Guidelines for Infrastructure Development through Build-Operate-Transfer (BOT) Projects' (*UNIDO*, 1996) <https://digitallibrary.un.org/record/195428?ln=en> accessed 20 November 2023.

for compensation; exemptions from the obligations to pay compensation; benefits gained from failure to perform; duty to mitigate the loss; currency of damages; exclusion of consequential damages in cases where the party in breach of contract has not acted with gross misconduct.[77]

Conclusions

The regime and the enforceability of penalty and liquidated damages clauses is still a central and very debated topic in comparative law. The advantages of such contractual tool in terms of efficiency makes it in fact extremely suitable for major and complex contracts. Notably, these kinds of clauses are standard in construction contracts.

In practice, there are some differences throughout the legal systems that suggest that the parties should carefully consider the regime of such clauses both according to the applicable law to the contract, as well as in the place of enforcement.

If the contract contains a choice of court clause, they should be aware that in most legal systems the judges have a power ex officio to reduce the amount of the penalty, if it is manifestly disproportionate, and in some cases they may award additional damages. Arbitral tribunals are usually bound to the requests of relief formulated by the parties, so they are unlikely to reduce the amount of the penalty on their own motion. Further, if a party requests additional damages on top of the clause, provided that the applicable law and the contractual clause leave room for this request, they will have to clearly state so in their requests for relief.

Once a decision/award granting penalty clauses' damages has been issued, obstacles may still arise if enforcement is sought in countries that do not allow penalty clauses. Even if common law courts tend to reject such arguments and grant enforcement of decisions/ awards granting penalty clauses' damages, courts with stricter approaches (including on punitive damages) may nonetheless assess whether public policy is respected and whether the domestic rules prohibiting penalty clauses are to be considered overriding mandatory provisions, thus precluding the enforcement of the decision.

---

77 ibid 236–237.

PART IV

DISPUTE RESOLUTION

CHAPTER 14

Adjudication since 1998

Matt Molloy

This chapter will be necessarily brief and focus on some headline observations regarding three key areas. I start with a reflection on the pre May 1998 landscape before statutory adjudication was brought into force in the UK. I then consider how adjudication has evolved and where adjudication is now. Finally, I share my thoughts on what the future holds and where adjudication may be going.

The pre–May 1998 landscape

The genesis of adjudication in the UK is well documented.[1] The concerns of the day were highlighted in Sir Michael Latham's 'Constructing the Team' ('the Latham Report') published in July 1994 which recommended a system of mandatory adjudication. That recommendation was realised through the Housing Grants Construction and Regeneration Act 1996 ('the Construction Act') which came into force on 1 May 1998. To the extent a construction contract did not provide for adjudication which complied with Section 108 of the Construction Act, then the adjudication provisions of the Scheme for Construction Contracts (England and Wales) Regulations 1998 (or their equivalents in Scotland and Northern Ireland) ('the Scheme') would apply.

The options for resolving construction industry disputes prior to May 1998 were limited. In the event parties were unable to resolve their dispute amicably their choice was between litigation before an official referee or arbitration. Save for the fact that litigation was conducting with 'wigs and gowns' and in public, there was arguably little difference between the two options in terms of time and expense, i.e., they were typically both lengthy and expensive:

> From my experience as an advocate, both before official referees and arbitrators, I do not think that in most cases of complexity there was much difference in the length of a hearing of a dispute whether it was heard in court or in an arbitration. **It might be said that this is because, once counsel is briefed in an arbitration, he dictates the manner in which the case will be presented and by training will follow court procedure**.[2]

Ten years prior to the publication of the Latham Report, the then Master of the Rolls, Sir John Donaldson, opined on the 'state of the official referees list' in the following terms:

---

1 For a good summary, see Peter Coulson, *Coulson on Construction Adjudication* (4th edn, OUP 2020), Ch 1.

2 James Fox-Andrews, 'Construction industry disputes: Official Referee or technical arbitrator – the pros and cons' (1992) 8(1) Const LJ 2, 9 (emphasis added).

DOI: 10.4324/9781032663975-19

217

The delays in disposing of business before the official referees, through no fault of their own, [is] wholly unacceptable … if this reduction in the length of the lists does not occur or seems unlikely to occur, urgent consideration should be given to conferring upon the official referees, a power analogous to that contemplated by section 92 of the County Courts Act 1959 (power to judge to refer to arbitration] to enable official referees, whether sitting as such or arbitrators, to refer, or sub-refer, the 'nuts and bolts' of the suit to suitably qualified arbitrator for inquiry and report. This would result in the official referees becoming, in effect, the construction industry court, having the same relationship to the construction industry as the Commercial Court has to the financial and commercial activities of the City of London.[3]

Additionally, it was permissible for parties to constrain references to arbitration and litigation until the end of a project, e.g. after a final statement or certificate had been issued. Thus, the reality was that it was only those with 'deep pockets' and the means to fund arbitration or litigation who were able to pursue claims. The perception was that the odds were heavily stacked in favour of the larger organisations or those with access to limitless funds who had the ability to stay the course of litigation or arbitration.

In many ways the advent of adjudication can be seen as the product of successful lobbying on the part of the specialist contracting organisations and/or more general contracting bodies in order to redress that perceived imbalance of power. However, the proposed introduction of adjudication was not universally welcomed. Had I been delivering this talk as an aspiring adjudicator in this room 25 years ago, I suspect that I may not have received such a warm reception as I have today. I see in the audience some of those who took an active part in the debate at the time concerning the proposed introduction of statutory adjudication. The subtitle of a collection of papers published in 1997 and edited by the former Director of the King's College Centre of Construction Law, Professor John Uff KC, is informative of the opposition to the proposed reforms – Contemporary Issues in Construction Law Volume II – Construction Contract Reform: A plea for sanity ('Plea for Sanity').[4]

The papers in Plea for Sanity spanned the period 1995 to 1997 and were stated to represent a collection of papers in opposition to the reform proposals. In his editorial Professor Uff said that the:

> publication is not a plea for abandonment of the reform programme started in 1992, but for a pause to allow proper debate. Particularly, the impending introduction of compulsory adjudication will have far-reaching and irreversible effects on all sides of the UK construction industry.[5]

An article from the late Ian Norman Duncan Wallace QC published in the Construction Law Journal in 1997[6] also gives a flavour of the mood of the day with (for him) a characteristically strong and colourful account of the perceived shortcomings of 'industry' arbitrators or adjudicators and their seeming bias against the client or 'paymaster parties':

> Even when adjudicators are nominated by those traditional institutions in the construction industry (including the Chartered Institute of Arbitrators) which currently nominate arbitrators failing agreement, **the present writer has already drawn attention in Hudson and**

---

3 *Northern RHA v Derek Crouch Construction Co Ltd* [1984] QB 644, 674–675.

4 John Uff, *Contemporary Issues in Construction Law. Vol II A Plea for Sanity* (Construction Law Press 1997).

5 Ibid.

6 Ian ND Wallace, 'HGRA adjudication: swarms of wannabes' (1997) Const LJ (emphasis added).

elsewhere to the seeming bias of 'industry' arbitrators against client or paymaster parties (i.e. against the owner or, in a sub-contract setting, the main contractor), indicated by the reported misconduct cases, in England and Australia in particular. **Moreover, there is a class of aggressive and over-confident arbitrator in the construction industry, with a confirmed belief in the superiority of his own technical expertise** combined with inquisitorial activism (the latter unfortunately expressly encouraged by the 'take the initiative' language of article 13 of the Scheme, no doubt borrowed from section 34(g) of the Arbitration Act), in contrast to hearing witnesses tested by cross-examination and analysis of contemporaneous documentation presented by the parties, for the satisfactory resolution of disputes.[7]

As well as a concern regarding the ability of the aspiring adjudicators more generally, was a concern as to the appropriateness of having a complex construction industry disputes determined, albeit temporarily, within a 28 day timetable. If one looks at the list of contributors to Plea for Sanity, it is evident that much of the opposition and concern was held by legal practitioners and/or experienced arbitrators. A cynical view may be that the proposed reforms presented a threat to those who benefited from the then status quo of lengthy and expensive arbitration or litigation. A more benevolent view may be that those concerns were well founded – how could disputes regarding a final account, extension of time, loss and expense, allegations of professional negligence or alleged defects possibly be resolved in 28 days?

The evolution of adjudication – where are we now?

It is fair to say that today adjudication is very much an embedded part of the construction industry litigation landscape. It is also fair to say that at the outset in 1998 there was uncertainty as to the nature of adjudication and the form it would take. It is perhaps instructive that the adjudication provisions of the Scheme do not prescribe for any submissions to the adjudicator beyond the Referral of the dispute. Allied with the inquisitorial powers conferred upon the adjudicator (consistent with Section 34(g) of the Arbitration Act referred to by Duncan Wallace[8]) indicates that the original concept for adjudication was that the process would be more akin to expert determination, whereby an experienced and suitably trained industry professional would be presented with a 'dispute' consisting of the parties' previously canvassed and exchanged arguments, conduct an investigation and make a decision without the need for formal sequential submissions. Indeed the ICE Conditions of Contract at the time attempted to define the word 'dispute' by limiting it to matters which had already been referred to the Engineer for a decision and which had been subject to a notice of dissatisfaction. This concept was also referred to by one practitioner as the 'black bag' approach, whereby the parties would package up all their previously rehearsed arguments in a 'sack' and hand them over to the adjudicator for a decision.[9]

In contrast to the Scheme, the JCT Adjudication Rules did provide for a Response to be provided within 7 days service of the Referral. Perhaps as a result of familiarity with an adversarial system, the 'norm' in adjudication is now for an exchange of sequential submissions, e.g. Referral, Response and Reply and more (e.g. Rejoinder, Surrejoinder,

---

7 Ibid.

8 ibid.

9 E.g. Dominic Helps, referring to the judgment in *Edmund Nuttall v RG Carter* [2002] EWHC 400 (TCC).

Rebutter, Surrebutter, First Final Submission, Second Final Submission etc. etc.!). My view is that one of the reasons for this is that the adjudicators were initially drawn and/or trained by individuals from a pool of practitioners who had been trained in arbitration and were familiar with the adversarial common law system of resolving construction industry disputes. The TCC has also made it clear that parties are entitled to advance new arguments and evidence within an adjudication subject to the other party having a reasonable opportunity to present its case.[10] The adjudicator has also arguably been given a de-facto power to adopt an extended timetable in the event they consider that it would not be possible to conduct an adjudication in a procedurally fair manner as a result of its size and complexity.[11] Consequently it could be said that adjudication has become in reality a fast track system of arbitration.

Perhaps the turning point for adjudication was the first adjudication enforcement action by Dyson J (as he then was) in *Macob Civil Engineering Limited v Morrison Construction* [12]on 12th February 1999. The statistics of the number of adjudication appointments made by adjudicator nominating bodies ('ANBs') in the UK show that *Macob* triggered a marked increase in the numbers of adjudications which, apart from a drop in 2011 (and post the 2008 financial crisis and associated economic downturn), have continued at a sustained rate since that time.[13] Another contributory factor to the growth and continued use of adjudication may also be the historic drive towards more cost efficient litigation. At the outset we had the Woolf Reforms of 1996 and the Arbitration Act 1996, both of which were aimed at addressing concerns regarding the delays and costs associated with litigation and arbitration. Since then we have had the Jackson Cost Review of 2004 which had similar aims.

Another significant factor which in my view has contributed to the development of adjudication is the evolution of official referees to High Court Judges and the integration of the Technology and Construction Court ('TCC') as part of the Business and Property Courts of England and Wales with TCC Judges having the same status as Commercial Court Judges. In many ways I consider an analogy can be drawn between the role fulfilled by the official referee of the past and that of the present day adjudicator.

The official referee was created by Section 82 of the Judicature Act 1873. Its origin arose from the increased use of arbitration business in contrast to a jury trial or litigation for technical disputes. Although the official referee was abolished by Section 25 of the Courts Act 1971, 'official referees' business' continued. However, in some circles, the official referee was seen as inferior to High Court Judges. For example, Sir Antony Edwards-Stuart has referred to a perception of the official referees as the 'cadet branch' of the High Court.[14]

The change in status from 'cadet judges' to High Court Judges can perhaps best be seen in the appointment of Dyson J and subsequently Forbes J (who was the first Official

---

10 E.g. *Cantillon Limited v Urvasco Limited* [2008] EWHC 282 (TCC).

11 E.g. *CIB Properties Limited v Birse Construction* [2004] EWHC 2365 (TCC); *Dorchester Hotels Limited v Vivid Interiors* [2009] EWHC 70 (TCC).

12 [1999] 2 WLUK 258.

13 See e.g. Renato Nazzini and Aleksander Kalisz, '2022 Construction Adjudication in the United Kingdom: Tracing trends and guiding reform' (*King's College London*, 3 November 2022) <10.18742/pub01-160> accessed 27 October 2023.

14 See Antony Edwards-Stuart, 'The Jackson Reforms and Technology & Construction Court Litigation' in Julian Bailey (ed), *A Festschrift for Lord Justice Jackson* (Bloomsbury Publishing 2018).

Referee to become a High Court Judge). This was followed by the appointment of Jackson J (as he then was) and the 'Jackson 5' (Ramsey J, Akenhead J, Coulson J and Edwards-Stuart J) who have all played their role in elevating the status of the judges who dealt with construction industry disputes and also the TCC more generally. It can be seen from the caselaw and development of the jurisprudence concerning adjudication that a key part of the role of the TCC is to support and police adjudication and in particular the conduct of adjudicators and parties to adjudication. It can also be suggested that, as the status of the TCC has been raised and the pressure on the judicial budget has increased, adjudication has become the natural home for dealing with domestic commercial construction industry disputes. I would suggest that there is a correlation between the increased status of the TCC and that of the adjudicator. Three examples of this can be seen in the judgments of Coulson LJ in the Court of Appeal:

- *S&T (UK) Limited v Grove Developments Limited*: *[2018] EWHC 123 (TCC)*:-
  70. Mr Speaight properly conceded that, if the court had the power to do something, then so too did an adjudicator. **I agree: in any case where the parties have conferred upon an adjudicator the power to decide all disputes between them, the adjudicator has the same wide powers as the court.**[15]
- *Bresco Electrical Services Limited (in liquidation) v Michael J Lonsdale (Electrical) Limited and Cannon Corporate Limited v Primus Build Limited*:
  31. On analysis, **I can see no reason why, purely as a matter of jurisdiction (as opposed to utility), a reference to adjudication should be treated any differently to a reference to arbitration**.[16]
- *John Doyle Construction Limited (in Liquidation) v Erith Construction Limited*:
  29. Although it has come at some cost to other court users in the TCC (because they can sometimes be bumped down the queue for interim appointments in order to prioritise adjudication enforcement hearings), it has generally been regarded as a great success. It is one of the reasons why, speaking personally, **I rather cavil at the suggestion that construction adjudication is somehow 'just a part of ADR'.** In my view, that damns it with faint praise. In reality, it is the only system of compulsory dispute resolution of which I am aware which requires a decision by a specialist professional within 28 days, backed up by a specialist court enforcement scheme which (subject to jurisdiction and natural justice issues only) provides a judgment within weeks thereafter. **It is not an alternative to anything; for most construction disputes, it is the only game in town.**[17]

Lord Briggs' opinion in the UK Supreme Court in *Bresco* has added even greater weight to the increased status and importance of adjudication to the construction industry.

The TCC has also been seen to chastise parties for opting to litigate disputes in the TCC when adjudication may have been more appropriate:

---

15 [2018] EWHC 123 (TCC) (emphasis added).
16 [2019] EWCA Civ 27 (emphasis added).
17 [2021] EWCA Civ 1452 (emphasis added).

Finally, there is an adjudication scheme for claims in professional negligence, operated by the Professional Negligence Bar Association … It is a great pity that the parties did not adopt that method of resolving their dispute in this case. It would have been far quicker, and much more economical, than conducting a High Court trial … Using the scheme to which I have referred, to resolve a dispute such as this one, would have been a far better way for the parties to have proceeded.[18]

However, with increased status comes increased responsibility and scrutiny of the conduct of adjudicators and the parties to adjudication. For present purposes I have just looked at 2019 (but there are many more examples in different years), but some examples of the extent to which the conduct of adjudicators has been the subject an interrogation of the TCC are listed below: *J J Rhatigan & Co (UK) Ltd v Rosemary Lodge Developments Ltd*,[19] *RGB P&C Ltd v Victory House General Partner Ltd*,[20] *Willow Corp SÀRL v MTD Contractors Ltd*,[21] *Corebuild Ltd v Cleaver & Anor.*[22] [2019] EWHC 2170 (TCC).

Another aspect of the increase in status of adjudication is the increase in complexity of the process. Allied with this is the effect it has on the cost of the process. As well as an increased need for accountability, comes an increased need for quality. Thankfully, there has been some progress in this regard, with the advent of low value dispute schemes, such as the CIC LVD Model Adjudication Procedure and the TeCSA LVD Scheme, and the increase in more extensive training and education of adjudicators by professional bodies than was available at the outset as well as the increased inclusion of adjudication modules by Universities as part of their post graduate LLM and MSc programmes.

The future – where are we going?

Oscar Wilde is attributed as saying that 'imitation is the sincerest form of flattery that mediocrity can pay to greatness'. With that quip in mind, there are signs that UK construction adjudication is likely to be the subject of increased use in the future or used as a model to be adopted elsewhere in other areas, industries or jurisdictions.

As things currently stand statutory adjudication in the UK is restricted to 'construction contracts' as defined by the Construction Act. Thus there are notable exclusions, such as construction contracts with residential owner occupiers or contracts which involve power generation. I predict that in the future there is likely to be a widening of the UK adjudication process by virtue of some erosion of the excluded operations currently caught by S.105 of the Construction Act.

I also predict that there may be a widening of the adjudication process to other industries. I have already alluded to voluntary adjudication schemes being adopted in other industries, e.g., the Professional Negligence Bar Association,[23] and the Society of Computers and Law has also introduced an adjudication scheme for IT disputes. Although strictly a statutory 'arbitration scheme', the creation of a Pubs Code Adjudicator (a product of the last UK coalition government) to address disputes between tied tenants and

---

18 *Beattie Passive Norse Limited (2) NPS Property Consultants Limited v NPS Property Consultants Limited* [2021] EWHC 1116 (TCC) [152] (Fraser J).

19 [2019] EWHC 1152 (TCC).

20 [2019] EWHC 1188 (TCC).

21 [2019] EWHC 1591 (TCC).

22 [2019] EWHC 2170 (TCC).

23 ibid.

large pub-owning businesses/landlords bears similarities in the use of a statutory backed private dispute resolution regime as a means of dealing with disputes which would have otherwise occupied Court time and burdened the judicial budget.

There has also been an increased uptake of adjudication internationally. Perhaps understandably, this has thus far been predominantly confined to common law and/or or commonwealth countries, but there are signs that this may not always be the case, e.g. a civil law jurisdiction such as Germany has been considering the process and Quebec has a pilot adjudication scheme. FIDIC has also recently instigated increased training and a new accreditation regime in order to cater for an anticipated increased demand for adjudicators on projects where its contracts are used as a result of a requirement of funders of international construction projects in developing countries (such as the World Bank) to adopt FIDIC contracts and a commitment to fund dispute adjudication/avoidance boards.

I also perceive an export or transfer of the skills acquired by construction industry adjudicators to other areas, such as dispute/conflict avoidance (or adjudication) boards or panels where board/panel members are able to use their experience to assist on live projects in order to prevent the escalation of disputes to a formal referral to adjudication or arbitration. Other areas where adjudicators are being used is where parties are seeking a more evaluative mediation process, e.g. the RICS evaluative mediation model where the evaluative mediator may be asked to provide an opinion or recommendation in the event a settlement is not achieved.

Although training and qualification of adjudicators has developed in line with the increase in complexity, one concern amongst those who have invested in the training is the difficulty of developing a practice as an adjudicator. The situation is arguably similar to mediation and arbitration. However, the difference is that, historically, newly trained or qualified arbitrators or mediators were able to act as pupils or observers in order to get hands on experience and receive guidance from experienced practitioners which they could then use in support of getting onto panels and getting their first appointment. My view is that there is a real need for adjudication to follow suit in this respect. This is something that I have pioneered over the recent years. My hope is that the ANBs/professional bodies now take the lead in the roll out and recognition of pupillage and mentoring schemes as in many ways they are the gatekeepers to the future of adjudication.

Conclusion and final thoughts

With the benefit of hindsight, the naysayers have been proved to be wrong. Adjudication in the UK has become an overwhelming success. It owes its success in many ways to the support it has received from the Courts and the evolution and increased status of the TCC. Adjudication is now a mature, complex and highly legal process. With this, comes expense and an increased need for quality and accountability. Recent moves to make adjudication more accessible to smaller and medium sized entities in order to resolve low value disputes are welcome. However, low value does not necessarily equate with simplicity or an absence of complexity. Thus the training requirements, case management and decision making skills are as much, if not more, demanding for these types of disputes as for high value, complex disputes with sophisticated and experienced representatives. This provides a challenge. It also provides an opportunity.

CHAPTER 15

Arbitration and insolvency in civil law European countries

Crenguta Leaua and Corina Tanase

Arbitration and insolvency are two institutions that do not easily coexist. Both insolvency and arbitration have their own very specific legal provisions within a jurisdiction, each providing a special regime for settlement of disputes that deviates from the general rule (*specialia generalibus derogant*). In short, the application of arbitration and insolvency in the same dispute involves an analysis of 'special vs special' regulations.

The purpose of the national insolvency laws is to implement a collective procedure for covering the debts of the insolvent company opened in their jurisdictions, limiting or forestalling parties' rights to freely dispose or enforce their claims in relation with the insolvent company. Under such procedure, usually, all creditors of the insolvent company are required to file their claims in the insolvency procedure which are subject to the verification by the appointed insolvency practitioner.[1] These provisions are in most European civil law countries mandatory provisions of public policy, from which the parties are not entitled to deviate. The national insolvency laws regulate different insolvency proceedings, with the most common being the reorganization of the company[2] and the liquidation of the company[3].

On the other hand, arbitration by definition is a private alternative jurisdiction, its purpose being to enable the parties to use such alternative means for solving their disputes under procedural rules designed by them and the tribunal, either as ad-hoc arbitration or by making use of the rules of arbitration provided by arbitration institutions.[4] Also, the international conventions set the purpose of the arbitration as settling disputes arising from the commercial relationship of the parties (be them physical or legal persons).[5]

---

1 The appointed insolvency practitioner, depending on the type of insolvency, has different names under different jurisdictions: for example, in Romanian 'administrator judiciar' or 'lichidator judiciar'; in France 'liquidateur' or 'administrateur judiciaire'; in Spain 'administrador concursal' or 'mediador concursal'.

2 In essence, the reorganization of the company aims to cover the debts of the insolvent company, the reorganization of the business of the insolvent company and its reintegration in the economic circuit at the end of the proceedings.

3 In essence, the liquidation of the company aims to cover the debts of the insolvent company, the liquidation of the entire estate of the insolvent company and the dissolution of the company at the end of the proceedings.

4 National laws usually regulate the scope of the arbitration, in relation to domestic and international arbitration. See e.g., Romanian Civil Procedure Code, arts 541–542, 1112, and 1115.

5 See e.g. European Convention on International Commercial Arbitration (adopted 21 April 1961, entered into force 7 January 1964) 484 UNTS 349 (Geneva Convention) art 1; UNCITRAL Arbitration Rules, art 1; Convention on the Recognition and enforcement of Foreign Arbitral Awards (adopted 10 June 1958, entered into force 7 June 1959) 330 UNTS 3 (New York Convention).

224   DOI: 10.4324/9781032663975-20

Consequently, while the rationale of arbitration special provisions is to give room for parties' autonomy for solving their disputes in a business-to-business relationship, the rationale of insolvency is totally the opposite, namely, to set up a collective procedure, with the aim to remove the arbitrary and reduce the parties' autonomy in a business-to-business relationship.

This is a philosophical clash between arbitration and insolvency that make them so difficult to coexist, especially that in most jurisdictions, there are no express provisions regulating the effects of the opening of the insolvency on the arbitration agreement and/or the arbitration proceedings. In addition to the national laws, the EU laws must be also considered in relation with the European countries that are also EU Member States. Thus, when the relevant parties are nationals of the EU Member States, then the provisions of the Regulation (EU) 2015/848 of the European Parliament and of the Council of 20 May 2015 on insolvency proceedings (recast) in force since 2017 become applicable (the 'EU Insolvency Regulation').[6]

As such, the interaction between insolvency and arbitration remains of interest and current even with the continuous evolution of the arbitral practice, as the problems it poses may affect the very core of an arbitration, leaving an award against an insolvent company without effects or subject to annulment or refusal to recognize and enforce if such award is rendered without the observance of the effects of the opening of the insolvency.[7]

Is the impact of the opening of the insolvency proceedings in arbitration a matter of jurisdiction?

As shown above, in certain European civil law countries, the insolvency law creates a special tool concentrating creditors' claims against the estate of the insolvent debtor before the specialized insolvency court (applying the principle of *vis attractiva concursus*). To this end, the national insolvency courts where the insolvency was opened assert an exclusive jurisdiction on insolvency.[8] In such case, the rational is that, allowing creditors' individual claims for receivables against the estate outside the insolvency procedure carried out in front of the insolvency court, may negatively affect the rights of the other creditors, and create imbalance between the creditors.

The impact of insolvency on arbitration arises in cases in which one (or more) of the creditors and the debtor have concluded arbitration agreements for the resolution of their respective claims against each other and an arbitration procedure is either pending or a claim is filed after the opening of the insolvency proceedings.

In these circumstances, the main questions that arise in connection with the exclusive jurisdiction of the insolvency court are: (i) what law the arbitral tribunal should consider in relation to its jurisdiction when the national insolvency law institutes an exclusive

---

6 Regulation (EU) 2015/848 of the European Parliament and of the Council of 20 May 2015 on insolvency proceedings (recast) [2015] OJ L141/19 (EU Insolvency Regulation). The EU Insolvency Regulation represents a general rule, but at the EU level there are also other special provisions regulating insolvency that apply solely in certain cases and those are not part of this comparative study. See Miguel Virgos and Francisco Garcimartin, *The European Insolvency Regulation: Law and Practice* (Kluwer Law International, 2004) 8–10.

7 For example, under Italian law an award rendered without observing the insolvency provisions regulating expressly the termination of the arbitration agreement is subject to annulment. See Massimo V Benedettelli, 'International Arbitration in Italy (Kluwer Law International 2020) 410.

8 See for example Romania, France, Poland, Spain etc.

jurisdiction of the insolvency court, and does the fact that the arbitration is pending at the time of the opening of the insolvency creates any difference, and (ii) does such an exclusive jurisdiction of the insolvency courts render an arbitration agreement inoperable?

Under national laws the effects in arbitration of the opening of the insolvency proceedings against one of the parties to an arbitration agreement vary greatly from jurisdiction to jurisdiction, and do not find an overall consensus. This variation is very relevant especially in the case of international arbitration from the perspective of the application of multiple and competitive jurisdictions and laws in the same dispute.

In addition, the EU insolvency Regulation has direct applicability in an EU Member State, providing in Article 92 that it is 'binding in its entirety and directly applicable in the Member States in accordance with the Treaties'. So, if EU Member States are involved the EU Insolvency Regulation plays an important part because it regulates, inter alia, the effects that the opening of the insolvency proceeding may produce, as well as a series of conflict of laws and substantive provisions. However, the EU Insolvency Regulation does not override the applicability of the national legislations regulating the insolvency proceedings.[9]

As a general comment, Article 3(1) of the EU Insolvency Regulation establishes that the jurisdiction to open insolvency proceedings belongs to the courts of the Member State within the territory of which the centre of the debtor's main interests is situated. Also, Article 19(1) expressly provides that a judgment for the opening of the insolvency proceedings in an EU Member State is automatically recognized in another EU Member State, without any formality. This principle also applies to the judgments rendered in relation with the course and closure of insolvency proceedings, and the judgments deriving directly from the insolvency proceedings, and which are closely linked with them.[10]

Another aspect to be mentioned in relation with the EU Insolvency Regulation is the evolution in regulating the effects of insolvency proceedings on pending court and arbitration cases. Previously, at the EU level, the insolvency proceedings were regulated by the Council Regulation (EC) No 1346/2000 of 29 May 2000 on insolvency proceedings which was repealed since 25 June 2017 which was silent on such effects in case of pending arbitration proceedings[11]. This raised much debate in the international arbitral practice on the law to be considered when determining the effects of the opening of the insolvency proceedings in arbitration: was it the national law from the place where the insolvency was opened or was it the national law from the place of arbitration?

This debate led to the need for the EU Insolvency Regulation to provide expressly the law regulating the effects of insolvency proceedings on pending arbitral proceedings. The EU Insolvency Regulation currently provides expressly in Article 18 that '[t]he effects of insolvency proceedings on (...) pending arbitral proceedings concerning an asset or a right which forms part of a debtor's insolvency estate shall be governed solely by the law of the Member State in which (...) the arbitral tribunal has its seat'.

This regulation is important for determining the law governing the effects of the insolvency in arbitration, but it is applicable only when the insolvency is opened in an EU

---

9 Virgos and Garcimartín (n 6) 7–8.

10 EU Insolvency Regulation, art 32.

11 Council regulation (EC) No 1346/2000 of 29 May 2000 on insolvency proceedings [2000] OJ L160/1, art 15 regulated expressly only the law governing the effects of insolvency on 'lawsuit pending'.

Member State and the place of arbitration is in another EU Member State. For all the other cases, the EU Insolvency Regulation does not find direct applicability.

In the following paragraphs, few considerations on the applicable law from the perspective of Article 18 of the EU Insolvency Regulation are set down.

First, this provision regulates only the situation in which the arbitration proceedings are already pending at the date of the opening of the insolvency against one of its parties. However, it does not regulate the situation in which the arbitration agreement itself is declared invalid/ inoperable/ terminated under the national insolvency law where the insolvency is opened or in which the legal capacity of the insolvent company is affected.

Thus, the law determining, inter alia, the continuation of the arbitration proceedings and the type of claims that may be decided upon by the tribunal is the law at the place of arbitration.

One of the most common effects under national insolvency laws, is that the disputes pending when the insolvency procedure is opened are de jure suspended upon the opening of the insolvency. Even if in many jurisdictions such stay does not refer expressly to arbitration proceedings, usually the relevant jurisprudence in those jurisdictions makes no difference between court proceedings and arbitration proceedings from this perspective. The purpose of the stay of a pending dispute, either in front of a national court or an arbitral tribunal, is not uniform. In certain jurisdictions, this suspension means that a claim falling under exclusive jurisdiction of insolvency court must be filed by a creditor within the insolvency proceedings in order to be recovered within such procedure (including submission of the receivable for the verification by the insolvency practitioner). The stay is related to the essential condition for a creditor of the insolvent company to register its receivables in the insolvency proceedings within a certain period in order for such to be reviewed by the appointed insolvency practitioner and for the respective creditor to preserve its right to recover its receivables. However, under other jurisdictions the stay is not mandatory, or it only aims to bring the appointed insolvency practitioner as party to the arbitration proceedings.

For example, under Romanian Insolvency Law, Article 75(1) provides that all disputes pending at the date of the opening are suspended de jure, as their capitalization may be sought only in the insolvency proceedings by filing a statement of receivables with the administrator of the estate (the judicial administrator) and that once the decision to open the insolvency proceedings remains final (either by not being challenged or by the challenges being dismissed) all such disputes pending outside the insolvency proceedings are terminated.[12] Even if not expressly provided, this provision refers also to the arbitration disputes, which should be suspended and subsequently terminated. If the place of arbitration is Romania, this poses no problems, the arbitration practice confirms such automatic

---

12 Law no 85/2014 on the proceedings for preventing insolvency and on the insolvency proceedings, art 75(1): 'As of the date of the opening of the procedure shall be de iure suspended all legal court, off-court actions or enforcement procedures to recover receivables upon the debtor's estate. The capitalization of their rights may be made only within the insolvency procedure by filing the request for admission of the receivables. It is possible to resume such procedures only in case the decision for opening the procedure is annulled, the order for opening the procedure is revoked or the procedure is closed in the conditions of Article 178. If the decision for opening the procedure is annulled or revoked, as the case may be, legal court or off-court actions or enforcement procedures to recover receivables upon the debtor's estate and the enforcement may be resumed. At the date the decision for opening the procedure remains final, both the legal court and off-court actions, as well as the enforcement stayed shall terminate.'

stay. The issue arises if the place of arbitration is outside Romania, with an arbitral tribunal that does not give effects to this provision, with a distinction to be made in case the EU Insolvency Regulation applies or not. In such a case, even if the arbitration proceeds and may pass scrutiny at the place of arbitration, it is questionable if an award establishing payment obligations or declarations against the estate of the insolvent company may be recognized and enforced in Romania.

The situation is similar in France which regulates the stay and prohibition to file a claim outside the insolvency proceedings if such aims to obtain an order to pay or the termination of a contract due to the non-payment of debts.[13] The distinction is that under French law an arbitration may proceed with establishing the existence of a claim, in case the existence of such claim is denied in the insolvency proceedings, without the arbitral tribunal having the possibility to order the payment.[14] The core issue is for such a claim to be submitted prior to the insolvency proceedings for verification and for the arbitral tribunal not to order payment or other attachments regarding the estate.[15] Italy also prohibits the continuation or commencement of litigations against the debtor's estate that is part of the insolvency proceedings.[16]

On the other hand, the Spanish Insolvency Law, regulating expressly the effects of the opening of the insolvency in arbitration, provides that such will not impact the effectiveness of an arbitration agreement and that the arbitration proceedings pending at the date of opening of the insolvency shall continue.[17] The situation is similar in Germany, where

---

13 French Code de Commerce, Article L 622-21: 'I. – The decision to open stays or prohibits every legal actions of all creditors whose receivable is not referred to under Article L. 622-17 (I) seeking to obtain:

1 an order against the debtor to pay a sum of money.

2 the rescission of a contract for non-payment of a sum of money.

II. – It also stays or prohibits any proceedings for enforcement on the part of these creditors on both movable and immovable properties as well as any distribution procedure that did not produce an attributive effect prior to the decision to open.

III. – Hence, all time limits, to be observed under the penalty of loss or rescission of rights, are stayed.' See also ICC award no 6697 of 26.12.1990 [Pascal Ancel, Note – *Sentence partielle du 26 décembre 1990 dans l'affaire CCI No 6697, Revue de l'Arbitrage*, Comité Français de l'Arbitrage; Comité Français de l'Arbitrage 1992, Volume 1992 Issue 1) pp 146–151] where on the basis of the same principles of suspension of individual claims and equality of creditors which are fundamental principles of collective procedure of insolvency, an arbitral tribunal with its seat in Paris dismissed a creditor's claim aiming at the delivery of a bank guarantee by the debtor undergoing insolvency proceedings in Luxembourg.

14 Cour de Cassation, Chambre civile 1 rendered on 8 March 1988; Cour de Cassation, Chambre comm. rendered on 9 January 1990.

15 Yves Derains, Laurence Kiffer, 'National Report for France (2013)' in Jan Paulsson and Lise Bosman (eds), *ICCA International Handbook on Commercial Arbitration*, (Kluwer Law International 2013); Flore Poloni, Nicolas Partouche, 'IBA Toolkit on Insolvency and Arbitration. Questionnaire. National Report of France.' (*IBA*, January 2021) <https://www.ibanet.org/MediaHandler?id=097400CE-C218-4FA4-9114 -88A2BC57960D> accessed 20 November 2023. See also *Societe Gaussin et autres v Societe Alstom Power Turbomachines, Cour de Cassation (Ch Com), 2 June 2004*, where the dispute concerned a request for arbitration filed against an insolvent company which had as object a declaratory relief with respect to plaintiff's receivable, deriving from agreements concluded between the parties prior to the commencement of the insolvency procedure. The Court of Cassation stated that the public policy principle of stay of individual actions prohibits, after insolvency proceedings have been opened, the initiation of arbitral proceedings without undergoing the procedure of verification of receivables beforehand.

16 Italian Insolvency Code, art 150: 'Unless otherwise provided by law, from the day of the declaration of the opening of the judicial liquidation no individual enforcement or precautionary action, including for claims accrued during the judicial liquidation, may be commenced or continued on the assets included in the proceedings.'

17 Francisco Garcimartín, Manuel Penades, 'IBA Toolkit on Insolvency and Arbitration. Questionnaire. National Report of Spain' (*IBA*, January 2021) <https://www.ibanet.org/MediaHandler?id=4D3C244E-F98A -42EB-B769-08B7C208B8F7> accessed 20 November 2023; Real Decreto Legislativo 1/2020, de 5 de mayo, por el que se aprueba el texto refundido de la Ley Concursal (Spanish Insolvency Law), art 140.

an automatic stay of a pending arbitration proceedings is not regulated by the German Insolvency Code, but a stay may be ordered by the Tribunal for reasons of due process.[18]

Second, if the arbitration is initiated after the insolvency proceedings are opened, such will not fall under the provisions of Article 18 of the EU Insolvency Regulation, and it is possible for such to fall under Article 7(2)(f) of the EU Insolvency Regulation. Based on this provision, the law at the place of opening the insolvency proceedings shall determine 'the effects of the insolvency proceedings on proceedings brought by individual creditors, with the exception of pending lawsuits'. Thus, in relation with arbitration, after the opening of the insolvency, the possibility to file an individual outside the insolvency proceedings may be solely a matter of the validity/ effectiveness of the arbitration agreement.

On the applicable law from the perspective of non-EU European countries, mention is made that, in absence of the EU Insolvency Regulation, this shall be determined on a case by case basis, the arbitral tribunals usually taking into account the law at the place of arbitration to determine the effects of the opening of the insolvency proceedings.

In general, regardless of the applicable law, the issue is to what extent the exclusive jurisdiction of the insolvency court and the stay of the proceedings may equate with a lack of validity or effectiveness of the arbitration agreement.

Validity and effectiveness are two different legal concepts, considering that even if an arbitration agreement may be valid at the date of its signing, it may nevertheless be prevented to produce effects due to lack of effectiveness.[19]

The concept of ineffective or inoperable arbitration agreement as distinct from the concept of validity is also envisaged in article II (3) of the New York Convention:

> The court of a Contracting State, when seized of an action in a matter in respect of which the parties have made an agreement within the meaning of this article, shall, at the request of one of the parties, refer the parties to arbitration, unless it finds that the said agreement is null and void, inoperative or incapable of being performed.[20]

While the insolvency law that regulates the insolvency proceedings themselves is the insolvency law where the insolvency proceedings are opened against the insolvent company with little to no debate, the issue is different in relation with the law applicable to the arbitration agreement and to the arbitration proceedings in case of insolvency.

As shown above, once the insolvency proceedings are opened usually the insolvency court has exclusive jurisdiction. Thus, a matter to be considered is if the choice of the parties to defer their disputes to arbitration supersedes the provisions of national insolvency laws? And, similarly, if a validly concluded arbitration agreement becomes ineffective/ inoperable at the opening of the insolvency?

---

18 Philipp K Wagner, Carl-Christian Kramer, 'IBA Toolkit on Insolvency and Arbitration. Questionnaire. National Report of Germany' (*IBA*, January 2021) <https://www.ibanet.org/MediaHandler?id=7C3981B3 -B3C2-4912-810A-D1EA92F6531D> accessed 20 November 2023.

19 Vesna Lazic, *Insolvency Proceedings and Commercial Arbitration* (Kluwer Law International 1998) 1811–183.

20 New York Convention 1958, Article II(3).

For example, in the Italian Insolvency Code it is expressly provided that the termination in accordance with the insolvency law of a contract which includes an arbitration agreement will also lead to the termination of a pending arbitral case.[21]

The arbitral tribunals were reluctant to guide themselves on this matter in light of the national insolvency law, but they preferred to give prevalence to the operability of the arbitration agreement, using the arbitral laws at the place of arbitration to determine the validity and operability of the arbitration agreement.

Is the impact of the opening of the insolvency proceedings in arbitration a matter of subject-matter arbitrability?

Another question is to what extent the arbitration agreement is operable if the subject matter consists in claims insolvency or placed outside the power of the parties to arbitrate on them. This is a matter which does not affect the validity of the arbitration clause, but its effectiveness in relation with certain subject-matters.

In essence the matters brought in front of an arbitral tribunal must be covered by an arbitration agreement, namely the parties must have agreed to place the respective matter within the power of the arbitral tribunal to hear and decide on them. There are situations in which there are subject matters that fall outside the scope of the arbitration agreement as the parties are not entitled to dispose freely on those respective rights.

This is accepted by the international conventions such as 1927 Geneva Convention and the New York Conventions. The New York Convention, Article II(1) provides that an arbitration agreement shall be recognized if it concerns 'a subject matter capable of settlement by arbitration'.

Usually, the arbitrability is also defined by the national arbitration legislation, but no consensus may be found.

For example, under Romanian Code of Civil Procedure it is expressly provided in Article 542 of that the arbitration agreements may not be concluded in relation with the rights on which the parties may not dispose of, and in Article 1112 entitled the Arbitrability of the Dispute, it is provided that 'any claim of patrimonial nature may form the subject-matter of the arbitration if it concerns rights on which the parties may freely dispose, and the law of the state from the seat of the arbitral court does not reserve the exclusive jurisdiction of the courts of law'.

Under Swiss law, Article 177(1) of the Swiss Private International Law Act of 18 December 1987 regulates the subject-matter arbitrability providing that any claim involving a 'financial interest' may be submitted to arbitration.[22]

Under Article 2060 of the French Civil Code an arbitration agreement may not be concluded by parties 'in matters of status and capacity of the persons, in those relating to

---

21 Italian Insolvency Code, art 192 [Arbitration clause]: 'If the contract containing an arbitration clause is terminated in accordance with the provisions of this Section, the pending arbitration proceedings may not be continued.' This corresponds to the provisions of art 83-bis of the Italian Insolvency Law of 1942.

22 See also Swiss Federal Supreme Court, Decision 4A_200/2021 of 21 July 2021, based on awards in CAS 2019/A/6404 et CAS 2019/A/6405, ASA Bull 1/2022, p 230 cited in Matthias Scherer, 'Introduction to the Case Law Section' (2022) 40(1) *ASA Bulletin* 97.

divorce and judicial separation or on matters of disputes concerning public bodies and institutions and more generally in all matters in which public policy is concerned'.

Section 1030(1) [Arbitrability] of the German Code of Civil Procedure (Zivilprozessordnung – ZPO), provides that are arbitrable claims 'involving an economic interest' or if the parties are entitled to conclude a settlement on the respective claim. The following paragraphs of Section 1030 of ZPO provide subject-matters that are not arbitrable.

Usually, the parties are entitled to freely dispose by means of an arbitration agreement the rights on which they are entitled to freely reach a settlement agreement. However, as shown above the national laws do not have a unanimous approach on what matters are arbitrable, raising a lot of questions as to the law applicable to the arbitrability issue.

The arbitral tribunals tend not to go automatically with the law at the place of arbitration, but in some cases the arbitral tribunals are also inclined to a certain extent to consider the laws at the most probable location of the enforcement of an award, the law governing the contract, or the law governing the arbitration agreement as per the parties' choice.

Thus, the issue that arises in connection with insolvency is what claims may still be arbitrable after the opening of the insolvency proceedings, but the scope of the dispute/ claim brought in front of an arbitral tribunal is important in determining the arbitrability. In principle, disputes originating out of the insolvency proceedings or related to the proceedings are not arbitrable.[23] For example, an arbitral tribunal shall not have jurisdiction to decide opening of the insolvency proceedings, closing such proceedings, appointment of the insolvency practitioner.

Again, the laws are very different as there are certain laws that do not allow any claim against the insolvent company during the insolvency proceeding, while there are laws that prevent only certain type of claims (for example under French law an arbitral tribunal may not order payment of claims, but may determine their existence).[24]

Is the impact of the opening of the insolvency proceedings in arbitration a matter of legal capacity or legal standing of the insolvent party?

The issue of legal capacity (substantive capacity) and legal standing (procedural capacity) in arbitration arises from the fact that, usually, under the insolvency laws, the insolvent company's activity and estate may no longer be freely run by the company, but it is usually conducted or supervised by a court appointed insolvency practitioner, by the insolvency court, by the creditors registered in the insolvency proceedings, or even the appointed insolvency practitioner replaces the insolvent company in claims and administration of the estate.

The main question is what legal provisions apply to these two legal concepts and to what extent the diminishing or loss of the legal capacity of the insolvent company from the moment the insolvency proceedings against it are opened, impact the legal standing of the insolvent company in arbitration.

The legal capacity is usually seen from the perspective of a party's capacity to validly conclude an arbitration agreement. In accordance with national laws, usually, a party is required to have legal capacity in order to conclude an arbitration agreement. Even if no

---

23 See e.g. France: Cour de Cassation, Chambre comm, rendered on 4 February 1986.
24 Cour de Cassation, Chambre comm, rendered on 4 November 1980.

express provision to this end is found in the arbitration laws, the general contract law provisions apply. For example, under Romanian law a party to the arbitration agreement is required to have 'full capacity to exercise its rights and obligations',[25] while under French law it is provided that 'any person may conclude arbitration agreement in connection with rights that they are free to dispose of'. Thus, under French law the capacity provided by the contract law must also be considered, as no express provisions were included in the ones regulating the arbitration agreement.

The capacity of a party to arbitration is also addressed by international conventions. Article V(a) of the New York Convention provides that recognition and enforcement of an award in case the parties to the arbitration agreement were 'under the law applicable to them, under some capacity' may be refused.

While it is generally accepted by the tribunals that the law applicable to determine whether a party has legal capacity is the national law of the respective party, the legal standing in arbitration is another matter altogether that was differently considered by the Tribunals.

The number of available cases, either national or arbitral, related to this matter is reduced. The issue of the legal capacity and legal standing of an insolvent company to be a party to an arbitration was previously addressed in Switzerland. The first case is *Vivendi-Elecktrim case* whereby the Swiss Federal Supreme Court held that the capacity was governed by the Polish law and that from the perspective of that law the insolvent company lacked legal capacity and thus could not have been a party to an international arbitration.[26] This decision met criticism from the arbitration community as it was considered that the matter was not a matter related to the capacity of the insolvent company, but a matter of validity of the arbitration agreement that should have been analysed in light of the Swiss law.[27] The approach taken in *Vivendi-Elektrim* was subsequently indirectly abandoned by the Swiss Federal Supreme Court in the *Portuguese case*.[28] While upholding the principle that the legal capacity of a party is determined in accordance with the law in the country of its incorporation, the Swiss Federal Supreme Court held that the Portuguese Insolvency Law did not regulate a lack of capacity of the insolvent company.[29]

---

25 Romanian Civil Procedure Code, art 542(1).

26 Decision of the Swiss Federal Supreme Court No 4A_428/2008 of 31 March 2009, published in 1-3 Consol., Swiss Int'l Arb L Rep (2007-2009), Case no 12, pp 241–258.

27 The Decision in *Vivendi-Elektrim* rendered by the Swiss Federal Supreme Court, upholding the arbitral award rendered in the same sense, was based on the provisions of the Polish Bankruptcy and Reorganization Act in force at that time that provided in Article 142 that '[a]ny arbitration clause concluded by the bankrupt shall lose its legal effect as at the date bankruptcy is declared and any pending arbitration proceedings shall be discontinued'/

28 The Decision of the Swiss Federal Supreme Court No 138 III 714 of 16 October 2012.

29 ibid. The Court held that 'Article 87 (1) P-IL [Portuguese Insolvency Law] leaves the legal personality of a bankrupt Portuguese entity untouched and therefore also its capacity to be a party in an international arbitration seated in Switzerland. According to the Swiss lex arbitri, Art 87(1) P-IL therefore regulates one aspect of the substantive validity of the arbitration agreement, which is to be assessed according to Art 178(2) P-IL. Under Swiss law at least, bankruptcy does not affect the validity of an arbitration agreement (...) and therefore Art 87(1) P-IL may not deprive the arbitration clause of its validity.'

Article 87 (1) of the Portugues Insolvency Law in force at that time provided that '[w]ithout prejudice to provisions contained in applicable international treaties, the efficacy of the arbitral agreements relating to disputes that may potentially affect the value of the insolvency estate and to which the insolvent party shall be suspended'.

On this matter, when discussing the legal capacity of a company, there are arbitral tribunals in international arbitrations with the seat of arbitration in Switzerland, that specify that the relevant legal capacity is the legal capacity of the company to be holder of rights and obligations (for example in Romania this is 'capacitatea de folosinţă' – capacity of use; in Switzerland this is 'Rechtsfàhigkeit') and that a limitation to the capacity to exercise the respective rights in case of insolvency are not relevant for determining the legal standing as party in arbitration.[30]

In one international arbitration having the place of arbitration in Switzerland and involving a Romanian company undergoing insolvency, one arbitral tribunal held that 'a distinction must be made between, on the one hand, the capacity to be a holder of rights and obligations (Rechtsfàhigkeit) and, on the other hand, the capacity to stand as a party in Swiss proceedings, and in particular in international arbitrations seated in Switzerland (Parteifàhigkeit)'.[31] The same arbitral tribunal went further to state that:

> The Rechtsfàhigkeit is governed by the law of the place of incorporation, pursuant to Articles 154 and 155(c) PILA. By contrast, the Parteifàhigkeit in relation to Swiss proceedings is governed by Swiss law, according to which all natural persons and legal entities with the capacity to be the holder of rights and obligations are capable of being parties in Swiss proceedings. The upshot of this is that under Swiss law, if a company has legal capacity to hold rights and obligations (Rechtsfàhigkeit) under the law of the place of incorporation, it automatically has the capacity to be a party to Swiss arbitration proceedings (Parteifàhigkeit).[32]

A similar decision was reached in another arbitration case.[33] However, these awards are based on the specific provisions of Swiss law.

Under Spanish law, the insolvent company acting as claimant must be replaced in any pending arbitration by the appointed insolvency practitioner (trustee) and subsequently only the appointed insolvency practitioner may initiate claims. A failure to observe these provisions may lead to the impossibility to enforce a favourable award against the estate. The situation is more interesting in case of payment claims filed against the insolvent company, as it seems that is the amounts claimed in arbitration are challenged in the insolvency proceedings by the trustee or by the creditors, the arbitration proceedings should not continue with the insolvent company as defendant but with the trustee or creditors.[34] The situation seems to be similar in Germany[35], when the position as debtor is taken over by the appointed insolvency practitioner,[36] and failure to consider such in an arbitral case may lead to the rejection of enforcing the respective claim.[37]

---

30 For an interesting discussion on terminology, including on the types of legal capacity (the substantive capacity) and the legal standing (the procedural capacity) please see Simon Vorburger, *International Arbitration and Cross-Border Insolvency. Comparative Perspectives* (Kluwer Law International 2014), 145–147.

31 Partial Award on Jurisdiction dated 7 January 2016 rendered in an ad-hoc arbitration before a tribunal constituted in accordance with the 1976 UNCITRAL Arbitration Rules, para 84 (unpublished).

32 ibid.

33 Final Award in ICC Case no 20444 (unpublished).

34 Garcimartín and Penades (n 17) 8–10.

35 Alicja Zielińska-Eisen and Tobias Strecker, 'Annex II: Report on Main Features of Declarations in Germany', in Beata Gessel-Kalinowska vel Kalisz, *The Legal, Real and Converged Interest in Declaratory Relief* (Kluwer Law International 2019) 247–248.

36 Wagner and Kramer (n 18) 21.

37 Patrick Gerardy and Harry Nettlau, '*BayObLG – 102 Sch 142/21, Highest Regional Court of Bavaria, 102 Sch 142/21, 18 November 2021*', A contribution by the ITA Board of Reporters; Kluwer Law International.

Final remarks

When analysing the impact of the opening of the insolvency proceedings in relation to arbitration proceedings, there are a number of important factors that must be considered. For example, what law applies to the insolvency proceedings, what law applies to the arbitration agreement, what law applies to the effects of the insolvency on arbitration proceedings, what is the status of the arbitration proceedings, namely if it is pending before the tribunal when the insolvency proceedings against one of the parties is opened or the arbitration proceedings are initiated after the opening of the insolvency proceedings. Also, it may prove to be quite important if it is a domestic or international arbitration in the discussion.

As in most cases the insolvency legislation is of international public policy of the state where the insolvency it is opened, an award breaching such provisions bears the risk of being annulled at the seat of arbitration or of being prevented from recognition in the state of enforcement.

The Tribunal should have a care in order for the arbitration not to be used by the interested party as an extra option, instead of an alternative jurisdiction to the state courts.

CHAPTER 16

Construction projects in investor–State arbitration

Insights from the latest trends and statistics

Renato Nazzini[1] and Aleksander Godhe[2]

Introduction and background

Following the relaxation of international sanctions against Libya in 2003, the Austrian company Strabag decided to pursue large construction projects in the country. It got engaged in several road projects under six contracts around the cities of Misurata and Benghazi.[3]

However, Libya was affected by the anti-government Arab Spring resulting in a 2011 civil war between the government of Muammar Gaddafi and rebel forces. Strabag alleged that it suffered considerable losses in the midst of the crisis which were directly attributable to state organs including its armed forces, police, and various authorities responsible for Libyan infrastructure. It argued that, due to the hostilities, the construction project was interrupted and ongoing security concerns prevented the works from resuming. Strabag also claimed that it suffered various types of damage including loss of equipment, outstanding amounts owed under payment certificates and for additional works done, unpaid retention amounts and staff evacuation during the times of disturbance.[4]

Strabag hence brought an investment claim in the amount of €112 million pursuant to the Austria–Libya Bilateral Investment Treaty ('BIT') against the state of Libya. Libya resisted the claim by challenging the jurisdiction of the constituted arbitral tribunal and denying all liability.[5] The tribunal found in favour of Strabag and ordered compensation of US\$75 million plus 75% of the Claimant's legal costs and costs of the arbitration – one of the highest amounts awarded to any investment claim brought in relation to a construction project.[6]

The *Strabag v Libya* case demonstrates that, in some circumstances, a construction project may be protected through the operation of international investment law and applicable international investment treaties, including BITs. This right to a remedy exists outside

---

1 Professor of Law and Director of the Centre of Construction Law & Dispute Resolution, the Dickson Poon School of Law, King's College London. Independent arbitrator and partner at LMS Legal LLP, London.

2 Research Associate (Dispute Resolution) at the Centre of Construction Law & Dispute Resolution, the Dickson Poon School of Law, King's College London. Visiting Fellow at the Stockholm Centre for Commercial Law, Stockholm University.

3 *Strabag SE v Libya*, ICSID Case No ARB(AF)/15/1, Award (29 June 2020) [1–8], [56–60].

4 ibid [245].

5 ibid [2], [101].

6 ibid [979].

DOI: 10.4324/9781032663975-21

235

of the construction contract although quantum must be carefully assessed, pleaded and proven. Investment arbitration is not a 'free-for-all' against states either.

There are 2,219 BITs in force around the world at the time of writing and an additional 364 treaties with investment provisions (such as free trade agreements or multilateral investment treaties) conferring rights on foreign investors.[7] States far and wide have signed these investment treaties to promote and protect one another's foreign investments. The United Kingdom, by way of example, has BITs in force with 85 other states including Nigeria, Mexico and China. Pursuant to these treaties, if the host state breaches its obligations to protect a British foreign investment, the investor may have the right to bring a claim in arbitration directly against the host state.

There are several characteristics of international investment law that can affect the claimant's decision to pursue a claim. First, treaty protection can only be invoked if it was the host state that harmed the investment through its actions, including through legislative or regulatory measures. This means that pure contractual disputes between two companies are not eligible for investment treaty protection. Second, investment arbitration – the typical investor–State dispute settlement ('ISDS') mechanism provided for in investment treaties – allows the claimant to avoid suing the host state in its own domestic courts. Arbitral tribunals offer a neutral forum for resolving disputes. Thirdly, decisions of investment tribunals are almost always publicly available with some hearings being recorded. Finally, investment awards are easily enforceable and often even more easily so than commercial arbitral awards.

The International Centre for Settlement of Investment Disputes ('ICSID') Convention provides a procedural framework for resolving investment disputes and established ICSID – the arbitral institution that can administer these disputes and publishes its own arbitration rules. Disputes conducted pursuant to the ICSID Convention and its Arbitration Rules are most common in ISDS, accounting for 473 out of 890 concluded and publicly-available investment cases at the time of writing.[8] However, the Convention is not an investment treaty – it contains neither standards of investment protection nor consent to arbitration. Therefore, it works in symbiosis with other investment treaties such as BITs that would often reference it.[9]

Looking closer at enforcement, the ICSID Convention specifies that an arbitral award is treated as a judgment of the highest court in the jurisdiction where it is enforced.[10] In non-ICSID cases, such as those under the UNCITRAL Arbitration Rules or the ICC Rules, enforcement relies on the New York Convention on the Recognition and Enforcement of Foreign Arbitral Awards 1958. The New York Convention specifies only limited grounds on which the enforcement of an award can be refused.[11]

---

7 See UNCTAD, 'International Investment Agreements Navigator' (*Investment Policy Hub*) <https://investmentpolicy.unctad.org/international-investment-agreements> accessed 20 November 2023.

8 See UNCTAD 'Investment Dispute Settlement Navigator' (*Investment Policy Hub*, 31 December 2022) <https://investmentpolicy.unctad.org/investment-dispute-settlement/advanced-search> accessed 20 November 2023.

9 Rudolf Dolzer and others, *Principles of International Investment Law* (3rd edn, OUP 2022) 16.

10 Convention on the Settlement of Investment Disputes between States and Nationals of Other States (adopted 18 March 1965, entered into force 14 October 1966) 575 UNTS 159 (ICSID Convention) art 54(1).

11 Convention on the Recognition and Enforcement of Foreign Arbitral Awards (adopted 10 June 1958, entered into force 7 June 1959) 330 UNTS 3 (New York Convention) art V.

This article provides a practical overview of the use and utility of investment arbitration in relation to investments in the construction sector. First, it discusses the trends and statistics relating to construction investment ICSID cases. Second, it looks at the standards of investment protection alleged and breached in all publicly-available investment arbitrations concerning construction investments. Third, it considers the jurisdictional issues that may arise in such cases starting with contractors being 'investors' for the purposes of investment treaties and moving to construction projects constituting 'investments'. Finally, the article looks deeper at the standards of investment protection that appear in treaties, pointing to the appropriate legal tests and illustrating how they can apply to construction investment disputes.

Trends and statistics

Disputes related to construction sector investments are becoming increasingly significant in ISDS. This chapter analysed the biannual ICSID caseload statistics spanning ten years: from 2012 to the end of December 2022.[12] Figure 16.1 compares the proportion of newly registered ICSID disputes relating to construction projects in any given year with the overall proportion of such disputes in all ICSID cases in the particular year. ICSID statistics were relied upon not only because they represent the majority of investment arbitrations, but also because they are regularly reported.

Figure 16.1 illustrates that in 2012 construction investment disputes accounted for 7% of all ICSID cases up until that point. In the same year, construction sector disputes accounted for 8% of all new cases registered with ICSID. These two values remained the same in the next year. In 2014 and 2015 there was some fluctuation in the number of new registrations but the average in these two years remained at 8%.

However, something changed in 2016; the proportion of newly registered construction sector investment ICSID cases started climbing. By the end of 2021, ICSID reported 16.5% of all newly registered cases to relate to construction sector investments. This was the third most represented economic sector, surpassed only by the (i) oil, gas and mining, and (ii) electric power & other energy sectors. However, in 2022, the proportion of new registrations fell to 8% while the overall proportion rose to 11%.[13] There could be several reasons for this sudden drop. It could have been partially caused by the overall small number of registered ICSID cases in 2022 at 41 compared to 66 in 2021.

This being said, the number of construction sector ISDS cases is considerable and on an upward trend. In fact, the number of construction-related cases is inevitably higher than just the number of cases relating to investments specifically in the construction sector. Some cases in the oil, gas and mining or energy sectors would also concern construction projects although the investor is not a construction company. For instance, the *PSEG v Turkey* case concerned the performance of a concession agreement for the construction of a thermal power plant. Although the economic sector relevant to the case was the

---

12 See ICSID, 'The ICSID Caseload – Statistics' (*International Centre for Settlement of Investment Disputes, World Bank Group*) <https://icsid.worldbank.org/resources/publications/icsid-caseload-statistics> accessed 20 November 2023.

13 ICSID, 'The ICSID Caseload – Statistics Issue 2023-1' (*International Centre for Settlement of Investment Disputes, World Bank Group*, 2023) <https://icsid.worldbank.org/sites/default/files/Caseload%20Statistics%20Charts/The_ICSID_Caseload_Statistics.1_Edition_ENG.pdf> accessed 5 June 2023.

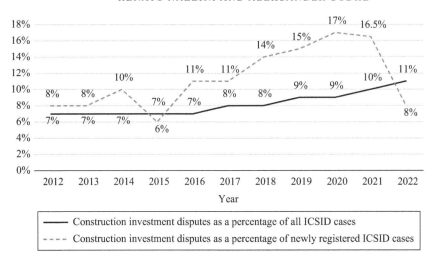

Figure 16.1 Share of ICSID cases relating to construction sector investments over time

energy sector, and the investor was a US-based energy company, the underlying dispute concerned a construction project and its financing.[14] Further, an investment may relate to a different sector despite it relating to a construction project and the investor being a construction company. The case of *Impregilo v Pakistan (I)* illustrates that well since the dispute concerned the construction of a hydroelectric power plant in Pakistan by a leading Italian construction company.[15] Nonetheless, the United Nations Conference on Trade and Development ('UNCTAD'), responsible for maintaining the databases of known ISDS disputes, classified the case as one in the energy sector.

This points to the fact that the distinction between 'construction disputes' and other cases is considered somewhat artificial in the context of ISDS. After all, regardless of the relevant economic sector, the substantive law applied by tribunals would be the same in all cases. Anecdotally, this might have contributed to poor awareness of the ISDS system among construction professionals. This paper, however, challenges this accepted wisdom and discusses the trends and key contributions of construction cases to ISDS. The issue is significant – given that ICSID has been consistently registering more cases in most years since the early 1990s,[16] the number of construction-related cases and their importance to ISDS is likely to continue growing.

Evidence for the importance of construction disputes in ISDS is also clear from broader economic data. The global construction sector is expected to grow by 42% between 2020 and 2030, amounting to an additional US$4.5 trillion worth of investment, driven by India,

---

14 *PSEG Global Inc and Konya Ilgin Elektrik Üretim ve Ticaret Limited Sirketi v Republic of Turkey*, ICSID Case No ARB/02/5, Award (19 January 2007).

15 *Impregilo SpA v Islamic Republic of Pakistan (I)*, ICSID Case No ARB/02/2, Order taking note of the discontinuance of the proceeding issued by the Secretary General dated 11 June 2002, pursuant to Arbitration Rule 44 (11 June 2002).

16 ICSID (n 12).

China and the United States. In fact, the construction sector is predicted to be the motor of economic growth out of the pandemic and recession. Construction will also increasingly shift to emerging markets,[17] which would lay a good foundation for more investment claims as such jurisdictions are riskier and tend to rely more on foreign investors rather than domestic contractors for their construction projects.[18]

Standards of investment protection and ISDS disputes relating to construction investments

The Investment Dispute Settlement Navigator published by UNCTAD provides the most complete database of ISDS cases.[19] At the time of writing, the database identifies 149 investment arbitrations relating to construction investments under ICSID and other arbitration rules.

An analysis of these cases demonstrates that the following standards of investment protection were alleged by investors in their claims against states:

- **Fair and Equitable Treatment ('FET'): 61 cases.**
- **Indirect expropriation: 53 cases.**
- Full Protection and Security ('FPS'): 31 cases.
- Umbrella clauses: 23 cases.
- Arbitrary or discriminatory measures: 22 cases.
- Most Favoured Nation ('MFN'): 16 cases.
- National treatment: 14 cases.
- Other: 8 cases.
- Direct expropriation: 3 cases.
- War/insurrection loss: 3 cases.
- Performance requirements: 1 case.
- Customary international law: 0 cases.
- Transfer of funds: 1 cases.

Out of the 149 cases, 44 are still pending. In 38 cases the tribunal found in favour of the state and in 25 in favour of the investor (in two further cases the tribunal found that the state was liable but awarded no damages). A further 19 disputes were settled and 16 were discontinued. Data relating to the outcome of the case was unavailable for five cases. Therefore, excluding pending cases, a claim relating to an investment in the construction sector appears to have a 44% chance of either resulting in settlement or an award in investors' favour although not necessarily for the full amount claimed.

Looking at the disputes in which the claim succeeded, the tribunal found breaches of the following standards of investment protection:

---

17 Graham Robinson and others, 'Future of Construction: A Global Forecast for Construction to 2030' (*Marsh & Guy Carpenter and Oxford Economics*, September 2021) <https://resources.oxfordeconomics.com/hubfs/Africa/Future-of-Construction-Full-Report.pdf> accessed 20 July 2023.

18 Robert Ginsburg, 'Country Risk Analysis and Investor–State Dispute Settlement: A New Approach' (2020) *Georgetown Journal of International Law* 425.

19 See UNCTAD, 'Investment Dispute Settlement Navigator' (n 8).

- **FET: 15 cases.**
- **Indirect expropriation: 8 cases.**
- Umbrella clauses: 3 cases.
- Arbitrary or discriminatory measures: 2 cases.
- FPS: 2 cases.
- Direct expropriation: 1 case.
- MFN: 1 case.
- War/insurrection loss: 1 case.
- National treatment: 0 cases.
- Performance requirements: 0 cases.
- Customary international law: 0 cases.
- Transfer of funds: 0 cases.
- Other: 0 cases.

The popularity of FET and indirect expropriation appears in line with overall ISDS trends. Across all ISDS cases in which the investor succeeded or liability was found but no damages were awarded, 65% related to FET and 32% related to indirect expropriation.[20] The statistics are similar for the construction sector investment ISDS cases at 55% and 30% respectively. Turning to the success rate of allegations, a FET allegation succeeded in 25% of cases while indirect expropriation in 15% of cases. Naturally, investors would bring several allegations to support their claim and maximise their chances of success.

Jurisdiction

Contractors as 'investors'

Although ISDS cases concerning construction investments are increasing in number, international investment law contains principles that make the process of suing states often difficult to navigate. This may contribute to the apparently low success rate of claims.

To begin with, in order to make a claim against a state, a construction company must clear a few essential jurisdictional hurdles.

First, a frequent jurisdictional precondition under BITs is that the contractor bringing the claim must be an 'investor' as defined by the investment treaty. The Austria–Libya BIT of 2002 relevant in the *Strabag v Libya* arbitration, required that an investor be 'making or having made' an investment. This provision came under scrutiny by the tribunal since Strabag indirectly held 60% shares in a joint venture that set up a Libyan company to carry out the construction. However, these shares were held by the German wholly-owned subsidiary of the investor. Such a vehicle was put in place to comply with Libyan law requiring companies carrying out construction projects to engage a local partner. Therefore, the remaining 40% of shares in the joint venture were held by the Libyan Investment and Development Company ('LIDC'). The LIDC was a company owned by the government-controlled Libyan Social Development Fund.

---

20 UNCTAD, 'Special Update on Investor–State Dispute Settlement: Facts and Figures' (*UNCTAD*, 2017) <https://unctad.org/system/files/official-document/diaepcb2017d7_en.pdf> accessed 21 July 2023.

On the basis of the above corporate structure, Respondent argued that Strabag fell short of the jurisdictional requirements of the BIT and did not qualify as an 'investor' as it made the investment indirectly through 'two layers of wholly owned subsidiary companies'. It argued that the treaty required Strabag to have made the investment itself without utilising an intermediate vehicle. However, the tribunal quickly dismissed the argument by noting that in a subsequent provision, the BIT expressly permits the investments to be controlled indirectly.[21]

In a different claim brought by a British construction company Garanti Koza, against Turkmenistan, the UK-Turkmenistan BIT of 1995 contained no definition of an investor at all, merely requiring the investor to be a national of the UK or Turkmenistan or a company incorporated or constituted in either country.[22] Therefore, the tribunal had no issue finding that the claimant qualified as an investor under the BIT, despite allegedly being a mere UK 'facade' of a Turkish parent company.[23]

The two cases hence point to the importance of the language of the treaty for clearing jurisdictional hurdles associated with bringing an investment claim. Although the treaties in question were worded quite broadly, this is not always the case. Other, particularly more modern, BITs contain far more restrictive definitions. For instance, the Netherlands Model Investment Agreement of 2019 contains the following wording:

> For the purposes of this Agreement:
> (...)
> (b) 'investor' means with regard to either Contracting Party:
>> (i) any natural person having the nationality of that Contracting Party under its applicable law;
>> (ii) any legal person constituted under the law of that Contracting Party and **having substantial business activities in the territory of that Contracting Party**; or
>> (iii) any legal person that is constituted under the law of that Contracting Party and is **directly or indirectly owned or controlled by a natural person as defined in (i) or by a legal person as defined in (ii)**.
>
> A natural person who has the nationality of the Kingdom of the Netherlands and the other Contracting Party is deemed to be exclusively a natural person of the Contracting Party of his or her **dominant and effective nationality**. (emphasis added)

The language of the Netherlands Model Investment Treaty points to another difficulty – the need for investors to have the nationality of a contracting state. Given that nationality is determined by domestic law and not international law, investors must remain alert to the nationality requirements of the state of origin if they wish to benefit from investment protection treaties that the state has entered into. In *Soufraki v UAE,* the investor – holder of a concession agreement to develop a UAE port – attempted to rely on the Italy–UAE BIT of 1995 as the basis for his $580 million claim for the cancellation of the concession agreement. However, unbeknown to him, he lost his Italian nationality upon the acquisition of Canadian nationality. He was only made aware of the change as a result of expert

---

21 *Strabag* (n 3) [113-20].

22 Agreement Between the Government of the United Kingdom of Great Britain and Northern Ireland and the Government of Turkmenistan for the Promotion and Protection of Investments (adopted 9 February 1995, entered into force 9 February 1995) (UK–Turkmenistan BIT 1995) art 1.

23 *Garanti Koza LLP v Turkmenistan*, ICSID Case No ARB/11/20, Award (19 December 2016) [221–2] and [225].

evidence submitted in the arbitration. Therefore, the tribunal quickly dismissed the claim on jurisdictional grounds.[24]

The *Soufraki* case shows that domestic laws may complicate issues of jurisdictions further in investment cases, justifying the need for local legal advice. Such matters may become further complicated in cases of complex, multinational corporate entities.

The discrepancies in definitions of an 'investor' prove that the wording of the investment treaty can make or break an ISDS claim. Construction companies are likely to satisfy the test for 'investor' but care should be exercised when determining whether they are an investor of the state that is a party to the relevant BIT. Mere incorporation in that state may not be sufficient. On the other hand, a construction company incorporated in country A, which is not a party to the relevant BIT, may be an investor of country B, which is a party to the relevant BIT, depending on its shareholding and control structure.[25]

Construction projects as 'investments'

The second jurisdictional precondition is that the investor must have made an 'investment' covered by the treaty. For example, the UK–Turkmenistan BIT, which was applied in the construction case *Garanti Koza v Turkmenistan*, contains the following definition in Article 1:

> For the purposes of this Agreement:
> (a) 'investment' means every kind of asset and in particular, though not exclusively, includes:
> > (i) movable and immovable property and any other property rights such as mortgages, liens or pledges;
> > (ii) shares in and stock debentures of a company and any other form of participation in a company;
> > (iii) claims to money or to any performance under contract having a financial value;
> > (iv) intellectual property rights, goodwill, technical processes and know-how;
> > (v) business concessions conferred by law or under contract, including concessions to search for, cultivate, extract or exploit natural resources.
> A change in the form in which assets are invested does not affect their character as investments and the term 'investment' includes all investments, whether made before or after the date of entry into force of this Agreement;

The *Garanti Koza* tribunal found that the investment did fall within the above definition under the heading (i) as it involved the transfer of movable property – equipment and materials – used for the construction of bridges.[26] Several subsequent tribunals also held that the construction of a power plant,[27] a hotel[28] or the dredging of a canal[29] constitute 'investments' under the respective investment treaties. Therefore, as a general rule, claim-

---

24 *Hussein Nauman Soufraki v United Arab Emirates*, ICSID Case No ARB/02/7, Award (7 July 2004) [51–2], [86].

25 E.g. *Standard Chartered Bank v The United Republic of Tanzania*, ICSID Case No ARB/10/12, Award (2 November 2012) [200], [257].

26 *Garanti Koza* (n 23) [234].

27 *Blusun SA, Jean-Pierre Lecorcier and Michael Stein v Italian Republic*, ICSID Case No ARB/14/3, Award (27 December 2016) [271].

28 *Sistem Mühendislik Insaat Sanayi ve Ticaret AS v Kyrgyz Republic*, ICSID Case No ARB(AF)/06/1, Decision on Jurisdiction (13 September 2007) [96].

29 *Jan de Nul NV and Dredging International NV v Arab Republic of Egypt*, ICSID Case No ARB/04/13, Decision on Jurisdiction (16 June 2006) [104], [106].

ants should relatively easily meet the requirement of an 'investment' given that construction projects tend to involve the moving of physical assets.

However, ISDS cases concerning construction investments face a particular challenge in this area if the investment treaty contains a legality clause, i.e., provides that the investment must have been made 'in accordance with host state law'. For instance, Article 23(1) of the Austria–Libya BIT, applied in *Strabag v Libya*, provides:

> This Agreement shall apply to investments made in the territory of either Contracting Party in accordance with its legislation by investors of the other Contracting Party prior as well as after the entry into force of this Agreement.

In order to make the investment 'in accordance with [Libyan] legislation' Strabag was prompted to establish a joint venture with the LIDC – a move that made them compliant with the legality clause of the BIT, but one that Libya unsuccessfully attempted to use against them in the arbitral proceedings.[30] Such requirements imposed at domestic law, frequently in relation to the construction of infrastructure, may pose a particular challenge to construction-related claims.

If an investment arbitration is brought under the ICSID Convention, the claimant must also demonstrate that the dispute arises 'in direct relation to an investment, pursuant to Article 25 of the ICSID Convention'.[31] This is separate from and independent of the claimant having an 'investment' as defined by the underlying investment treaty. Therefore, if a claim is brought under the ICSID Arbitration Rules, the investment must be covered by both the ICSID Convention and the BIT. There is a significant overlap between the two and most investments would satisfy both definitions. However, the Convention does not provide a definition of an investment. Therefore, the definition evolved through the decisions of tribunals. Although ISDS has no formal system of precedent, decisions of tribunals are considered persuasive authority,[32] so the views of tribunals in this respect have weighed on subsequent cases.

The Decision on Jurisdiction in *Salini v Morocco*[33] is the leading authority on the point. The tribunal stated that investments under the ICSID Convention should meet the following criteria that encompass:

1. A contribution.
2. A certain duration of the operation.
3. Participation in the risks of the transaction.
4. Contribution to the economic development of the host state.[34]

The *Salini* case related to the construction of a highway in Morocco by an Italian investor. In applying the above test, the tribunal found that the construction project did meet the definition of an investment under the ICSID Convention.[35]

---

30 *Strabag* (n 3) [103–11].

31 *Garanti Koza* (n 23) [235].

32 E.g. *Saipem SpA v The People's Republic of Bangladesh*, ICSID Case No ARB/05/07, Decision on Jurisdiction and Recommendation on Provisional Measures (21 March 2007) [67].

33 *Salini Costruttori SpA and Italstrade SpA v Kingdom of Morocco*, ICSID Case No ARB/00/4, Decision on Jurisdiction (31 July 2001).

34 ibid [52].

35 ibid [58].

There is some debate about whether the 'Salini test' is exhaustive or merely indicative.[36] Some tribunals suggested that the test is not sufficient,[37] while, on the other hand, it may be argued that it requires too much, particularly under its fourth limb. Nonetheless, *Salini* definitely carries persuasive authority and should be considered by construction practitioners. The tribunal in *Garanti Koza* expressly mentioned the test in the award despite neither party pleading it.[38] The tribunal in *Bayindir v Pakistan* expressly stated that 'The construction of a highway is more than construction in the traditional sense' as it involves the spending of significant resources over a significant period of time. Therefore, it clearly qualifies as an investment under the ICSID Convention.[39] By extension, presumably, most investments that involve the construction of a structure would, for the same reason, constitute an investment under the Convention.

This was confirmed by the tribunal in *Strabag v Libya* that found no difficulty in arguing that the construction of roads would satisfy the *Salini* test. It stated:

> The evidence shows that Claimant committed substantial amounts of material and human capital to its investment over a period of several years, acquiring property in Libya, building large facilities, and importing large quantities of heavy equipment, including material such as rock crushers that only made economic sense in the context of a long-term presence in Libya.[40]

Therefore, it appears that it would be difficult for a construction project not to constitute an investment for the purposes of the test.

Standards of investment protection

The six most common standards of investment protection appearing in investment agreements are:

- MFN.
- National treatment.
- FET.
- Compensation for expropriation (direct and indirect).
- Umbrella clause.
- Free transfer of funds.[41]

Out of the above standards, FET and compensation for expropriation are most frequently successful in cases concerning an investment in the construction sector.

There are also a few other, less common standards: arbitrary or discriminatory measures, FPS, war/insurrection loss, performance requirements and customary international law. Investment treaties may also contain bespoke standards of investment protection. In *Strabag v Libya,* by way of an example, the investor alleged breaches of several of the

---

36 E.g. *Philip Morris Brands Sàrl, Abal Hermanos SA v Oriental Republic of Uruguay*, ICSID Case No ARB/10/7, Decision on Jurisdiction (2 July 2013) [204].

37 *Phoenix Action, Ltd. v The Czech Republic*, ICSID Case No ARB/06/5, Award (15 April 2009) [100–14].

38 *Garanti Koza* (n 23) [235-42].

39 *Bayindir Insaat Turizm Ticaret Ve Sanayi AS v Islamic Republic of Pakistan*, ICSID Case No ARB/03/29, Decision on Jurisdiction (14 November 2005) [128].

40 *Strabag SE v Libya*, ICSID Case No ARB(AF)/15/1, Award (29 June 2020) [110].

41 Jonathan Bonnitcha and others, *The Political Economy of the Investment Treaty Regime* (OUP 2017) 93.

above: (i) war/insurrection loss, (ii) FPS, (iii) umbrella clause, (iv) FET, (v) indirect expropriation, and (vi) arbitrary, unreasonable, and/or discriminatory measure.[42]

Most-favoured nation treatment

The purpose of MFN clauses is to avoid discrimination between different foreign investors. These clauses oblige states to treat one another's investors no less favourably than they treat the investors of third states. In practice, this means that, through this clause, an investor can import standards of investment protection and other rights from treaties that the host states signed with third states.[43] In *ATA Construction v Jordan*, a case concerning the construction of a waterway dike, a Turkish investor successfully relied on the FET standard and the 'obligation to afford the investor treatment no less favourable than that required by international law' in other treaties, through the MFN provision in the applicable treaty. The claimant was subsequently awarded non-pecuniary relief.[44]

The MFN clause cannot be, however, used to broaden the definition of an 'investment' or 'investor' under the treaty so as to broaden the scope of the tribunal's jurisdiction.[45] Investment tribunals are split on whether the MFN clause can be used to import entire dispute resolution clauses between different instruments – a dilemma acknowledged in the *Garanti Koza* award.[46] UK BITs avoid this problem by specifying clearly the provisions to which MFN applies.[47]

National treatment

Along MFNs, national treatment is the second non-discrimination standard of investment protection. It states that foreign investors shall be treated no less favourably than local, domestic investors. National treatment intends to create a level playing field between foreign investors and their local competitors.[48] It is a standard of investment protection that, so far, has not been successfully argued in an ISDS case concerning a construction investment, despite being alleged in 14 disputes.

The tribunal in the leading case *Methanex v United States* applied a three-step analysis to substantiate an allegation of breach of national treatment:

1. Whether the domestic investor is in 'like circumstances' to the foreign investor.
2. If so, whether the domestic investor received better treatment than the foreign investor.

---

42 *Strabag* (n 3) [211].

43 E.g. *National Grid plc v The Argentine Republic*, UNCITRAL, Decision on Jurisdiction (20 June 2006) [92].

44 *ATA Construction, Industrial and Trading Company v The Hashemite Kingdom of Jordan*, ICSID Case No ARB/08/2 (18 May 2010) [73], [125].

45 E.g. *Krederi Ltd. v Ukraine*, ICSID Case No ARB/14/17, Award (2 July 2018) [295]; *Société Générale In respect of DR Energy Holdings Limited and Empresa Distribuidora de Electricidad del Este, SA v The Dominican Republic*, UNCITRAL, LCIA Case No UN 7927, Award on Preliminary Objections to Jurisdiction (19 September 2008) [40–1]; *ST-AD GmbH v Republic of Bulgaria*, UNCITRAL, PCA Case No 2011-06, Award on Jurisdiction (18 July 2013) [397].

46 *Garanti Koza* (n 23), Decision on the Objection to Jurisdiction for Lack of Consent (3 July 2013) [40–1].

47 United Kingdom Model Investment Promotion and Protection Agreement (IPPA 2008) art 3(3).

48 Dolzer (n 9) 253–4.

3. If the treatment is less favourable, whether the discrimination was justified, shifting the burden of proof onto the respondent state.[49]

SD Myers v Canada, the tribunal highlighted that the analysis of 'like circumstances' analysis places high emphasis on the economic or business sector.[50] Other cases also emphasised the relevance of similar regulatory regimes.[51] In *ADF v USA*, a case concerning the construction of a highway, the claimant alleged that the USA introduced subsidies that favoured domestic steel manufacturers. However, the tribunal held that the allegation was not substantiated since the measure did not appear to prejudice foreign steel manufacturers,[52] hence falling short of the second step in the *Methanex* test.

Fair and equitable treatment

FET is one of the most common standards of investment protection in investment treaties. Investors also allege its breach most frequently. In *Saluka v Czech Republic*, the tribunal said that FET requires the host state not to act in a manner that is manifestly inconsistent, non-transparent, unreasonable or discriminatory.[53] The *Genin v Estonia* tribunal stated that FET breaches 'would include acts showing a wilful neglect of duty, an insufficiency of action falling far below international standards, or even subjective bad faith.'[54]

The tribunal in *Glencore v Colombia* added the following factors relevant to a FET breach:

- Whether the host state engaged in harassment, coercion, abuse of power, or other bad-faith conduct against the investor.
- Whether the state made specific representations to the investor before the investment was made and then acted contrary to such representations.
- Whether the state respected the principles of due process, consistency, and transparency when adopting the measures at issue.
- Whether the state failed to offer a stable and predictable legal framework, in breach of the investor's legitimate expectations.[55]

FET was one of the two breaches found by the tribunal in *Garanti Koza*. The tribunal held that Turkmenistan's insistence on the Smeta payment system breached this standard of investment protection as it was not a contractual requirement.[56] In another construction case, *Alpha Projektholding v Ukraine*, the claimant sought to use the FET standard

---

49 *Methanex Corporation v United States of America*, UNCITRAL, Final Award (3 August 2005), Part IV, Chapter B [13].

50 *SD Myers, Inc v Government of Canada*, UNCITRAL, Partial Award (13 November 2000).

51 *Apotex Holdings Inc and Apotex Inc v United States of America*, ICSID Case No ARB(AF)/12/1, Award (25 August 2014).

52 *ADF Group Inc v United States of America*, ICSID Case No ARB(AF)/00/1 (9 January 2003) [61], [158–9].

53 *Saluka Investments BV v The Czech Republic*, UNCITRAL, Partial Award (17 March 2006) [309].

54 *Alex Genin, Eastern Credit Limited, Inc and AS Baltoil v The Republic of Estonia*, ICSID Case No ARB/99/2, Award (25 June 2001) [367].

55 *Glencore International AG and CI Prodeco SA v Republic of Colombia*, ICSID Case No ARB/16/6, Award (27 August 2019) [1310].

56 *Garanti Koza* (n 23) [400].

to challenge the Ukrainian privatisation of hotels that they had helped construct. The tribunal agreed, holding that the measure interfered with the claimant's contract with the hotel on future joint activities.[57]

Compensation for expropriation

Expropriation refers to the taking away or destruction of rights acquired by the investor. A typical asset capable of being expropriated is a contractual right. Expropriation can be direct or indirect. Direct expropriation refers to the transfer of an investor's legal title to their right or asset to a third party. In *Burlington v Ecuador*, the tribunal found that (i) the imposition of a 99% windfall levy on foreign oil revenues, (ii) seizure and auction of investor's share of oil production, (iii) physical takeover of investor's facilities, and (iv) termination of contracts amounted to direct expropriation.[58]

Indirect expropriation covers measures that, although on their face do not transfer the legal title to the investor's rights away from the investor, have a similar effect in practice. Today, direct expropriations are rare. States would think twice before taking such an unambiguous measure as to directly deprive the investor of their legal title with no compensation.[59] Indirect expropriations are, therefore, far more common. In *Middle East Cement v Egypt*, the tribunal found that the withdrawal of the investor's licence to import cement into Egypt amounted to indirect expropriation. The investor's entire business was centred around this activity, so the state measure effectively prevented the investor from operating.[60]

Indirect expropriation may also take forms that appear legitimate. Taxation provides one such example. In *Manolium-Processing v Belarus*, the investor was engaged to develop land for the construction of a luxury hotel. The tribunal held that the imposition of 'confiscatory and discriminatory' taxation on the investor, resulting in the subsequent transfer of assets to the state municipality by presidential order, amounted to indirect expropriation.[61]

The case of *Metalclad v Mexico* also provides useful guidance. In this case, Mexico revoked the investor's permit to develop and operate a hazardous waste landfill and designated the land in question as a national area for the protection of cacti. The tribunal found a violation of the standard against expropriation and said:

> [E]xpropriation under NAFTA includes not only open, deliberate and acknowledged takings of property, such as outright seizure or formal or obligatory transfer of title in favour of the host State, but also covert or incidental interference with the use of property which has the effect of depriving the owner, in whole or in significant part, of the use or reasonably-to-be-expected economic benefit of property even if not neces- sarily to the obvious benefit of the host State.[62]

---

57 *Alpha Projektholding GmbH v Ukraine*, ICSID Case No ARB/07/16, Award (8 November 2010) [415], [422].

58 *Burlington Resources Inc v Republic of Ecuador*, ICSID Case No ARB/08/5, Decision on Liability (14 December 2012) [337] and [506].

59 Dolzer (n 9) 153.

60 *Middle East Cement Shipping and Handling Co SA v Arab Republic of Egypt*, ICSID Case No ARB/99/6, Award (12 April 2002) [107].

61 *OOO Manolium-Processing v The Republic of Belarus*, PCA Case No 2018-06, Award (22 June 2021) [464].

62 *Metalclad Corporation v The United Mexican States*, ICSID Case No ARB(AF)/97/1, Award (30 August 2000) [103].

Other tribunals have also suggested that expropriation might be evidenced through a combination of several state measures,[63] the depravation of investors' rights should last for a substantial period of time but need not be permanent,[64] and expropriation should be assessed in the light of the effect of the state measures and not their purpose or intention.[65]

However, expropriation is not by itself unlawful. States may expropriate investors but must compensate them for doing so. Therefore, an investor can only successfully allege expropriation if they were not compensated or the compensation was inadequate.[66]

Umbrella clauses

The purpose of umbrella clauses is to escalate a breach of contract, and breaches of other commitments that the state made to the investor, to a breach of the investment treaty. As the tribunal in *Noble Ventures v Romania* put it:

> [T]wo States may include in a bilateral investment treaty a provision to the effect that, in the interest of achieving the objects and goals of the treaty, the host State may incur international responsibility by reason of a breach of its contractual obligations towards the private investor of the other Party, the breach of contract being thus 'internationalized', i.e. assimilated to a breach of the treaty. In such a case, an international tribunal will be bound to seek to give useful effect to the provision that the parties have adopted.[67]

By way of example, the UK Model Bilateral Investment Treaty contains the following umbrella clause in Article 2(2):

> Each Contracting Party shall observe any obligation it may have entered into with regard to investments of nationals or companies of the other Contracting Party.

Umbrella clauses may also be worded more narrowly. They can, for instance, only cover breaches of obligations caused by state conduct or contracts that the investor entered into directly with the state.[68] The umbrella clause was a standard of investment protection breached in *Garanti Koza* case concerning a construction project. The tribunal found that Turkmenistan breached the contract for the construction of the highway bridges by requiring invoices to be submitted in a specific, post-Soviet Smeta system. That did not form a part of the investor's obligations under a contract and the umbrella clause escalated that breach into a breach of the BIT.[69]

Nonetheless, some tribunals prefer a more guarded interpretation of umbrella clauses. In *Sempra v Argentina*, the tribunal held that ordinary commercial breaches of a contract would not violate the umbrella clause. Instead, the state should have breached the contract

---

63 *Compañiá de Aguas del Aconquija S.A. and Vivendi Universal SA v Argentine Republic*, ICSID Case No ARB/97/3, Award (20 August 2007) [7.5.11] to [7.5.20].

64 *Biwater Gauff (Tanzania) Ltd v United Republic of Tanzania*, ICSID Case No ARB/05/22, Award (24 July 2008) [463].

65 *Suez, Sociedad General de Aguas de Barcelona, SA and Vivendi Universal, SA v Argentine Republic*, ICSID Case No ARB/03/1, Decision on Liability (30 July 2010) [122].

66 *Rumeli Telekom AS and Telsim Mobil Telekomunikasyon Hizmetleri AS v Republic of Kazakhstan*, ICSID Case No ARB/05/16, Award (29 July 2008) [706].

67 *Noble Ventures, Inc v Romania*, ICSID Case No ARB/01/11, Award (12 October 2005) [54].

68 *SGS Société Générale de Surveillance SA v Islamic Republic of Pakistan*, ICSID Case No. ARB/01/13, Decision of the Tribunal on Objections to Jurisdiction (6 August 2003) [167].

69 *Garanti Koza* (n 23) [400].

through some exercise of a sovereign state function.[70] Such restrictions were criticised by other tribunals as unsupported by the wording of the investment treaties.[71]

Another important issue surrounding umbrella clauses was addressed in *Strabag v Libya*. As was mentioned, the investor entered into construction contracts with several Libyan state entities. The umbrella clause in the applicable Article 8 of the Austria-Libya BIT provided that '[e]ach Contracting Party shall observe any obligation it may have entered into with regard to specific investments by investors of the other Contracting Party'. The issue was whether Libya (as a state) entered into the construction contracts through the state-owned entities. The tribunal noted that the contracts concerned significant public infrastructure projects and the state-owned enterprises performed public functions. Therefore, Libya's arguments of privity of contract failed.[72] Nonetheless, other tribunals have emphasized the importance of establishing the connection between the state and the signatories to the contract if the umbrella clause is to be relied upon.[73]

Free transfer of funds

Foreign investors, when making an investment abroad, most often plan to transfer some of the profit back to their home jurisdiction. As one tribunal said, the right to transfer funds freely is 'fundamental to the freedom to make a foreign investment and an essential element of the promotional role of BITs'.[74] Therefore, any restrictions on transfers to and from the host state are a significant concern to investors. Equally, however, the host state must be able to monitor cashflows for the proposes of national policies.[75] This is why most investment treaties contain clauses regulating restrictions on the free transfer of funds.

The transfer clause hence typically permits the investor to make all or certain types of transfers. Most clauses allow the investor to make transfers specifically in relation to the investment.[76] For instance, in *von Pezold v Zimbabwe*, the tribunal held that Zimbabwe's refusal to release the investor's foreign currency to repay loans amounted to a breach of the free transfer of funds clause under the BIT.[77] However, cases concerning the free transfer of funds are rare. There is, for instance, no construction ISDS case where the investor alleged a breach of this standard.

Nonetheless, several tribunals have grappled with the issue of whether a particular transfer was protected by the applicable treaty. In *Rusoro v Venezuela*, the tribunal found that gold was a commodity and not a currency and hence fell outside of the protection

---

70 *Sempra Energy International v The Argentine Republic*, ICSID Case No ARB/02/16, Award (28 September 2007) [305–314].

71 *Burlington Resources Inc v Republic of Ecuador*, ICSID Case No ARB/08/5, Decision on Jurisdiction (2 June 2010) [190].

72 *Strabag* (n 3) [173–188].

73 *Impregilo SpA. v Islamic Republic of Pakistan*, ICSID Case No ARB/03/3, Decision on Jurisdiction (22 April 2005) [223].

74 *Continental Casualty Company v The Argentine Republic*, ICSID Case No ARB/03/9, Award (5 September 2008) [239].

75 Dolzer (n 9) 290.

76 Rudolf Dolzer and Margarete Stevens, *Bilateral Investment Treaties* (Martinus Nijhof 1995) 87.

77 *Bernhard von Pezold and Others v Republic of Zimbabwe*, ICSID Case No ARB/10/15, Award (28 July 2015) [608].

of the transfer of funds clause.[78] In *Valores Mundiales v Venezuela* accrued investment income was held to be protected.[79] Interestingly, the tribunal in *Karkey v Pakistan* adopted a broad definition of assets under the treaty and decided that the detention of vessels breached the provision for the free transfer of funds.[80]

Other standards of investment protection

Apart from the six above, there are several, less common standards of investment protection. Full protection and security (FPS) mainly relates to the physical and legal security of the investment necessary to protect against harm. This typically encompasses (i) acts of insurgents or rioting groups, (ii) acts of government forces such as police or the military and (iii) governmental regulatory acts that disrupt the investment.[81] It places an obligation on the state to protect the investment from, for instance, civil unrest, and provide the necessary legal framework for such protection.[82] Although this standard was alleged in many construction cases, it succeeded in just one – *Cengiz v Libya*. The claimant alleged that the looting of its construction equipment by armed groups during the Libyan revolution was attributable to the state and the state failed to put in place measures for the protection of the investment. Therefore, the state allegedly breached both the negative and positive obligation of FET to, respectively, refrain from harming the investment and take precautionary steps to prevent harm. The tribunal agreed with the claimant on both accounts.[83]

Other treaties protect against arbitrary or discriminatory treatment. This means that the investor should be protected from arbitrariness and benefit from the rule of law. In practice, the standard requires the investor to be afforded 'a rational process' before the state makes a decision affecting it.[84] For instance, the absence of reasons for taking measures would amount to arbitrary treatment. If the investor, as a result of this arbitrary state conduct, is treated differently to another person in similar circumstances, that would amount to discriminatory treatment.[85]

Some treaties, on the other hand, refer to 'unreasonable' treatment instead of 'arbitrary'. However, the tribunal in *National Grid v Argentina* held that the two terms are substantially the same and refer to something being done capriciously and without reason.[86] In terms of 'discrimination' the concept here is different from discrimination under the national treatment and MFN provisions which are restricted to discrimination on the basis of nationality.[87] For instance, in *von Pezold v Zimbabwe*, the state expropriated the inves-

---

78 *Rusoro Mining Ltd. v Bolivarian Republic of Venezuela*, ICSID Case No ARB(AF)/12/5, Award (22 August 2016) [574].

79 *Valores Mundiales, SL and Consorcio Andino SL v Bolivarian Republic of Venezuela*, ICSID Case No ARB/13/11, Award (25 July 2017) [635].

80 *Karkey Karadeniz Elektrik Uretim AS v Islamic Republic of Pakistan*, ICSID Case No ARB/13/1, Award (22 August 2017) [654–5].

81 Dolzer (n 9) 231.

82 *Frontier Petroleum Services Ltd v The Czech Republic*, UNCITRAL, Final Award (12 November 2010) [296].

83 *Cengiz İnşaat Sanayi ve Ticaret AS v Libya*, ICC Case No 21537/ZF/AYZ, Award (7 November 2018) [435], [451–2].

84 *Saluka Investments BV v The Czech Republic*, UNCITRAL, Partial Award (17 March 2006) [460].

85 *Plama Consortium Ltd v Republic of Bulgaria*, ICSID Case No ARB/03/24, Award (27 August 2008) [184].

86 *National Grid plc v The Argentine Republic*, UNCITRAL, Award (3 November 2008) [197].

87 *Ulysseas, Inc v The Republic of Ecuador*, UNCITRAL, Final Award (12 June 2012) [293].

tors on the basis of their skin colour and it was found to amount to discrimination under this standard of investment protection.[88]

Some obligations of states stem not from the investment treaty, but from international law directly. If states establish a certain repeated practice followed by a belief that this practice is legally binding in international law (the 'opinio juris'), it may amount to a principle of customary international law.[89] Many of the aforementioned standards of investment protection, such as FET, are codified principles of customary international law. However, a treaty may for some reason not contain a FET provision. If so, the argument could be made that a state is bound by it regardless as it stems not from the treaty but from custom.[90]

Further, a BIT may contain an investment protection standard applicable in specific circumstances. Some treaties contain an express reference to loss arising from war or insurrection.[91] These are often an extension of the principle of non-discrimination, but also add that the state should afford compensation or restitution to the investor if, as a result of conduct relating to war, insurrection or similar events, the investor suffers losses.[92] In fact, the construction case of *Strabag v Libya* was one of the few cases where the state was found to breach this standard. As was discussed above in greater detail, the investor's assets were stolen during the Libyan revolution. The investor successfully claimed for losses sustained due to insurrection or war, as well as under an umbrella clause. The tribunal awarded the investor €74.9 million in the award.[93]

Finally, BITs may sometimes contain clauses relating to state performance requirements. States can set conditions under which they admit investments. These obligations are imposed on the investors through domestic law and may require them to meet prescribed objectives relating to the establishment or operation of the investments. For instance, the investor might be obliged to hire local employees, only obtain supplies from domestic producers or form a joint venture with a state-owned company.[94] In order to avoid states overly burdening the investors with such rules, some BITs contain clauses that prohibit or limit the ability of states to insist on performance requirements.[95]

---

88 *Bernhard von Pezold and Others v Republic of Zimbabwe*, ICSID Case No ARB/10/15, Award (28 July 2015) [501].

89 Jean d'Aspremont, 'International Customary Investment Law: Story of a Paradox' in Tarcisio Gazzini, Eric De Brabandere (eds) *International Investment Law: the Sources of Rights and Obligations* (Martinus Nijhoff, 2012) 15–23.

90 E.g., *Koch Minerals Sàrl and Koch Nitrogen International Sàrl v Bolivarian Republic of Venezuela*, ICSID Case No ARB/11/19, Award (30 October 2017) [8.44].

91 E.g., Agreement between the Republic of Austria and the Great Socialist People's Libyan Arab Jmahiriya for the Promotion and Protection of Investments (signed 18 June 2002, entered into force 1 January 2004) ('Austria–Libya BIT 2002'), art 15.

92 Christoph Schreuer, 'The protection of investments in armed conflict' in Freya Baetens, *Investment Law within International Law* (CUP 2013) 13.

93 ibid [979–80].

94 Suzy H Nikièma, 'Performance Requirements in Investment Treaties' (*IISD*, December 2014) <https://www.iisd.org/system/files/publications/best-practices-performance-requirements-investment-treaties-en.pdf> accessed 21 July 2023.

95 E.g., Agreement between the State of Kuwait and the Republic of India for the Encourgaement and Reciprocal Protection of Investment (adopted 16 May 2001, entered into force 28 June 2003) (India–Kuwait BIT 2001) art 4.4: 'Once established, investment shall not be subjected in the host Contracting State to additional performance requirements which may hinder or restrict their expansion or maintenance or adversely affect or be considered as detrimental to their viability, unless such requirements are deemed vital for reasons of public order, public health or environmental concerns and are enforced by law of general application.'

Conclusion

Trends and statistics support greater awareness of ISDS in relation to the protection of construction investments. At ICSID, the number of disputes brought by investors operating in the construction sector has been growing significantly and already accounts for a considerable share of all disputes, ranking as the third most-represented economic sector. Construction companies have so far been successful, in whole or in part, or settled the dispute in 44% of the cases. This may be due to the complexity of the ISDS system, which may be difficult to navigate. This paper shows, however, that there are numerous standards of protection that can be successfully relied upon, provided the jurisdictional hurdles are cleared and the quantum is carefully assessed, properly pleaded and proven to the satisfaction of the tribunal. Investment protection is a useful, additional avenue for redress for contractors but it must be skillfully planned and managed so that its increased use results in just outcomes for contractors engaged in international projects.

CHAPTER 17

Construction and the energy sector

The transition to a clean energy and the Energy Charter Treaty

Crina Baltag

Introduction: energy construction projects

Complex infrastructure projects in the energy sector are expanding, in particular in the context of the transition to clean energy. Typical energy construction projects include turnkey projects of hydropower plants and dams, laying of pipelines, construction of refineries, construction of LNG facilities – including port facilities, construction of power transmission infrastructure. In the past years, the climate change mitigation measures adopted by States have significantly increased solar and wind farms projects,[1] rare-earth processing facilities,[2] rare earth magnet plants,[3] etc.

Energy construction projects are prone to the actions taken by States, the governments, and local authorities. Moreover, by their nature, these projects are of high value and cannot be relocated elsewhere. It is also relevant to note that, although contractors' rights are found in the contract, when the actions or inactions of the State or of its organs come into play, the contractor may resort to the protection offered by international investment treaties. Construction disputes related to energy projects usually raise the same issues as construction projects generally, such as claims relating to time and delay, variation disputes, defects, etc. Nonetheless, the scale of energy construction projects, the likely involvement of a State, the increased regulatory framework, and State participation in the projects, turn these disputes of the highest complexity.[4] Furthermore, some energy construction projects, such as the lying of pipelines or the building of dams, involve the crossing international borders, while others, such as offshore oil platforms, are made in tough environments.[5] With the mounting pressure to deliver on the climate change mitigation obligations and to comply with the harsher environmental requirements, more generally,

---

1 For example, the Ivanpah Solar Energy Generating System in the Mojave Desert, US. See 'Ivanpah Solar Energy Generating' (*California Energy Commission*) <https://www.energy.ca.gov/powerplant/solar-thermal/ivanpah-solar-energy-generating> accessed 29 August 2023.

2 See e.g., Maddie Stone-Grist, 'A once-shuttered California mine is trying to transform the rare earth industry' (*Fast Company*, 19 June 2023) <https://www.fastcompany.com/90910530/a-once-shuttered-california-mine-is-trying-to-transform-the-rare-earth-industry> accessed 29 August 2023.

3 See e.g., Lanre-Peter Elufisan, 'Neo begins building Europe's first rare earth facility' (*Mining Digital*, 11 July 2023) <https://miningdigital.com/articles/neo-begins-building-europes-first-rare-earth-facility> accessed 29 August 2023.

4 James L Loftis, Scott Stiegler, and Charles Aitchison, 'Energy Sector Construction Disputes' in Stavros Brekoulakis and David Brynmor Thomas (eds), *The Guide to Construction Arbitration*, (4th edn, Global Arbitration Review, 2021) 264.

5 ibid 265.

DOI: 10.4324/9781032663975-22

energy construction projects have to stay on top of the rapidly developing technologies, in particular in the renewables sector, the political pressure to deliver projects on time to comply with the commitments undertaken, and to avoid environmental damage.[6]

The most recent statistics of the International Centre for Settlement of Investment Disputes ('ICSID') show that out of the 844 arbitrations, 42% are in the oil, gas and mining, electric power and other energy sectors,[7] while 10% of the disputes before ICSID are related to investments in the construction sector.[8] Construction and energy sector investment disputes dominate investment arbitration before ICSID, and, arguably, a large portion of the disputes categorized as energy disputes may be primarily arising out of energy construction projects. It is to be noted that 13% of the ICSID arbitrations are brought under the Energy Charter Treaty ('ECT').[9] Examples of energy construction investment disputes relate to the construction of canals,[10] hydro-electric facilities,[11] power stations,[12] coal-fired plants,[13] hazardous waste landfills,[14] gas pipelines,[15] oil refineries,[16] dams,[17] or the ownership of a participating share in a joint venture of construction companies.[18]

Energy transition, dispute resolution, and energy construction projects

The 2022 Energy Arbitration Survey conducted by Queen Mary University of London with Pinsent Masons predicts that energy disputes will likely rise in the future because of the increased regulatory measures adopted by States in implementing transition measures in compliance with their climate change mitigation obligations.[19] As further explained by the Survey, '[t]his rapidly changing regulatory environment will also likely give rise to tensions between project partners, whether as a result of disagreements over the correct

---

6 ibid.

7 'The ICSID Caseload – Statistics. Issue 2023-2' (*ICSID*) <https://icsid.worldbank.org/sites/default/files/publications/2023.ENG_The_ICSID_Caseload_Statistics_Issue.2_ENG.pdf> accessed 4 September 2023, p 11.

8 ibid.

9 The *Energy Charter Treaty* was signed on 17 December 1994 and entered into force on 16 April 1998. The references in this chapter are made to the version printed in International Legal Materials 34 (1995): 373–454.

10 *Jan de Nul NV and Dredging International NV v Arab Republic of Egypt*, ICSID Case No ARB/04/13, Award (6 November 2008).

11 *Impregilo SpA v Islamic Republic of Pakistan*, ICSID Case No ARB/03/3, Decision on Jurisdiction (22 April 2005).

12 *Mihaly International Corporation v Democratic Socialist Republic of Sri Lanka*, ICSID Case No ARB/00/2, Award (15 March 2002).

13 *PSEG Global Inc, The North American Coal Corporation, and Konya Ingin Electrick Üretim ve Ticaret Ltd Sirketi v Republic of Turkey*, ICSID Case No ARB/02/5, Decision on Jurisdiction (4 June 2004).

14 *Metalclad Corporation v The United Mexican States*, ICSID Case No ARB(AF)/97/1, Award (30 August 2000).

15 *Saipem SpA v People's Republic of Bangladesh*, ICSID Case No ARB/05/07, Award (30 June 2009).

16 *Samsung Engineering Co, Ltd v Sultanate of Oman*, ICSID Case No ARB/15/30.

17 *Salini Construttori SpA and Italstrade SpA v Hashemite Kingdom of Jordan*, ICSID Case No ARB/02/13, Award (31 January 2006); *ATA Construction, Industrial and Trading Company v The Hashemite Kingdom of Jordan*, ICSID Case No ARB/08/2, Award (18 May 2010); *Desert Line Projects LLC v The Republic of Yemen*, ICSID Case No ARB/05/17, Award (6 February 2008); *Pantechniki SA Contractors & Engineers v the Republic of Albania*, ICSID Case No ARB/07/21, Award (30 July 2009).

18 *Impregilo* (n 11).

19 Queen Mary University of London and Pinsent Masons, 'Future of International Energy Arbitration Survey Report 2022' (*Queen Mary University of London*, 20 January 2023) <https://arbitration.qmul.ac.uk/media/arbitration/docs/Future-of-International-Energy-Arbitration-Survey-Report.pdf> accessed 4 September 2023, p 11 (QMUL Report).

interpretation of the new regulations and/or as an inevitable result of developers and operators navigating through and implementing an ever-changing regulatory framework'.[20]

The transition to a clean energy and the compliance with the goals set in mitigating the climate change consequences are said to increase not only the investments in the renewable energy resources, and, by consequence, the renewable energy construction projects, but also to intensify the decarbonization of the existing economies, which, similarly, involves significant construction projects, including decommissioning existing energy facilities or, more generally, how goods and services are produced and delivered. Furthermore, the construction industry, in itself, is targeted by the climate change mitigation goals, and hence forced to implement its own measures in this respect,[21] such as:

> 1) introducing biomass for renewable transportation fuels for use in construction equipment and heavy transport; 2) electrification of transport and industrial processes; 3) substitution as part of transitioning from fossil fuel use; and 4) applying carbon capture and storage technologies in the production of basic materials, such as cement and steel.[22]

In a bid to meet the transition to clean energy goals, it is submitted that investors in the energy sector, as well as contractors of energy-related projects, will have to keep up with the new technology.[23] Furthermore, it is already visible that 'smaller-scale investors are entering into the clean energy space', which, arguably, will lead to an increase in the number of disputes, as the '"new" investors have less familiarity with government regulation and do not have established relationships with energy businesses'.[24] On these future disputes, the respondents of the 2022 Energy Arbitration Survey conducted by Queen Mary University of London with Pinsent Masons have identified '"infrastructure (including construction)" (51%) and "price volatility" (39%)' as being the likely causes of energy-related disputes.[25]

Already, the investment arbitration landscape has seen, as mentioned above, various construction disputes related to energy projects.

For example, in *TransCanada v US*, the dispute related to the application submitted by TransCanada to the US Department of State, for a Presidential Permit to build the Keystone XL Pipeline which would carry crude oil from Alberta, Canada to the US. The US Department of State denied the permit raising the issue of significant impact on climate change of such project.[26] The laying of pipeline, in general, is a complex project, involving numerous operations, including securing thousands of land easements, the purchase of necessary equipment, the purchase of pipe, entering into long-term contracts

---

20 ibid.

21 The construction industry is responsible for 37% of global carbon emissions, of which 16% represents embodied carbon mainly from material manufacturing. See Shell and Deloitte, 'Decarbonising Construction: Building a Low-Carbon Future' (*Shell*) <https://www.shell.com/business-customers/construction-and-road/decarbonising-construction/_jcr_content/root/main/section/promo_951320074/links/item0.stream/1680587833348/699d1386fc20237fa60f387e43c010bef2c896b5/decarbonising-construction-building-a-low-carbon-future-industry-report.pdf> accessed 30 August 2023.

22 Filip Johnsson and others, 'The framing of a sustainable development goals assessment in decarbonizing the construction industry – Avoiding "Greenwashing"' (2020) 131 *Renewable and Sustainable Energy Reviews* 1, 1.

23 QMUL Report (n 19) p 17.

24 ibid.

25 ibid.

26 *TransCanada Corporation and TransCanada PipeLines Limited v The United States of America*, ICSID Case No. ARB/16/21, Request for Arbitration (24 June 2016) p 4. The case was discontinued in 2017.

with oil suppliers etc. In *Ioannis Kardassopoulos v Georgia*, an arbitration under the ECT, the dispute related to the development of an oil pipeline for the transport of oil from Azerbaijan oil fields to the Black Sea, through Georgia, which was a significant project for Georgia in particular in increasing the ties with the West.[27]

In *Nord Stream 2 AG v European Union*, also under the ECT, the dispute related to the construction and subsequent operation of the Nord Stream 2 pipeline, a major gas infrastructure project, involving the construction of an offshore import pipeline set to transmit natural gas from Ust-Luga in Russia to Lubmin in Germany.[28] Allegedly, Nord Stream 2 AG had 'contractual commitments in relation to Nord Stream 2, involving over 670 companies from 25 countries', and which included 'significant contracts for the supply of line pipes, their concrete weight coating, subsequent laying, and the construction of landfall facilities in Germany'.[29] Furthermore, Nord Stream 2 AG concluded a long term gas transportation agreement with Gazprom Export and financing agreements were entered into with PJSC Gazprom, Engie Energy Management Holding Switzerland AG, OMV Gas Marketing Trading & Finance BV, Shell Exploration and Production (LXXI) BV, Uniper Gas Transportation & Finance BV and Wintershall Nederland Transport and Trading BV for the financing of the cost of the project'.[30] Nord Stream 2 AG relied on the provisions of the ECT and submitted that the construction of Nord Stream 2 and related activities constituted an 'Investment' for the purposes of Article 1(6) of the ECT. As explained by the claimant, its investments included (i) the pipeline itself, which constitutes tangible property within Article 1(6)(a) of the ECT; (ii) the land purchased in Germany where the pipeline makes landfall, which constitutes property and property rights within Article 1(6)(a) of the ECT; (iii) the contracts with various companies for the performance of services or provision of materials connected with the construction and operation of Nord Stream 2, which constitute claims to performance pursuant to contract having an economic value and associated with an Investment within Article 1(6)(c) of the ECT; and (iv) the permits obtained from Finland, Sweden and Germany to authorise the construction and/or operation of Nord Stream 2 in those areas, which constitute a right conferred by virtue of licences and permits granted pursuant to law to undertake any Economic Activity in the Energy Sector within Article 1(6)(f) of the ECT.[31] Furthermore, Nord Stream 2 AG submitted that the investment is associated with an 'Economic Activity in the Energy Sector', as required by Article 1(6) of the ECT, and with reference to Article 1(4) and Annex EM I (Article 27.11) of the ECT, since it was associated with the transmission, distribution, trade, marketing and sale of natural gas through the construction and operation of Nord Stream 2.[32]

In the significant number of investment arbitrations, the ECT stands out as the suitable treaty for the protection of energy construction investments. Article 1(6) of the ECT is broad enough to cover every kind of asset, owned or controlled directly or indirectly by an investor, including property rights, shares, intellectual property rights conferred by

---

27 *Ioannis Kardassopoulos v the Republic of Georgia*, ICSID Case No ARB/05/18, Decision on Jurisdiction (6 July 2007) p 4.

28 *Nord Stream 2 AG v European Union*, PCA Case No 2020-07, Notice of Arbitration (26 September 2019) para 8.

29 ibid para 9.

30 ibid para 10.

31 ibid para 18.

32 ibid para 24.

licences and permits etc.[33] However, this broad definition is limited by the final paragraph of Article 1(6) which provides that investments pursuant to the ECT are only those 'associated with an Economic Activity in the Energy Sector', while Article 1(5) of the ECT defines the 'Economic Activity in the Energy Sector' as 'an economic activity concerning the exploration, extraction, refining, production, storage, land transport, transmission, distribution, trade, marketing, or sale of Energy Materials and Products'. The Understanding with respect to Article 1(5) gives examples of Economic Activities in the Energy Sector:

(i) prospecting and exploration for, and extraction of, e.g., oil, gas, coal, and uranium;

(ii) construction and operation of power generation facilities, including those powered by wind and other renewable energy sources;

(iii) land transportation, distribution, storage and supply of Energy Materials and Products, e.g., by way of transmission and distribution grids and pipelines or dedicated rail lines, and construction of facilities for such, including the laying of oil, gas, and coal-slurry pipelines;

(iv) removal and disposal of wastes from energy related facilities such as power stations, including radioactive wastes from nuclear power stations;

(v) decommissioning of energy related facilities, including oil rigs, oil refineries, and power generating plants;

(vi) marketing and sale of, and trade in Energy Materials and Products, e.g., retail sales of gasoline; and

(vii) research, consulting, planning, management, and design activities related to the activities mentioned above, including those aimed at Improving Energy Efficiency.

Energy construction projects and the future of the Energy Charter Treaty

The examples above of investment arbitrations under the ECT show the complexity of energy construction disputes and, perhaps, give an indication as to the need of having a specialized instrument under which such disputes should be adjudicated.

The ECT stands out as a unique multilateral treaty specialized in the energy field, which promotes and protects investments, as well as addresses important concerns related to them, including trade, transit and environmental issues. The ECT is peculiar not only by

---

33 Article 1(6) of the ECT:

'Investment' means every kind of asset, owned or controlled directly or indirectly by an Investor and includes:

(a) tangible and intangible, and movable and immovable, property, and any property rights such as leases, mortgages, liens, and pledges;

(b) a company or business enterprise, or shares, stock, or other forms of equity participation in a company or business enterprise, and bonds and other debt of a company or business enterprise;

(c) claims to money and claims to performance pursuant to contract having an economic value and associated with an Investment;

(d) Intellectual Property;

(e) Returns;

(f) any right conferred by law or contract or by virtue of any licences and permits granted pursuant to law to undertake any Economic Activity in the Energy Sector.

its specialization, but also because the European Union and EURATOM are Contracting Parties to it.[34]

However, almost 25 years after its entry into force, the ECT was set to undergo a vital transformation, aligning it with the goals of a transition to a clean energy.[35] This reform was also triggered by the necessity to align the ECT with the ongoing reform of investor–State dispute settlement (ISDS).[36] In November 2017, the Energy Charter Conference confirmed the launching of a discussion on the potential modernisation of the ECT and, a year later, in November 2018, the Conference approved the list of topics for the modernisation of the ECT,[37] which included the definitions of 'economic activity in the energy sector', 'investment', 'investor', 'transit', the right to regulate, sustainable development and corporate social responsibility, etc. The ECT Modernisation Group announced the successful conclusion of the modernisation discussions in June 2022, with the Contracting Parties to the ECT reaching an agreement in principle.[38] While the text of the modernised ECT was expected to be approved immediately by the Energy Charter Conference,[39] it has been postponed since 2022, without a date set for such approval. One reason for the delay in the approval of the modernised ECT is the criticism from the Member States of the EU, which are also Contracting Parties to the ECT, that the updated version of the ECT will not succeed in allowing the phase out of fossil fuel investments and the transition to a clean energy. While the updated version of the ECT would contain the phase out of fossil fuel investments, the European Commission itself has stated that this would not be sufficient to address the concerns that the ECT will prevent effective climate change mitigation measures from being implemented.[40]

The version of Article 1(5) defining the notion of 'Economic Activity in the Energy Sector', in its modernized version, provides how different sources of energy will be protected under the ECT, in the context of the obligations undertaken by the Contracting Parties for a transition to a clean energy. In particular, the EU and the United Kingdom will carve out fossil fuel related investments from the protection under Part III to the ECT on investment promotion and protection, after ten years from the entry into force of the modernised ECT.[41] Such changes in the approach to the protection of fossil fuel investment have a direct impact on the energy construction projects associated with the energy

---

34 For the complete list of the Contracting Parties, see 'Contracting Parties and Signatories of the Energy Charter Treaty' (*Energy Charter Treaty*) <https://www.energychartertreaty.org/treaty/contracting-parties-and-signatories/> accessed 2 September 2023.

35 See e.g., Kluwer Arbitration Blog, *ECT Modernization Perspectives,* available at https://arbitrationblog.kluwerarbitration.com/category/ect-modernisation/?doing_wp_cron=1594687733.4135251045227050781250, last visited 2 September 2023.

36 See 'Working Group III: Investor–State Dispute Settlement Reform' (*UNCITRAL*) <https://uncitral.un.org/en/working_groups/3/investor-state> accessed 5 June 2023.

37 Energy Charter Secretariat, *Report by the Chair of the Subgroup on Modernisation* (CCDEC 2018 21 NOT).

38 Energy Charter Conference, 'Finalisation of the negotiations on the Modernisation of the Energy Charter Treaty' (*Energy Charter Treaty,*24 June 2022) <https://www.energychartertreaty.org/modernisation-of-the-treaty/> accessed 4 September 2023.

39 ibid.

40 European Commission, 'Recommendation for a Council Decision on the approval of the withdrawal of the European Atomic Energy Community from the Energy Charter Treaty' COM (2023) 446 final, p 2.

41 The 24 June 2022 Draft ECT provides the revised Annex NI addressing Energy Materials and Products. See: Council of the EU, 'Working Document WK 9218/2022 INIT' (*bilaterals.org*, 27 June 2022) <https://www.bilaterals.org/IMG/pdf/reformed_ect_text.pdf> accessed 2 September 2023 (Draft ECT).

resources. While the modernisation process still sees a gradual phase out of the fossil fuel energy investments up to a cut-off date, it is to be noted that certain Economic Activities in the Energy Sector will still be protected by the ECT, even after this date, such as the 'transport, transmission, and distribution of petroleum gases and other gaseous hydrocarbons ... through pipelines provided the pipelines are capable of transporting renewable and low carbon gases'.[42] As such, certain pipeline construction projects may still fall under the ECT's application even in its modernized version.

Nonetheless, the suggested amendments of Article 1(6) of the ECT indicate that the broad definition of 'investment' as 'every kind of asset' will be particularized only to investment which are 'made or acquired in accordance with the applicable laws' in the host Contracting Party.[43] The suggested draft addresses the concerns of the host Contracting Parties that investment must be lawful, meaning that they should also comply with any climate change regulations implemented at the national level by that Contracting Parties. This is supported by the additional proposal that the modernised ECT include an express provision on the sovereign right of the Contracting Parties to regulate, which reads as follows: 'The Contracting Parties reaffirm the right to regulate within their territories to achieve legitimate policy objectives, such as the protection of the environment, including climate change mitigation and adaptation, protection of public health, safety or public morals'.[44] Furthermore, a new paragraph in the Preamble of the modernised ECT is set to acknowledge 'the inherent rights of the Contracting Parties to regulate investments within their territories in order to meet legitimate and public policy objectives'.[45] Other suggested new provisions to be implemented in the modernised ECT address 'Climate Change and Clean Energy Transition', recognizing the:

> urgent need of pursuing the ultimate objective of the United Nations Framework Convention on Climate Change (UNFCCC), the purpose and goals of the Paris Agreement in order to effectively combat climate change and its adverse impacts (...) [and] effectively implement (...) commitments and obligations under the UNFCCC and the Paris Agreement.[46]

Conclusion

The predictions by the 2022 Energy Arbitration Survey conducted by Queen Mary University of London with Pinsent Masons appear to be confirmed by the approach taken by the modernised ECT, that the next years will see an increase of energy disputes related to regulatory measures adopted by States in the implementation of their obligations of climate change mitigation and adaptation. However, while the transition to a clean energy, including the transformation of the economies, will necessarily imply the phase out of polluting energy resources and the termination of such energy investment projects, we will see an increasing need of energy construction projects for the renewable energy projects or for the adaptation or decommissioning of the fossil fuel facilities.

Therefore, the protection of energy investments, including of energy construction investments, will be a key element in the successful transition to a clean energy.

---

42 Draft ECT (n 41) Annex NI.
43 Draft ECT (n 41).
44 ibid.
45 ibid.
46 ibid.

International treaties, in particular the ECT, will be essential in ensuring that such investments are protected and promoted. The United Nations' Sharm el-Sheikh Climate Change Conference Implementation Plan has anticipated that 'USD 4 trillion per year needs to be invested in renewable energy up until 2030 to be able to reach net zero emissions by 2050, and that, furthermore, a global transformation to a low-carbon economy is expected to require investment of at least USD 4–6 trillion per year'.[47] Such massive investments will need to benefit from the meaningful protection, in particular by international treaties.

---

47 UNFCC, 'Decision -/CP.27 Sharm el-Sheikh Implementation Plan' (*United Nations Climate Change*, 20 November 2022) <https://unfccc.int/sites/default/files/resource/cop27_auv_2_cover%20decision.pdf?download accessed> 4 September 2023, para 30.

CHAPTER 18

Is there a role for AI in the determination of construction disputes?

Paula Gerber

Introduction

The resolution of construction disputes is an expensive exercise in terms of both time and money as well as an enormous drain on emotional and intellectual energy. Although the degree of suffering can to some extent be mitigated by choosing the most appropriate form of dispute resolution – adjudication, mediation, expert determination, arbitration, litigation, etc. – it always involves some degree of pain. Indeed, it has been observed that if construction disputes were a patient they would be declared 'seriously, if not critically, ill', and while all commercial parties complain about the problems associated with litigation, it is construction disputes where 'the disease is most advanced'.[1]

It is therefore not surprising that the construction industry is constantly looking for ways to reduce the suffering inflicted by construction disputes. We can respond to the pain of construction disputes in two ways; (i) take action to *prevent* disputes arising, and (ii) take action to more efficiently and effectively *resolve* disputes that cannot be avoided. There are undoubtedly opportunities for AI to play a positive role in *preventing* construction disputes, (for example, through the use of smart contracts, blockchain and the digitisation of construction projects). What is less clear is whether there is a role for AI in *resolving* construction disputes. In particular, could AI replace human judges in deciding construction disputes? Could AI be the cure to the disease that is construction litigation? Can AI make better and faster decisions in construction cases? This chapter seeks to answer these questions.

What is AI?

Many people think of artificial intelligence has a modern invention and are surprised to learn that the term actually emerged in the 1950s. Mathematician and computer scientist, John McCarthy coined the phrase during a workshop he organised in Dartmouth, New Hampshire, in the summer of 1956. He later admitted that the term artificial intelligence was not well liked by his peers, because the goal was *genuine*, not 'artificial', intelligence.[2] Nonetheless the term has survived almost three quarters of a century, and appears here to stay.

Although there is a lot of jargon around AI, it is a term that has so far eluded precise definition.[3] Yet defining AI is critical if we want to regulate it. And many accept that

---

1 Justice David Byrne, 'The future of litigation of construction law disputes' (2007) 23 *Building and Construction Law Journal* 398.

2 Melanie Mitchell, *Artificial Intelligence: A Guide for Thinking Humans* (Pelican Books, 2020) 4.

3 Pei Wang, 'On Defining Artificial Intelligence' (2019) 10(2) *Journal of Artificial General Intelligence* 1.

DOI: 10.4324/9781032663975-23

regulating AI is both appropriate and necessary.[4] Although legislators and policymakers require a precise legal definition of AI, in order to regulate it, for the purpose of this chapter, a general understanding of relevant terms suffices. With this in mind, a simple glossary is provided.

Term	Definition
Artificial Intelligence	Computer systems which behave and appear 'intelligent'. The core idea of AI involves machines mimicking human intelligence to perform tasks and improve themselves iteratively based on the information they collect.[5]
Machine Learning	This refers to the technical capability of AI, and the ability to improve itself by learning from the data. The machine analyses large amounts of data to detect patterns and produce predictions.[6] Machine learning can be further divided into: (i) *Supervised machine learning*: software which requires an ongoing exposure of input data and the associated output data to learn the complex underlying relationship between the inputs and outputs. An example of supervised machine learning is your Netflix recommendations;[7] and (ii) *Unsupervised machine learning*: software which can detect patterns within input data without human training and association to outputs. The technology automatically develops relationships between characteristics within the uncategorised input data.[8] There is no particular output goal required or trained for, instead the machine tries to make sense of the data without human supervision.[9] This is useful when you don't know what you are looking for; the machine discovers unknown patterns and provides useful insights.
Deep Learning	Deep learning is a relatively recent subset of machine learning. It refers to computers learning to do what comes naturally to humans. For example, deep learning is a key technology behind driverless cars, enabling them to recognise a stop sign, or to distinguish a pedestrian from a lamppost. Deep learning uses artificial neural networks to mimic the learning process of the human brain.[10]
Turing Test	A test that examines a machine's ability to show intelligence indistinguishable from that of human beings. A machine that succeeds in the test is qualified to be labelled as artificial intelligence.[11]

---

4 Amitai Etzioni and Oren Etzioni, 'Should Artificial Intelligence Be Regulated?' 2017(4) Issues in Science and Technology 33.

5 Yongjun Xu et al, 'Artificial intelligence: A powerful paradigm for scientific research' (2021) 2(4) *The Innovation.*

6 Matthias Schonlau, *Applied Statistical Learning with Case Studies in Strata,* (Springer, 2023) Ch 2.2.

7 Taeho Jo, *Machine Learning Foundations: Supervised, Unsupervised, and Advanced Learning* (Springer, 2021).

8 Schonlau (n 6) Ch 2.3.3.

9 Ibid.

10 Albert Chun Chen Liu, Oscar Ming Kin Law, and Iain Law, *Understanding Artificial Intelligence: Fundamentals and Applications* (The Institute of Electrical and Electronic Engineers, 2022) 6–7.

11 Ryan Abbott, *the Reasonable Robot: Artificial Intelligence and the Law,* (Cambridge University Press, 2020) 25.

Applying these definitions to the context of resolving construction disputes, this chapter seeks to determine whether there are machines that can pass the Turing Test. That is, do we have technology that is able to evaluate the vast quantum of data that sits behind construction disputes and reach correct conclusions about how cases should be decided, in a manner similar, or superior, to a human judge. If such machines exist, the next question that has to be asked is, *should* such machines decide construction disputes in place of human judges? Are they capable of administering justice and respecting the human rights of the parties?

The current use of AI judges

It has been observed that, 'Science fiction's visions of the future include many versions of artificial intelligence (AI), but relatively few examples where software replaces human judges. For once, the real world seems to be changing in ways that are not predicted in stories.'[12] Robot judges appear to be being used in place of human judges in the courts within two countries. Estonia is reportedly working on a pilot program whereby AI will adjudicate claims less than €7,000,[13] while China is even further along the path of using AI judges, having established smart courts where non-human judges powered by artificial intelligence decide a wide variety of disputes, including,

> intellectual property, e-commerce, financial disputes related to online conduct, loans acquired or performed online, domain name issues, property and civil rights cases involving the Internet, product liability arising from online purchases and certain administrative disputes.[14]

The Chinese AI judges are holograms which look like a person wearing a black robe. These virtual judges ask questions of the parties, set schedules, take evidence and issue dispositive rulings.[15]

Figure 18.1 Scan QR code to view a short video of China's robot judges in action

---

12 Rónán Kennedy, 'AI: why installing 'robot judges' in courtrooms is a really bad idea', 11 July 2023, *The Conversation*. Accessed at: https://theconversation.com/ai-why-installing-robot-judges-in-courtrooms-is-a-really-bad-idea-208718.

13 Tara Vasdani, 'Estonia set to introduce 'AI judge' in small claims court to clear court backlog' 10 April 2019, *LexisNexis*. Accessed at: https://www.law360.ca/articles/11582/estonia-set-to-introduce-ai-judge-in-small-claims-court-to-clear-court-backlog-. Note, however, a statement from the Estonian Ministry of Justice denying reports that it is developing AI judges to replace human judges: https://www.just.ee/en/news/estonia-does-not-deve lop-ai-judge.

14 Tara Vasdani, 'Robot justice: China's use of Internet courts' 5 February 2020, *LexisNexis*. Accessed at: https://www.law360.ca/artiles/17741/robot-justice-china-s-use-of-internet-courts.

15 Ibid.

The AI judges in the Hangzhou Internet Court are proving highly efficient at getting through the backlog of cases. Over three million disputes have been decided by the AI judges,[16] but are litigants happy to have their dispute decided by AI, with no real judge present? In China, the statistics suggest that parties may indeed be happy to have their dispute decided within an entirely non-human adjudication process. However, it is important to be conscious of cultural differences that may sit behind this willingness to accept the determination of disputes by AI judges. One of the only evaluations of China's internet courts found that:

> initiatives for administering justice simply, swiftly, and singly have blossomed because they correspond to the demands of the Chinese legal order, a system that privileges above all the maintenance of social harmony and stability.[17]

Thus, different expectations of the justice system, and different priorities relating to the resolution of disputes, will influence how willing humans are to accept AI judges. If the speed at which cases are finalised has the highest priority, then expedition of cases will make AI judges a more attractive alternative to human judges. In addition, if a judiciary is perceived as corrupt or incompetent, then decisions made by AI may might be preferable because they are viewed as being impartial, precise, objective and trustworthy.[18]

The factors that influence how acceptable AI judges are to the parties varies according to legal systems and cultures. Two studies that gauged the attitudes of Americans to AI judges found that respondents to the surveys overwhelmingly perceived robot judges as being *less* procedurally fair than human judges.[19] The vast majority of the 6,000 adults surveyed, viewed machine-adjudicated proceedings as inferior to human-adjudicated proceedings, when it comes to fairness.

However, this perception of unfairness is not insurmountable. The nuanced questions that the researchers included in the surveys, elicited responses that revealed what changes would be required for AI judges to be perceived as being as fair as human judges. The researchers found that, what they called the 'human–AI fairness gap', could be reduced if two issues relating to AI judging were addressed, namely;

I. Hearings

Parties' perception of fairness is linked to whether they feel they have 'had their day in court'. In order for a decision-making process to be perceived as fair, litigants require that a hearing is conducted, *but* it does not seem to matter whether that hearing is before a human judge or an algorithmic judge.[20]

II. Interpretability

Parties are more likely to think a decision is fair if there is 'transparency into – and knowledge of – how the outcome is derived.'[21] A tree-based model is

---

16 Agence France-Presse, 'Chinese Digital Courts: A Brave New World' 6 December 2019 *Courthouse News Service*. Accessed at: www.courthousenews.com/chinese-digital-courts-a-brave-new-world/.

17 Benjamin Minhao Chen & Zhiyu Li, 'How will technology change the face of Chinese justice? (2020) 34(1) *Columbia Journal of Asian Law* 1, 6.

18 Ibid 50.

19 Benjamin Minhao Chen, Alexander Stremitzer and Kevin Tobia 'Having your Day in Robot Court' (2022) 36(1) *Harvard Journal of Law* and Technology 128.

20 Ibid 156.

21 Ibid 145.

useful for providing this sort of explanation. Tree-based methods are a form of supervised machine learning that use 'if-then' rules to assess different inputs and reach an outcome. How a judgement was arrived at through the use of a decision tree-based model can be illustrated with a flowchart that sets out how relevant factors were considered at each stage leading to a determination around whether particular criteria were satisfied.[22] Including such an explanation would make it possible for the parties, and anyone else, to determine how much each factor mattered to the AI's ultimate decision. Moreover, it would be possible for someone (or something) to replicate the decision-maker's reasoning to see how a change in any of the factors might impact the decision.[23]

The authors of these studies argue that knowing that the conduct of hearings and the interpretability of a decision impact on a person's perception of the fairness of the process, means that we can undertake 'algorithmic offsetting' that incorporates a hearing, into the AI process, and enhances the interpretability of the decision.[24] Such measures are likely to have a positive impact on opinion relating to the fairness of AI judges, which will influence the acceptability of any future initiatives to introduce robot judges into any common law jurisdiction. However, conducting hearings before non-human judges and improving the interpretability of algorithmic decisions will not overcome other barriers to AI judging that are explored in this chapter.

Can AI make *better* decisions than human judges?

When considering whether AI can make better decisions than human judges, it is worth noting that 'All human decisions are susceptible to prejudice and all judicial systems suffer from unconscious bias, despite the best of intentions.'[25] There is widespread familiarity with the saying that 'justice is blind', and with the image of Lady Justice wearing a blindfold. The message that this expression and image seek to convey, is that judges are impartial; that the judicial system is fair and has integrity. Yet all human decisions are susceptible to prejudice and all judicial systems suffer from implicit bias.[26] Given these inherent flaws in human decision-making, it is understandable that there is interest in exploring whether AI represents a better alternative.

Every human – including judges – has implicit biases, and implicit bias influences our judgment. Implicit bias refers to 'stereotypical associations so subtle that people who hold them might not even be aware of them'.[27] The idea that implicit bias could be removed from decision-making by replacing human judges with AI, is therefore very appealing. Surely justice would be more readily achieved if algorithms were designed that ignored factors that have no legal bearing on a particular case, for example, gender and race?

---

22 Ibid 145–146.

23 Ibid.

24 Ibid 161.

25 Briony Harris, 'Could an AI ever replace a judge in court?' 7 November 2017, World Governments Summit *Observer*. Accessed at: https://www.worldgovernmentsummit.org/observer/articles/2017/detail/could-an-ai-ever-replace-a-judge-in-court.

26 Jeffrey Rachlinski et al, 'Does unconscious racial bias affect trial judges?' (2009) 84 *Notre Dame Law Review* 1195, 1203.

27 Ibid.

Unfortunately, as with many aspects of AI, the answer is not that simple. AI can theoretically remove irrelevant factors from consideration, but AI learns and mimics the biases of its programmers and the data they are programmed with. And every human – has implicit biases, including programmers.

Machine learning involves AI learning from its inputs in a way that improves its outputs. This is referred to as a feedback loop, and while it results in continuous learning and improvement of outputs, it has been described as AI's 'Achilles' heel, since it is prone to reinforcing the unconscious bias of its developers.'[28] Thus AI has biases, just as human judges have biases, but AI's are embedded in the design of the algorithm and/or in the data used to train the algorithm.[29]

This AI bias is well illustrated in COMPAS, the tool used in many US courts to assist judges in criminal matters, make decisions about pretrial release and sentencing. COMPAS issues a statistical score between 1 and 10 that quantifies how likely a person is to be rearrested if released.[30] However, a problem was identified with COMPAS because of the data used to design the algorithms. Historically police have arrested more black men, than white men, meaning that the risk of a black person being assessed as likely to be rearrested is higher than other races.[31] Although AI was introduced to the criminal justice system in an effort to make the system less biased, the opposite appears to be true.[32]

There is increasing evidence suggesting that human prejudices have been baked into these tools because the machine-learning models are trained on biased police data. Far from avoiding racism, AI may simply be better at hiding it.[33] Many critics now view these tools as a form of tech-washing, where a veneer of objectivity covers mechanisms that perpetuate inequities in society.[34]

Thus, AI judges remove the subjective biases of human judges, but replaces them with subjective biases of the programmer and of history. In the construction context, this may result in a bias towards claimants in security of payment adjudications, given that a study found that in security of payment claims in New South Wales, Australia, 57.1% of claimants recovered the full amount claimed and a further 23.5% of claimants received more than half of their claim, but less than the full amount sought.[35]

Embedded bias in algorithms is more problematic than implicit bias in judges (or adjudicators or arbitrators), because it is more difficult to identify and correct. Robots cannot 'unlearn' their biases unless their algorithms can be corrected, which is difficult given the

---

28 Maud Piers and Christian Aschauer, 'Administering AI in Arbitration' Chapter 5 in Renato Nazzini (ed) *Construction Arbitration and Alternative Dispute Resolution* (2021) Informa Law from Routledge, 64.

29 Ibid.

30 Will Douglas Heaven 'Predictive policing algorithms are racist. They need to be dismantled' 17 July 2020, *MIT Technology Review*. Accessed at: www.technologyreview.com/2020/07/17/1005396/predictive -policing-algorithms-racist-dismantled-machine-learning-bias-criminal-justice/.

31 Taylor, E., Guy-Walls, P., Wilkerson, P., et al. 'The Historical Perspectives of Stereotypes on African-American Males' (2019) 4 *Journal of Human Rights and Social Work* 213, 217–218.

32 Molly Callahan, 'Algorithms were supposed to Reduce Bias in Criminal Justice – Do They?', *The Brink: Pioneering Research from Boston University*, (Research Post, 23 February 2023). Accessed at: www.bu.edu/articles/2023/do-algorithms-reduce-bias-in-criminal-justice/.

33 Heaven, above n 30.

34 Callahan, above n 32.

35 Thomas E. Uher and Michael C. Brand, 'Analysis of adjudication determinations made under security of payment legislation in New South Wales' (2005) 23 *International Journal of Project Management* 474, 479.

opaqueness of AI.[36] Implicit bias in human judges, on the other hand, is capable of being identified and mitigated. For example, there are tests that can be used to assess levels of implicit bias[37] and once judges are alerted to their own unconscious biases, steps can be taken to correct those biases so that they do not influence their decision-making, by, for example, providing targeted training.[38]

Lady Justice not only wears a blindfold, she also holds a set of scales, representing the solemn task of weighing the arguments and evidence presented by both parties and reaching a just outcome.[39] Can AI do the same job; can it evaluate the arguments and evidence and reach a correct decision?

Given the sophisticated and multifarious nature of construction disputes, it is natural that we are drawn to the idea of using AI to analyse the data and reach a decision on the appropriate outcome. However, machine learning, even deep learning, rely on binary codes.[40] Yet, real-world construction disputes involve much complexity, uncertainties and ambiguities, and are difficult to reduce to reduce to a series of numbers. Take, for example, the Australian case that followed a fire in the 21-storey Lacrosse apartment building in Melbourne.[41] A French backpacker left a cigarette butt in a plastic food container that was being used as an ashtray on a timber table on the balcony of the apartment where he was staying. That smouldering cigarette started a fire that spread rapidly from the level 8 to the top of the building due to the highly combustible aluminium composite panels (ACPs) that were installed on the outside of the building. Unlike the Grenfell Fire in London, there was, thankfully, no loss of life.[42]

In 2016, the owners of the building commenced proceedings seeking in excess of AU$12 million for reinstatement of property damaged by the fire and the cost of replacing noncompliant cladding. There were eight respondents, including the builder, building surveyor, architect, fire engineer and the French backpacker. Following a six-week hearing, His Honour Judge Woodward published his decision and reasons which filled 227 pages. His Honour apportioned liability as follows:

   i. building surveyor (33%);
   ii. architect (25%);
   iii. fire engineer (39%); and
   iv. French backpacker (3%).[43]

---

36 Piers and Aschauer, above n 28, 65.

37 See, for example, the Harvard Implicit Association Test, accessed at: https://implicit.harvard.edu/implicit/takeatest.html.

38 Jeffrey J Rachlinski, Sheri Lynn Johnson, Andrew J Wistrich and Chris Guthrie, 'Does unconscious racial bias affect trial judges?' (2009) 84 *Notre Dame L Rev* 1203

39 Love, L. P. 'Images of justice' (2000) 1(1) *Pepperdine Dispute Resolution Law Journal* 29.

40 Savesh Tanwar, Sumit Bdotra and Ajay Rana, *Machine learning, blockchain, and cyber security in smart environments: application and challenges,* (CRC Press LLC, 2023) 194.

41 ABC News 'Docklands fire: Melbourne high-rise apartment blaze forces evacuation of hundreds' 25 November 2014. Accessed at: www.abc.net.au/news/2014-11-25/residents-evacuated-after-fire-in-melbourne-cbd-apartment-build/5914978.

42 *Owners Corporation No 1 of BS613436T v LU Simon Builders Pty Ltd ('Lacrosse')* [2019] VCAT 286, [7].

43 Ibid, [896].

The builder was found to have breached the statutory warranties,[44] but not its duty of care.[45] Although the builder breached the warranties, the other respondents were held to be concurrent wrongdoers who were liable to the builder for the damages it had to pay to the homeowners. On appeal there was a minor reallocation of liability; the fire engineer was found to be liable for 42% of the loss i.e. an additional 3% and the building surveyor liable for 30% i.e., 3% less than at first instance.[46]

The decisions at first instance and on appeal are noteworthy for the comprehensive analysis of the law and its application to the facts, including the operation of the 'peer professional opinion' defence; how breaches of statutory warranties can occur in the absence of any negligence, causation and remoteness, proportionate liability, concurrent wrongdoers and quantum of damages. It is difficult to envisage AI being able to exercise such nuanced analysis and reach such an insightful, reasoned and rigorous decision. It would be an interesting exercise to give the Lacrosse fire fact scenario to an AI judge and see whether it is able to balance the scales of justice and reach a transparent and just decision.

Another factor to consider when evaluating whether AI judges can make better decisions than human judges, is what knowledge and skills human judges use in reaching their decisions. Humans invariably use a vast array of knowledge, intellect and experience – not purely legal – when undertaking the task of applying law to facts. This is best illustrated in Lord Aitkin's seminal judgment in the case of *Donoghue v Stevenson*[47] which established the law of negligence. It has been observed that,

> When looking to establish an underlying foundation determining duties owed between parties, Lord Atkin turned to the biblical parable of the Good Samaritan as a basis for what would become known as the neighbour principle.[48]

AI cannot replicate the knowledge that human judges, like Lord Aitken, acquire through long-term engagement and active perception of the real physical world.[49] Ultimately, AI cannot capture or respond *'to intangible human factors that go into real-life decision-making – the ethical, moral, and other human considerations that guide the course of business, life, and society at large'.*[50] Without access to these intangible factors, AI cannot make better decisions than human judges.

Should AI replace human judges?

Irrespective of whether AI can make *better* decisions than human judges, it is necessary to also consider whether AI *should* be used in place of human judges. For it has been noted

---

44 Warranties relating to suitability of materials, compliance with the law and fitness for purpose pursuant to section 8 of the *Domestic Building Contracts Act 1995* (Vic).

45 See *Owners Corporation No 1 of BS613436T v LU Simon Builders Pty Ltd* [302]–[303] and *Tanah Merah Vic Pty Ltd v Owners Corp No 1 of PS613436 (No 1)* [2021] VSCA 72, [62]–[63].

46 *Tanah Merah Vic Pty Ltd v Owners Corp No 1 of PS613436 (No 2) ('Lacrosse No 2')* [2021] VSCA 122, [26].

47 [1932] AC 562.

48 Sir Harry Gibbs Legal Heritage Centre. Accessed at: https://legalheritage.sclqld.org.au/donoghue-v-stevenson-1932-ac-562

49 Joe McKendrick and Andy Thurai, 'AI Isn't Ready to Make Unsupervised Decisions', 15 September 2022, *Harvard Business Review*. Accessed at: https://hbr.org/2022/09/ai-isnt-ready-to-make-unsupervised-decisions.

50 Ibid.

that 'The use of AI in the legal system raises significant moral implications, including questions about the value of human judgment, the role of technology in society, and the appropriate balance between efficiency and fairness in the legal system.[51]

This section considers two reasons why AI should not be used as a decision maker in construction disputes, in place of human judges, namely, AI's inability to provide transparent reasons for its decisions and the risk it poses to human rights.

Lack of reasons

A defining characteristic of our justice system is that judicial decisions are accompanied by reasons[52] and the 'primary responsibility of judges is reasoned decision-making.'[53] Judicial reasons are essential for

(a) enabling the parties to see the extent to which their arguments have been understood and accepted as well as the basis of the judge's decision;
(b) ensuring judicial accountability; reasons enable decisions to be scrutinised, by appellate courts and the public; and
(c) providing predictability regarding how like cases will probably be decided in the future.[54]

In the context of AI deciding construction disputes, it is the first two of these rationales that are most significant. Justice is not served by a judge delivering a decision without an explanation of the basis for that decision. This is encapsulated in the expression that 'justice should not only be done, but should manifestly and undoubtedly be seen to be done'.[55] The giving of reasons for the decision allows the parties to understand whether justice has been done. That is, they can see exactly how the judge considered the submissions, arguments and evidence; what weight they gave to them. A reasoned judgment can be contrasted with an arbitrary decision, which is the anthesis of justice.[56]

How AI reaches a decision is opaque, meaning it is difficult to 'look inside' and decipher the reasons for the decision. This is a phenomenon dubbed the 'Black Box Problem'.[57] It has been described in the following terms:

> [because programmers] do not themselves set a system's parameter values, they might not actually know what these values are. But even if they do know the values of individual parameters, the fact that these values are often numerous and nonlinearly coupled means that developers cannot readily track the way individual inputs are transformed into specific outputs. For this reason, they are often unable to understand the solution.[58]

---

51 Dom Watts, 'Could AI replace Judges?' *Ministry of Injustice*. Accessed at: https://ministryofinjustice.co .uk/ai-replace-judges/#:~:text=Disadvantages%20of%20AI%20Replacing%20Judges&text=Potential%20Bia s%3A%20AI%20systems%20are,trust%20in%20the%20legal%20system.

52 Luke Beck, 'The constitutional duty to give reasons for judicial decisions' (2017) 40(3) *UNSW Law Journal* 923.

53 *Soulemezis v Dudley* (1987) 10 N.S.W.L.R. 247 CA at 278 per McHugh J.A.

54 McHugh JA (as he then was) in *Soulemezis v Dudley (Holdings) Pty Ltd*, above n. 13, at p. 279.

55 *R v Sussex Justices; Ex parte McCarthy* [1924] KB 256, 259 (Lord Hewart CJ).

56 Jason Bosland and Jonathan Gill, 'The principle of open justice and the judicial duty to give public reasons' (2014) 38 *Melbourne University Law Review* 482, 487–488.

57 Carlos Zednik, 'Solving the Black Box Problem: A Normative Framework for Explainable Artificial Intelligence' (2021) 34(2) *Philosophy and Technology* 265.

58 Ibid, 268.

Parties to a construction dispute are unlikely to accept a decision when they do not understand how it was arrived at. Until such time as AI becomes transparent – that is, it can provide sound, discernible reasons for its decision – it is unlikely to be a viable alternative to human judges.

An absence of reasons for a decision is also problematic because it limits judicial accountability by precluding scrutiny of the decision by an appellate court.[59] The inability of AI to provide reasoning and justification for decisions, makes verifiability impossible.

Current AI models of adjudication do not provide reasons for how they came to a decision. The result is that while AI experts may potentially be able to comprehend why AI decided the case in favour of one party, lay individuals will struggle to understand the basis for the decision. The precise reasons are inscrutable.[60] This is highly problematic and raises questions about whether AI adjudication affords disputants due process rights.

Violation of human rights

Construction law and human rights law are not natural bedfellows. Lawyers rarely think of these areas of private law and public law as being connected, and yet there are many instances where they converge. Examples include designing buildings which are as accessible to people with a disability as they are to able bodied people,[61] and striving for gender equality and non-discrimination within the construction industry.[62] Another emerging area of convergence between human rights law and construction law is the potential use of AI to resolve construction disputes.

The International Covenant on Civil and Political Rights (ICCPR) sets out the universal standards relating to the rights of individuals when they interact with the legal system. Article 14(1) of the ICCPR provides that 'everyone shall be entitled to a fair and public hearing by a competent, independent and impartial tribunal established by law.' There are several aspects of this right that warrant further consideration.

Fair hearing
The United Nations Human Rights Committee (the body responsible for monitoring compliance with the ICCPR) has stated that:

> the concept of a fair hearing in the context of article 14(1) of the Covenant should be interpreted as requiring a number of conditions, such as equality of arms, respect for the principle of adversary proceedings, preclusion of *ex officio reformatio in pejus* [worsening of an earlier verdict], and expeditious procedure.[63]

These are only examples of the criteria to be considered, not an exhaustive list. Perhaps not surprisingly, the Human Rights Committee has yet to consider how the use of AI in judicial decision-making might potentially violate the right to a fair trial. It is, however,

---

59 Michael Kirby, 'Ex Tempore Judgments; Reasons on the Run' (1995) 25 *University of Western Australia Law Review* 213, 221.

60 Piers and Aschauer (n 28) 65.

61 Aimi Hamraie, *Building Access: Universal Design and the Politics of Disability* (2017) University of Minnesota Press.

62 Natalie Galea, Abigail Powell, Martin Loosemore and Louise Chappell 'The gendered dimensions of informal institutions in the Australian construction industry' (2020) *Gender, Work and Organization*.

63 *Yves Morael v. France*, Communication No. 207/1986, para [9.3].

an issue that scholars have considered and the conclusion reached is that there is a high risk of breaches of the right set out in Article 14 of the ICCPR. In particular, when AI is used to make judicial decisions, the right to a fair hearing is jeopardised by the opacity of the algorithm.[64]

Another aspect of the right to a fair trial that AI judges may breach is the requirement of independence of the judiciary. This means ensuring that judges are free from influence or intervention by not only the executive and legislative branches of government, but also other third parties.[65] Potentially the persons responsible for designing robot judges could threaten the independence of the judiciary since they are pursuing economic interests that may 'not fully align with the lawful administration of justice'.[66]

Public hearing

Jeremy Bentham observed that 'Where there is no publicity there is no justice'.[67] Open justice in the form of public hearings is the hallmark of the judicial branch of government.[68] The rationale for public hearings include that they facilitate:

> public and professional scrutiny and criticism [of judges], without which abuses may flourish undetected. Further, the public administration of justice tends to maintain confidence in the integrity and independence of the courts. The fact that courts of law are held openly and not in secret is an essential aspect of their character. It distinguishes their activities from those of administrative officials.[69]

Former Australian High Court Judge, The Hon. Michael Kirby has questioned whether AI adjudication conforms with this requirement that disputes in the court system be openly and publicly adjudicated.[70] Do virtual hearings shut the door to public hearings?

During the early days of the COVID pandemic, when courts had to rapidly pivot to conducting online hearings, there were challenges in ensuring public hearings. Indeed, it was observed that remote or virtual hearings were akin to 'enclosed, non-public and informal sites that do not reflect the legal civic space of a physical courtroom'.[71]

However, the manner in which virtual hearings are now organised, publicised and conducted, including with live streams and more readily available recordings of court hearings,[72] means that online hearings do not necessarily equate to non-public hearings. The right to a fair trial will be 'effectively upheld in systems where, similarly to a human judge, the public can observe AI judges administering court proceedings'.[73]

---

64 Kalliopi Terzidou 'The Use of Artificial Intelligence in the Judiciary and Its Compliance with the Right to a Fair Trial' (2022) 31(3) *Journal of Judicial Administration* 154.

65 Ibid, 160.

66 Ibid,

67 Jeremy Bentham, quoted in *Scott v Scott* [1913] AC 417, 477 (Lord Shaw).

68 Kieran Pender, 'Open Justice, Closed Courts and the 'Constitution': Australian and Comparative Perspective' (2023) 42(2) *The University of Queensland Law Journal,* 155.

69 Gibbs J in *Russell v Russell* (1976) 134 CLR 495, [8].

70 Michael Kirby, 'The Future of Courts – Do They Have One?' (Conference Paper, Judicial Conference of Australia Third Annual Colloquium, 2020).

71 Michael Legg and Anthony Song, 'The Courts, the Remote Hearing and the Pandemic: From Action to Reflection' (2021) 44(1) *UNSW Law Journal* 126, 142.

72 See, for example, 'The Court of Appeal (Civil Division) – Live Streaming of Court Hearings', *Courts and Tribunals Judiciary,* at www.judiciary.uk/the-court-of-appeal-civil-division-live-streaming-of-court -hearings/.

73 Tom Salmon, 'Locking the court doors? AI judges and the right to a public hearing' (2022) *Australian Human Rights Institute Blog.* Accessed at: www.humanrights.unsw.edu.au/students/blogs/artificial

Of course, having AI judges does not mean hearings have to be virtual. Judicial avatars in physical courtrooms could be the new reality. Anyone who has seen the ABBA Voyage performance in London knows that we have the technology to make it 'almost impossible to tell you're not watching human beings', with one reviewer commenting that 'Any sense you're not actually in the presence of the band dissolves' as soon as they start playing their hits.[74] Maybe one day we will be able to walk into a courtroom and believe we are appearing before Lord Denning!

Competent, independent, and impartial tribunal established by law

Laws governing judicial appointments generally require that judges have full legal capacity – the ability to comprehend, interpret, and apply the law effectively within a legal context.[75] In Australia, section 6 (2)(b) of the *Federal Court of Australia Act 1976* specifically states that 'a person is not to be appointed as a Judge unless the person has appropriate knowledge, skills and experience to deal with the kinds of matters that may come before the Court".[76] Similarly, in the UK, the *Constitutional Reform Act 2005* sets out the qualifications for appointment of 'a person' as a judge of the Supreme Court.[77]

A robot judge, not being a person, does not satisfy the requirement for cases to be decided by a competent, independent and impartial tribunal established by law, which is a key component of the right to a fair trial articulated in Article 14 of the ICCPR.

The ongoing development of private law

A final argument against the use of robot judges for construction disputes lies in the manner in which the common law and equity are constantly evolving. While private law seeks to provide consistency and certainty it also incorporates flexibility that allows justice to be provided according to the unique facts of each case. The ability of judges to adapt and develop the common law means that it continues to be relevant and applicable as societies change and evolve.

Construction disputes have proven to be fertile ground for the expansion of private law, particularly in the area of remedies. The 2019 Australian High Court decision in *Mann v Paterson Constructions Pty Ltd* is illustrative of this evolution.[78] Angela and Peter Mann engaged Paterson Constructions Pty Ltd to build two townhouses on land they owned in the Melbourne suburb of Blackburn. The standard form domestic building contract specified a contract sum of AU$971,000. The relationship between the homeowners and the builder broke down before the completion of the second townhouse. The Manns sought to terminate the contract following delays in completing the works which they alleged constituted a repudiation of the contract by the contractor. The owners purported to accept the

---

-intelligence-judges-right-to-public-hearing#:~:text=In%20the%20AI%20judging%20context,finding%20are %20fair%20and%20accurate.

74 Alexis Petridis, 'Abba Voyage review: jaw-dropping avatar act that's destined to be copied' 26 May 2022, *The Guardian*. Accessed at: https://www.theguardian.com/music/2022/may/26/abba-voyage-review-jaw -dropping-avatar-act-thats-destined-to-be-copied.

75 Tania Sourdin, 'Judge v Robot? Artificial Intelligence and Judicial Decision-making' (2018) 41(4) *UNSW Law Journal*, 1123.

76 *Federal Court of Australia Act 1976* (Cth) s 6.

77 *Constitutional Reform Act 2005* (UK) s 25.

78 (2019) 267 CLR 560.

contractor's repudiation and excluded the contractor from the site. Paterson Construction claimed that the Manns' conduct in denying it access to the site constituted a repudiation, which it accepted. The Manns claimed damages for delay and defective work. The contractor sought damages for breach of contract or restitution on a quantum meruit basis. The contractor's claim was for $944,898 (based on an assessment that the total value of work and labour done under the contract amounted to $1,898,673, which, after deduction of payments already made under the contract, yielded a balance of $944,898).

At first instance, the contractor was awarded $660,526.41 on a quantum meruit basis, that being the sum that was assessed as being the fair and reasonable value of the work it had performed. This calculation was not based on the builder's entitlement under the contract but rather, the value of the benefit that the owners received from Paterson Construction. The result was an award of restitution substantially in excess of the contract price, which was consistent with a long line of authorities that held that if a contract is rescinded, it is to be regarded as 'abandoned' and thus has no application to acts done and rights accrued up to the point of rescission.[79]

The Australian High Court in *Mann v Paterson Construction* turned this thinking on its head. While not entirely killing off quantum meruit claims, the court significantly restricted when quantum meruit can be used[80] and such claims can no longer be considered the 'pot of gold at the end of the rainbow' that they once were. In a significant shift from the prior position, the High Court held that a contractor is *not* entitled to recover a quantum meruit for work carried out before termination of the contract and for which a contractual right to payment had accrued at the time of termination. In those circumstances a contractor's *only* entitlement is to sue for damages for breach of contract or for a debt accrued under the contract. Where there is an entitlement to recover on a quantum meruit basis for work carried out before termination, but for which no contractual right to payment had accrued at the time of termination, the price stipulated in the contract may limit the value of the claim in quantum meruit.

Thus, the High Court significantly shifted the law relating to the remedy that a contractor is entitled to when a principal repudiates a contract. Contractors can no longer elect between claiming quantum meruit or the contractually agreed price in debt, for work carried out prior to the termination. They only have a right to sue for the debt.[81] Further, the contract sum is no longer an irrelevant consideration in assessing a quantum meruit claim; it may act as a ceiling or cap on the amount of restitution awarded.

This High Court decision clarifies the relationship between the law of contract and unjust enrichment in Australia. The seven judges, in three separate judgments, spanning 222 paragraphs, and almost 100 pages, in a nuanced and insightful way, changed the direction of the law. No amount of algorithms could have achieved this outcome. If AI was presented with the facts in *Mann v Paterson*, it would, no doubt, have comprehensively researched the law to date, applied that reasoning to the facts, and reached an entirely

---

79 Ibid [202].

80 Wayne Jocic, 'A tale of two townhouses and quantum meruit: *Mann v Paterson Constructions Pty Ltd*' 16 October 2019, Melbourne Law School, *Opinions on High*. Accessed at: https://blogs.unimelb.edu.au/opinionsonhigh/2019/10/16/jocic-mann/.

81 David Winterton and Timothy Pilkington '*Mann v Paterson Constructions Pty Ltd*: The intersection of debt, damages and quantum meruit' (2020) 44(2) *Melbourne University Law Review* 678.

different decision to that of the Australian High Court. The law would have continued in a static and unchanging manner, rather than be a dynamic and evolving body of rules.

What role should AI play in determining construction disputes?

Almost 50 years ago, Joseph Weizenbaum reflected that 'Since we do not have ways of making computers wise, we ought not now to give computers tasks that demand wisdom'.[82] Notwithstanding rapid advancements in AI, computers still lack the capacity to be wise, and wisdom is still a key aspect of judicial decision-making. In light of this, it has been suggested that rather than standing for artificial intelligence, it would be better if, in the context of judicial decision-making, if AI was understood as standing for *Augmented* Intelligence.[83] Augmented intelligence could *assist* judicial decision-making in three distinct ways:

    i. first-level supportive technology;
    ii. second-level replacement technology; and
    iii. third-level disruptive technology.[84]

As a supportive technology, augmented intelligence can help judges with research, including identifying cases, legislations and commentaries. However, the use of AI in this way needs to be treated with caution, due to the risk that AI will make up fake cases. One of the most astonishing illustrations of this occurred in a New York Federal District court in June 2023 when two lawyers were sanctioned for submitting a legal brief to the court that included 'non-existent judicial opinions with fake quotes and citations created by the artificial intelligence tool ChatGPT'.[85] The plaintiff had commenced proceedings against the defendant airline alleging that he was injured when a metal serving cart struck his left knee during a flight from El Salvador to John F. Kennedy Airport. The defendant applied to have the action dismissed on the basis that it was time-barred. The plaintiff's brief in response to the application to dismiss cited cases with relevant sound names such as, *Martinez v. Delta Air Lines*, *Zicherman v. Korean Air Lines* and *Varghese v. China Southern Airlines*. The problem was ChatGPT had made up these cases; a phenomenon known as 'hallucinations', where AI creates 'outputs that are nonsensical or altogether inaccurate'.[86]

The lawyers responsible for submitting the brief referencing non-existent case law were fined US$5,000 for their bad faith in making false and misleading statements to the court. The judge held that the lawyers' conduct promoted 'cynicism about the legal profession and the American judicial system'.[87] There is already evidence of judges using AI to draft their decisions.[88] It does not take a huge leap to imagine a judge, rather than a lawyer

---

82 Joseph Weizenbaum, *Computer Power and Human Reason, from Judgement to Calculation* (1976) W H Freeman & Co, 253.

83 Piers and Aschauer (n 28) 69–70.

84 Sourdin, (n 76), 1117.

85 *Mata v. Avianca, Inc.*, United States District Court, S.D. New York, 22-cv-1461 (PKC), 22 June, 2023.

86 IBM 'What are AI hallucinations?' Accessed at: https://www.ibm.com/topics/ai-hallucinations.

87 *Mata v. Avianca*, 2.

88 See Luke Taylor 'Colombian judge says he used ChatGPT in ruling' 3 February 2023, *The Guardian*. Accessed at: www.theguardian.com/technology/2023/feb/03/colombia-judge-chatgpt-ruling and 'Indian judge

relying on the hallucinations of AI, and the damage that would do to the reputation of the judicial system.

The second way augmented intelligence could be used by judges is to assist them to draft judgments and procedural orders.[89] Human judges can use a draft prepared by AI as the basis for their own decision; not as a substitute for their decision, but rather as a 'first draft' that they finalise using their extensive knowledge, skills and experience.

As discussed above, third-level disruptive technology is already being seen in lower courts in some countries, such as Estonia and China. However, 'for matters that involve some element of judicial discretion, automation will remain difficult. ... It is currently very challenging to automate most litigations as AI does not have the emotional intelligence to determine what is reasonable and what is misleading'.[90]

Ultimately, AI can augment the role of human judges in the resolution of construction disputes but it cannot replace them, for 'the human mind is the only place where original thought can occur based on billions of cognitive interactions taking place at the same time. Computers are faster at 'computing' but are restricted by their electronic make-up and circuitry from thinking in parallel like their human counterparts'.[91]

Conclusion

It is clear, that 'The role of the human judge though is not merely that of a data processor. To reduce judging to such a definition would be to reject not only the humanity of the judge, but also that of all those who come before them.'[92] In order to retain humanity within the court systems, it is essential that AI be recognised as a powerful tool that can *assist* judges in deciding construction cases, but cannot *replace* them.

AI is already proving valuable in improving the speed and quality of legal research and document analysis (but still requires close supervision and monitoring by humans, due to the risk of hallucinations). It is starting to be used in ADR where it is facilitating negotiations by analysing data from both parties, identifying areas of common ground and proposing potential solutions that could lead to settlements.[93] There is a place for AI in the court system, but as augmented intelligence, not artificial intelligence.

The idea of AI replacing human judges and making better and faster decisions in construction cases is not realistic, at least not in the near future. There are several reasons why robot judges will not be replacing human judges anytime soon, including issues around programmers' bias, the black box problem, lack of public confidence in decisions

---

used ChatGPT in a criminal case' 29 Mar 2023 *DigWatch.* Accessed at: https://dig.watch/updates/indian-judge-used-chatgpt-in-a-criminal-case

89 Tony Tung-Yang Chang, 'Taiwan's Judicial Yuan Introduces AI System for Drafting Judgments in Criminal Cases' 28 August 2023, *Lexology.* Accessed at: www.lexology.com/library/detail.aspx?g=479514a8-e3e2-4ca9-aba9-e0d08529ef2a.

90 Dawn Lo, 'Can AI replace a judge in the courtroom?' (quoting Dr Felicity Bell). 1 October 2021, *UNSW Sydney Newsroom.* Accessed at: https://newsroom.unsw.edu.au/news/business-law/can-ai-replace-judge-courtroom.

91 Jim Mason, *Innovating Construction Law: Towards the Digital Age* (2021) Routledge, 18.

92 Tania Sourdin & Richard Cornes 'Do Judges Need to Be Human? The Implications of Technology for Responsive Judging'

93 FTI Consulting 'Harnessing the Power of AI for Construction Disputes' 13 October 2023. Accessed at: https://www.fticonsulting.com/insights/articles/harnessing-power-ai-construction-disputes#:~:text=Natural%20Language%20Processing%20(NLP)%20algorithms,and%20quality%20of%20legal%20arguments.

rendered by AI judges and breaches of human rights. In addition, AI adjudication can lead to diminished confidence in the outcome and reduced feelings of justice due to the lack of transparent reasons and violations of the right to a fair trial.

For these reasons, AI can augment the role that judges perform and potentially improve efficiency, but it cannot, at least at this point in time, replace judges, because it cannot guarantee justice, or provide the parties with a feeling that justice has been served. There may come a time when a robot judge can successfully master judicial decision-making, but that seems to be in the very distant future, because,

> judicial decision-making is an area of daunting complexity, where highly sophisticated legal expertise merges with cognitive and emotional competence. Many of the central concepts in the judicial application of the law – such as 'justice', 'reasonable care', and 'intent' – are deeply enmeshed in the fabric of human life.[94]

Construction judges (and arbitrators) can rest easy; for the time being, robot judges do not pose a realistic threat to their positions.

---

94 G Sartori and L. Branting (eds) *Judicial Applications of Artificial Intelligence* quoted in David M. Masuhara 'Artificial intelligence and adjudication: Some perspectives' (Autumn 2017) 111 *Amicus Curiae* 1, 3.

INDEX

Note: Page numbers in **bold** indicate tables in the text, and references following "n" refer to notes.

1984 Building Act 143; Approved Document B 143–144

accountable person 150
adjudication schemes: low value dispute schemes 222; Professional Negligence Bar Association 222; Pubs Code Adjudicator 222; Society of Computers and Law 222; voluntary adjudication schemes 222
adjudication: ad hoc 136; bonds 102, 110; breach of natural justice 42; contractual 11, 136; enforcement 41; evolution of 219–222; lack of jurisdiction 42; pre–May 1998 landscape 217–219; 'pay now argue later' policy 42; review 41; statutory 41, 136; statutory procedure to set an adjudication decision aside 42; types of disputes that can be referred 41
adjudicator: powers 221; review adjudicator 42
Adjudicator Nominating Bodies (ANB) 136, 220
ADR *see* Alternative Dispute Resolution
advance payment guarantee bond 101
AI *see* artificial intelligence
algorithmic bias 265–268
Alternative Dispute Resolution (ADR) 58
ANB *see* Adjudicator Nominating Bodies 223
Anns 110–122; case law retreat 127–129; housing defect claimants 122–124; Law Lords' response 125–126; legal issues in 124–125
Anti-Corruption Authority (ANAC) 83
anti-suit injunction 26
arbitration agreement: effectiveness 229; inoperability 229; validity 229
arbitration rules: ICSID Rules 236, UNCITRAL Rules 236

artificial intelligence (AI): construction disputes 274–275; fair hearing 270–271; *vs* human judges 265–268; lack of reasons 269–270; public hearing 271–272; use of AI judges 263–265; violation of human rights 270
Australian West Coast model 38n249

balanced evaluation process 51
Banwell Report 54n38
bid bonds 101
Bilateral Investment Treaty (BIT) 235
BIT *see* Bilateral Investment Treaty
bonds: adjudication 102, 110; advance payment guarantee 101; bid 101; conditional 101; conditional *vs.* on-demand 103–104; on-demand 101
Brussels I Regulation (Recast) 25
BUILD (Building Users Insurance against Latent Defects) 10
Build-Operate-Transfer (BOT) Projects 213
Building Control Alliance (BCA) 146–147
building information modelling (BIM) 60, 61, 72
building regulation 142; Building Safety Act 2022 139; Defective Premises Act 1972 118; Factories Act 1937 142; Fire Precautions Act 1971 142; Public Health Act 1936 119, 127, 142–143; Public Health Act of 1961 142; Offices, Shops and Railway Premises Act 1963 142; the 1984 Building Act 143; the Regulatory Reform (Fire Safety) Order 2005 147; shops and offices 142
Building Research Establishment (BRE) 144
Building Safety Regulator 49

CAM (minimum environmental criteria) 82–85
carbon-neutral approach 78, 78n6

INDEX

Centre of Construction Law & Dispute Resolution: cash flow 10–12; changes to valuation 8–9; history of 7–8; King's College London Centre of Construction Law & Dispute Resolution 47; quality and fitness 9–10; time dimension 9

choice of law: use of English law internationally 15–17

classic liquidated damages/penalty rules 167–168, 184

Clean Construction Accelerator 68

collaborative practices, construction projects 48

collaborative procurement 57, 59

collateral objectives 86

collateral warranties 58

commercial arbitration: arbitrability 230–231; capacity 231–233; effect of insolvency on jurisdiction 225–230; insolvency and stay of proceedings 227; law governing the effects of insolvency on arbitral proceedings 226; standing 231–233

commercial documents 20

compensation for expropriation (direct and indirect) 247–248

conditional bonds 101

Construction Contract Policy 10

Construction Playbook 56, 57, 68, 73–74

contract administrator: role of 34–37

Cookham Wood Trial Project 62

cost-effectiveness approach 52

Crown Commercial Services 76

DAB/DAAB *see* Dispute Avoidance Board/ Dispute Avoidance and Adjudication Board

deep learning 262

Department for Levelling Up, Housing and Communities (DLUHC) 47

desktop studies 145–146

digital information management 60

Diplock, Lord 104, 105

Dispute Adjudication Boards 41n283

Dispute Avoidance Board/Dispute Avoidance and Adjudication Board (DAB/DAAB) 223

do no significant harm principle (DNSH) 82–85

duty of care: *Anns* 124–125; assumption of responsibility 127; special relationship 127

early supply chain involvement (ESI) 53, 55, 72

Edwards-Stuart J. 20

effective contracting 74

embedded carbon 77n4

Energy Charter Treaty ('ECT'): investment 256; reform 257–259

energy construction projects 253–254; dispute resolution 254–257; energy charter treaty (ECT) 257–259; energy transition 254–257

English contract law: commercial common sense 19–20, 178; fitness for purpose 91–100; impact of 27–37; international construction contracts 15–17, 15n5; prevalence of 17–27; prevention principle 27–28; procedural advantages of 22–24; substantive advantages of 18–21; textual interpretation 19; use of 15–17

English residential building law 113–115; balance sheet 129–131; statutory innovations 131–133

European Climate Law 68, 68n4

exclusive jurisdiction clauses 25

express FFP obligations 97–99

FAC-1 73, 75, 76

fair and equitable treatment (FET) 246–247

FIDIC *see* International Federation of Consulting Engineers

fitness for human habitation 92

fitness for purpose (FFP): express obligations 97–98; implied obligations 91–97

fixed price model 53

free transfer of funds 249–250

full protection and security (FPS) 250–251

gateways, regulatory reforms: gateway three 66; gateway two 63–65; between gateways two and three 65–66; planning gateway one 63

golden thread of information 60, 150

Great Fire of London 140; The London Building Act 1667 140; Regional Acts 141

Grenfell Tower disaster 47–50, 139

guarantee: advance payment guarantee bond 101; instruments of 104; law of guarantee 101; refund 101–102; retention and maintenance 102; tender 101

Guidance on Collaborative Procurement for Design and Construction to Support Building Safety 47–50

Hackitt, Dame Judith 47–48, 48n3, 50

Hackitt Report 147–148

Health and Safety Executive (HSE) 47

Hoffmann, Lord 21

home ombudsman 150

human–AI fairness gap 264: hearings 264; interpretability 264–265; *see also* artificial intelligence (AI)

INDEX

ICSID *see* International Centre for Settlement of Investment Disputes
implied FFP obligations: contractor without design responsibility 95–97; design and build 94–95; general considerations 91–94
Independent Review of Building Regulations and Fire Safety 47
indulgence clauses 108, 109
insolvency: in civil law European countries 224–225; jurisdiction 225–230; legal capacity 231–233; subject-matter arbitrability 230–231
integrated information management contract (IIMC) 62
Interim Payment Certificates 37
International Centre for Settlement of Investment Disputes (ICSID) 236, 254
International Chamber of Commerce (ICC) Commission 213
International Federation of Consulting Engineers (FIDIC)156
international investment treaties 235–236; BITs 235–236; Energy Charter Treaty ('ECT') 257–259
International Statutory Adjudication Forum 41, 41n282
Investor–State arbitration 26, 235–237; in civil law European countries 224–225; construction investments 239–240; enforcement 236; jurisdiction 240–244; standards of investment protection 244–251; trends and statistics 237–239
Italian legal framework: do no significant harm principle (DNSH) 82–85; minimum environmental criteria 82–85, 85–86; NZEB requirements 79–81; prospects for reforms 81–82

JCT 2016 construction phase contract 56
JCT Pre-Construction Services Agreement (PCSA) 56
Joint Contracts Tribunal (JCT) 32–33

King's College Construction Law Association (KCCLA) 13
King's College London report: action plans and leadership 71; client strategy and expectations 70; contract governance and joint risk management 70–71; early supply chain involvement and preconstruction activities 70; framework alliances and shared learning 71; long-term contracts and industry investment 70; Procuring Net Zero Construction 68–73; specialists and supply

chain collaboration 70; team evaluation and bidder proposals 70; whole life procurement and digital information 71

liability relating to construction products 149
life cycle assessment (LCA) methodologies 83
Linkage Agreement 16
liquidated damages: in arbitration 210–211; caps of liability 9, 177–178; classic test applied 168–170; clauses pénales 199–204; in construction arbitration 211–214; causative link 187; enforceability 208–209; international principles 205–208; loss sustained 187; in the Middle East 181–183; partial possession 173–175; penalty clauses 208–209; post-termination 177–178, 190; reduction 193–194, 201; secondary obligation 170–173, 200; specific breach 187; survive termination 175–177; variation 190; void for uncertainty 178–179

machine learning 262
modern methods of construction (MMC) 72
most-favoured nation (MFN) treatment 245–246
multi-party contracts 59

National Recovery and Resilience Plan (PNRR) 84–85
Nearly Zero Energy Buildings (NZEB) 78
negligence 118
Net Asset Value (NAV) 171
net zero and sustainable construction 73–74
Net Zero Carbon 77–79, 78n6

official referees 14, 217–220
on-demand bonds 101; *vs.* conditional bonds 103–104

Paris Agreement 67
pay-when-paid clauses 41
payments: advance payment guarantee bond 101; claim 40; direct methods of 9; Interim Payment Certificates 37; mechanisms 39–41; 'pay-when-certified clause' 41; 'pay-when-paid' clause 41; progress payments; schedule 40
penalty clauses 168
Piano Aria e Clima (the Air-quality and Climate Plan) 85
prevention principle 27–28, 3; act of prevention 28–29; extension of time 30–33
price-quality ratio 52
pure economic loss 127

INDEX

quantification: agreement 158–159; classification and approaches to 153–155; contract forms and practices 164–165; cost-based compensation 155–158; formula 161–163; modern complexities 163–164; price claims 159–161

reasonable skill and care 94
recognition and enforcement of judgments 24–26
refund guarantees 101–102
Reid, Lord 35
remediation contribution order 135
retention and maintenance guarantees 102
Rix, Lord Justice 178
rule against penalties 200

security of payment legislation 37–38
single-stage approach 53–54
single-stage procurement 54
standards of investment protection: arbitrary or discriminatory measures 239, 250; customary international law 239, 251; direct expropriation 239, 247–248; fair and equitable treatment 239, 246–247; full protection and security 239, 250; indirect expropriation 239, 247–248; most favoured nation ('MFN') 239, 245; national treatment 239, 245–246; performance

requirements 239, 251; transfer of funds 239, 249; umbrella clauses 239, 248–249; war/insurrection loss 239
supply chains 55, 74

target price contract 9
TCC *see* Technology and Construction Court
Technology and Construction Court (TCC) 14, **17**, 116; adjudication 221; procedural innovation 24; support for arbitration 22–23
tender documentation 86
tender guarantee 101
third-party commentary 185
third-party rights 58
Turing test 262

UAE: free zone laws 192–196
UK Office of Government Commerce 51, 52
umbrella clauses 248–249
United Nations Industrial Development Organization (UNIDO) 213
urban planning 85–86

valuation: based on agreement 158–159; based on cost 155–158; based on a formula 161–162; based on prices 159–161

whole life procurement 71–72